MEDIEVALISM AND THE GOTHIC

IN AUSTRALIAN CULTURE

For Mac,

with, I hope, good

memories of gargoyles

on a rainy Melbourne

night. —

love,

Stephanie

MAKING THE MIDDLE AGES

Publication of this work was assisted by a publication grant from the University of Melbourne and the Research and Graduate Studies Committee, Faculty of Arts, the University of Melbourne.

MEDIEVALISM AND THE GOTHIC

IN AUSTRALIAN CULTURE

Edited by

Stephanie Trigg

MELBOURNE
UNIVERSITY
PRESS

MELBOURNE UNIVERSITY PRESS

An imprint of Melbourne University Publishing Ltd

187 Grattan Street, Carlton, Victoria 3053, Australia

mup-info@unimelb.edu.au

www.mup.com.au

First published 2005, Brepols Publishers n.v., Turnhout, Belgium

First published in Australia and New Zealand 2006

Text © Brepols Publishers n.v., Turnhout, Belgium 2005

Design and typography © Ellis Creative and Brepols Publishers 2005

Printed in Australia by The University of Melbourne Design & Print Centre

National Library of Australia Cataloguing-in-Publication entry

Medievalism and the Gothic in Australia.

Bibliography.
Includes index.
ISBN 0 522 85247 5.

1. Medievalism — Australia — History. 2. Architecture, Gothic — Australia. 3. Gothic revival (Architecture) — Australia. 4. Gothic literature — Australia. 5. Gothic revival (Literature) — Australia. I. Trigg, Stephanie.

994

Contents

Part I—Re-writing Medieval and Gothic Literature

Acknowledgements

I would like to thank Geraldine Barnes, Margaret Clunies Ross and Simon Forde, who have warmly supported this project from its inception. Louise D'Arcens, Ken Gelder, Paul James, David Matthews and Peter Otto discussed many aspects of this collection with me, and it is the sharper for their advice. Helen Hickey provided exemplary research assistance, and Simon French and Maryna Mews provided excellent editorial support. I am especially grateful to Robert Colvin, for the front cover photograph, and to Andrew Preston for compiling the index.

Grateful acknowledgement is also made to the Publications Sub-Committee, the Faculty of Arts, and the Department of English, all of the University of Melbourne, for their support of this volume.

Illustrations

Introduction: Medieval and Gothic Australia

STEPHANIE TRIGG

For medieval writers, the Antipodes were a region of otherness, imaginable principally through a series of complex but static geo-cultural fantasies. The further one travelled from Jerusalem, the further one travelled from the heart of Christian truth, and from the centre of the world, according to an understanding framed in terms that were geographical, theological, and ethical. When John Mandeville, for example, in the fifteenth century, wrote about the Antipodes as proof that the world was a circumnavigable sphere, he argued that these regions were the 'opposite' of the more familiar world. Working from the observation that different stars are visible at different points, he remarks:

> Be the which I seye you certeynly that men may envirowne alle the erthe of all the world as wel vnder as abouen and turnen ayen to his contre, that hadde companye and schippynge and conduyt, and alleweys he scholde fynde men, londes, and yles als wel as in this contree.

> For yee wyten welle that they that ben toward the Antartyk, thei ben streght feet ayen feet of hem that dwellen vnder the Transmontane also wel as wee, and thei that dwellyn vnder vs ben feet ayenst feet. For alle the parties of see and of lond han here appositees habitables or trepassables and [yles] of this half and beyond half.[1]

Mandeville does not conceive of these lands as uninhabited; his earth is populated by 'opposite' communities, yet his understanding of these 'men, lands and isles' is conditioned by the expectation of oddity. His chief example of these lands under the star Antartyk is the country of Lamary, which scholars equate with modern Sumatra. Here the people go naked, as they say that is how God made Adam and Eve; they share sexual partners without marriage; they hold all land and goods in common; and they practise cannibalism. These are familiar tropes from many travel and explo-

---

[1] *Mandeville's Travels*, ed. by M. C. Seymour (Oxford: Clarendon Press, 1967), Chapter 20, p. 134.

ration narratives about various 'new worlds' in the medieval and early modern period. What is less often remarked is that such descriptions barely seem susceptible to historical change. Mandeville's Antipodes are conceived with considerable geographical precision, but they seem unaffected by historical change or progression. Their cultural features are as 'fixed' as the two stars, Transmontane and Antartyk, which hold up the axis around which the earth revolves.

Five hundred years later, relationships between the Antipodes and Europe are no longer defined by a binary opposition of difference; rather, they are part of a complex global network of social, cultural and political influences. In a further contrast with Mandeville's vision, these relationships are deeply conditioned by historical forces and the ideologies of fully-fledged colonialism: in spite of direct evidence to the contrary, the early settlers of the 1780s persisted in conceptualizing Australia as if it were uninhabited, virgin pastoral land, as *terra nullius*. Generally unwilling to recognize or assimilate indigenous tradition, they set about establishing visible, material and institutional links to the land they called 'home' for many generations, even as those links were often sorely tested by the very 'unhomely' nature of the new world. And indeed, in the various projects of colonial settlement, their underlying ideas of historical and cultural tradition were often conceived under the broad sign of the 'Gothic'.

As Chris Brooks shows in his recent study, *The Gothic Revival*, 'Gothic' signifies far more than a series of architectural, literary or cultural revivals. Certainly, it describes a sensibility concerned with the uncanny or 'unheimlich', the sublime or the irrational — the repressed others of enlightenment and modernity — but in historical terms, it also mobilized some deeply contested political and social ideologies that came to a head in the seventeenth century.[2] Gothic tradition could be linked to a medieval tradition of parliamentary resistance to royal power; but could equally be used to trace a feudal trajectory of private land ownership that lent itself to the idea of aristocratic inheritance under the benevolence of the crown. Similarly, Gothic style in religious architecture could signify a strong continuity with the Catholic Church of the Middle Ages and its close relationship to the monarchy, or it could be associated with a Saxon (and by implication, Protestant) understanding of the Church's independence from the crown.

For the Australian colonists, concerned to establish homogenous British rule and to reinforce their cultural supremacy over the subjects under their charge, the complexities of this inheritance were quickly subsumed and harmonized under the rubric of cultural style and architectural fashion, so that when it came to giving tangible, material form to the institutions of religion, education and the law that the settlers imported to their new model colonies, Gothic was often the uncontested first choice for building. This choice was also powered by the driving force of association: the choice of Gothic for churches and law courts lent the 'natural'

---

[2] Chris Brooks, *The Gothic Revival* (London: Phaidon, 1999), pp. 30–48.

authority of age and tradition to the spiritual and judicial authority of both penal colonies and civilian settlements.

By the second half of the century, the colonies of what would become Australia in the first Federal Parliament in 1901 were sufficiently wealthy (particularly Victoria, enriched by the discovery of substantial gold deposits) to construct cities on a large and sweeping scale, whose principal civic buildings were far more flamboyant and grand than anything constructed in similar-sized cities in Europe, particularly Britain. As a style, Gothic encourages conspicuous and ornate display, and it was warmly embraced by the prosperous cities of Melbourne, Sydney and Adelaide. As a result, this version of medieval style is a daily reminder of the European past for many Australians, while also signifying the past history, and the heritage culture, of their own cities.

In contrast, Canada and the United States register a much greater impact from Renaissance, seventeenth-century and Enlightenment thought — in short, from European modernity. Britain and other northern Protestant European countries share a tension between the rival claims of medieval and humanist inspiration. But Australia conceives the historical past primarily under the sign of late eighteenth- and nineteenth-century Gothic, while also frequently invoking a mythologized medieval past. This collection suggests that there is a substantial strand in Australian cultural history that reveals the Gothic and medievalist paradigms at their most exposed, even if the relationship between them is not always stable, as a number of these essays demonstrate.

Across a range of disciplines, Australian scholarship is often able to see things differently, at some distance from the main forcefields of both traditional scholarship and contemporary global culture. When it comes to examining our own past, similarly, contemporary Australian scholars are no longer content to re-trace familiar trajectories. Poised between the traditional ties with Britain, the successive waves of post-war European and Asian migration, a growing affinity with American culture, and an increasing consciousness of indigenous tradition, Australian critics deploy a sophisticated, global awareness of the working of cultural influence and historical tradition, at both an academic and a more popular level. This collection situates itself in that context, re-examining the various historical and mythological deployments of the medieval and Gothic past across a range of cultural fields, from exploration narratives, poetry and fiction, to historical re-enactments and Gothic recreations of various kinds in architecture, performance, ritual and urban subcultures, all in an Australian context. The essays also range from pre-settlement narratives to futuristic computer games or speculative fiction. This collection makes no claim to exhaust the field. On the contrary, we hope our work will open up other possibilities, other cultural spheres, and other interpretations of the material.

Both the key terms in our title — 'Medievalism' and the 'Gothic' — are problematic, in different ways, and both have long and complex histories in Britain and in mainland Europe, and in countries colonized by those powers. But both terms also invoke a series of subtle and varied triangulated relationships between the historical past, its cultural survival and its cultural revival: this is what makes them such powerful lenses for reading Australia's negotiations with its cultural and historical heritage. The relatively recent date of Australia's European settlement, moreover, has the effect of foregrounding questions of geographical, historical and cultural difference and discontinuity, on which the thematic concerns of medievalism and the Gothic thrive. If anything, Australians are increasingly conscious that everything brought to this country from Europe is very, very new, in comparison with indigenous traditions of custodianship, community, and the sacred, for example.

Interestingly, these two fields in Cultural and Literary Studies, at least, do not enjoy much overlap: 'medievalism' and 'Gothic' tend to name separate kinds of texts, scholarly debates, and institutional or academic groupings. This division results from a different kind of historical formation: the periodization of English literary studies. Most scholars of medievalism received their primary training in medieval studies, even if they later diverge to study the post-medieval reception of medieval texts and institutions, or the representation of medieval culture in fiction, film, architecture and design. Gothic studies, on the other hand, emerges primarily from the fields of eighteenth- and nineteenth-century literary studies, though with strong input from students of popular culture, film, and architecture. Of course there are exceptions to this pattern, but these broad developments do explain why each field has developed different understandings of the relationship between the historical period they name and its later transfiguration in other cultural forms; and indeed, why there is so little overlap in the conceptual and methodological structures of each field.

However, it is one of the central contentions of this book that the Australian context in which medievalism and the Gothic are played out has the potential to bring them together in new and distinctive ways. This collection articulates a new kind of relationship, or rapprochement, between these two scholarly fields; it also highlights the depth of both formations in Australian culture, where their influence is profound but not always acknowledged. Both these terms, 'medieval' and 'Gothic', rely on a certain degree of shock value, though for different thematic and historical reasons. Let us consider them in turn.

'Gothic Australia' immediately and dramatically suggests an unexpected contrast to the open skies and stretching landscapes that figure so powerfully in the Australian national imagination. The rhetorical force here depends on both surprise and melodrama; though on reflection, it is easy to see how Australian cultural history since the nineteenth century has constructed its convict past in Gothic terms, as the dark underside to colonial settlement; the punitive underbelly of Enlightenment. This is particularly the case in the disciplinary regimes established in New South Wales, on Norfolk Island and in Van Diemen's Land (now the state of Tasmania), and the ease with which they have been assimilated into Australian heritage tourism. As David Matthews remarks in his essay on Marcus Clarke, 'Convictism, the ruined monuments of which could still be seen on the landscape, was Australia's own equivalent of castellated culture, a repressed and melancholic past.' Postcolonial modernity needs something against which to define itself, a medievalized past against which we prove our own enlightenment. And once that sense of historical Gothic has been developed, it is relatively easy to extrapolate Gothic into its other senses, concerned less with historical understanding and more with sensibility, with consciousness, tapping into international movements that are less dependent on geography or history, or a sense of place. In a similar vein, Andrew Smith and William Hughes have recently argued that Gothic's fascination with both homeliness and otherness, with what it means to be human, means that it is easily mapped on to colonial anxieties about race and ethnicity.[3]

Gothic Australia is most easily recognized in the towering spires, arched windows and enclosed cloisters of so many of its churches, universities, and public buildings. These buildings already have a dual historical reference, signifying both nineteenth-century revivalism as well as medieval architecture: a very complex set of associations. The English Arts and Crafts movement, which grew out of the Gothic revival, but found its chief expression in domestic and interior furnishings, also enjoyed a long vogue in Australian colonial society. The Barr Smith family, in South Australia, for example, were the largest customers of William Morris's company, ordering carpets, wallpapers and furnishings of all kinds for their several houses in Adelaide and its environs.[4] Many of these furnishings are lost, of course, but the Victorian vogue for stained glass in this style has left a substantial inheritance in many Australian houses, in both grand mansions and humbler suburban homes.

However, this sense of Gothic — the one that has, perhaps, the closest and most tangible links to the medieval — represents only one dimension of this much broader cultural form. As many scholars have shown, the meaning and resonance of the term 'Gothic' are both deep and complex, even divided. It can be said to name a language, a historical period, a revivalist movement, and a fashion in literary sensibility that itself has generated a whole series of revivals. Peter Otto summarizes this range of cultural references and semantic connotations in his essay, 'Romantic Medievalism and Gothic Horror':

> By the middle of the nineteenth century, the word 'gothic' could be used to refer to a style of architecture, a form of literature (Gothic fictions), a cultural fashion (the Gothic revival), and an historical period (the medieval). It could designate the barbarous world from which the modern has emerged; a primitive (natural) world able to renovate a lifeless modernity; and the sense that the modern is *unable* to divide itself from the barbarous past.

---

[3] Andrew Smith and William Hughes, 'Introduction: The Enlightenment Gothic and Postcolonialism', *Empire and the Gothic: The Politics of Genre*, ed. by Smith and Hughes (New York: Palgrave Macmillan, 2003), pp. 1–3.

[4] See Christopher Menz, *Morris & Company: Pre-Raphaelites and the Arts and Crafts Movement in South Australia* (Adelaide: Art Gallery Board of South Australia, 1994).

Three recent Australian usages exemplify and help us track this trajectory. In 2001 Brian Andrews entitled his study of Australian Gothic revival architecture, mostly from the nineteenth century, *Australian Gothic*.[5] This is the obvious, most visible and material face of the Gothic. But the phrase was also used by Janine Burke to title her biography of the painter Albert Tucker, where it refers more precisely to an aesthetic or psychological sensibility.[6] And in 2002, Dmetri Kakmi also uses the phrase to characterize the work of Sonya Hartnett, the controversial fiction writer for children and adults: 'What she has done for our landscape is comparable to what Carson McCullers did for the American Deep South. She is the proponent of what I call Australian Gothic.'[7] Perhaps it is because 'Gothic' has so many different contested meanings that it is easier to conceptualize a number of intersections between the Gothic and Australian culture.

In contrast, 'Medieval Australia' enjoys the status of a provocative oxymoron, since the 'Medieval' initially has a much more restricted and at first glance, historical sense. Here the 'common sense' reaction is to say that Australia has no medieval past, separated as it is, so decisively, from the English or European Middle Ages. But as the emergent discipline of medievalism has taught us, the 'Medieval' is only partly a historical category. The afterlife of medieval culture runs long and deep, especially through the second half of the nineteenth century, whether this is realized through the continuous survival of medieval inventions, ideas and practices, or through deliberate acts of revival and recreation. The revivals we call medievalist, in turn, can be carried out under the sign of representation — more or less earnest attempts to understand the medieval as a historical, or even a mythological category — or under the postmodern order of simulation, or play. In these instances, medieval culture is understood as a source of images, narratives, roles and ideas, available to be combined with images from other periods and contexts, detached from any attempt to represent the historical or the real, or from any anxiety about authenticity or continuity of place.

We find both kinds of medievalism in Australian culture, as many of the essays in this collection reveal, across a range of literary texts and social or political practices of medieval revivalism or recuperation. Some of these essays also start to sketch out what might be distinctive about Australian Medievalism. As a preliminary generalization, we might suggest that Australian acts of revival are precisely that: there can be no pretence of medieval survival, except in the most general terms of cultural

---

[5] Brian Andrews, *Australian Gothic: The Gothic Revival in Australian Architecture from the 1840s to the 1950s* (Carlton: Miegunyah Press, 2001).

[6] Janine Burke, *Australian Gothic: A Life of Albert Tucker* (Milsons Point: Knopf, 2002).

[7] Dmetri Kakmi, 'Chaucer and Verse', *The Age* (Melbourne), 6 April 2002, Saturday Extra, p. 7. 'Strictly speaking, of course, Hartnett is not a horror or a fantasy writer, though her work borrows tropes from both; she melds reality with the uncanny in a wholly original manner that virtually redefines the genres from the inside out before charting its own unique territory.'

inheritance, terms that have become increasingly problematic under the searching critique of postcolonialism, multiculturalism and Aboriginal studies. In this regard, Australian medievalism is actually exemplary. Unable to mask the very real differences between the medieval and the modern through an implied physical continuity, it foregrounds the acts of recuperation that I argue condition and structure all such acts, even those that take place on medieval English, British or European sites, so privileged as 'authentic' in the popular imaginary.

The relations between medievalism and the Gothic are thus quite complex. Australian medievalism appears on the surface to be a kind of top-dressing, to represent a form of imported 'culture' that speaks primarily of loss, and distance from England. In contrast, at the time of settlement and colonization, the Gothic was undergoing a hotly contested debate about the cultural value of the medieval past, and beginning to generate a long and complex tradition in fiction and poetry. As a number of contributors to this collection point out, the Gothic in the Australian imaginary hints at the settler consciousness of something deeply unknowable and terrifying in the Australian landscape, the fear of the unknown, or of a terrible primitivism. These associations were strengthened, too, as Australia was gradually transformed from a scattering of penal colonies along the coastline to a settler culture, yearning for a sense of its own past to accompany, and even authorize its growing colonial domination of the land and its indigenous inhabitants. Almost inevitably, such a past was Gothic in orientation, whether this was a fascination with a convict past against which to define their later enlightenment and to celebrate their liberty, or a nostalgia for their own architectural ruins. St Mary's Cathedral in Sydney, for example, was almost more attractive after it had burnt down, than when it was first built, becoming Australia's first 'authentic' Gothic ruin. Brian Andrews quotes from a letter to the editor, in the *Tasmanian Catholic Standard*, of 1869, four years after the fire:

> Dear Sir — To a Catholic visiting Sydney, the ruins of St Mary's Cathedral constitute the most interesting sight in the city. Whilst gazing upon them he is filled with feelings of veneration and awe [...]. Seen on a calm moonlit eve, these ruins forcibly remind the beholder of one of England's ruined abbeys; the stillness of the night and the celestial rays of Diana giving a serene air to the pile, and rendering the visitor for a while oblivious of the fact that he is in Australia, where all works (excepting Nature's) are modern.[8]

The period between European settlement and the present is also, perhaps uncannily, co-extensive with the period of Gothic literature's major transformations. Chris Baldick's anthology of Gothic tales, for example, stretches from 1773 — just two years after the return to England of Captain James Cook, having charted the east coast of Australia — to the present. And as many of the essays in this collection

---

[8] Andrews, p. 4.

show, Australian writers deploy many familiar tropes and genres of the Gothic, while also rehearsing a number of anxieties about cultural belonging and tradition.

In many contemporary studies of the Gothic mode, however, the medieval is a topic that barely rates a mention in the index. And indeed, for some commentators, the medieval is virtually antithetical to the Gothic. Baldick points out, for example, that a great deal of Gothic fiction from the late eighteenth century, like Horace Walpole's *The Castle of Otranto*, is 'concerned with the brutality, cruelty, and superstition of the Middle Ages'. He goes on to argue that literary Gothicism diverges quite markedly from the medieval revivalism of Pugin and Ruskin, for example: 'the implied valuations of medieval life are so different in either case. Such a contrast helps to clarify the fact that the most troublesome aspect of the term "Gothic" is, indeed, that literary Gothic is really anti-Gothic'.[9] But it would be a gross simplification to assume that 'medievalism' necessarily implies a positive valuation of medieval culture, or the desire willy-nilly to import its meanings and ideologies into any context. Many of the essays in this collection that are concerned with literary texts offer much more complex readings of the cultural possibilities and significance of medieval culture, than simply celebratory ones. Louise D'Arcens, for example, draws a powerful contrast between the different symbolic uses made of the story of King Arthur in two novels by Jessica Anderson. Similarly, David Matthews on Marcus Clarke, Peter Otto on Henry Kendall, and Andrew Lynch on Francis Webb, all show these Australian writers actively negotiating contradictions between their medievalist and Gothic inheritance and their own poetics.

In most of the critical literature concerned with definitions, however, the Gothic is discussed primarily in terms of its relationship with romanticism.[10] And while the discipline of medievalism is less well established, it finds its chief points of focus in the study of individual examples (principally literary, visual, architectural or cinematic); the academic and institutional study of medieval culture; and occasionally, in the study of national cultures.[11] Certainly, the two fields are rarely discussed together.

---

[9] Chris Baldick, *The Oxford Book of Gothic Tales* (Oxford: Oxford University Press, 1992), pp. xii–xiii.

[10] See for example, the discussion in Michael Gamer, *Romanticism and the Gothic: Genre, Reception, and Canon Formation* (Cambridge: Cambridge University Press, 2000), especially pp. 8–23.

[11] In addition to the journal *Studies in Medievalism*, and a range of studies of the Robin Hood and Arthurian traditions, some key general texts are *Medievalism in American Culture*, ed. by Bernard Rosenthal and Paul E. Szarmach (Binghamton: Medieval and Renaissance Texts and Studies, 1989); Kathleen Biddick, *The Shock of Medievalism* (Durham: Duke University Press, 1998); *Medievalism in the Modern World: Essays in Honour of Leslie J. Workman*, ed. by Richard Utz and T. A. Shippey (Turnhout: Brepols, 1998); and Angela Weisl, *The Persistence of Medievalism: Narrative Adventures in Contemporary Culture* (New York: Palgrave Macmillan, 2003).

It would be fascinating in a more comprehensive study to trace the changing semantic resonances of the 'medieval' and the 'Gothic' in Australian cultural history, and the inter-relationships between those two formations. By examining selected instances in intensive detail, however, these essays help us sketch out some possible ways of thinking about that relationship, and articulating a closer than customary relation between them.

Conceptually, we can plot examples of both medievalism and the Gothic along two parallel axes, along a continuum that ranges from specific historical reference at one end and a much looser invocation of style, or sensibility at the other. This model also allows us to bypass the problematic formulated by Chris Baldick — that so much of what is named Gothic is actually anti-Gothic, or anti-medieval — because this heuristic tool is less concerned with value than reference. At the extreme end of one axis, then, is the medieval as a historical period, restricted in reference to Europe before the sixteenth century. At the other extreme of the second axis is Gothic as a non-historical sensibility, a mode of consciousness preoccupied with the repressed, the uncanny, or the subcultural other to the dominant culture. Each of these extremes can move towards each other, in both conceptual and thematic terms. The medieval can be detached from its historical and geographical points of reference: its stories can be re-told; its images relived in different contexts; and it can come to stand for a particular literary sensibility. The Gothic, too, can invoke both its own historical past in eighteenth- and nineteenth-century romanticism, as well as harking back to its origins as a version of critical or sympathetic medievalism.

To consider the cultural phenomena studied in this volume, then, at the one extreme we would place the Cistercian monastic foundation studied by Megan Cassidy-Welch which transports medieval religious tradition to rural Victoria, seeking a continuity with that practice in a new setting; at the other, the Gothic horror novels of Kim Wilkins read by Ken Gelder that make no reference to the medieval at all. These two examples, have, perhaps, little enough in common. And yet — and this is the point of the continuum model — it is a somewhat harder to say where, along these lines, we might place the recycled fragments of Victorian Gothic architecture in the buildings of Montsalvat, the artists' colony in outer-suburban Melbourne (Sarah Randles), or the associations of Aboriginal culture with the primitive with the poetry of Henry Kendall (Peter Otto), or the John Ruskin-inspired medievalism of the 'Daughters of the Court' in late nineteenth-century Melbourne (Victoria Emery). Each of these examples re-figures the relationship between medievalism and the Gothic differently: the model of the continuum is useful for thinking about the play between these conflicting impulses, and the way these texts are related to one another.

Medievalism and the Gothic in Australian Culture is divided into two halves. The first, 'Re-writing Medieval and Gothic Literature', studies primarily literary texts, and here we see the most complex set of inter-relationships between medievalism and the Gothic. This should not surprise us: works of the imagination thrive on ambiguity and tension between the literal and the symbolic. Generically, too, these texts fit more easily into older literary traditions and the textual world of fiction, drama and poetry, removed at least one level from the strikingly obvious disjunctions of the physical and material Australian landscape that feature so strongly in the second half.

This is not to say that Australian authors are not deeply conscious of writing from a position *outside* England: many of the texts studied here return obsessively to the question of Australia's difference from the 'castellated country' of the motherland. In David Matthews's reading, melancholy is the dominant trope here, figured around the perceived 'absence' of history, in the real absence of a medieval past. Marcus Clarke distinguishes his own writing from such nostalgia, but in turn works to 'Gothicize' the landscape, and to introduce some of Gothic's dominant tropes — 'vengeance and destruction leading to tragedy' — into narratives that otherwise owe significant debts to medieval romance tradition, with the opposite expectation of a fortunate or triumphal outcome for the hero.

Peter Otto also articulates a set of relationships, often antagonistic ones, between these two formations, 'romantic medievalism' and 'Gothic horror' in a range of British and Australian romantic poets, with a special focus on the poetic construction of Henry Kendall's understanding of 'Aboriginal Man' as an enabling trope for his own role as 'singer of a new, aboriginal/medieval/gothic dawn', and the poetic traditions that make that possible.

Andrew Lynch's essay looks at the problem from the perspective of the expatriate, exploring the poetry written by Francis Webb in England. Webb's poetry confronts the relationship between medievalist and Catholic traditions, and explores the sense of 'cultural and personal dispossession' in being a Catholic and an Australian in England. In Lynch's reading, Webb desires a fuller social community and sense of belonging, of being 'home', but is further excluded by the mental illness that has the effect of binding him to place, to Costessey, in Norfolk.

Jessica Anderson's *Tirra Lirra by the River* is one of the most famous Australian medievalist novels, with its direct invocation of Tennyson's Lady of Shalott as a powerful narrative and imaginative trope for projecting onto an inaccessible and romanticized medieval past. In contrasting this novel with Anderson's more recent *One of the Wattle Birds*, Louise D'Arcens shows the very different uses Anderson's heroines make of their Arthurianism, and how little we can take either the thematic content or the cultural meaning of medievalism for granted. D'Arcens also uses this comparison to sketch a larger trajectory in Australian literary culture, from an earlier 'colonial dependency' to the 'mature cultural sovereignty' of the late twentieth century.

Margaret Rogerson, similarly, studies a particular theme — that of the 'Everyman' — in Australian fiction and drama from the 1930s to the late twentieth century, tracing a movement from the concern to replicate 'the psychological "anywhere" of the old morality play tradition' in the plays of Dulcie Deamer, to a more distinctive medievalism, locked into an Australian consciousness of place, and anxiety about spiritual homogeneity or communication with Aboriginal spirituality, in Randolph Stow's *To the Islands*. Even where that spirituality is not specifically religious, as in Kate Grenville's *Idea of Perfection*, it is a powerful means of dramatizing the struggle between the demands of perfection and imperfection.

Jenna Mead shows how the traditions of English romantic poetry influenced the inscription of the Australian pastoral landscape, down to the castellated water tower and dovecot of Joseph Archer's properties in Tasmania, and uses these as the starting-point for a meditation on memory and the institutions of medieval studies and medievalism in Australia.

Valerie Krips looks at texts from the other end of the writerly spectrum: fantasy literature written mostly for children. Her essay is premised on the twinned ideas that childhood is 'the home we all acknowledge', and that children's texts are a crucial site for considering changes in a culture's understanding of its own heritage. In all three novels studied here, by Isobelle Carmody, Dave Luckett, and Catherine Jinks, the children who are their subjects find themselves in what Krips calls 'heritage time', where the past is represented 'in the service of present concerns'. In an era of reconciliation, so different from the first encounters of Europeans with Aboriginal people, these texts reveal 'some of the possibilities of resolution offered by heritage', by taking the reader into a sphere that is 'partly historical, partly mythological'.

Krips's essay is a fitting conclusion to the first half of the collection, in that it affirms the ongoing cultural work performed by Australian negotiations with the European past, and the possibilities of harnessing our fascination with that past in the service of further understanding and reconciliation with the much older traditions that had already shaped the landscape, and ways of being in this country.

The second section, 'Gothic Landscapes and Medieval Communities' is principally concerned with the different, even contradictory ways medievalist and Gothic modes have been used to describe, represent or transform the Australian landscape, and to construct relationships of community and identity. Unsurprisingly, perhaps, this is where one of the chief differences between the two modes emerges. The individual in a Gothicized landscape is usually alone, in a relationship with landscape or society that is problematic and troubled, seeking reconciliation, or a sense of 'home' but not always finding it in conventional ways. This is true, oddly, as much as it is for William Dampier (Barnes and Mitchell), struggling to make sense of 'the fabulous bigness and monstrousness of the southern latitudes', as it is for the urban, subcultural Goths in Ken Gelder's essay on 'The "UnAustralian" Goth'. Barnes and Mitchell suggest a new reading of the now infamous description of Australia as *terra nullius*, as a 'medieval signature' to signify that which resists being known, with the further effect of rendering the indigenous inhabitants invisible, beyond even ethnographic interest. Gelder shows how the Goth identity in Australia is rendered 'both less Australian and more homely-in-Australia: more otherworldly and yet *here*'. The theme of home, of homeliness, and its opposite, the *unheimlich*, or the 'uncanny', in Freud's formulation, is a profoundly suggestive one in most mobilizations of Gothic.

On the other hand, one of the primary manifestations of medievalism in Australia is its capacity to serve as a model for social organization and idealized forms of community, whether this applies to the specific importation of the continuous traditions of medieval monasticism (in Megan Cassidy-Welch's study of the Cistercian monastery at Tarrawarra), or the utopian or game-playing bricolage of medievalist re-enactment and community groups (Adina Hamilton) or fantasy role-playing games (Matthew Chrulew). As all three essays show, 'community' is never straightforward. Tarrawarra is built on a site colonized through armed attacks on the indigenous Wurundjeri people: while the Coranderrk station on the same site later housed many Aboriginal children who had been forcibly taken away from their families. In this context, medievalism is 'a historical choice' whose political implications can easily be buried under a European ideal of a spiritual site.

Fictionalized, or utopian medievalist communities are often more self-conscious about their ethical choices, as Hamilton shows. Her essay identifies some curious tensions between a scholarly and a more popular medievalism that is often utopian in form and structure, and analyzing different ways of sharing knowledge beyond the 'castle' of institutionalized medieval studies. Her examples range from the fiction of Kerry Greenwood, the Crossroads Medievalist community, and the activities of the Society for Creative Anachronism. In the society's revisionary topography, for example, Australia becomes the Kingdom of Lochac, with its own carefully articulated hierarchies and boundaries.

Topographic fantasy — or the imaginative re-inscription of the landscape — also plays a crucial role in the serious games like Dungeons and Dragons studied by Matthew Chrulew. These games mostly originate from the United States, though they are projected into a deeply globalized culture. Chrulew examines one game, *Shadowrun*, which constructs a series of analogies between Aboriginal culture and other non-Western cultures (from the Americas, and from Asia), and, by extension, with the Middle Ages as the 'Other' to modernity.

The two essays that discuss nineteenth-century medievalism in this section both show how medieval forms were deliberately invoked to create quite direct links, or associations, between the colonies and England. Sarah Randles discusses the perceived ideological links between nineteenth-century Australian Gothic architecture and its contemporary counterparts in nineteenth-century England, even while these buildings were so important in developing a version of Australian historical consciousness, and a sense of its own past. 'Gothic' constituted the obvious architectural vocabulary for such a sense. The late nineteenth-century women's society in Melbourne, 'The Daughters of the Court', examined by Victoria Emery, tapped into the current intellectual fashion for the writings of John Ruskin to mediate their own relations to medieval 'courts', combining a hierarchic social organization with a self-conscious 'modern' sense of women's role in the world. Medievalism is rarely theorized along gender lines, and Emery's essay traces some fascinating fault lines through an organization that was both woman-centred and yet also chivalric.

Australian medievalism in the social sphere is not restricted to community on this small scale, either. Paul James and I consider two key moments of nation-building in Australia — the federation of the separate colonies in 1901; and the recent Constitutional Convention that debated the possibility of Australia becoming a republic — to show how the formation of Australia as a nation-state depends heavily on a strong sense of continuity with British parliamentary tradition. That inheritance is often contradictory, however, as Australian debates and controversies about parliamentary ritual practice and its medieval accoutrements reveal.

As many of the essays in this collection show, Australia both is, and is not a 'castellated country', in the phrase debated by Cowling and Stephensen in the essay by David Matthews that opens the collection. Lacking a medieval past of their own, Australians have constructed an elaborate network of links to such a past, whether that past is idealized or the subject of critique, and whether those links are material, institutional, or imaginative. In doing so, they have also produced a series of rich and intriguing visions — medievalist and Gothic — of their own past, present, and future.

Part I

Re-writing Medieval and Gothic Literature

Marcus Clarke, Gothic, Romance

DAVID MATTHEWS

A ll Australians are familiar with the idea that their country lacks history and tradition, of the kind signalled by historic ruins and other traces of the past as conceived by a European settler culture. While this idea obviously lends itself to a certain kind of critique of Australia — and in the literary field, to anxieties about what there is to write about — it must also be recalled that Australian historical 'emptiness' has often been constructed positively. There have been few more dramatic examples of this than Joseph Furphy's (or rather Tom Collins's) vision of a 'virgin continent' waiting in 'serene loneliness [...] while the primordial civilizations of Copt, Accadian, Aryan and Mongol crept out, step by step, from paleolithic silence into the uncertain record of Tradition's earliest fable', and waiting still longer as the 'hard-won light' of empire made its way around the globe. For Furphy, although Australia's history was a 'blank' in its long waiting, this was positively conceived as conferring freedom on a 'recordless land [...] committed to no usages of petrified injustice [...] clogged by no fealty to shadowy idols [...] cursed by no memories of fanaticism and persecution [...]'.[1]

In his well-known 1856 essay, 'The Fiction Fields of Australia', Frederick Sinnett, albeit somewhat mockingly, pointed out the obvious ramifications for literature:

> No storied windows, richly dight, cast a dim, religious light over any Australian premises. There are no ruins for that rare old plant, the ivy green, to creep over and make his meal of. No Australian author can hope to extricate his hero or heroine, however pressing the emergency may be, by means of a spring panel and a subterranean passage, or such like relics of feudal barons [...].[2]

---

[1] *Such is Life* in *Joseph Furphy*, ed. and intro. by John Barnes, Portable Australian Authors (St Lucia: University of Queensland Press, 1981), pp. 65–66.

[2] Frederick Sinnett, 'The Fiction Fields of Australia', in *The Writer in Australia: A*

The same issue provoked a *querelle* with a sharper edge in the 1930s between G. H. Cowling, professor of English literature at the University of Melbourne, and the critic P. R. Stephensen. Cowling, while professing as an expatriate Englishman in Australia to 'love the country', complained that 'there are no ancient churches, castles, ruins — the memorials of generations departed. You need no Baedecker [*sic*] in Australia. From the point of view of literature this means that we can never hope to have a Scott, a Balzac, a Dumas [...].'[3] Stephensen, in a vehement reply, spoke anecdotally of his own years in England and of his 'yearning', while there, 'to be in a country *without* any castles or ruins, to be at liberty in a country in which there were thousands of square miles of ground *not* staled by history and tradition'. Like Furphy, Stephensen saw Australia as a primitive country and there was 'a difference between a primitive country and a castellated country, a profound difference — but what an impertinence for a denizen of the castellated country to decry the other country when he is visiting it; what bad manners, what an example of castellated culture!'[4]

By comparison with Furphy these writings of Sinnett, Cowling, and Stephensen show a narrow and quite specific sense of historical lack. Whether positively or negatively, each of them is concerned not with Australia's lack of history as such but the lack of a Middle Ages. It is castles and churches they are concerned with and, secondarily, the ruins of such buildings that, in the eighteenth century, contributed so substantially to the Gothic sensibility. Sinnett paraphrases Milton's lines in 'Il Penseroso', where 'storied Windows richly dight / Casting a dimm religious light' form part of a larger portrait of a ruined cloister. He mocks the narrative machinery of the Gothic novel, leading up to his rather gleeful conclusion 'that Mrs Radcliffe's genius would be quite thrown away here'.[5] At the same time, via his reference to 'feudal barons', he shows his understanding of Gothic as being based on a reading of the relics of medieval culture. Cowling, too, makes it clear that it is *medieval* artefacts he misses while Stephensen's riposte about 'castellated culture' shows that this is the way he has understood Cowling.

Early writers on Australia were just as likely to look to classical antiquity as the Middle Ages when defining Australia's historical lack. In 1838 William Woolls, the man who taught Rolf Boldrewood, referred to the absence of the Australian equivalent of the 'plains of Marathon, [the] pass of Thermopylae', *and* its lack of

---

Collection of Literary Documents, 1856 to 1964, ed. by John Barnes (Melbourne: Oxford University Press, 1969), pp. 8–32 (p. 9).

[3] G. H. Cowling, 'The Future of Australian Literature', *The Age* (Melbourne), 16 February 1935, p. 5; qtd. Leigh Dale, *The English Men: Professing Literature in Australian Universities* (Toowoomba: ASAL, 1997), p. 153.

[4] P. R. Stephensen, 'The Foundations of Culture in Australia' (1935), in Barnes, *Writer in Australia*, pp. 204–44 (p. 217).

[5] Barnes, *Writer in Australia*, p. 10.

'the triumphal arch, the high-raised battlement, the moated tower [...]'.[6] But later writers are more likely to appeal to medieval culture, reflecting the widespread rise of interest in medieval culture in Britain in the later nineteenth century and the consequent export of such interest to the colonies as medieval English texts became available as never before and the neo-Gothic architectural style reached its zenith.[7]

In an Australia that built its universities, cathedrals and many public buildings on neo-Gothic lines, writers located medieval culture as the bedrock of their own culture. In the 1900 poem by 'Oriel' in which a bushman asks why he is going to the war, his father gives him a stern history lesson about protecting freedom and democracy which looks back to Magna Carta, 'When mail-clad fingers pointed and the trembling tyrant signed / The Charter that our liberty decreed'.[8] Seeking, around the same time, to emphasize the lofty social origins of Sybylla Melvyn's mother in *My Brilliant Career*, Miles Franklin gives her an ancestor who sailed with William the Conqueror.[9]

The Middle Ages in Australia by the end of the century had become, just as they were in Britain, a storehouse of allusion and, as with all proverbial wisdom, could be drawn on to quite contradictory purposes. Stephensen's own critique of Cowling gives a neat example. For all his scorning of 'castellated culture', Stephensen draws on a *positive* vision of medieval culture by comparing the situation of the Australian writer in the 1930s to that of Wycliffe and Chaucer in the late fourteenth century. Just as these two writers had to develop the English vernacular, so modern Australian writers must work with the emergent Australian vernacular. Cowling, Stephensen suggests, is like those Latinists 'who [...] sniffed (no doubt) at the very idea of literature in English'. The situation of the late fourteenth-century writers is directly comparable with the Australian situation: 'Here we are on the threshold of Australian self-consciousness, at the point of developing Australian nationality, and with it Australian culture[;] we are in our Chaucerian phase [...]' (p. 211).

---

[6] William Woolls, 'The Beauties of Australia' (1838) in Michael Ackland, *The Penguin Book of 19th Century Australian Literature* (Ringwood: Penguin, 1993), p. 16.

[7] On the export of medieval texts to the colonies, see Kathleen Biddick, *The Shock of Medievalism* (Durham: Duke University Press, 1998), pp. 99–101, passim. Biddick discusses the activities of the EETS in relation to India but neglects the equally important case of Australia (which does not fit her postcolonialist paradigm so well). On Australia and medieval studies see my *The Making of Middle English, 1765–1910* (Minneapolis: University of Minnesota Press, 1999), pp. ix–x, xiv, 157, and Louise D'Arcens, 'From Holy War to Border Skirmish: The Colonial Chivalry of Sydney's First Professors', *Journal of Medieval and Early Modern Studies*, 30 (2000), 519–45.

[8] 'Oriel' (John Sandes), 'The Bushman's Question' (1900) in *Turning the Century: Writing of the 1890s*, ed. by Christopher Lee (St Lucia: University of Queensland Press, 1999), p. 33.

[9] Miles Franklin, *My Brilliant Career*, ed. by Elizabeth Webby (1901; Sydney: Angus and Robertson, 2001), p. 4.

This juxtaposition, occurring within one paragraph, seems peculiarly self-undermining. In order to *attack* Cowling's yearning for 'castellated culture', Stephensen makes a favourable comparison with perhaps the single most recognizable representative of that culture, Geoffrey Chaucer. A medieval comparison, in short, is used to demonstrate the invalidity of medieval comparisons. But the opposition makes sense as part of Stephensen's dichotomy of primitive culture and castellated culture. Chaucer is primitive (but nobly so); his struggle with the vernacular is an authentic medieval moment. Like 'Oriel', Stephensen is happy to see Australian culture as rooted in English medieval culture: 'Australian culture begins with a general background of Chaucer, Shakespeare, Herrick, Byron, Charles Dickens [...]' (p. 205). Chaucer is not in fact a part of 'castellated culture', which refers to the secondary, belated yearnings after medieval culture of later periods. Chaucer's struggle to refine the vernacular — reiterated in 1930s Australia — is an authentic and timeless writerly task.

This opposition between the authentic and the secondary is crucial to Stephensen's vision of the lineages of Australian literature. To him, such writers as Marcus Clarke, Rolf Boldrewood, Adam Lindsay Gordon, Henry Kendall, Price Warung, 'and other melancholics' form a bad, inauthentically Australian lineage (p. 230). On the positive side, there are Paterson, Lawson, Furphy, Miles Franklin, Steele Rudd, and the *Bulletin* school (p. 230–31). Clarke and the melancholics are obsessed with the notion of Australia 'as a permanent colony' and are responsible for perpetuating the theme of convictism (p. 230). They are 'English-minded' writers. Conversely, Stephensen's positive lineage consists of 'Australian-minded' writers, which is a matter of disposition rather than birth: 'Kendall, the Australian native, was as melancholy and English-minded as anyone English-born, in his attitude to Australia' (p. 231).

It is on the face of it a peculiar move to establish melancholy as the primary artistic criterion of judgement. It involves Stephensen in some sleight of hand given that Lawson, no stranger to the blues, is an important member of the right lineage (the idea seems to be that if he was a melancholic, at least he was *our* melancholic). This odd literary criterion, melancholia, results not so much from the undoubted melancholia of some of these writers of the first group (Kendall, Gordon, Clarke) but from the set of substitutions that began with the motif of the absence of history. 'History', as we have seen, contracts to the Middle Ages; medieval castles and ruins, therefore, define England; Gothic derives from castles and ruins; and melancholy derives from the Gothic sensibility. The imposition of melancholy on the landscape by Clarke, Kendall, and others is therefore constructed as a peculiarly English thing to do and something that produces an unacceptable Gothic Australia.

Whether positively or negatively, Sinnett, Cowling, Stephensen, and Furphy have in common the notion of historical *absence*, an essential Australian *lack*. But it would be truer to say that the absence they describe is based on repression rather than a real lack. Furphy's massive, empty *longue durée* can only be imagined by the forgetting of the continent's indigenous inhabitants which is the condition of its becoming a virgin. Stephensen's sense of consolation derived from a land not 'staled' by history requires a similar repression. In their context such repressions are hardly surprising when even today the great extent of indigenous history is often regarded as only an indifferent counter to the notion of historical lack. For many, Aboriginal tradition is the wrong kind of history, not a parallel history but a non-history. This was put very clearly by the then Reconciliation Minister, Philip Ruddock, in October 2000 when he told foreign newspapers that for all their long history in Australia, the Aborigines did not invent the wheel and did not have chariots.[10]

Fiction and 'terra nullius'

In July 1870, writing an obituary of Charles Dickens in the *Argus*, Marcus Clarke showed a very clear sense of the difference between the literature of 'castellated culture' and modern realism. Clarke bestows some respect on Walter Scott, who 'had cast the magic of his spells on tower and ruin, forest, moor, and fell. The knights had arisen and clanked in their stately armour through folios of commonplace; while distressed damsels and love-lorn squires outraged propriety with all the ease of fiction'.[11] But it took Dickens, with a new kind of romance that Clarke called 'the romance of reality', to create a more durable literature when 'the great London "public" recoiled before the mediaeval romance' (p. 630). Dickens's 'fame lies in the fact that he painted men and manners, not as they should be, but as they are' (p. 629) and he did more for England, Clarke concluded, than Scott had done for Scotland, precisely because he captured a real and present England while Scott, in effect, worked with castellated culture (p. 636).

    Whatever else he is doing here Clarke, as a *critic*, is engaged in a form of 'position-taking' as a *novelist*, in Pierre Bourdieu's sense, within the literary field of late nineteenth-century Australia. Clarke himself by this time had written one novel, *Long Odds*. By aligning himself as he does in the obituary Clarke is taking a position that defines a particular moment in his 'trajectory' as a writer.[12] Clarke looks to be

---

[10] See, for example,'Australian Minister Sparks Race Row', *BBC News*, 5 October 2000; 17 October 2001, http://news.bbc.co.uk/1/hi/world/asia-pacific/957544.stm; *Courier Mail* (Brisbane), 7 October 2000, late edition, p. 25.

[11] Marcus Clarke, 'Charles Dickens', in *Marcus Clarke*, ed. by Michael Wilding, Portable Australian Authors series (St Lucia: University of Queensland Press, 1976), p. 630.

[12] '[T]he trajectory describes the series of positions successively occupied by the same writer in the successive states of the literary field, it being understood that it is only in the structure of a field that the meaning of these successive positions can be defined [...]'. Pierre Bourdieu, *The Field of Cultural Production: Essays on Art and Literature*, ed. and intro. by Randal Johnson (Cambridge: Polity Press, 1993), p. 189.

known as a painter of men and manners, a realist, resolutely setting the romance of reality against the earlier form of romance pursued by Scott.

Clarke's literary career to this point had followed a Dickensian mode of production in quite obvious ways. Like Dickens, Clarke came to fiction via journalism. *Long Odds* was serialized in the *Colonial Monthly*, a journal Clarke founded and edited, and published as a book in 1869. This mode of journal serialization followed by book publication was of course perfected by Dickens; by publishing *Long Odds* in a journal he owned and ran himself, Clarke further mimicked Dickens's standard practice. Clarke's otherwise somewhat gratuitous point that Dickens did more for England than Scott for Scotland opens up the question of a novelist's national role and suggests that Clarke saw himself as being able to do something for Australia and, thereby, become Australia's great realist. This was a not unreasonable expectation for an ambitious young man planning a literary career in Australia in the 1870s. While there were several poets who might be put forward as Australian laureate, the position of Australia's novelist must have seemed relatively open. Overall, Clarke's endorsement of Dickens's success in the obituary is not disinterested but can be read as a manifesto of his own intentions as a literary figure.[13]

Position-taking is, of course, not solely a matter of manifesto-like pronouncements but relies in addition on what is actually done in the fiction itself. Clarke knew that whatever he had achieved in *Long Odds*, he had conspicuously failed to capture his own time and place. The novel was set in London and provincial England and had only one Australian character. The prefatory note that appeared in the 1869 book publication is very aware of this potential drawback where the Australian marketplace was concerned. In it, Clarke defers to Henry Kingsley's *The Recollections of Geoffrey Hamlyn* (1859) as the best Australian novel (demonstrating that the question of the leading Australian novelist is on his mind) and then says that the interest of *Long Odds* is in seeing how a character like Sam Buckley would 'get on in England'.[14]

At the time of writing the Dickens obituary, Clarke was several months into the serial that would eventually bring him the position he wanted: *His Natural Life* would ultimately bring Clarke fame and is still generally recognized as the major Australian novel of the nineteenth century. Yet it did so in spite of its author's particular ambitions. Clarke failed to become Australia's urban, middle class realist and his reputation was in eclipse at one point for precisely the same reasons that he held Scott to have been eclipsed by Dickens. Stephensen thought Clarke to be a writer of melancholic inauthenticity just as surely as Clarke held Scott to be finally

---

[13] On Clarke's 'belatedness' in relation to European writers, see Andrew McCann, 'Marcus Clarke and the Gothic Commodity', *Southern Review*, 31 (1998), 282–96.

[14] Marcus Clarke, *Long Odds* (Melbourne: Clarson, Massina, 1869), unpaginated preface.

inauthentic. Clarke's reputation did of course recover but with the qualification that he should never be taken as principally a realist.

The move Clarke made in his new serial — the move that lifted it beyond *Long Odds* — was a shift *away* from Dickensian urban realism towards the kind of romance written by Scott and Dumas, where romance is found in the past, specifically the repressed past. The history to which he went — the convict period — was of course still quite palpably real in the 1870s, as Clarke himself discovered when he visited Hobart and Port Arthur and saw the last living convicts there. But the system of transportation and the convict system were gone; on the east coast transportation had ceased ten years before Clarke's arrival in the country in 1863. Clarke wrote of 'Van Diemen's Land', but the place he visited had officially been Tasmania since 1854. Convictism, the ruined monuments of which could still be seen on the landscape, was Australia's own equivalent of castellated culture, a repressed and melancholic past.

Clarke was, then, cannier than Stephensen thought. Faced with a fictional *terra nullius*, he looked for the repressed and found it. Throughout his fiction, the Australian landscape is overloaded with significance. Stephensen seems to sense, in Clarke's overt Gothicizing of the landscape, the return of the repressed (in this case, the legacy of convictism), which in his view would be better forgotten. His rejection of the melancholy in Clarke, Kendall, and Gordon is an early version of the current rejection of the so-called 'black armband history' — the wrong history, the history which, at any given time, we do not want because it conflicts with an official idea of national character.

The production of Gothic is one of Clarke's two principal responses to Australian emptiness. The other is its inverse: shaping his narratives like traditional romance, Clarke proposes fictional escapes from Australia for his characters and release from any fear of what is or is not in it. A conflict therefore runs through Clarke's fiction between the ameliorative form of romance with its focus on the hero and his final, triumphant restoration, and the Gothic motifs of vengeance and destruction leading to tragedy.

The Pleasures of Melancholy and the Quest for Home

Clarke first saw Port Arthur 'beneath a leaden and sullen sky'. Approaching by boat he 'beheld barring our passage to the prison the low grey hummocks of the Isle of the Dead' and reflected 'that there was a grim propriety in the melancholy of nature'. In Tasmania, 'Everybody [...] begged that the loathly corpse of this dead wickedness called Transportation might be comfortably buried away and ignored of men and journalists'.[15] Recording this sentiment at the end of the three articles he wrote for

---

[15] Marcus Clarke, 'Port Arthur', nos 2 and 3 in *Marcus Clarke*, ed. by Wilding, pp. 519, 529.

the *Argus* on Port Arthur, Clarke has already ignored it. In melancholy and repression he had found the subject matter that would allow him to write about Australia.

A century-long tradition (or more, if William Dampier is included)[16] already existed of describing Australia principally in terms of the bizarre and strange: the uncanny, in short, which is so central to Gothic. But far from revelling in the uncanny, Clarke often shows signs of self-consciousness about it, frequently trying to resist Gothic and the Australian uncanny (as if anticipating such criticisms as Stephensen's) by placing distance between his narrating voice and his experiencing characters. So in *His Natural Life*, Dick Purfoy, in flight, wakes in the bush and sees 'close to him four huge monsters, which slowly advanced. He rose to his feet, and the monsters disappeared. They were wild turkeys, magnified into moas by the mists of morning' (p. 613). Neither reader nor character is left in any doubt here that monstrosity is a mirage. More dramatically, John Rex falls prey to his imagination in the cave beneath the blowhole while on the run:

> His imagination — always sufficiently vivid and spurred to unnatural effect by the exciting scenes of the previous night — painted the most outrageous monsters as dwelling in the vermicular labyrinths that twined beneath him. Each patch of shadow, clinging bat-like to the humid wall, seemed to him some globular sea-spider ready to drop upon him with its viscid and clay-cold body, and drain out his chilled blood, enfolding him in rough and hairy arms.[17]

Despite these and other horrors — 'All creatures that could be ingendered by slime and salt', 'countless blisterous and transparent shapelessnesses', 'Bloodless and bladdery things' — there is in fact nothing there but 'the harmless life of the Australian ocean'. It is Rex's guilty conscience that momentarily asserts itself, as he succumbs to 'imagination — the unconscious religion of the soul'. The point is clinched when Rex's own shadow 'seemed to take the shape of an avenging phantom, with arms upraised to warn him back' (pp. 542–43).

In Clarke's last story, the novella *The Mystery of Major Molineux*, this approach to and retreat from Gothic is central.[18] The story opens with the trappings of a Gothic

---

[16] See Geraldine Barnes and Adrian Mitchell, 'Passing through Customs: William Dampier's Medieval Baggage', in this collection.

[17] I quote the original serial version here: Marcus Clarke, *His Natural Life*, ed. by Stephen Murray-Smith (Harmondsworth: Penguin, 1970), p. 542. For the 1874 revision of the serial as a novel, see Marcus Clarke, *His Natural Life*, ed. by Graham Tulloch with an introduction by Michael Meehan (Oxford: Oxford University Press, 1997). Following Tulloch, I do not use the title *For the Term of His Natural Life*, which was not Clarke's. The episode of Dick Purfoy's flight does not appear in 1874 but the blowhole episode reappears almost word for word.

[18] For a cogent historicist analysis of the Gothic in this story, see Andrew McCann, 'Colonial Gothic: Morbid Anatomy, Commodification and Critique in Marcus Clarke's *The Mystery of Major Molineux*', *Australian Literary Studies*, 19 (2000), 399–412.

ghost story, narrated by Julius Fayre, who becomes intrigued by Major Molineux, a man never seen in society on a Thursday and whose young niece, Agnes Tremayne, has mysteriously died. Beatrice, the attractive young daughter of Fayre's friend Rochford, tells Fayre that she is repelled by the Major's gloomy dwelling, known as Castle Stuart, and its two servants: 'The closed windows, the desolate garden, that horrible old cripple, and Mary Pennithorne, with her toothless mouth — ugh! the thought of it makes me shudder.' The man of science, Fayre, puts a more rational view: 'But, my dear young lady, there is nothing horrible in lameness, and though the absence of teeth may render Mrs Pennithorne unsightly, the poor woman is to be pitied rather than shuddered at.'[19]

After a riding accident, Beatrice dies in mysterious circumstances at Castle Stuart while Fayre, attending her, learns the Major's secret. But Fayre does not reveal the secret; when the Major kills himself, the story tails away with Fayre's hyper-rational account of the autopsy of the Major's body and his discovery of a peculiar calcareous growth on 'the pneumo-gastric, or *vagus* nerve' (p. 65). With the death of Beatrice, the character most susceptible to Gothic explanations, we are left only with rational explanations. The narrative is as a result barely coherent: it is impossible to explain the deaths of the young women and they cannot be linked to the repressed crime from the convict days that is earlier mentioned. Beatrice apparently dies of terror; but as Fayre's conclusion is that there is nothing to terrify, her death is inexplicable. Fayre refuses to articulate terror: 'The mystery of Major Molineux has now been told', he says, 'at least as much as can be told without violating a confidence which I even now hold sacred. There are many points in this strange and dreadful history which I cannot attempt to explain' (p. 66).

Repeatedly distancing himself from the uncanny, Clarke anticipates Freud's complaint about the writer's insertion of the uncanny into otherwise realistic narratives. For Freud the uncanny derives from superstitions we have overcome, so to play upon them 'is in a sense betraying us to the superstitiousness which we have ostensibly surmounted; he [the writer] deceives us by promising to give us the sober truth, and then after all overstepping it.'[20]

This 'betrayal' is one that Clarke could not evade. He does not always manage to place distance between his narrating selves and the uncanny, as is evident throughout *His Natural Life*. Clarke the would-be realist frequently succumbed just as readily as John Rex to the Gothicizing tendency, which was perhaps as deep in his unconscious as it is in Rex's. In the blowhole, Rex is the phantom and the phantom is a shadow; Clarke is less successful at keeping at a metaphorical level the monstrosity of

---

[19] Marcus Clarke, *The Mystery of Major Molineux* (1881; Canberra: Mulini Press, 1996), p. 15.

[20] Sigmund Freud, 'The ''"Uncanny"'', *The Standard Edition of the Complete Psychological Works of Sigmund Freud*, trans. and ed. by James Strachey (London: Hogarth Press/Institute of Psycho-Analysis, 1953–75), XVII (1955), pp. 219–252 (p. 250).

Gabbett, the book's other major villain. Through Gabbett Clarke tries to portray the dehumanizing effect of the convict system. Recaptured after an escape, Gabbett appears as a beast, 'a spectacle to shudder at [...]'. He is described as an 'animal' who 'crouche[s], with one foot curled round the other [...] one hairy arm pendant between his knees [...]'. He is 'horribly unhuman [...]'. But Clarke forgets his avowed intention of showing how the convict system dehumanizes men as Gabbett's beastliness is linked to Gothicized nature rather than the system:

> in his slavering mouth, his slowly grinding jaws, his restless fingers, and his bloodshot, wandering eyes, there seemed to live a hint of some terror more awful than the terror of starvation — a memory of a tragedy played out in the gloomy depths of that forest which had vomited him forth again [...]. (p. 256)

Cannibalism is the horror that is unarticulated at this point. But the malign agency of the 'forest' is unmistakable. The attribution of such agency, shading into outright personification, is a favourite technique of Clarke's, usually linked to Gothic effect. In his account of the western Tasmanian penal settlement of Macquarie Harbour Clarke notes how 'the black sides' of the harbour are 'gloomed by overhanging rocks, and shadowed by gigantic forests'. The description of the Gordon River is striking:

> The turbulent stream is the colour of indigo, and, being fed by numerous rivulets, that ooze through masses of decaying vegetable matter, is of so poisonous a nature that it is not only undrinkable, but absolutely kills the fish that in stormy weather are driven in from the sea. (pp. 242–43)

Neither the ideas here, nor many of the words, were Clarke's — he never set eyes on Macquarie Harbour. In fact he is intensifying the account in John West's *History of Tasmania*:

> The torrents, which pour down the mountains, mingle with decayed vegetable matter, and impregnated with its acids discolour the waters of the harbour; and the fish that approach the coast, often rise on the waves, and float poisoned to the shores.[21]

In West's account we are left to *assume* that the acidic waters poison the fish; a sense of malign agency is more evident in Clarke's, achieved at the price of an awkwardly placed adverb.

Like Clarke after him, West projects a vision of the place as deriving its terror from association with convictism: 'The name of *Macquarie Harbour* is associated exclusively with remembrance of inexpressible depravity, degradation, and woe. [...] There, man lost the aspect, and the heart of man!' (II, 181–82). Yet, again like Clarke, he finds misery in the natural features of the place: 'every object wore the air of rigour, ferocity, and sadness' (p. 182). Despite trying to emphasize the link of

---

[21] John West, *The History of Tasmania*, 2 vols (1852; Adelaide: Libraries Board of South Australia, 1966), II, p. 182.

Macquarie Harbour to convictism, both West and Clarke end up finding a more ancient and chthonic horror, an uncanny landscape to which convictism is belatedly but appropriately drawn.

This malign personification is most famously expressed in the account of the 'mountain forests [...] funereal, secret, stern' in the 1876 preface to Gordon's *Sea Spray and Smoke Drift*. Here, 'the savage winds shout among the rock clefts', cockatoos 'stream out, shrieking like evil souls [...] the mopokes burst out into horrible peals of semi-human laughter'.[22] Writing in his own voice as critic rather than hiding behind a narrator, Clarke gives himself away entirely, saying that 'the dweller in the wilderness acknowledges the subtle charm of this fantastic land of monstrosities. He becomes familiar with the beauty of loneliness'.[23] Clarke suggests that 'a poem like "L'Allegro", could never be written by an Australian' because it is too happy. He does not need to add that the mood he is invoking is that of the parallel poem, 'Il Penseroso', because he has clearly enough ventriloquized the speaker's last lines in that poem: 'These pleasures, Melancholy, give; / And I with thee will choose to live'.

The moment of *identification* is striking; for all the silent, rustling horror of the Australian bush Clarke finally identifies it as his *place*, in a moment reminiscent of Cowling's later assertion of love for Australia even as he complains of the fact that a Baedeker's Guide is not required. Even here, though, there is equivocation; it is not, strictly speaking, *Clarke* who learns to love the Australian bush, but 'the dweller in the wilderness'.

This tendentious moment in which romance is nowhere to be seen and the uncanny is rendered acceptable, even desirable, is rarely seen in Clarke's fiction. There, he is obsessed with the motifs of return and restoration: escape from the bush. He had, of course, every personal reason to meditate on these possibilities. An only child whose mother had died when he was young, Clarke was sixteen when his father fell ill with a brain condition. He had lived in expectation of a substantial inheritance but now learnt that the fortune his lawyer father had been accumulating had disappeared, probably through bad speculation. Without prospects, Clarke was advised to emigrate to Australia.[24] Thereafter, he seems to have lived in expectation of return, being by turns upbeat and pessimistic about it in his letters to his friend Cyril Hopkins back in England.[25] In his fiction, counter to the typical Gothic motifs

---

[22] Marcus Clarke, Preface to Adam Lindsay Gordon, *Sea Spray and Smoke Drift* (Melbourne: Clarson, Massina, 1876); repr. in Ackland, *19th Century Australian Literature*, pp. 43–46 (p. 45). The Aborigines, by contrast, are curiously marginal: 'From a corner of the silent forest rises a dismal chant, and around a fire dance natives painted like skeletons'. This relatively non-threatening appearance contrasts with that of Charles Harpur's Aborigines, who complement and complete the menace of the bush in 'The Creek of the Four Graves'.

[23] Ackland, *19th Century Australian Literature*, p. 46.

[24] Elliott, *Marcus Clarke*, pp. 20–22.

[25] See, for example, Elliott, *Marcus Clarke*, pp. 70, 72, 174–75, 180.

of vengeance and destruction, Clarke seeks the romance narrative pattern of triumphant heroic return. These motifs have everything to do with the question of being at home and where one is at home, and this, in turn, is inescapably connected to the uncanny.

As Freud famously made clear, the 'uncanny' derives its force (in the German language) from its being 'the opposite of what is familiar', literally that which is not 'homely'. Whether or not Australia could truly be 'home' was problematic for many immigrants and native inhabitants in colonial times and after. So Cowling professes love for Australia, but misses the medieval/Gothic trappings of his former English home, which for him constitute history. Stephensen, in a completely opposite move, welcomes being home in Australia, away from such historical trappings. For the exile Clarke, the problem of home and whether he could ever find Australia 'homely' is a deep one that ultimately drives all of his fiction.

Clarke had been in the colony five years when he began serializing *Long Odds*. In it, the fates of the two major characters contrast. Cyril Chatteris, English, heir to his father's fortune, falls from his father's favour, murders his enemy Dacre who schemed to bring him undone and flees. This narrative runs alongside that of Bob Calverly, an Australian who is visiting England. Calverly and Chatteris are rivals for the same woman, Kate Ffrench; Calverly, who is rich, is also targeted by the scheming Dacre and loses much of his money. Ultimately he turns the tables and, enriched by a massive win at the races, goes back to Australia, taking Kate. An epilogue takes place five years later on the spacious station Calverly has bought with his race winnings. A dying swaggie is brought in and he expires in front of Calverly and Kate — it is Cyril Chatteris.

In the preface, Clarke writes that England is a place 'which young Australians still call "Home"'.[26] *Long Odds* is very clearly a novel about 'home' and the attempt to return there. Cyril Chatteris at the beginning of the novel is blocked from returning to his family seat in 'Loamshire' because his father disapproves of his bohemian life and activities as a radical journalist. Ultimately, Chatteris is forced into a more permanent exile in Australia, forever away from home. Bob Calverly meanwhile is a willing visitor to 'that country which young Australians still call "Home"' but is threatened with being marooned there by the loss of his fortune. He emerges as the novel's true hero when he is able to return, triumphantly, to what must now be regarded as his true home in Australia. The plot of romance is perfected, and the novel closes with the reflection that 'every man has a romance once in his life [...]' (p. 344).

There are many parallels between Cyril Chatteris and Marcus Clarke: both bohemian journalists, both live in expectation of an inheritance from their fathers, which is snatched away from each. Chatteris's miserable exile to Australia is an extreme version of Clarke's similar enforced stay. The enviable figure in the book is

---

[26] Clarke, *Long Odds*, unpaginated preface.

Calverly, the omnicompetent Australian who defeats the villains, wins a fortune, gets the girl (and the sheep station) and, crucially, is 'at home' wherever he goes.

His Natural Life begins with the same story: the ne'er-do-well son who has fallen from his father's favour misses out on his inheritance and is exiled to Australia. It is now that Clarke adds Gothic, not apparent in *Long Odds*, to the formula. The repressed material he discovered at Port Arthur takes Gothic shape in his hands and Rufus Dawes/Richard Devine is subjected to the full Gothic horror of the penal colony. But in the serial version of the novel, as Michael Meehan has pointed out, the second sequence, in which Dawes escapes and becomes Tom Crosbie, the prosperous goldfields storekeeper, 'proceeds in an explicitly anti-tragic and anti-gothic mode [...]'.[27] Instead, the pattern of romance is restored. While John Rex initially usurps Rufus Dawes's position back in England by returning as an impostor, Rex is only the false hero of the tale, in Vladimir Propp's terminology.[28] His return prefigures Dawes's own triumphant occupation of the hero's role, and final return home.

Both books are simultaneously fearful of banishment and death (Rex, Chatteris) and hopeful about return and restoration (Dawes, Calverly). The moral scheme is entirely traditional and logical: Rex and Chatteris are guilty characters, Dawes and Calverly entirely innocent. The 1874 revision of *His Natural Life* is more brutal: Rex still goes back as an impostor but now he offers only a grim parody of the romance hero's return, one that can never happen. Dawes dies, albeit achieving redemption at the last; there is no return, no fortune. For all the optimism of its redemptive ending in which Dawes returns to his humanity (while Rex, a stroke victim, dies 'a mere animal, lacking the intellect he had in his selfish wickedness abused'), the new narrative, without 'Crosbie', and the regenerative sequence, is pessimistic about the heroic return to England.[29] It therefore enters more fully the Gothic-melancholic narrative: Dawes can only win in the terms of Gothic melancholy, by self-sacrifice and death.

Bourdieu's concept of authorial trajectory is designed to replace that of authorial biography.[30] In Clarke's case, the early announcements of trajectory give way to later stories that appear to invite collocation with biographical details. The permutations of Gothic in 'Holiday Peak', published in *The Australasian* in January 1873, and *The Mystery of Major Molineux* can be read as offering highly ironic commentary on a failed trajectory by an author who, burdened with debt, a growing family to support and later, illness, seems to have viewed his own return to England as unlikely.

---

[27] *His Natural Life*, ed. by Tulloch, p. xix.

[28] V. I. Propp, *Morphology of the Folktale*, trans. by Laurence Scott, 2nd edn (Austin: University of Texas Press, 1968), p. 80.

[29] *His Natural Life*, ed. by Tulloch, p. 430.

[30] See n. 12, above.

The narrator of 'Holiday Peak' is Marston (who appears in other stories as a Clarke-figure). At the opening he is astray in the bush, described in ways that anticipate the later preface to Gordon's poems: 'There is an indescribable ghastliness about the mountain bush at night which has affected most imaginative people'.[31] Personification is a frequent device — 'a few blasted trees crouch together like withered witches' — and animal life is sinister — 'a whirr of wings and a harsh cry disturb you from time to time, hideous and mocking laughter peals above and about you, and huge grey ghosts with little red eyes hop away in gigantic but noiseless bounds' (p. 594).

Marston then happens on a place of ancient ritual and human sacrifice. There is a self-conscious moment as Marston thinks of himself as 'a usurping white man within the mystic temple of a dead forgotten creed [...]' (p. 595). What follows is a sudden filling of the landscape with the entire history of world religion. Mithra, Isis, Osiris, Tammuz, and a host of other figures are invoked 'and now, in this strange and barren land, long deemed worthless to the tread of white feet, did I meet again the traces of the old religion' (pp. 595–96). Beyond this place lies a shangri-la, the land of what might have been as Marston calls it. This is a nineteenth-century literary utopia (leaving little doubt that the story has tipped over into parody): here, Byron is a family man and devoted husband, Dickens and Thackeray are friendly again, and Marston himself is 'an author whose readers are counted in millions, and to whom Chapman and Hall give £5,000 a volume' (p. 601). Marston is told that although he did have to go to Australia, his time of poverty lasted only a year and then, instead of exile to 'Bush Land' his 'fortune was recovered' (p. 600). The romance return is this time effected through utopian fantasy.

Marston then goes to a fairy-tale castle, a kind of utopia within utopia. 'This, then, was the world of which I had dreamt, and that other sordid one in which I had lived so long was but a dream!' (p. 606). The castle proves to be a pan-medieval version of Valhalla where the hosts of Barbarossa, Charlemagne and Arthur sit on horseback in the hall.

> As one entranced in waking slumber, I moved through the portal [...]. Yes, it was true! — chivalry lived still, and smug tradesmen, rejoicing in their science of money-breeding, had not beaten honesty and love to death with their yard-measures. All around me were beauty, truth, and honour, and serene in the midst of great and noble souls. (p. 607)

At this point a hitherto unannounced character, Lady Lenore, enters, evidently Marston's lost love. Inevitably, as he speaks to her of romantic fulfilment, the vision vanishes and Marston finds himself alone on the hill in Australia.

The medievalism here is of the kind rejected by Clarke in the Dickens obituary. Momentarily, it is positively envisioned, in a form in which medieval chivalry, explicitly anti-mercantile (and hence anti-modern), is emplaced as the other to

---

[31] *Marcus Clarke*, ed. by Wilding, p. 593.

Gothic horror. The chivalric Middle Ages operate as a kind of antidote to Gothic. The chivalric romance, however, is finally unavailable, the yearnings of the narrator (and by extension, the author) for home destined to be frustrated.

Clarke's last fiction, *The Mystery of Major Molineux* (discussed above), is equally pessimistic. Julius Fayre falls in love with the much younger Beatrice but before he can ask her to marry him, she is made an heiress by a bequest from the Major and he now feels that his proposal cannot be made without his appearing mercenary. While this kind of problem is solvable in traditional romance, Beatrice then dies. She is the victim of the Gothic elements in the story and her death is the most intense moment of a Gothic plot. But it also takes the Gothic out of the story. If *The Mystery of Major Molineux* is not, finally, a Gothic story, then the Australian landscape is once again emptied of melancholic possibility. The characteristic tendency to overload *terra nullius* with significance is averted.

Yet there is no romance return, either. Fayre, out riding with Rochford, remarks that the scenery around Hobart reminds him of 'one of the mountain counties of England. Rochford agrees and replies, 'I wonder if either of us will see them again?' (p. 18). No answer is given. Soon after, Beatrice has the accident that leads her to the fatal stay in Castle Stuart.

The answer to Rochford's question is obviously 'no'. In Clarke's last and most Gothic romance, the idea of heroic return has become the idle talk of middle-aged men. This is a fiction that opens by proposing in Tasmania a landscape overloaded with Gothic significance, only then to empty it again. The cost is that finally Tasmania is only a place like another place but not that place, a simulacrum of the desired utopia. At the end of his career, Clarke writes of landscapes that are loaded with the weight of civilizations past or which stand in for the desired landscape of home, only to be evacuated of history and significance and to become once again melancholic wildernesses, equivocally Gothic, certainly anti-romantic, in which the birds scream a harsh song of loneliness and love perishes unrequited.

Romantic Medievalism and Gothic Horror: Wordsworth, Tennyson, Kendall, and the Dilemmas of Antipodean Gothic

PETER OTTO

Civilization has been the scourge of the Natives; Disease, Crime, Misery and Death, have hitherto been the sure attendants of our intercourse with them.

— A Letter from a Gentleman in New South Wales (1826)[1]

By the middle of the nineteenth century, the word 'Gothic' could be used to refer to a style of architecture, a form of literature (Gothic fictions), a cultural fashion (the Gothic revival), and an historical period (the medieval). It could designate the barbarous world from which the modern has emerged; a primitive (natural) world able to renovate a lifeless modernity; and the sense that the modern is *unable* to divide itself from the barbarous past. Rather than having a univocal 'meaning', Gothic at times seems to name a network of antagonistic meanings that define some of the most important debates of modernity. In the following pages, I will look at some of the antagonistic senses of the Gothic as they appear in what may seem to some readers an unlikely location: the late poetry and prose of Henry Kendall, arguably 'the most substantial [Australian] poet of the colonial period'.[2] I will focus on the ways in which Kendall uses the Gothic —

---

[1] 'A Letter from a Gentleman in New South Wales', Methodist Missionary Society, in *Correspondence: Australia, 1812–26*, Australian Joint Copying Project, quoted in *Dispossession: Black Australians and White Invaders*, compiled by Henry Reynolds (Sydney: Allen and Unwin, 1989), p. 2.

[2] William H. Wilde, Joy Hooton and Barry Andrews, *The Oxford Companion to Australian Literature* (Melbourne: Oxford University Press, 1985), p. 385.

Gothic medievalism and Gothic primitivism, in particular — to generate a sense of belonging in an alien locale and, often at the same time, a disabling awareness of alienation, violence and chaos.

During his lifetime and until the 1930s, Kendall was often described as a quintessentially Australian poet.[3] George Oakley, writing in *The Australian Monthly Magazine* for August 1867, argued that 'Kendall's poetry which is as original in style as Ossian, is alone national in the sense of being evolved as it were from the country he inhabits. It is not so much he that speaks as Australia in him'.[4] As late as 1940, A. M. Hamilton-Grey was calling Kendall 'Our "God-Made Chief" — "A Singer of the Dawn"'.[5] Yet this same poet includes as one of his *Songs from the Mountains* a poem 'On a Spanish Cathedral'; hears in the sublime landscapes near Brisbane Water 'sounds like the melancholy wail that one seems to hear in the august Athurian [*sic*] *epos*'[6]; believes that the 'story of Arthur' is the 'only possible English epic of the nineteenth century'[7]; and on one occasion compares his own plight with that of Sir Bedivere mourning the loss of his king.[8]

The question of why a quintessentially Australian poet could see himself as Sir Bedivere — or why a poet associated with Ossian, a fictional third-century bard from the Scottish highlands, could also be described as Australia's 'God-Made Chief' — takes us to the heart of the Gothic and its role in nineteenth-century Australia. Before broaching these matters, however, we must turn first to Wordsworth and Tennyson, who mediated Kendall's reception of the Gothic.

---

[3] Thomas Thornton Reed, *Henry Kendall: A Critical Appreciation* (Adelaide: Rigby, 1960), p. 6.

[4] George Oakley, *The Australian Monthly Magazine*, August 1867. Quoted in Reed, *Henry Kendall*, p. 3.

[5] A. M. Hamilton-Grey, *Kendall: Our 'God-Made Chief' — 'A Singer of the Dawn'* (Sydney: Publicity Press, 1940).

[6] Henry Kendall, 'Arcadia at our Gates', *The Australian Town and Country Journal*, 27 Feburary 1875, p. 339 and 6 March 1875, pp. 379–80. The reference to 'the august Athurian [*sic*] *epos*' is on p. 379 of the second instalment.

[7] Henry Kendall, 'The Holy Grail', reprinted in part in *Henry Kendall: Poetry, Prose and Selected Correspondence*, ed. by Michael Ackland (St Lucia: University of Queensland Press, 1993), pp. 158–59 (p. 158).

[8] Henry Kendall, 'The Late Mr. A. L. Gordon: In Memoriam', in *The Poetical Works of Henry Kendall*, ed. by T. T. Reed (Adelaide: Libraries Board of South Australia, 1966), pp. 371–72, lines 52–55. All quotations from Kendall's poetry are taken from this volume and will be cited parenthetically in the text, giving line numbers (e.g. 52–55).

Visions of Paradise

Wordsworth recalls the years immediately following the French Revolution as a time when desire and reality, myth and history, seemed to have converged.[9] This idyll was short-lived. By the close of the eighteenth century, the terror in France, repression at home, and war between England and France had opened an abyss between the present and the dreams of the revolutionary past. In the 'Prospectus' to *The Recluse*, early drafts of which may date from 1798, 'Paradise, and groves / Elysian', no longer the soon-to-be-achieved goal of history, reappear as the future-present of the individual, the end towards which his labours are directed. 'Beauty [...] waits upon my steps', Wordsworth writes, 'Pitches her tents before me as I move, / An hourly neighbour'. But what is the status of this vision, Wordsworth asks. Must it be read as a history of 'departed things'? Or, worse, should we unmask such dreams and myths as mere fictions 'of what never was'?[10]

Wordsworth's answer to both questions is no. When 'the discerning intellect of Man' is 'wedded to this goodly universe / In love and holy passion', paradise becomes a present reality, 'A simple produce of the common day'. Moreover, as an emblem of our true nature and destiny, of what we are able (individually and collectively) to become, it anticipates an apocalypse of the imagination, in which history and nature return to their source in the imagination.

In this scheme of things, the poet rather than the revolutionary is the prime agent of change, which he incites by singing of what humanity is and what it could become. Wordsworth's great tasks are therefore to 'chant [...] the spousal verse / Of this great consummation' and, using 'words / Which speak of nothing more than what we are', to rouse 'the sensual from their sleep / Of Death'.[11] For 'the sensual', human desire is at odds with the objective world, and history is in discord with the ultimate source of things. When 'the sensual' wake they discover within themselves an active power, a counterpart to the shaping spirit that animates nature. As Wordsworth exclaims:

> How exquisitely the individual Mind
> (And the progressive powers perhaps no less
> Of the whole species) to the external World
> Is fitted: — and how exquisitely, too —
> Theme this but little heard of among men —

---

[9] William Wordsworth, *The Prelude: 1799, 1805, 1850*, ed. by Jonathan Wordsworth, M. H. Abrams, and Stephen Gill (New York: Norton, 1979), Book 11 (1850), lines 136–43.

[10] William Wordsworth, 'Prospectus' to *The Recluse*, in *The Poetical Works of William Wordsworth*, ed. by E. De Selincourt and Helen Darbishire, 5 vols. (Oxford: Clarendon Press, 1940–49), vol. 5, p. 4, lines 42–50.

[11] Wordsworth, 'Prospectus' to *The Recluse*, in *Poetical Works*, ed. by Selincourt and Darbishire, vol. 5, p. 4, lines 57–61.

The external World is fitted to the Mind;
And the creation (by no lower name
Can it be called) which they with blended might
Accomplish: — this is our high argument.[12]

Wordsworth's view of the prophetic role played by the poet and of the relation between the poet's vision and history closely structure the work of Henry Kendall. His *oeuvre* returns again and again to a group of closely related themes: the significance of the paradise or transcendent beauty glimpsed in childhood, landscape, mythology and so on; the innocent, passionate lives for whom paradise and beauty are 'the simple produce of the common day'; and the possibilities of self-transformation and, ultimately, of cultural transformation, opened by such visions.

Visions of paradise are for Kendall not as omnipresent as Wordsworth claims them to be; nevertheless, in poems such as 'Dedication — To a Mountain', he reports experiences in which the congruence between mind, nature, and the divine becomes a present (albeit still subjective) reality:

walking in exalted woods
Of naked glory — in the green and gold
Of forest sunshine — I have paused like one
With all the life transfigured; and a flood
Of light ineffable has made me feel
As felt the grand old prophets caught away
By flames of inspiration. (31–37)

Jesus's transfiguration, reported in Mark 9. 2–8, is usually understood as a revelation of his true identity as Son of God and of the glory he will assume at his second coming. Kendall's transfiguration reveals his kinship (as poet) with the creative force that animates nature and, in so doing, provides a glimpse of a future state in which mind, nature, and the divine are in harmony. At the same time, it authorizes his vocation as prophet and poet, and rationalizes the difficulties that will beset his attempt to 'arouse the sensual from their sleep' by singing the 'spousal verse' of a future 'great consummation'.

For Kendall and Wordsworth, poetry offers us a vision of a future paradise because it takes us back to the origin of things, in effect to the moment before our expulsion from Eden. Poetry therefore offers, according to Kendall, 'a revelation of Divinity beyond all revelations: a religion past religion'. As he writes in a letter to Mrs Selwyn dated 9 April 1864:

When I face the face of things, through the eyes of this Agent [Poetry], I am as it were, an *Aboriginal* Man. I look about me, as one might have looked on the first morning of Creation, with a surpassing wonder. The Visible becomes everlastingly new — everlastingly suggestive. There is a gloss for me on things, — a gloss, which once seen

---

[12] Wordsworth, 'Prospectus' to *The Recluse*, in *Poetical Works*, ed. by Selincourt and Darbishire, vol. 5, pp. 4–5, lines 63–71.

never leaves a man without the companionship and the exceeding great comfort of Beauty.[13]

One of the many odd things about Kendall's white, 'civilized', '*Aboriginal* Man' is that, as he looks about him in the same way as he 'might have looked on the first morning of Creation', he sees (amongst other things) the medieval. To understand why, we must turn first to the Gothic and then to Tennyson, the most important of Wordsworth's Victorian followers, who provided one of the chief models for Kendall's role as singer of a new, Aboriginal/medieval/Gothic dawn.

Romantic Medievalism

The root meaning of the word Gothic refers to the language and customs of the Goths or, more broadly, the Germanic peoples who invaded Europe in the third to fifth centuries AD, capturing Athens in 267–68 and sacking Rome in 410. For this reason, the Renaissance routinely opposed the Gothic to the classical: the former signified the barbaric, chaotic and violent, all which was opposed to classical civilization, order and peace. By the middle of the eighteenth century, however, Gothic had come to mean 'medieval' and therefore 'barbaric'. As such, the term plays an important role in the founding narratives of a modernity that defines itself in opposition to a (supposedly) barbaric past, 'in expectation of the differentness of the future'.[14] The fall of the Bastille on 14 July 1789 provides a paradigmatic instance of this narrative: for the revolutionaries, it exemplified not simply the emergence of the civilized from the barbaric, but the modern from the medieval, the present from the barbaric institutions of the past.

In the second half of the eighteenth century, many of the attributes ascribed to the Gothic were re-valued. Although its association with barbarism persisted, the distance of the Gothic from classical civilization could now also be taken as proof of the former's truth to nature and the latter's artifice. In *Letters on Chivalry and Romance* (1762), Hurd argues that 'The *gallantry*, which inspirited the feudal times' furnished 'the poet with finer scenes and subjects of description in every view, than the simple and uncontrolled barbarity of the Grecian'.[15]

This re-valuation of the Gothic (and the primitive) is taken a step further in romanticism. Wordsworth writes that his poetic 'Prospectus' to *The Recluse* bears the same relation to the major poem as 'the ante-chapel has to the body of a Gothic

---

[13] Henry Kendall, Letter to Mrs Selwyn, 25 March 1865, in *Henry Kendall*, ed. by Ackland, pp. 211–14 (p. 213).

[14] Jürgen Habermas, *The Philosophical Discourse of Modernity: Twelve Lectures*, trans. by Frederick Lawrence (Cambridge: Polity Press; Oxford: Blackwell, 1987), p. 6.

[15] Richard Hurd, *Letters on Chivalry and Romance, with the Third Elizabethan Dialogue*, ed. by Edith J. Morley (London: Frowde, 1911), p. 108.

church'. His earlier poems bear the same relation to 'the main Work as may give them claim to be likened to the little cells, oratories, and sepulchral recesses' that are normally part of 'those edifices'.[16] This comparison does not imply that Wordsworth modelled his poetry on Gothic precursors: *The Recluse* and its 'Prospectus' are unashamedly modern poems. Their form is Gothic, however, to the extent that Wordsworth draws his inspiration from the same primitive (and therefore authentic) springs as poets in less civilized times. The Gothic (the medieval and the primitive) grounds in human nature the visions of paradise that, for Wordsworth, provide a sense of what we could become.

The late eighteenth-century revaluation of the medieval/Gothic led to renewed interest in the legendary King Arthur. Hurd, for example, regrets that Milton's 'growing fanaticism' convinced him not to write an epic on '*Arthur and his Knights of the Round Table*', although this was 'his favourite subject'.[17] In *The Prelude*, Wordsworth recalls that, while searching for an appropriate theme for his 'life's work', he had at first thought to tell this 'Romantic tale by Milton left unsung'.[18] Blake writes that 'the fables of Arthur and his round table [...] Arthur's conquest of the whole world; [...] his death, or sleep, and promise to return again' are objects of his 'visionary contemplations, relating to his own country and its ancient glory, when it was as it again shall be, the source of learning and inspiration'.[19] Notwithstanding his 'visionary contemplations', Blake, like Milton and Wordsworth, did not write an Arthurian epic.

This reticence provided an opportunity for later generations of romantic medievalists. For the Victorian age it seemed, in Kendall's words, that the story of Arthur was 'The only possible English epic of the nineteenth century'.[20] Of the many attempts to write this epic, the most influential was Tennyson's *Idylls of the King*.[21] For Victorian audiences, arguably the most significant of this poem's twelve books

---

[16] Wordsworth, *Poetical Works*, ed. by Selincourt and Darbishire, vol. 5, p. 2.

[17] Hurd, *Letters*, p. 115.

[18] Wordsworth, *The Prelude*, Book I (1805), ll. 179–80.

[19] William Blake, *The Complete Poetry and Prose of William Blake*, ed. by David V. Erdman, newly rev. edn (New York: Anchor, 1988), p. 542.

[20] For a discussion of some of the most important attempts to write for the nineteenth century an Arthurian epic, or part thereof, see Laura Cooner Lambdin and Robert Thomas Lambdin, *Camelot in the Nineteenth Century: Arthurian Characters in the Poems of Tennyson, Arnold, Morris, and Swinburne* (London: Greenwood Press, 2000).

[21] James W. Hood, *Divining Desire: Tennyson and the Poetics of Transcendence* (Aldershot: Ashgate, 2000), p. 156, notes that 'forty thousand copies of the 1859 first edition [of Tennyson's *Idylls*] were printed, over ten thousand of which sold in the first week'.

was the last, *The Passing of Arthur* (1869), which incorporated Tennyson's first major Arthurian work, 'Morte d'Arthur' (written 1833–34; published in 1842).[22]

Tennyson's 'Morte d'Arthur' begins in *medias res*: Arthur is mortally wounded; Mordred, his brother and foe, is dead; and of all his knights only Sir Bedivere is still alive. The poem's brief retrospect of the battle leading to this crisis is expanded in *The Passing of Arthur*. It took place, Tennyson writes, in Lyonnesse:

> A land of old upheaven from the abyss
> By fire, to sink into the abyss again;
> Where fragments of forgotten peoples dwelt,
> And the long mountains ended in a coast
> Of ever-shifting sand.[23]

At this equivocal border between land and sea, existence and non-existence, the founding distinctions that once divided Arthurian civilization from chaos are undone, even the boundaries between friend and foe, past and present, life and death, become uncertain.

In both 'Morte d'Arthur' and *The Passing of Arthur*, following Thomas Malory's *Le Morte D'Arthur* (completed in 1470; printed 1485),[24] Arthur's mortal life can be brought to its conclusion only when Sir Bedivere throws Arthur's sword, Excalibur, into the lake, an act that has important consequences. First, it signals that the present is now radically divided from the past. As Bedivere recognizes, 'now [...] the true old times are dead', 'the whole Round Table is dissolved', and he is doomed to 'go forth companionless [...] Among new men, strange faces, other minds' (III, 559: 397, 402, 404, 406).

Second, the loss of Excalibur (and the division signalled by this event) is presented as a necessary precondition for Arthur's journey 'To the island-valley of Avilion' (427). Paradoxically, the collapse of Arthurian civilization is a triumph that removes the fleshly obstacles dividing Arthur (and his knights) from the Grail and, therefore, from paradise. Third, this radical break with the immediate past, and the return of Arthur to Avilion, together locate the present in a history that stretches back, not to a heroic past now departed, but to the timeless ideal (briefly and

---

[22] In *The Passing of Arthur* 198 lines were added to the 272 lines of the 'Morte d'Arthur'. The latter was published with a framing narrative, 'The Epic', not reproduced in the former.

[23] Alfred Tennyson, *The Poems of Tennyson*, ed. by Christopher Ricks, 3 vols (1969; 2nd edn, Harlow: Longman, 1987), vol. III, p. 551, lines 82–86. All quotations from Tennyson's work are taken from this edition of his poems and will be cited parenthetically in the text, giving volume and page numbers, unless clear from the context, and line numbers (e.g. III, 551: 82–86).

[24] For a detailed account of the relation between Tennyson's *Idylls* and Malory's *Le Morte D'Arthur*, see David Staines, *Tennyson's Camelot: The Idylls of the King and its Medieval Sources* (Waterloo: Wilfrid Laurier University Press, 1982).

inadequately) embodied by that past. This ideal in turn opens a future defined by the expectation that Arthur will return, that the ideal will once more be realized in time.

Tennyson's Arthurian ideal, Wordsworth's vision of paradise, and Blake's 'visionary contemplations' of his nation's 'ancient glory' are all *Gothic* visions of a primitive state in which myth, history and human desire converge. In this sense, they are precisely what a romantic poet like Kendall might be expected to see in the antipodes, on the margins of the civilized world. To stand at the primitive, Gothic spring of human history and culture is to see the world as it 'might have looked on the first morning of creation'. It is to glimpse what Kendall calls '"that aboriginal and plenary power which constitutes the authentic insignia [...] of genius", and whose presence is essential to the growth of any culture'.[25]

Historical time is, of course, always moving away from its beginning. Romantic poetry is, therefore, written under the sign of actual or potential loss. Wordsworth writes in *The Prelude* that

> The days gone by
> Come back upon me from the dawn almost
> Of life; the hiding-places of my power
> Seem open, I approach, and then they close;
> I see by glimpses now, when age comes on
> May scarcely see at all;

This loss, however, adds urgency to his role as poet: 'I would give', Wordsworth writes,

> While yet we may, as far as words can give,
> A substance and a life to what I feel:
> I would enshrine the spirit of the past
> For future restoration.[26]

In 'Morte d'Arthur' and *The Passing of Arthur*, the poet (represented by Sir Bedivere) has the same urgent responsibility: namely to enshrine 'the spirit' of Arthurian civilization 'for future restoration'. Kendall assumes a similar role; however, it is now the dawn of colonial settlement that must be enshrined for future restoration, the 'aboriginal' power and potential that, in the first encounter with an alien landscape, provides a sense of what the colony could become. Some of the difficulties that arise as Kendall attempts to carry out this role can be seen in 'Arcadia at our Gates', an essay first published in two parts, in *The Australian Town and Country Journal* of 27 February and 6 March 1875.

---

[25] Henry Kendall, 'Men of Letters in New South Wales', *Punch Staff Papers*, 1872. Quoted in Robert Dingley, 'Double Vision: Aspects of Aboriginality in Kendall's Writing', in *Henry Kendall: The Muse of Australia*, ed. by Russell McDougall (Armidale: Centre for Australian Language and Literature Studies, 1992), pp. 405–17 (p. 412).

[26] Wordsworth, *The Prelude*, Book 12 (1805), lines 333–42.

'On the Brink of the Beautiful'

In the late eighteenth and early nineteenth century, first impressions of Australia often associated the landscape with a classical, Gothic, or mythical past. Lieutenant Southwall, who arrived in Port Jackson with the First Fleet on 26 January 1788, wrote in his diary that

> nothing can be conceived more picturesque than the app'e of the country while running up this extra[ordinary] harbour. [...] The scene is beautifully height'ed by a number of small islands that are dispers'd here and there, on which may be seen charm'g seats, superb buildings, the grand ruins of stately edifices, etc. etc. which as we pass'd were visible, but at intervals the view being pr'ty agreably interrupted by the intervention of some proud eminence, or lost in the labyrynth of the inchanting glens that so abound in this fascinating scenery.[27]

In *Letters from an Exile at Botany Bay to his Aunt in Dumfries* (1794), George Watling strikes a similar tone:

> Perhaps nothing can surpass the circumambient windings, and romantic banks of a narrow arm of the sea, that leads from this to *Parramatta*, another settlement about fourteen miles off. The Poet may there descry numberless beauties; nor can there be fitter haunts for his imagination. The elysian scenery of a Telemachus; — the secret recesses for a Thompson's musidor; — arcadian shades; or classic bowers, present themselves at every winding to the ravished eye.[28]

In the decades that divide these remarks from the publication of 'Arcadia at our Gates', the landscapes they describe had become, for the settlers, part of the known. Immersed in the familiar, the colonists had lost sight of the wilderness that lay just beyond their purview. They were, according to Kendall, 'standing blind on the brink of the beautiful'.

In making this assessment, Kendall is repeating Anthony Trollope's observation, published in *Australia and New Zealand* (1873), that in England and Australia it is so commonly believed that Australian landscape 'is monotonous' that few visitors or settlers bother to 'make a search after the beauties of nature'; yet there is 'grand scenery in [...] all the Australian colonies'.[29] In New South Wales, Trollope singles out the Hawkesbury as a river that can be favourably compared even with the Mississippi and the Rhine.

---

[27] Daniel Southwall, 'Diary', in *Historical Records of New South Wales*, vol. II, p. 666. Quoted in Bernard Smith, *European Vision and the South Pacific 1768–1850* (Oxford: Oxford University Press, 1960), pp. 134–35.

[28] George Watling, *Letters from an Exile at Botany Bay to his Aunt in Dumfries* (Penrith: Ann Bell, 1794), pp. 22–23. Quoted in Smith, *European Vision*, p. 135.

[29] Anthony Trollope, *Australia and New Zealand*, 2 vols (1873; 2nd edn, repr. London: Dawsons, 1968), vol. 1, p. 315. Trollope visited Australia from 1871 to 1872.

Trollope's enthusiasm was roused, Kendall confides, even though he had seen only a small portion of the Gothic magnificence before him. What he took to be 'an august cathedral of scenery' was in fact merely 'the portico of the temple'. 'A mere lingerer', Trollope did not realize 'he was coasting waters far more striking in their lovely reality than the fabled lakes lying to the west of the sunset'. Kendall is referring to Brisbane Water, the vast lake and estuary lying north of Broken Bay and the mouth of the Hawkesbury, described in the *Sydney Gazette* of 16 June 1825 as 'resembling [...] in extent and smoothness the beautiful water of Loch Lomond'.[30]

When Kendall published 'Arcadia at our Gates' in 1875, although the Hawkesbury and Brisbane Water may not have been popular tourist destinations, they were hardly unknown. Settlement of the Hawkesbury region dates from 1794, while the towns of Windsor, Richmond, Wilberforce, Pitt Town and Castlereagh date from 1810.[31] Indeed, Trollope was surprised to see 'a large dilapidated and unused church', which he took as evidence of 'how soon ruins may be instituted in a new country'.[32] Work began on the task of surveying the Brisbane Water district in 1825. By 1829 a settler could enthuse that 'the calm bosom' of Brisbane Water 'is daily ruffled by the busy oar of the settler, the blue gum cutter and the lime burner, each pursuing his own vocation'.[33]

If settlers and tourists are to (re)discover the Arcadia at their gates they must, in effect, recover the state of wonder experienced by the first white visitors to Brisbane Water. Unfortunately, as Kendall notes, 'The early history of civilization at Brisbane Water has been, to a considerable extent, forgotten by even its oldest European inhabitants'.[34] He therefore finds himself in the unenviable position of having to draw on his own experience of Brisbane Water in order to imagine what Charles Webb (presented by Kendall as the first white settler in the area) might have seen on his first voyage to this region, so that readers of 'Arcadia at our Gates' can see the landscape as it might have looked 'on the first morning of creation'.

---

[30] Charles Swancott, *Gosford and the Kendall Country* (Woy Woy: Brisbane Water Historical Society, 1966), p. 8. Loch Lomond was the 'picturesque highlight' of the 'Short Tour' of the Highlands, 'established as a fashionable amusement from about 1760'. See Peter Womack, *Improvement and Romance: Constructing the Myth of the Highlands* (London: Macmillan, 1989), pp. 62–63.

[31] Stan Stevens, *Hawkesbury Heritage* (Windsor: Hawkesbury Shire Council, 1984), p. 7.

[32] Trollope, *Australia and New Zealand*, p. 324.

[33] Swancott, *Gosford and the Kendall Country*, pp. 8, 9.

[34] Swancott describes the Brisbane Water area as 'bounded on the east and south by the Pacific Ocean and the Hawkesbury River, to a point in the vicinity of Wiseman's Ferry. The northern boundary runs from a point below Catherine Hill, across country below Lake Macquarie and the village of Wyee, to the Judge Dowling Range'. See Swancott, *Gosford and the Kendall Country*, p. 7.

In *The Passing of Arthur*, Sir Bedivere must reach the limits of Arthurian civilization before he wins a glimpse of Avilion and of Arthur's apotheosis. An analogous pattern appears, albeit in a more literal register, in Kendall's 'Pytheas', named after the 'Gray old sailor of Massilia' who (supposedly) discovered 'England in the misty dawn of Time'. Pytheas's journey 'From the fair calm bays Hellenic' takes him first to 'the limits of the world', the shores of the Arctic. It is only after he has traversed this realm of 'Dumb dead chaos' that he turns the 'prow' of his boat and moves on to 'The sweet green fields of England'.

Webb's antipodean journey follows an analogous path. Leaving Sydney behind, and passing the 'gloomy North Head', he journeys to the margins of the known where, after passing several 'cruel menacing rocks', and a 'great gaping battle-field of antagonistic waters', he reaches 'the terminus of the beautiful Hawkesbury'. Even now Webb's trials are not at an end, for he must battle 'the white wrath of rock-baffled waters' before he can enter the new/ancient world:

> First the monster, and then the Hesperides. As the harsh fierce coast of Attica fences in the green valleys beyond Athens so this league or two of passionate surge shuts a way a new Beulah, from the blind fury of outer waters. Borne swiftly by the tide [...] we come to where the roar of the ocean is like the voice of thunder calling out of other lands. Here the Spenserian dream is realised.

The first sentence of this quotation compares Webb's voyage to Brisbane Water with Hercules' entry into the garden of the Hesperides. Both must slay the monster that guards the entrance to paradise before they can enter and seize its treasures. The paradise discovered by Webb is identified by Kendall as a 'new Beulah', one of the names to be given to Jerusalem after the Exile: 'Thou shalt no more be termed Forsaken; neither shall thy land any more be termed Desolate: but thou shalt be called Hephzibah ["My delight is in her"], and thy land Beulah ["married"]' (Isaiah 62. 4). As this suggests, Webb's voyage is at one and the same time a journey into the future and a homecoming, which brings the temporal back into relation with the divine.

Still mixing mythological associations, Kendall claims that in this 'new Beulah [...] the Spenserian dream is realised'. This second denomination refers to *The Faerie Queene*, a poem in which, as Spenser explains in his introductory Letter addressed to 'Sir Walter Raleigh knight', he labours 'to pourtraict in Arthure, before he was king, the image of a brave knight, perfected in the twelve private morall vertues'. The young Arthur, Spenser continues, saw 'in a dream or vision the Faery Queen, with whose excellent beauty ravished, he awaking resolved to seeke her out, and so [...] went to seeke her forth in Faerye land'.[35] Brisbane Water, first associated with the Garden of the Hesperides and described as a 'new Beulah', is now a 'Faerye

---

[35] Edmund Spenser, 'The Faerie Queene: A Letter of the Authors Expounding his Whole Intention in the Course of This Work', in *Spenser: Selected Writings*, ed. by Elizabeth Porges Watson (London: Routledge, 1992), pp. 280–84 (pp. 281, 282).

land' in which Webb (first seen as Hercules, then as Israel and now as Arthur) sets out as chivalrous settler to obtain the object of his desire.

Despite their initial enthusiasm, Southwall and Watling come to the view that their first experience of Sydney Harbour had been misleading. Watling believed he had been deceived by 'the specious external'. Southwall was equally dismissive: 'Tis greatly to be wish'd these appearances were not so delusive as in reality they are'.[36] Kendall is willing to allow that Sydney Harbour offers only an 'evanescent beauty which [...] swims on the light of forms'. In contrast, 'the actual loveliness' of Brisbane Water 'is so surprising, that the mere creations of the eye pass into nothing before we have the leisure to look for them'. As merely subjective beauty dissolves, the observer catches sight of the divine:

> Even to the eyes of the rough bushman, whose voyage has been followed so far, these superb illuminations of rock, wood, and water must have come like a supernatural revelation. Into every beautiful object viewed — however insufficiently — for the first time, there enters something immeasurable and divine; and our conception of this will be always determined by our powers of *second sight*.

This revelation takes the reader (with Webb and Kendall) from temporal to eternal things, from the temporal beginning of white settlement to the divine origin of all (European) civilizations. As Webb moves past the terminus of the Hawkesbury and then into Brisbane Water, the landscape therefore evokes many of the founding myths of European civilization. 'The dazzling spectacle of the "Broadwater"' flashes and glows like 'the shield of a Miltonic archangel'. Narrara Creek winds 'like some splendid serpent of the Pre-Adamite days'. The same creek has, 'here and there',

> all the grace and delicacy of an old world scene. All the nooks, openings, large-like avenues, hedges, arbours, tiny banks, and fairy inlets, which form the association of a dear dead English childhood are here.

In 'the darkly magnificent valley of Mooni Mooni', one can see 'caves of stalactite and stalagmite, vaulted and groined like a cathedral — domes of cliff, and clumps of black crag grouped about like the relics of a mighty Druidical temple'. And in more sheltered spaces, 'the roar of the tempest on the ranges sounds like the melancholy wail that one seems to hear in the august Athurian [*sic*] *epos*'.

This powerful congruence between the white settler/poet/tourist, the 'surprising beauty' discovered in his/her first encounter with the Australian landscape, and the divine origin of [European] things makes the settler an 'aboriginal' inhabitant of a new (colonial) world.

One might complain that Webb is a 'rough bushman', whose 'persistent desire' is not to embrace the Faery Queen but to find 'fresh fields and pastures new', and that Kendall, by his own admission, has 'more knowledge of [Webb's] path, than ability

---

[36] Watling, *Letters*, p. 23. Southwall, 'Diary'. Both quoted in Smith, *European Vision*, p. 135.

to describe its surroundings'. 'Fancy one of the hierophants of medieval Italy in the place of Charles Webb!', Kendall ejaculates; 'Fancy a robed and crowned Levite like Turner, entering yonder temple of the Almighty! Why the effect would have been something like transfiguration!' Yet, paradoxically, Webb's material preoccupations and Kendall's poetic failings reveal rather than obscure the presence of beauty: their human shortcomings negatively define that 'ancient glory, when it was as it again shall be'.

A more direct threat to the claims of transcendent beauty and the settler society it authorizes can be found in the historical context of Webb's journey. In *Idylls*, the collapse of Arthurian civilization and the emergence of a new world occurs in a landscape where 'fragments of forgotten peoples' dwell. If one were to focus on Kendall's account of Webb's first night on the shores of Brisbane Water, one might assume that the region was uninhabited. One should remember, however, that in, say 1820 (Kendall writes that Webb's journey took place 'more than half a century ago'), despite the ravages of diseases brought by white civilization, such as small-pox, venereal disease and pneumonia, the indigenous inhabitants of the region were a significant force.[37]

Kendall's attempt to see Brisbane Water through Charles Webb's eyes stops on the morning of his first day in the region. This 'clear blue morning', he writes, 'might receive from our hands some fitting furniture of scenery and events. But the picture is closed'. It is closed, one assumes, in order to quarantine Webb's 'supernatural revelation' from the work of colonization about to begin, conflict with the indigenous inhabitants of this 'new Beulah', and the possibility that Webb's arrival is belated, perhaps even illegitimate. At the same time, as a romantic poet intent on transforming the real by invoking the ideal, Kendall cannot completely ignore the former. In 'Arcadia at our Gates', Webb's experience of transcendent beauty is therefore collocated with a radically different observation:

> Between the early settlers and the blacks there appears to have been constant warfare
> — the savages having to be kept under by means of fire-arms. About 1830 things
> became comparatively quiet, and continued so until 1842. In this year, the Aborigines,
> for some reason not handed down, re-commenced their hostility; and many of them,
> committed crimes of such a serious character that the Government had to send down a
> body of soldiers. [...] from what I can learn, the military displayed great barbarity. In
> the middle of the night, camp after camp was surprised, and the occupants, men,
> women, and children, shot down like native dogs.

The vision of transcendent beauty is, of course, meant to judge and offer an alternative to this brutality. Yet as the essay progresses, the boundary between the real and the ideal, the natural and the supernatural, becomes less and less secure. As

---

[37] Henry Reynolds writes that in 1795, when settlement of the Hawkesbury began, 'an "open war" started with the Hawkesbury River clans'. See *Frontier: Aborigines, Settlers and Land* (Sydney: Allen and Unwin, 1987), p. 5.

I have suggested, the 'rock-baffled waters' through which Webb must pass are a physical and psychological barrier. Yet at the same time Kendall implies, perhaps unconsciously, that they also symbolize Aboriginal resistance to settlement. The primary obstacle delaying settlement of Brisbane Water was human not geographical:

> its reputation was anything but inviting — owing to the ferocity of the blacks. About six or seven hundred of these savages held possession of all the coast country lying between the Hawkesbury and the majestic waters of Lake Macquarie.

Although 'Defended by one of the largest and fiercest tribe of aborigines that ever threw the aggressive boomerang', Brisbane Water 'was nevertheless penetrated by the persevering white man; and one by one its hills and bays were discovered and mapped off in the memory of the intruder'. This last clause implies that exercise of memory, even the kind rehearsed in Kendall's 'Arcadia at our Gates', may not be in all regards as therapeutic as Wordsworth would like it to be. Indeed, memory is here isomorphic with dispossession.

For the romantic settler/tourist, the experience and recollection of transcendental beauty plays an important set of roles. First, it validates European settlement of the region by providing an origin able to displace questions of merely temporal precedence. In his experience of 'surprising beauty', Webb is more Aboriginal than the Aborigines. Second, the fiction of transcendental beauty provides a defence against an alien landscape and culture by locating ultimate reality in a realm not touched by the temporal and spatial processes of colonization. In both of these roles, beauty diverts attention from, and legitimates the outcome of, a struggle *between* civilizations.

Third, it offers a resolution of the problems of dependence and independence that beset a colonial culture. The latter can break from the former and yet remain its heir. By breaking from the past, the colonial world returns to the same springs that nourish European civilization. The settler is therefore a prodigal *and* faithful son: even as he leaves home, he is always already returning to his father. The movement from the centre to the periphery, where surprising beauty is discovered, displaces the struggle between colonizer and colonized.

'The melancholy wail [...] in the august Athurian [*sic*] *epos*' recalls the fate of those peoples destroyed by the periodic rise and fall of (European) civilization. Heard in the valley of Mooni Mooni and at the sources of the Wy Wy and Narrara, it evokes the destruction of Aboriginal peoples. For Trollope, this is an inevitable side-effect of the arrival of European civilization. He urges only that the Aborigines be allowed to 'perish without unnecessary suffering'.[38] Their fate is no more relevant to settler society than Tennyson's 'forgotten fragments of peoples' are to the peoples who will in later ages draw inspiration from Arthur. For Kendall, however, the

---

[38] Trollope, *Australia and New Zealand*, p. 76.

relations between the ideal and the real, beauty and violence, civilization and barbarity, are more difficult to untangle.

At the close of 'Arcadia at our Gates', Kendall imagines the elders of Gosford pointing 'out to their children spots mossed with its old traditions'. Rather than recalling Webb's encounter with 'surprising beauty', the white elders recall (although without appearing to register either its significance or its affective force) a landscape of violence:

> 'Here', they may say, 'was the camp where the poor blind black-fellow, "Pannikan", was shot down by the soldiers like a vulture.' 'Up that Hosee's Gully, Mick Brady, the left-handed sawyer, was murdered a hundred and twenty years ago.' 'Here Jem Wells lived, the bushman who had all the notions and accomplishments of a blackfellow.' 'There, on that slope, stood the lone hut of Jack Hayes, the brave old cripple who lived by himself and worked till there was no work left in him.' 'At the head of this Popran Creek, Billy Fawkner, the last of the blacks, killed his mate, Long Dick.' 'Over yonder is the cave where Tom Desmond slept, the giant convict who tied the savage that speared him to a tree, and then cut his hands off.' 'And here, by this large hotel, was warm-hearted Hugh Campbell's Bushman's Home, where the sawyers and shingle-splitters used to come; and, over their grog and pipes, discuss quaintly the great questions of the day.'

The bucolic community of Hugh Campbell's Bushman's Home and the lonely heroism of Jack Hayes is remembered alongside an internecine strife between white and black and within both white and black communities.

The 'constant warfare' that marked early settlement of Brisbane Water is not quite forgotten; yet, at the same time, the elders seem unable to make it an object for consciousness. Although they allude to this violence, it does not ruffle the surface of the anecdotes they believe are fit for children. For Kendall, this 'underside' to beauty is a much more disturbing presence. It problematizes the role that, as poet, he hopes to play in colonial society. It also conditions the strong current of Gothic horror in his *oeuvre*, which threatens to engulf his evanescent visions of beauty.

Explanations for Kendall's preoccupation with Gothic horrors usually draw on his troubled personal life, culminating in his 'admission to the Gladesville Mental Asylum in 1871 and 1873 — for alcoholism, addiction to opiates, depression and melancholia — and, between these two dates, the year of mental and physical breakdown that he was later to refer to as "The Shadow"'.[39] Ackland adds that Kendall's despair is strongly influenced by 'the mid-century crisis of faith'.[40] Without understating these factors, it seems likely that the current of Gothic horror in Kendall's *oeuvre* also derives from the attempt to think through the implications

---

[39] Peter Otto, 'Kendall's Sublime Melancholy', in McDougall, *Henry Kendall*, pp. 418–43 (p. 421).

[40] Michael Ackland, 'Towards "The Shadow": Henry Kendall and the Mid-Century Crisis of Faith', in McDougall, *Henry Kendall*, pp. 275–88 (p. 276).

of Romantic aesthetics and romantic medievalism in a colonial context. We can explore this possibility by turning briefly to *Songs from the Mountains*.

The Spirit of the Past

In 'Dedication — To a Mountain', the first of Kendall's *Songs from the Mountains*, the narrator/poet plays the part of a poetic Charles Webb: walking amongst 'exalted woods / Of naked glory', he is transfigured by transcendent beauty (31–32). In this experience, his soul hears 'The higher worship'; he gathers 'The broad foundations of a finer hope' and, like 'the grand old prophets', is 'caught away / By flames of inspiration' (27, 28, 36–37).

The content of this revelation and the kind of vocation it demands are suggested by 'Hy-Brasil' and 'On a Spanish Cathedral'. In the former, a woman made perfect by fasting and prayer is touched and transfigured by 'the glory of the Saviour', giving her 'the eyes of saints of Heaven — all their glory in her hair' (8, 28). Where those less pure are able only fleetingly to experience transcendent beauty, for this pure woman the experience of 'glory' (later described as 'a radiant spirit' following the instructions of 'God the Father') turns her eyes to the west, where she sees the legendary Hy-Brasil (Eden) floating on the sea (29).

While pure women fast and pray in order to make their bodies congruent with the divine, in 'On a Spanish Cathedral' inspired men struggle to make matter conform to their dream of heaven, 'the spire and tower and dome of their thought' (30). Through their prayers and dreams 'A soul of unspeakable fire' descends, inspiring them to fight to realize their dream (29). The result is a building filled and transfigured with 'the glory of Godhead' (6).

Kendall makes no attempt to disguise the distance dividing him from the woman's purity and the builders' zeal. He describes the Spanish cathedral as 'a luminous dream of the Heaven I never may see' (50) and admits that 'We can never find Hy-Brasil — never see its hills again!' (38). This sense of personal failure — the subject of 'Mooni', 'The Voice in the Wild Oak', 'Narrara Creek', 'Names upon a Stone' and 'After Many Years' — makes more poignant his plea in 'The Sydney International Exhibition' for 'one hour'

> Of life pre-eminent with perfect power,
> That I may leave a song whose lonely rays
> May shine hereafter from these songless days. (51–54)

In this song, Sydney appears as an antipodean Camelot, a 'shining City of a hundred spires! / In mists of gold' (71–72) that emerged when

> Arthur Phillip [stood] in a day of dream:
> What time the mists of morning westward rolled,
> And heaven flowered on a bay of gold! (151–53)

In that distance past, the 'Strong sons of Europe [...] Faced ghastly foes and felt the alien spear!' (87–88); but now the ideal has emerged from 'immemorial silence'. Now, the poem concludes, the ideal glimpsed in the first moments of colonization can rise from the darkness:

> The gracious Love [Christ] that helped us long ago
> Will on us like a summer sunrise flow;
> And be a light to guide the Nation's feet
> On holy paths — on sacred ways, and sweet. (286–89)

This imagined moment in which, for poet and colony, the gap between desire and achievement is closed, underwrites Michael Ackland's argument in *That Shining Band* that we should see *Songs from the Mountains* as Kendall's 'climactic attempt to fulfil a life-long sense of mission'. Although the result 'was hardly the prophetic triumph which the young man had dreamed of', nevertheless, Ackland concludes, we can hope that 'in his final years' he was not deprived 'of the satisfaction involved in [...] knowing that [...] he had nevertheless raised enduring verbal monuments to an article of personal faith, that inspired individual efforts could still advance the creation of "A new Age 'cast in a diviner mould"'.[41]

This reading of *Songs* is, however, qualified by a counter-narrative that suggests, not simply that Kendall is unworthy of his vocation or that the ideal remains forever out of reach, but that the desire for 'A new Age' is in some sense intertwined with the barbaric world it is designed to displace. We can outline this narrative by turning to three poems from *Songs*: 'Beyond Kerguluen', 'Cooranbean', and 'The Curse of Mother Flood'.

In the first of these poems, the gleams and glitters of landscape reveal chaos rather than order, and startle the observer with horror rather than beauty. The bays that mark the borders of this world tell a

> Tale of distress from the dawn of the world!
> *There* are the gaps with the surges that seethe in them —
> Gaps in whose jaws is a menace that glares!
> *There*, the wan reefs with the merciless teeth in them
> Gleam on a chaos that startles and scares. (156–60)

This polar landscape is hundreds of kilometres south of the living landscapes and forests described by Kendall in poems such as 'Dedication — To a Mountain'. Many thousands of years divide it from its own springtime, when 'Dells of the daffodil — spaces impearled, / Flowered and flashed' (70–71). Yet this division is difficult to sustain, for the landscape described in 'Beyond Kerguluen' is produced by the

---

[41] Michael Ackland, *That Shining Band: A Study of Australian Colonial Verse Tradition* (St Lucia: University of Queensland Press, 1994), pp. 184, 192–93. See also, 'No Easy Age for Faith or Verse: *Songs from the Mountains* and Henry Kendall's Burden of Election', in McDougall, *Henry Kendall*, pp. 385–404.

withdrawal of the ideal. Moreover, the 'Tale of distress' written on its surface speaks of a reality more primitive and much more persistent than the romantic 'Dells of the daffodil' that once bloomed on its surface.[42]

In 'Cooranbean' and 'Beyond Kerguluen', Gothic horror registers a more recent distress. 'Cooranbean' describes a glen that has been deserted for only fifty-seven years. Here the landscape is marked by 'The brand of black devil'; 'There is doom, there is death in the air: a curse groweth up from the ground!' (3–4). 'The Curse of Mother Flood' describes an equally dismal locale: a 'gorge with a grave in the mouth of it', where there is never 'a hope of the Spring in it — / Never a glimmer of yellow and green' (27, 29–30).

These landscapes are associated with terrible crimes. In the former, they are committed by 'black Tom', a 'black devil' who escaped from 'shackle and gyve' to become 'mate of red talon and paw — a wolf in the shape of a man' (33, 3, 34, 36). In the latter, the narrator speaks more obliquely of a 'Crime that would startle a fiend from his lair' (58). The poems draw readers toward these landscapes and the crimes they memorialize, as if demanding we remember them. Yet at the same time, they insist that these crimes cannot be known: they are 'unspeakable'; a 'terrible mystery'; 'without name — man never heard of it'; and so on.

Wordsworth hoped to 'enshrine the spirit of the past for future restoration'. In 'Cooranbean' and 'The Curse of Mother Flood', the spirit of a violent past, and the locale that enshrines it, threatens to disable the present and future of white settlement. In 'Cooranbean', merely asking a 'white-headed man of the woods' about the glen turns him into a 'phanton' [sic] (9, 12). In 'The Curse of Mother Flood', those who see the gorge hurry away aghast, speechless, their hair 'frozen with horror' (37–38).

Both poems appear to recommend, therefore, that readers try not to see what they are being drawn towards. Having described a landscape that is convulsed with unnamed suffering — 'bloody-red sedge' that stands 'In the throat of a feculent pit', and 'a foam like the foam of a fit [that] sweats out of the lips of the ledge' — the narrator of 'Cooranbean' recommends that the viewer *Bow low with inaudible breath: beseech with the hands to the face!'* (21–22, 24). While evoking the 'wild witch' of the pit that squats in the gorge 'with a ghoul at her throat!', 'The Curse of Mother Flood' warns that 'Just the one glimpse' of her will turn the viewer into a 'white leper', who poses a risk, presumably, of contaminating the entire community (52, 45, 48).

---

[42] For a different view, see Michael Ackland, 'No Easy Age for Faith or Verse', in McDougall, *Henry Kendall*, p. 395. Ackland argues that 'The polar region is [...] a measure of celestial deprivation and alienation from a wonderful, paradisial past'. The former, he argues, is 'a haunting spectre now lying far away' from the poet's world. In my view, the extent to which the polar region is defined by the absence of its 'paradisial past' suggests a closer relation between these poles.

The poems' attempts to quarantine readers from this primal horror are barely effective. For the first forty-four lines of 'Cooranbean', 'doom' and 'death' seem confined to the glen while the 'white-headed [men] of the woods' range freely over the rest of the landscape. In the last four lines, however, this relation is reversed. At night, 'doom' and 'death' well up from the glen, threatening to engulf the settlers, now confined to their huts. At such times, 'the white fathers fasten the door, and often and often they start / At a sound like a foot on the floor and a touch like a hand on the heart' (47–48). The last lines of 'The Curse of Mother Flood' seem more reassuring. They turn from the 'wild witch' to 'the strong shining Hawkesbury — / Spacious and splendid' (73–74). Yet the witch and her Valley of Death are only 'Twenty miles' north and, on numerous occasions in the late eighteenth and the nineteenth century, gathered sufficient power to devastate the Hawkesbury valley. In 1799, 1806 and 1809, the new settlements were inundated. Even after they had been moved to higher ground, the settlers were defenceless before the great flood of June 1867 that reduced Windsor, Richmond and Pitt Town to islands in 'a vast inland sea'.[43]

The Gothic vision implied in these poems, of a violence that once helped establish, but now returns to haunt white settlement, implies that the existence of an ideal not entwined with violence can be no more than an article of faith. While this faith gives the poet/settler the courage to go on, it intensifies the gloom of the present. As Kendall remarks in 'Eighteen Hundred and Sixty Four':

> God help us all! If that lone Faith we have
> Were reft from us by any ruthless fate,
> Who, sisters, looking down a gloomy grave,
> Would have the strength to stay behind and wait? (57–60)

An Antipodean Brotherhood

In 'The Late Mr. A. L. Gordon: In Memoriam', Kendall represents his friend, Adam Lindsay Gordon, as white Australia's 'aboriginal' bard and one of its 'medieval' knights. He 'sang the first great songs these lands can claim / To be their own', while living the 'open-hearted', moral life that 'keeps / The splendid fire of English chivalry / From dying out' (7–8, 18–20). Gordon and Kendall, along with Charles Harpur and Lionel Michael, together form an antipodean brotherhood of the round table: they are 'a shining band', a 'bright company this sin-stained world / Can ill afford to lose' (43, 27–28).

In Tennyson's *Idylls*, Arthur's knights live a 'twofold life': they struggle in the temporal world to find the eternal reality of the grail. The former provides the obstacles that impede their quest; yet at the same time, it is only in time (through

---

[43] Stevens, *Hawkesbury Heritage*, pp. 61–62.

duty, chivalry, morality), that a path to the latter can be found. Analogous difficulties confront the antipodean poets, who, as poets, also labour under 'The wild specific curse which seems to cling / Forever to the Poet's twofold life!' (36–37). Like Arthur's knights, members of the 'shining band' live in a world divided between material reality and their visions of the ideal, in which they struggle to realize the latter in the former.

In the eighth book of the *Idylls*, Arthur offers a gloomy summary of the little achieved by his knights in their search for the Holy Grail. Most, he complains, have been 'lost to me and gone, / And left me gazing at a barren board, / And a lean Order — scarce returned a tithe' (III, 490: 888–90). For the antipodean brotherhood, their quest to lay the foundations of an Australian poetic tradition had still more disastrous results. 'The Late Mr. A. L. Gordon' was published in *The Australasian* on 2 July 1870, eight days after Gordon committed suicide. 'Charles Harpur died in June 1868, a bitterly disappointed man'.[44] And on the 29 April 1868, the body of Lionel Michael was found in the Clarence River, close to the city of Grafton. It was impossible to determine from his injuries whether he had been murdered, taken his own life, or been the victim of an accident. For Kendall, however, death provided Michael with an escape from the pain of life. As he gloomily observed in 'James Lionel Michael': 'Safely housed at last from rack [...] Who would wish to have him back?'

In Tennyson's poem, the failure of Arthur's knights prompts a remarkable affirmation of a reality beyond appearances. There are visions that the king has seen, Arthur says, that come again and again,

> Until this earth he walks on seems not earth,
> This light that strikes his eyeball is not light,
> This air that smites his forehead is not air
> But vision [...].

Under the pressure of these visions, the 'sleeping woods' of time are discovered to be a 'specious external'. Behind them lies the absolute world glimpsed in myth and poetry: Arthur's true self, Jesus, God. In the antipodes, however, the death of Michael, Harpur and Gordon sparks no comparable illumination.

The failures of Arthur's knights weaken but do not immediately destroy Arthurian civilization. In 'The late Mr. A. L. Gordon', the two events are conflated. Kendall writes:

> having wove and proffered this poor wreath,
> I stand to-day as lone as he who saw
> At nightfall through the glimmering moony mists,
> The last of Arthur on the wailing mere,
> And strained in vain to hear the going voice.

---

[44] Ackland, *That Shining Band*, p. 114.

At the close of *The Passing of Arthur*, Sir Bedivere is the last survivor of 'the old order' as it changes, 'yielding place to new' (559). In contrast, Kendall is the last survivor of a new order that had proved unable to displace 'the old'. Some of the consequences of this radically different situation are implied by Kendall's curious misrepresentation of Sir Bedivere's plight.

The antipodean Sir Bedivere strains 'in vain to hear the going voice'. Gordon, it seems, merely vanishes into silence leaving the narrator alone. In contrast, in the last pages of Tennyson's recension of the myth, Arthur and Avilion are vocal. Arthur's last words are proffered and clearly heard by Sir Bedivere, before he sets sail with the three queens. When the barge is no more than 'one black dot against the verge of dawn', Sir Bedivere distinctly hears, although faint, 'Sounds, as if some fair city were one voice / Around a king returning from his wars'. Arguably, these differences register the absence in Kendall's poem of an antipodean Arthur.

Tennyson is reported to have described 'King Arthur as the "soul" and the Round Table as the "passions and capacities of *a man*"'.[45] More broadly, he is the spiritual centre of the community of the Round Table that, Sir Bedivere claims, 'was an image of the mighty world'. As we have seen, in 'Morte d'Arthur' and *The Passing of Arthur*, Arthur's death divides the present from the past, reveals the timeless ideal that informed the Arthurian world, and provides a point of reference in relation to which the beginning and end of future civilizations can be mapped. In contrast, in 'The Late Mr. A. L. Gordon', collapse of the 'new order' leaves the antipodean Sir Bedivere in a present without centre or soul, and in a history that lacks an untainted beginning to which it could one day return in triumph. Once more, it seems, Gothic horror threatens to eclipse the spiritual realities adumbrated in Kendall's Gothic medievalism.

As in 'The Past', it is possible to argue that beyond the 'sleeping woods' in which the narrator is enclosed, the (spiritual/imaginative) sun will one day rise. Kendall writes that 'if 'tis true' that beyond 'the darkness of the grave, the soul / Becomes omniscient', then Gordon may receive his poetic 'offering' and 'read it with a sigh for human friends, / In human bonds, and grey with human griefs'. But, once again, this uncertain consolation is achieved at the cost of confirming the present darkness. The Sir Bedivere of Kendall's poem is an exile from the European past, swept along by an antipodean history without purchase in the ideal.

I am, of course, not suggesting that 'The Late Mr. A. L. Gordon: In Memoriam' discredits, at least in any simple way, Kendall's romantic medievalism. To do so would be to diminish the remarkable sense of displacement generated by the tension here and elsewhere in Kendall's *oeuvre* between Gothic horror and Gothic medievalism. The poem measures not simply the distance between the real and the ideal, but the remarkable sense of disorientation generated when the one is found to

---

[45] William E. Buckler, *Man and His Myths: Tennyson's 'Idylls of the King' in Critical Context* (New York: New York University Press, 1984), p. 13.

be enmeshed with the other. In Kendall's *oeuvre*, the tension between Gothic horror and Gothic medievalism provides a vehicle for exploring the experience of *not* belonging, of living in a world where the [European] Mind and the 'external World' are *not* fitted to each other.

Seen in this light, Kendall's *oeuvre* looks forward to the contemporary debate about 'belonging' represented by Peter Read's *Belonging: Australians, Place and Aboriginal Ownership*.[46] This debate is too wide-ranging adequately to be discussed in this chapter. Nevertheless, one of the strands informing contributions of white Australians can perhaps be summarized by the following quotation from Manning Clark's 'Australia, Whose Country Is It?':

> Sometimes when I stand in the Australian bush on a clear windless day I am visited with strange thoughts: am I living in a country where history has not begun, or where history is all over? I wonder whether I belong [...] I am ready, and so are others, to understand the Aboriginal view that no human being can ever know heart's ease in a foreign land, because in a foreign land there live foreign ancestral spirits. We white people are condemned to live in a country where we have no ancestral spirits. The conqueror has become the eternal outsider, the eternal alien. We must either become assimilated or live the empty life of a people exiled from their source of spiritual strength.[47]

Although Kendall is no longer widely thought to be an Australian Ossian, he may nevertheless be the first, albeit unwilling, cartographer of this dis-ease.

---

[46] Peter Read, *Belonging: Australians, Place and Aboriginal Ownership* (Cambridge: Cambridge University Press, 2000).

[47] Manning Clark, *Speaking out of Turn: Lectures and Speeches 1940–1991* (Melbourne: Melbourne University Press, 1997), p. 144. Quoted in Read, *Belonging*, p. 17.

'I See a Strangeness': Francis Webb's Norfolk and English Catholic Medievalism

ANDREW LYNCH

For many Australian writers of the 1950s, living in England seems to have aroused simultaneous feelings of belonging and alienation, unpredictably inflected by education, class, religion and other factors. Religion is a factor of particular importance in the case of the poet Francis Webb (1925–73), resident in England from 1953 to 1960, where he initiated an outstanding body of poems later collected in *Socrates* (1961) and *The Ghost of the Cock* (1964).[1] Webb's English experience was a very unusual one, since most of his time was spent in Norfolk mental hospitals, but that should not discourage interest in him as an Australian expatriate writer of the period, especially as his work achieved some local recognition. Poems were published in journals,[2] plays broadcast by the BBC, and he was even the subject of newspaper attention.[3] Webb's Norfolk poems should be part of any understanding of Australia's post-war re-alignment to English and European tradition.[4] His English poetry, some of it completed after his return to Australia in 1960, traces an experience of exile and isolation; of all Australian expatriates Webb was the least personally exposed to the broader English scene, and probably also the most cut off from home. But his work remained engaged and adventurous, responding passionately to the new environment. It charts the developing response of

---

[1] Both books were published by Angus and Robertson in Sydney. Some new writing and revisions were undertaken after Webb's return to Australia in 1960.

[2] *The Listener*; *The Times Literary Supplement*; *John O'London's Weekly*.

[3] Michael Griffith, *God's Fool: The Life and Poetry of Francis Webb* (Sydney: Angus and Robertson, 1991), pp. 218–27.

[4] For a discussion of the expatriate Australian poet, see Bruce Bennett, *Spirit of Exile: Peter Porter and his Poetry* (Oxford: Oxford University Press, 1991).

a modern Australian subject, abroad in England, to the 'strangeness' of his surroundings and of himself in them.

More specifically, a number of Webb's Norfolk poems are important for the study of Australian medievalism, as instances of how the medieval is confronted and deployed within the formation of an Australian identity. These texts are deeply reliant on medievalist and Catholic traditions for their historicizing structures, many of which were already part of Webb's culture in Australia. A long sequence on St Francis of Assisi had just been published when he left.[5] Yet Webb's medievalism is so thoroughly politicized and acculturated within contemporary terms that it becomes one with his modernity. Catholicism and the idea of the Catholic artist, the strangeness of England and his being a stranger there, medieval and Reformation English history, Cold War politics, the Norfolk landscape — in Webb's text these are not only omnipresent and inseparable but broadly constitutive of each other's meaning. It is the purpose of this study to trace their connectedness within his sequence of ten poems, 'Around Costessey', work he began in England in 1959 and completed in Australia in the following years. The poem is too long and dense to allow for detailed attention to all its sections. Discussion is mainly limited to Sections 1–4 and 6, as the most directly connected with the issue of English literary medievalism. Section 7, 'In Memoriam: Anthony Sandys, 1806–83', deserves a substantial study in its own right and must be omitted here, despite its relevance to the themes of 'strangeness' and poetic creativity.[6]

'What frightens you must be a ruin, and waste'[7]

Webb's poetry is usually considered difficult to understand, and this poem-sequence is no exception, raising immediate interpretative challenges. The lack of conventional elements of structure, such as narrative continuity, obvious homogeneity of topic, or even a single physical setting — '*Around* Costessey' is a set of mental propositions as much as a local sketch-book — inclines the reader to rely on contextual paradigms (religious, historical, aesthetic) and internal patterns of verbal organization to make sense of the whole. There is a danger in this. Whilst scholarly investigation and close reading establish the suggestiveness and coherence of the poem, they also risk making it seem over-planned and heavily thematized,

---

[5] 'The Canticle', in Francis Webb, *Birthday*, Adelaide, 1953. See Andrew Lynch, 'Re-making the Middle Ages in Australia: Francis Webb's "The Canticle" (1953)', *Australian Literary Studies*, 19 (1999), 44–56.

[6] For a reading, see Bill Ashcroft, *The Gimbals of Unease: The Poetry of Francis Webb* (Nedlands: Centre for Studies in Australian Literature, 1996).

[7] '6. The Tower', in 'Around Costessey', Francis Webb, *Collected Poems* (Sydney: Angus and Robertson, 1969), p. 205. All subsequent references to Webb's poetry are to this edition.

simply because to the reading experience it is just the opposite: heterogeneous, elusive and processual. The loose, juxtapositional structure paradoxically invites belief in implicit explanations that might bind the scattered leaves into one volume. It is especially tempting to read Webb as a poet with a complete intellectual master plan, simply to protect him against naive biographical criticisms. My aim in this study is to show how 'Around Costessey' makes poetic sense, but in a way that resists the elision of history often involved in thematized unitary readings. Reading sections of the poem as 'medievalist', in their specific cultural contexts, I hope to articulate what is odd and inassimilable, what marks them as distinct and fluid in their moment of production. Certainly, I stress the significance of the poem's 'omnitemporality', which sees it share some of the characteristic anachronism and anatopism of medieval religious art and poetry: '2. Our Lady's Birthday' and '10. Good Friday, Norfolk', are written in a mode familiar to any reader who knows medieval lyrics like 'Now goth sonne under wod'. But the main aim here is not to justify Webb's aesthetic by reference to 'timeless' religious doctrine: I am mainly trying to understand his mid-twentieth-century Catholic culture through an historicized reading of the poetry itself, including its medievalist aspects.

Part of Webb's poetic difference is intensely personal. In his mental hospital life, identity as a poet, a maker, gave Webb distinction and privilege, including a cherished 'side-room' that offered respite from the general ward, a place for books, wireless and his small art collection, and above all the chance to write. 'Side-room' became his metonymy for poetry itself and for the state of psychic trust in which he was able to compose it.[8] Poetry was, in these circumstances, a kind of ordination for Webb, a field of sanctuary for the exercise of a religious function. He was a Catholic, and since *Birthday* in 1953, had dedicated himself to writing as such. Rather unusually in the Anglo-Celtic Australia of his childhood, he did not identify himself as an 'Irish' Catholic. Despite an education by the Christian Brothers in Sydney, and a professed love of Yeats, his poetry gives no evidence of imaginative investment in Ireland. In 1953, then determined never to return to Australia, Webb briefly entertained the Franciscan notion of adopting the life of an agricultural labourer in the Republic of Ireland, but this was quashed by his immediate detainment on arrival in Dublin and forced return to England after a few weeks.[9]

Self-exiled from Australia, unwanted in Catholic Ireland, Webb's relation to England was unusually difficult to negotiate. More easily than an Australian Catholic of Irish descent, he could assert his place in a long-standing English religious tradition, one whose medieval origins and their nineteenth-century revivals were everywhere visible. Nevertheless, any Catholic's potential to 'belong' in England was overshadowed by history: the Reformation, the break from papal

---

[8] See its use in '9. Father Jones' of 'Around Costessey': '[...] there is rising / Stack and side-room on your chosen ground, / Of star-stature in my brain'.

[9] See Griffith, *God's Fool*, pp. 214–16.

authority, the dissolution of the monasteries, subsequent persecution and disenfranchisement of Catholics, and a long legacy of cultural mistrust. For a Catholic with roots in Ireland, the history of religious persecution could be readily assimilated into a collective discourse of struggle and endurance. By contrast, Webb's position in England was isolated. Not only was he far from home and removed from normal society, but his membership of the 'universal' church became a further mark of cultural difference. During his period as an inmate of the Rice Hospital at Drayton, Webb frequently walked to hear mass at St Walstan's in the historic Catholic enclave of Costessey,[10] about two miles away. These walks to Costessey, along Green Lane by the River Wensum, evidently focussed for him a strong emotional association between his own life and the troubled traditions of English Catholicism.

This was also a strong literary association. Unlike an Australian Catholic poet such as Vincent Buckley, a cultural Anglophile who remained preoccupied with Ireland, Webb resembled an English intellectual convert to Catholicism, and he was very familiar with the writings of converts such as G. M. Hopkins and G. K. Chesterton, who had revealed themselves as strong stakeholders in the medieval past. Webb habitually carried W. H. Gardner's Penguin selection of Hopkins's poems and prose in his pocket, wearing out many successive copies, and he expressed an enthusiasm for Chesterton that was typical of Australian Catholic taste in this period.[11] A major link between Hopkins, Chesterton and Webb is that for each in different ways the idea of the medieval focussed strong feelings of cultural and personal dispossession, but also symbolized a strong desire for fuller community.

The situation of the medieval in English Catholicism was double: the medieval associations of 'Rome' were potentially a weak spot in Catholic cultural identity, attracting criticism and contempt. On the other hand, after two centuries of medievalist revival, the Middle Ages carried with them many favourable associations of antiquity, national heritage, chivalric glamour and pre-industrial integrity in labour, and these could all be annexed in the struggle to dignify Catholic identity. In this latter scenario, from Pugin onwards, the medieval was often represented as both truly nationally English and international, a kind of core state of European culture without the unpleasant accretions of later times, much as Hopkins imagines 'Duns Scotus' Oxford' as a place where stone towers merge organically with country fields, no modern 'graceless growth' between them.[12] Such a Middle

---

[10] For St Walstan's, Costessey, and the cult of St Walstan, see Ernest G. Gage, *Costessey Hall* (Old Costessey: n. pub. 1991), pp. 35–39; Carol Twinch, *In Search of St Walstan* (Norwich: Media Associates, 1995); Eamon Duffy, *The Stripping of the Altars* (New Haven: Yale University Press, 1992), pp. 195–205.

[11] For Chesterton and Australia, see Katharine Massam, *Sacred Threads: Catholic Spirituality in Australia 1922–1962* (Sydney: University of New South Wales Press, 1996).

[12] Hopkins, p. 40.

Ages became a model era for many Catholics, whose alienation from unbelieving 'modernism' found more positive expression in allegiance to the medieval past. The 'modern' became the unnatural and aberrant — urban blight, industrial pollution and bourgeois dullness — into which medieval youth and vitality had suffered a fall. In terms of religious history this fall was the Reformation itself.

English historiography was a long-running sectarian battlefield, in which Catholics tended to become apologists for the Middle Ages mainly because their religion, however misleadingly, identified them with a 'medieval' institution usually seen as ritualist and illiberal. For all its potential glamour, 'Going over to Rome' was often traumatic for all concerned. Hopkins's family treated his change as a tragic loss; his father, already imagining him in 'the cold limbo which Rome assigns to her English converts',[13] wrote 'O Gerard my darling boy are you indeed gone from me?'[14] Hopkins himself, as a Catholic priest self-exiled from Balliol in the 'base and brickish skirt'[15] of Oxford, grew suspicious of his once-beloved university: 'I could not but feel how alien it was, how chilling, and deeply to be distrusted'.[16] Religious community took precedence for him over all other kinds — 'In reality it is the deepest impression I have in speaking to people, that they are or that they are not of my religion'[17] — but it is clear that he missed his former attachments and through class feelings was uncomfortable with many of the new ones. 'Duns Scotus' Oxford' — 'Towery city, and branchy between towers' — became an easier space for him to inhabit than the modern city. Hopkins yearned for an unspoiled medieval home, unified by its dedication to the Immaculate Mary, as he always yearned for figures of childhood unpolluted by sinful maturity.

Hopkins's example shows how hard it was for converts to reconcile their feelings of Englishness with the separation from family, university and cultural privilege that followed the change to Catholicism. Whilst a Catholic viewpoint gave him a more critical angle on English culture and policy, it also lessened his power to comment effectively. The result was a deep sense of isolation — 'To seem the stranger lies my lot, my life / Among strangers' — and frustration that his voice should have become that of the outsider:

---

[13] Manley Hopkins to the Rev. H. P. Liddon, 15 October 1866, in *Further Letters of Gerard Manley Hopkins*, ed. by C. C. Abbot (London: Oxford University Press, 1956), p. 435.

[14] Letter 47A, 18 October 1866, in *Further Letters*, p. 97.

[15] 'Duns Scotus' Oxford', *Gerard Manley Hopkins: Poems and Prose*, ed. by W. H. Gardner (Harmondsworth: Penguin, 1953), p. 40.

[16] Norman White, *Hopkins: A Literary Biography* (Oxford: Clarendon Press, 1992), p. 306.

[17] White, *Hopkins*, p. 306.

> England, whose honour O all my heart woos, wife
> To my creating thought, would neither hear
> Me, were I pleading, plead nor do I: I wear
> y of idle a being but by where wars are rife.[18]

A much more widely known Catholic cultural commentator was G. K. Chesterton (1874–1936) who in many works staked out the medieval as a strategic area to reclaim for Englishness. In journalistic pieces he attacked 'the queer, automatic assumption that it must always mean throwing mud at a thing to call it a relic of medievalism'.[19] His priest-detective Fr Brown sardonically tells the local vicar 'We take some interest, you know [...] in old English churches'.[20] In *The Flying Inn* Chesterton's hero inspires a 'renewal of that laughter that has slept since the Middle Ages'.[21] In his biography of Chaucer, the medieval Catholic poet becomes an unsung nationalist hero, the inventor both of 'Modern Fiction' and of England:

> Nobody waves a Union Jack and cries, 'England made jolly stories for the whole earth.' It is not too much to say that Chaucer made not only a new nation but a new world [...] And he did so in a language that was hardly useable until he used it; and to the glory of a nation that had hardly existed till he made it glorious.[22]

Chesterton devotes a whole chapter to 'Chaucer as an Englishman'. As in all this work, praise of the medieval becomes a function of his overall project to redeem Catholicism from its long cultural marginalization in modern England.

As in Irish Catholic nationalism, there was the danger that all this praise for the lost pre-modern world would tend to political conservatism, and subject religion to inherited class and ethnic prejudices. Some Catholics could invoke their 'old' religious status as a badge of true Englishness and social status, but they did so at the risk of severe alienation from modernity, and from many fellow Catholics. Evelyn Waugh provides a good example. In his *Men at Arms* (1952), for instance, the hero Guy Crouchback is the son of

> two English families which had suffered for their Faith and yet retained a round share of material greatness. The chapel at Broome had never lacked a priest through all the penal years and the lands of Broome stretched undiminished and unencumbered from the Quantocks to the Blackdown Hills. Forbears of both their names had died on the scaffold. The City, lapped now by the tide of illustrious converts, still remembered with honour its old companions in arms.[23]

---

[18] Hopkins, *Poems*, p. 62: 'To seem the stranger lies my lot, my life'. The poem was written in Ireland, 'at a third / Remove'.

[19] 'On Turnpikes and Medievalism', *All I Survey* (London: Methuen, 1933).

[20] 'The Hammer of God', in *The Father Brown Stories* (London: Cassell, 1929), p. 127.

[21] G. K. Chesterton, *The Flying Inn* (London: Methuen, 1914), p. 51.

[22] G. K. Chesterton, *Geoffrey Chaucer*, 2nd edn (London: Faber, 1942), p. 15.

[23] Evelyn Waugh, *Men at Arms* (London: Chapman and Hall), p. 1.

'Old' Catholicism here confers a status at once romantically distinguished and comfortably established: 'a priest' is supplied along with the house and lands; the distant 'sufferings' of the family vouch for its ancient *noblesse*, as do the medievalist touches — 'forbears', 'honour', 'companions in arms'. Guy Crouchback's medieval ancestry is there to put him above the Box-Benders of this world, but it also serves to prove his lack of political community with other, less acceptable, co-religionists.[24]

Despite their differences, in all these versions the Middle Ages are made to stand for a fullness of English community that has been lost, and for a fullness of Englishness that has been wrongly taken away from Catholics, putting them (at least symbolically) beyond the pale. For the same reason the Middle Ages becomes the desired space within which the return of psychic wholeness for Catholics and their restoration to the wider community can be imagined, a converted world where Englishness and Catholicism have again become one. This desired outcome is ideologically complex. The idea of medieval 'England' satisfies a nationalist consciousness that is mainly a product of the post-medieval era, but also seeks to transcend it through a return to the supposed pan-European 'Christendom' of the pre-Reformation. In line with the later 'Pirenne thesis', Chesterton's idea of Europe depends on an anti-Islamic identification in both *The Flying Inn* and his 'Lepanto'. Against this oriental threat, Christendom is made the common cause uniting Europe; a medievalized Spanish knight of 1571 saves Western civilization, in a polemical departure from the usual post-Armada English myth:

> The last knight of Europe takes weapons from the wall,
> The last and lingering troubadour to whom the bird has sung,
> That once went singing southward when all the world was young.
> In that enormous silence, tiny and unafraid,
> Comes up along a winding road the noise of the Crusade.[25]

For Webb, as an extreme outsider, but a man steeped in English literature, the idea of Catholic identity in England was therefore complex. It offered him an imaginative place in English history through a bond with co-religionists, and by implication with all whom he thought upheld a persecuted, 'out of fashion' or 'dated' faith in modern times.[26] But it also provided an acknowledgement of cultural difference and exclusion, which matched his Australianness and his physical isolation. Unlike Hopkins, Chesterton and Waugh, Webb was not seeking Catholic admission to an 'Englishness' whose meaning was already historically marked out. An Australian outsider, able to identify with the religion but not the nationalist

---

[24] In *Edmund Campion* (London: Longmans, Green, 1935), Waugh cites Campion's view that Ireland was 'much beholden to God for suffering them to be conquered, whereby many of their enormities were cured, and more might be, would themselves be pliable'.

[25] G. K. Chesterton, 'Lepanto'.

[26] For these terms in 'Around Costessey', see '7. In Memoriam: Anthony Sandys, 1806–1883'.

aspirations of English Catholics, he saw England as a 'strange' place to which he had still to learn his relation, and whose history he, as a stranger, did not fully inherit.

Nationalism, let alone Empire, is not Webb's interest in England, but religion is. Despite the 'green' setting, with its pastoral tropes and close local associations, 'Around Costessey' always seeks a broader inclusivity and constantly shifts or elides time-periods and discourses. The painterly and immediate Norfolk landscape is also viewed under the aspect of neo-Platonic 'Form'; the material world of plants, animals and humans is consciously likened to the universal 'body of Christ'; time moves cyclically according to the rhythms of the seasons, the harvest and the liturgical year, more than by linear progression of dates and eras. Denied ordinary freedom in English society, Webb celebrates a unilaterally constituted community of the dispossessed, the persecuted and the marginalized, who redeem their present age by a continuing act of conversion through faith. The poem's anthological structure is a function of this desire for company. He centres the poem on a series of 'artist'-figures who are seen to have transmuted the pain of their temporal existence into an enduring vision of God. They form a heterogeneous set of companions for the poet-persona who is the 'I'/eye of the text, and whose meditations summon them: Christ and the Virgin Mary; an Elizabethan Jesuit, John Gerard; the Viennese composer, Anton Bruckner (1818–96); the Victorian painter, Anthony Sandys (1806–83); and 'Father Jones', a priest who had visited Webb in his mental hospital near Norwich. Though without the same spiritualist basis, the poem's structure as a whole is comparable to Yeats's *All Souls' Night*, except that Webb does not only comment on figures summoned from personal memory; before his community can be realized, he must first make its members part of him, in a 'mystical body' through which their association can continue unbroken. For Webb, community is homage to his chosen dead, the memory of others' kindness,[27] and daring to accept the gifts of strangers and strangeness. These actions are seen as instances in his own life of the universal grace given by Christ and mediated by the Virgin Mary; through such moments he learns to see the wreckage of history, including himself, as capable of redemption.

'History halts but one hour'[28]

'Around Costessey' is a poem in ten sections, advancing uncertainly from the Norman Conquest to the present:

1. Hastings

2. Our Lady's Birthday

---

[27] See '10. Good Friday, Norfolk'. The 'remembered airletter' acknowledges that friends like David Campbell and Rosemary Dobson had written to Webb in England.

[28] '1. Hastings', from 'Around Costessey'.

3. The Horses

4. Gerard, S. J.

5. Scherzo and Adagio of Bruckner's Ninth

6. The Tower

7. In Memoriam: Anthony Sandys, 1806–83

> I. 'Bird-song is your reverberating touch'
> II. Self-portrait
> III. Death
> IV. *Art*

8. Rookery

9. Father Jones

10. Good Friday, Norfolk

The sequence has an overall linear movement from the Middle Ages to the present day, but it appeals throughout to the principle of omnitemporality,[29] a feature of medieval lyric and drama, which connects past, present and future in terms of their common alignment to the unchanging truths of religion. For all that, this text is always implicated in historical consciousness; every section is situational, present tense, and specified by a time, place or perception in which we see the redemptive process in action. The relation of temporal moments to each other and to the present is always open to fluid and disruptive inter-connections. Webb catches himself in the act of creating history, or rather, of continually making present meaning through intense contemplation of what survives the wreck of the past. In this way, history, modern experience and creative utterance are inseparable for him; history is what he is enabled to perceive in gifted moments of poetic reflection. The overall structure of the sequence celebrates this power of *poiesis* to change fear and alienation to warm engagement with 'strangeness'. Typologically, the 'neutral ravenous mills' of Part 1 ('Hastings') are known by Part 10 ('Good Friday, Norfolk') as signs of 'the Cross', with an assurance that the sufferings of history are redeemable. Within this outer framework the poem mainly follows the Genesis order of creation, passing from light and water (2) to plants, fish, animals (3) and birds (8), and centring on humankind (4–7, 9).

Though the theme of the whole poem is praise of creation, Webb's poem begins with a scene of mass destruction — the Battle of Hastings in 1066. From the start 'Around Costessey' abandons the idea of the medieval as model of cultural or political unity that in their different ways Hopkins, Chesterton and Waugh had employed. His Middle Ages are from the outset associated with ruin and dispersal,

---

[29] For 'omnitemporal' poetry, see Douglas Gray, *Themes and Images in the Medieval English Religious Lyric* (London: Routledge and Kegan Paul, 1972).

and the ruin does not invite an idealizing restoration of 'Christendom'. Rather, it accompanies a resistance to totalizing views of history with their falsely coherent divisions. '1. Hastings' destroys belief in a pre-Reformation Catholic 'world' by presenting a scene already marked by the crass functionalism which medievalism often attributes to modernity. Webb's 1066 is an efficient colonialist land-grab, proleptic of Australia's European settlement in 1788.[30] The 'indoctrinate' Normans inevitably take power from 'illiterate', 'improvident' Harold, forever inscribing state control, class, and commodity values on the landscape:

> Pasture, embryo hills,
> The Dwelling by the Waterside,
> Cotesia, open eye,
> Improvident Harold has died:
> The two neutral ravenous mills
> Munch apathetic rye,
> Buried the old laissez faire.
> Totalitarian herald,
> Domesday Book and banner
> Deride the schoolboy Harold,
> Twirl militant arms in the air,
> Much ecstatic florin and tanner.
> So four strict carucates of land;
> Villein, villein, villein;
> Pannage for one hundred hogs (Illiterate Harold is slain).

Modern and medieval usages are so interlaced here that re-staging of the battle to match present-day 'sides' becomes impossible. 'Laissez-faire', a 'Norman' term usually applied to capitalism, oddly describes Harold's archaic regime; Webb's Normans combine a scary Cold War view of communist take-over, ('totalitarian', 'secret documents', 'indoctrinate') with Domesday Book's language of feudal land tenure ('carucates', 'villein', 'pannage', 'escheating'),[31] and the chivalric panache of the Bayeux Tapestry ('herald', 'banner', 'militant arms in the air'). In such a version, 'the medieval' is not tenable as a coherent or inviolate temporal category; Webb parodies the guided-tour exemplary history of Bad Kings and Good Things:

> Welcome reconnoitring groups,
> History halts but one hour,
> All the Harolds must die in battle
> Before the indoctrinate troops.

---

[30] For comparisons with Australian and New Guinea colonialism in Webb's work see 'End of the Picnic', *Collected Poems*, p. 98, and 'A Papuan Shepherd', *Collected Poems*, p. 26.

[31] 'Carucates' is a pre-Domesday usage. See T. B. Norgate, *The History of Costessey* (Taverham: n. pub., 1972), p. 58.

As an introduction to 'Around Costessey', therefore, '1. Hastings' does not provide either a stable historical origin or a confident appropriation of the past for modern purposes. Rather, Webb exposes both these moves as themselves instances of totalizing imposition in which power is the only truth, mentally alienating the place from its 'fullness' and foreclosing its potential meaning for the present onlooker — 'Cotesia, open eye'.

'2. Our Lady's Birthday' offers the poem another point of origin, one that sets itself against the historiography of discrete eras marked by human power shifts like 1066. Instead, the idea of history becomes cyclical, linked to a recurring feast of the Church — 8 September, nine months after the feast of the Immaculate Conception. The feast commemorates Mary's birth within the broad scheme of incarnation and redemption, rather than as a single historical event. The poem achieves that impression of breadth in many ways: its parataxis; the imaginary, composite landscape (there is no sea near Costessey); reference to Scripture, liturgy and traditional typology ('Calvary', 'the seven rainbow sorrows',[32] 'Immaculate', 'Original Sin'), and the fluid evocation of light as if in a watercolour 'wash' technique:

> Eleven o'clock. Reservoirs of Heaven,
> Waters of the sun,
> No-colour; and a rippling
> Before the prospecting nervous eye.
> And a tenderness wherein Calvary is begun
> And sunset foreboded, a tenderness coupling
> White heat with goldenness; and the seven
> Rainbow sorrows; and the urchin sea
> Clambering about; and the haystack library,
> Academic decorous morocco and vellum
> Bound, stalled in the heavy light upon a calm.
> (2. 1–11)

The 'tenderness' of the scene comes from its psychic survival of the Fall, and of all the sorrows in the spectrum of human history. As white holds in itself all other colours, the Immaculate contains all suffering. Mary's birth delivers her to the world of time and pain, 'In the lewd snake-bodied wind', but anticipates her mediation of its redemption, as Christ's mother and through her intercession for sinners:

> And you are an arch hurled across the wicked chasm
> By your Playfellow, of the matchless mind.[33]

---

[32] The Seven Sorrows of Mary are: 1. The Prophecy of Simeon; 2. The Flight into Egypt; 3. Losing the Child Jesus; 4. Meeting Jesus on the Way to Calvary; 5. Witnessing the Death of Jesus on the Cross; 6. The Pietà — Holding the Dead Jesus; 7. Jesus's Entombment.

[33] 'Matchless' comes from the famous fifteenth-century Marian lyric: 'I sing of a maiden / That is makeles; / King of all kings / To her son she ches.'

This is not an idly devotional poem. Mary is Webb's image for his (and the world's) ability to survive trauma; she intercedes in his struggle to overcome fear and aggression and to delight again in the play of creation. 'Playfellow', like the unruly sea, comes from the Epistle for the feast of the Nativity of the Virgin, Wisdom (Proverbs) 8. 22–35:[34]

> The Lord possessed me in the beginning of his ways, before He made anything from the beginning. I was set up from eternity, and of old, before the earth was made.[...] when He compassed the sea with its bounds, and set a law to the waters that they should not pass their limits [...] I was with him, forming all things, and was delighted every day, playing before him at all times, playing in the world; and my delight is to be with the children of men.[35]

The 'haystack library' points to this learned link between Mary and divine Wisdom, the 'efficient cause' of creation.[36] Scriptural texts which 'exalt the Wisdom of God [...] in the liturgy are applied to Mary, the most beautiful work of God's Wisdom'.[37] The idea is also found in the popular Litany of the Virgin:

> Mirror of justice, pray for us.
> Seat of wisdom, pray for us.
> Cause of our joy, pray for us.
> Spiritual vessel, pray for us.[38]

Mary is therefore made the mediatrix of Webb's own version of creation, his poetry. Her delight in the material world encourages his 'prospecting nervous eye' to see its goodness. In various medieval traditions, Nature and Mary are each 'vicars' of God;[39] each helps in the *creatio continua*, the ongoing divine process that conserves the world: 'as thus continuous, [...] [creation] is called conservation, an act, therefore, which is nothing else than the unceasing influx of the creative cause upon

---

[34] Webb uses this liturgy for another great Marian poem, 'Harry', in 'Ward Two': 'She cries: *Ab aeterno ordinata sum*'.

[35] Nativity of the Blessed Virgin Mary, *St Andrew Daily Missal* (Bruges: Liturgical Apostolate, Abbey of Saint-André, 1953), p. 1546. This is also the epistle for 8 December, Feast of the Immaculate Conception (p. 1178). Mary and divine Wisdom are also associated with Ecclesiasticus 24, 'Ab initio et ante saecula creata sum'.

[36] See *Catholic Encyclopedia* online, 'Creation',

http://www.newadvent.org/cathen/04470a.htm, accessed 31 May 2005.

[37] *Catholic Encyclopedia* online, 'Immaculate Conception',
http://www.newadvent.org/cathen/047674d.htm, accessed 31 May 2005.

[38] *St Andrew Daily Missal*, Appendix, pp. 78–79.

[39] See Geoffrey Chaucer, *The Parlement of Foulys*, ed. by D. S. Brewer (London: Nelson, 1960), p. 29, n. 2.

the existence of the creature'.[40] Mary stands for Webb's confidence that God is immanent in history, for all its pain.

This confidence continues into '3. The Horses', where it is extended from Wisdom and the 'rational' intellect to the 'vegetative soul', which is part of the 'irrational' faculties and is the 'passive' seat of the senses in the Aristotelian division adopted by Aquinas. The passive, vegetable world, 'ungirt with passion or reflection', praises its creator simply by 'naked growing'. The irrational 'animal soul', Aristotle's active seat of 'desire', is symbolized for Webb by the River Wensum ('consecrated, ordered Wish') and present in 'two old horses' who stand 'Licking each other's sides with great slow tongues'; their mutual action assuages the heat and flies of summer, the historical world of time and pain —

> Memory, rumour and an hour spin in the guise
> Of the buzzing swarming flies.

Through the animal soul's humble version of Pentecost (and of poetry), the landscape within time still communicates its maker. The 'he' of Webb's last stanza is undifferentiated, showing the undisrupted closeness between God and his 'irrational' creation:

> He will give his body to the gesticulating
> Green grass without forethought. He will lie beating, awaiting
> The perfect town of water, going, gone.
> He is the listing hulk or bale of straw
> In silt of the inorganic; pang of law
> Tides him into the rivers and the sun.
> Light plays throughout his muddied, floating things,
> His action, desire, his gift of tongues.

In the 'rational', human creation, pain becomes deeply intensified. '4. Gerard, S. J.' is based on the autobiography of John Gerard (1564–1637), an Elizabethan priest. Webb probably associated him with Costessey Hall, home of the recusant Jerningham family, a major centre for East Anglian Catholics in the era of persecution and beyond.[41] Gerard's autobiography, translated by Philip Caraman, was one of several books about underground priests to gain popularity after the war.[42] Evelyn Waugh also revised his *Edmund Campion* (1935) in 1946 with a new

---

[40] *Catholic Encyclopedia* online, 'Creation', http://www.newadvent.org/cathen/04470a.htm, accessed 31 May 2005: 'the creative act once placed is coextensive in duration with the creature's existence'.

[41] For the history of Costessey Hall, its priest-hole, attic chapel, etc., see Ernest G. Gage, *Costessey Hall* (Old Costessey, 1991), pp. 7–13; Norgate, *The History of Costessey*, pp. 48–49. Gerard had landed in Norfolk on his return to England in 1588. See *John Gerard: The Autobiography of an Elizabethan*, trans. by Philip Caraman, with an introduction by Graham Greene (London: Longmans, Green, 1951), p. 9, n. 2.

[42] *William Weston: The Autobiography of an Elizabethan*, trans. by Philip Caraman, with a

Preface.[43] In words that seem to have stuck with Webb, Waugh wrote that the nineteenth century's toleration of the Church was only 'a brief truce in the unending war'[44] against it:

> We have seen the Church driven underground in one country after another. [...] In fragments and whispers we get news of other saints in the prison camps of Eastern and South Eastern Europe, of cruelty and degradation more frightful than anything in Tudor England and of the same pure light shining in the darkness, uncomprehended. The hunted, trapped, murdered priest is amongst us again [...][45]

Language like this could be dangerously attractive to Webb, who suffered periodically from feelings of persecution and sometimes responded with violence. His poetry often seems a way of escaping that syndrome. The central sections of 'Around Costessey' (4–7) outline a breakthrough beyond the traditional scenario of persecution and victimage to renewed trust and acts of love. '4. Gerard, S. J.' assembles all the elements of Waugh's nightmare, but in a way that breaks up their battle-lines. Waugh's 'pure light shining in the darkness, uncomprehended'[46] establishes an absolute distinction between saint and tormentor, the Church and its enemies. Webb will have none of this dualism. For him, by contrast, the persecution is part of a general pre-creative chaos, a 'wilderness' of darkness for all:

> The dinghy runs aground. This tiny bay
> Is clenched in the obsessive bowels of night,
> Cannot abide the broadening vent of day
> [...]
> A wilderness of approaching hands and feet,
> The frightened country family and the giant
> Queen, and the nomad goatherd are my band:
> Assemble them in one lean Tudor Street
> And let me talk of darkness and the pliant
> Ocean and wading into light and land.

Relief can only come through the birth of a newly creative 'light' within the psyche, a benign *poiesis* that would allow a new beginning for all.

---

foreword by Evelyn Waugh (London: Longmans, Green, [1955]; Philip Caraman, *Henry Morse: Priest of the Plague* (New York: Farrar, Strauss and Cudahy, 1957); Christopher Devlin, *The Life of Robert Southwell, Poet and Martyr* (London : Longmans, Green, 1956).

[43] Evelyn Waugh, *Edmund Campion* (Boston: Little, Brown, 1946).

[44] Waugh, *Edmund Campion* (1946), Preface. See 'Around Costessey', '6. The Tower': 'And to the ceaseless causeless war / Brought truce'.

[45] Waugh, *Edmund Campion* (1946), Preface.

[46] John 1. 5, and also in the 'last gospel' of every mass in Webb's time.

Webb's attention was drawn to this landing scene by Graham Greene's introduction to Caraman's book,[47] where it is singled out for its 'sense of excitement' and 'immediacy'. Greene has also drawn fearful Cold War Parallels:

> We can read the *Autobiography* like a contemporary document or perhaps as something still a little ahead of our time, as though in a dream we had been allowed to read an account of life in 1960.[48]

Greene also highlights the section in which John Gerard is tortured by suspension from his wrists in the 'gauntlets', and quotes his interrogator, the pursuivant Topcliffe:

> 'I will see that you are brought to me and placed in my power. I will hang you up in the air and will have no pity on you; and then I shall watch and see whether God will snatch you from my grasp.'[49]

For Gerard, Topcliffe is pure enemy — 'old and hoary and a veteran in evil', 'a cruel creature [...] [who] thirsted for the blood of Catholics';[50] for Greene he is that and also the enemy within, an Elizabethan 'Mr Hyde'.[51] In Webb's version Topcliffe resembles the fallen earth, an arid volcanic landscape, but still not beyond potential witness to his creator, and still with a likeness to his victim. In this new type of Calvary and the mass, with its echoes of the vilification of Christ, Gerard and his tormentor are equally left in suspense, until the priest, as if in a sacramental action, brings forth a new meaning out of his enemy:

> I dangle, Topcliffe dangles. Which grows dim?
> If this should not be death, I'll pace again
> The fenland of his temples and the shale
> Of the pocked skin below his cheekbones, ask
> A cloud to bawl and beg some show of rain,
> Till there erupt from him the rose-en-soleil
> Dangling and swinging. That is all my task.

The 'rose-en-soleil', a rose surrounded by the rays of the sun, is best known as a Yorkist badge of Edward IV. In Webb it is perhaps meant for the Jesuit emblem which places the letters I H S (for Jesus), surmounted by a cross, above the nails of

---

[47] Caraman, *John Gerard*, pp. vi–viii.

[48] Caraman, *John Gerard*, p. vii.

[49] Caraman, *John Gerard*, p. 70. The last sentence would recall the taunting of Christ crucified to Gerard's readers — Matthew 27. 43: 'He trusted in God: let him deliver him now, if he will have him.'

[50] Caraman, *John Gerard*, pp. x, 68.

[51] Caraman, p. x. Compare the Pauline refrain 'Old man, old man' in '5. Scherzo and Adagio of Bruckner's Ninth'.

the Passion, within a sunburst.[52] There may be further reference to the closing imagery of Dante's *Inferno* and Eliot's 'Little Gidding': 'And the fire and the rose are one'. The point seems to be that each of the two 'dangling' figures, Gerard and Topcliffe, holds redemption in potential for the other. If the priest-victim is the one likened to Christ, it is mainly because he knows that his tormentor is redeemed and can show him the divine image. Webb's religious understanding of the scene breaks through the dualist rhetoric of Catholic Reformation narrative, especially in the Cold War applications where he found it, and abandons the polemics of sectarian historiography. Neither the Reformation (as the bane of English Catholicism) nor the contemporary histories which English Catholics had likened to it were granted power to define his poem's course.

'I see a strangeness stretch and flap a wing'[53]

In the preceding sections of this study I have traced the poem's success in breaking free of some restrictive cultural traditions that I have loosely called 'medievalist'. In what remains, on Section 6, 'The Tower', I wish to explore some of the new territory into which it was liberated. There is little need to demonstrate the text's overall thematic coherence, which is also thoroughly medievalist. The poem moves on to a final Good Friday vision, in which the omnitemporal significance of Calvary telescopes eight hundred years of history into one moment:

> Peter de Draiton, hasten from your shroud
> To the church of St Margaret, your beloved bird.
> But voices. Eight static centuries pry as wind
> Into His darkness; staccato forgiven hammer
> Broods in the third hour; and the omnibus
> With portly moon-faced grief
> Blunders up and down certain hills to know His Cross.

If anything, some of these final symbolic correspondences are too controlled, and seem constrictive of the landscape in their own way: willed, rather than found. Yet Webb, despite his conscious anachronism, occasional Platonic vocabulary and temporal elision, does not 'transcend' history in the sense of abandoning the material and temporal world. The urge to leave everything behind is present, but always understood as a loss of courage and faith. Resisting it, Webb finds in the world an immanent meaning that belies the standard histories, including his own, giving him the confidence to return to delight in creation. '6. The Tower' charts this process. In the overall landscape of this poetic sequence, 'The Tower' is the central evocation of Costessey 'around' which all else gathers.

---

[52] Jesuits under torture traditionally called on the name of Jesus.

[53] '6. The Tower', from 'Around Costessey'.

The title refers to the ruinous but imposing 'Thornbury Tower', part of the mid-Victorian 'medieval' addition to Costessey Hall, and still standing in Webb's time.[54] The Hall had been under demolition since 1920, after the death of Lord Stafford in 1913.[55] Fetes had been held in the park earlier in the century, but by the 1950s it was 'a semi-desert or scrubland', a 'scene of desolation', and the tower was 'unsafe'.[56] Before 1900, Costessey also had an annual Easter Monday custom known as the 'Cossey Guild' or 'Gyle', held to elect the 'mayor' for Whit-Sunday.[57] At the inauguration, after much ceremony and merry-making, in which children took a major part, '[...] [t]he procession finished up at Costessey Hall where a dinner was laid out in a barn'.[58] From some source Webb may have learned of these customs and conflated them, for 'The Tower' is an Easter Monday poem in which the desolate park landscape is a symbolic fairground thronged with children:

> Come on Easter Monday to our Poor Meadow.
> Here is a childhood: the florin of the sun aglow,
> A twopenny rook dipping home like Bleriot,
> The elm's engraved and hypostatic shadow,
> And the river wickered with working profiles of an eddy.
> You are young, young, cradling the sacred bowl
> And knife of flint. Ages leap in your body
> And flood into the unselfconscious soul.

In medieval times, the 'Poor Meadow' was land where the parish poor were allowed to graze their animals; by analogy, this place sustains Webb, on his outing from the hospital. It is spring, at the dawn of the resurrected year, imaginatively linked with all other Easters that have passed, including the rites of the Germanic dawn-goddess *Eostre* that were celebrated at the vernal equinox.[59] Although this particular day is a fleeting moment in time, it has its *hypostasis*, an essential underlying principle, which for Webb is the Divine.[60] A trusting, childlike sensibility is moved to find Edenic pleasure in the place, but another, 'old lag's' voice urges the child to leave — 'only go now, go' — because it knows from history how this world will be corrupted

---

[54] That is, not the Elizabethan Belfry Block pictured in Griffith, *God's Fool* following p. 168; see Griffith, p. 245. A photograph of the Thornbury Tower in 1951 is on p. 102 of Gage, *Costessey Hall*. See also Gage, pp. 95–107. The Thornbury Tower was red in colour, though of brick rather than stone, according to information received from Mr Tom Barley of Bentley, WA, who has kindly lent materials on Costessey.

[55] Gage, *Costessey Hall*, pp. 94–95.

[56] Gage, *Costesesy Hall*, p. 105.

[57] See Norgate, *The History of Costessey*, p. 56–57, for a full account.

[58] Norgate, *The History of Costessey*, p. 57.

[59] *OED*, Easter, n. 1.

[60] *OED*, hypostasis, 4, 5.

— 'Refined / Out of its nature, drifting in rotten slag'. Webb catches himself here in the act of emulating Hopkins's 'Spring', where young Eden is also clouded by adult knowledge:

> [...] Have, get, before it cloy,
> Before it cloud, Christ, lord, and sour with sinning,
> Innocent mind and Mayday in girl and boy.[61]

Norman White has said of this poem that Hopkins 'was unable to go on facing the human world, picturing it as fallen and degenerate'.[62] The difference for Webb is that he refuses to allow the Fall such power over the immanent divine in the world. Instead, he treats it as a bad episode within his familiar recurring cycle of mental illness and recovery:

> Yes, I have seen Costessey in every weather
> Enslaved and bowing in the rubbing heat
> Upon the abrasive sands of self-deceit
> At the time of gathering the stones together;
> Seen sun, tree, river, all distorted, straining
> With lever and pulley; the dead gutted bird
> Lolloping in the wind; the mad process gaining;
> I could not stand and feel, nor write a word.

Webb resists the urge to project evil on to the exterior scene as an irrevocable fact of history. That would be to deny the continual creation, the recurring renewal of the world signified to him by Easter, but present before Christianity came to England, and still present though this historic Catholic hall is in ruins. History is acknowledged, but stripped of its dominance, both in a personal and a general application. Ruin and renewal are accepted as inevitable. Though the Gothic-looking tower Webb sees looks 'old', it is not even part of the original Elizabethan building but a latecomer like himself, a construction after the fact. As such, it shares his own 'strangeness' to the place, and several other attributes as well: hard times, fearfulness, 'play', and a poetic gift that survives countless psychic relapses:

> Out of the quicksands and the anarchy
> I see a strangeness stretch and flap a wing:
> This tower of a red stone, eroded whistling ghost
> Where bush and grasses cross themselves and cower
> And juvenile pigeons play at being lost
> And the airman's[63] initials rest one single hour.
>
> What frightens you must be a ruin, and waste,
> But on this Easter Monday I will drink

---

[61] Hopkins, 'Spring', *Poems*, p. 28.

[62] White, *Hopkins*, p. 280.

[63] Webb qualified as a wireless air gunner in Canada in 1944.

> Your Costessey to the dregs, and likely think
> To find in these red stones the selfsame taste
> For out of my soul one hundred times before
> Has leapt a ghostly thing, bare in its power,
> As faith, and to the ceaseless, causeless war
> Brought truce, bearing itself like this old tower.

By understanding the meaning of the scene in relation to himself, rather than an original, general 'Fall', Webb continues to dispute the notion of solid 'eras' of history: pre- and post-lapsarian; medieval and modern; he also refuses to read history, including his own, as an essentialist combat between purity and evil, whether in the Reformation or the present day. 'Around Costessey' takes up these dualist hypostatizations to reveal them as constrictive, no more than historiographical moods and fashions with which the past is already littered. Worse, in their attempted enforcement of temporal hierarchies the divisions of historiography deny the omnitemporal persistence of grace, and mimic past traumas — conquest, intolerance, persecution of difference — so that they revive the 'ceaseless causeless war' of history. In a more personal way, the poet of 'The Tower' knows this partisan tendency as paranoid aggression, 'the time of gathering the stones together'. His struggle against mistrust is also a wider one for him as a Catholic writer in England, to escape the alluring posture of religious champion in the battle-lines of cultural commentary. Refusing to project his anxiety onto a vilified opponent (for this is the logic of persecution itself), and keeping his openness to 'strangeness', Webb radically departs from the English Catholic medievalism he knew.

'Where No Knight in Armour Has Ever Trod': The Arthurianism of Jessica Anderson's Heroines

LOUISE D'ARCENS

that landscape had become a region of my mind, where infinite expansion was possible, and where no obtrusion, such as the discomfort of knees imprinted by the cane of a chair, or a magpie alighting on the grass [...] could prevent the emergence of Sir Lancelot.[1]

Nora Porteous has returned to Brisbane only to find herself confronted with Camelot. Bedridden with pneumonia on arrival, the septuagenarian narrator of Jessica Anderson's *Tirra Lirra by the River* (1978) passes her convalescence by embarking on a retrospect of her life — a life which has taken her in a slow orbit from the Brisbane of her girlhood to London, where she lived for some thirty years, and finally back to Brisbane, where she has grudgingly resigned herself to living out her remaining years. Rallying to the unwelcome prospect of her Queensland twilight, Nora sets out to untangle a life-long sense of alienation from her subtropical surroundings. This sense of alienation has prompted her in her youth to view Brisbane through the prism of romantic Arthurianism, casting herself as a kind of antipodean Lady of Shalott, exiled from both life and love. It is only through comprehending the personal and cultural motives for her 'Arthurianising' that Nora can accomplish her final, inverse act of transformation: turning Camelot back into Brisbane, a Brisbane to which she can reconcile herself in old age.

In this respect Nora is both like, and unlike, Cecily Ambruss, the heroine-narrator of Anderson's later novel, *One of the Wattle Birds* (1994). On first inspection, the two could not seem less similar: Nora is seventy and lives alone in Brisbane, while Cecily is nineteen and lives in inner Sydney with her partner Wil. Nora has

---

[1] Jessica Anderson, *Tirra Lirra by the River* (Sydney: Picador, 1997), pp. 12–13. All further references are to this edition.

experienced the oppressions of pre-feminist womanhood, while Cecily, a young woman of the early 1990s, accepts without question her right to financial, intellectual, and sexual independence. Nora is looking back over her life, while Cecily tries to grasp how to go forward in the aftermath of her mother's recent death and her own dawning recognition of the transience of relationships. Cecily also differs markedly from Nora in her complete immersion in Sydney life, whose freedoms she embraces in preference to the bourgeois constrictions of her Italian heritage. The significant link that unites this unlikely pair is their shared devotion to Arthurian legend. For both Cecily and Nora the tales of Arthur become central to their self-understanding, functioning sometimes to obscure but more often to illuminate their sense of themselves as women and, more particularly, as Australian women.

In featuring the relationship between place and personal identity, these novels are hardly atypical of Anderson's work. Although almost nothing has been written about this relationship in *One of the Wattle Birds*[2] — an oversight I wish to rectify — numerous commentators have analyzed the author's preoccupation with place and identity, especially as explored through ex- and repatriation, in novels such as *The Commandant* (1975), *The Impersonators* (1980), and *Tirra Lirra*.[3] The particular distinction of *Tirra Lirra* and *Wattle Birds* lies rather in their use of medievalism, and especially Arthurian medievalism, as a conduit for Anderson's abiding theme.

A considerable amount has been written on Nora's predilection for Tennysonian romanticism.[4] This scholarship does not, however, dwell either on the special cultural significance given to the Arthurian world within this romanticism, or on its specific valency within colonial and postcolonial Australia. Moreover, despite the remarkable fact that Anderson has featured Camelot-obsessed heroines in two of her novels, no more than a few comments have been devoted to a comparison of these heroines' Arthurianism.[5] A sustained analysis of Nora and Cecily as Arthurians, and a comparative examination of these two examples of Australian medievalism will show how the heroines' differing readings of the Arthurian legends reflect the major contrasts between colonial and postcolonial Australia. I want to suggest that the transition between the two heroines' medievalisms reflects the changing significance

---

[2] Elaine Barry devotes less than a paragraph to it in her *Fabricating the Self: The Fictions of Jessica Anderson* (St Lucia: University of Queensland Press, 1996), p. 184.

[3] See Elaine Barry, 'The Expatriate Vision of Jessica Anderson', *Meridian*, 3 (1984), 3–11; Alrene Sykes, 'Jessica Anderson: Arrivals and Places', *Southerly*, 46 (1986), 57–71; and Elizabeth Ferrier, 'Mapping the Local in the Unreal City', *Island*, 41 (1989), 65–69.

[4] See, for instance, Ros Haynes, 'Art as Reflection in Jessica Anderson's *Tirra Lirra by the River*', *Australian Literary Studies*, 12 (1986), 316–23, and Harriet Waugh's review 'Living Without Lancelot', *New York Times Book Review*, 19 Feb 1982, p. 24.

[5] Barry devotes a paragraph to it in *Fabricating the Self*, p. 168, and Julian Croft notes it in passing in his review 'King Arthur faced in Coogee', *The Weekend Australian* (Sydney), 9–10 July 1994, Review, p. 7.

of the Middle Ages as an imaginative prism through which Australian experience has been refracted. The development they embody — from Nora's Victorian-inflected recreation of Camelot to Cecily's postmodern collapsing of the medieval into the present — is an index of Australia's transition from colonial dependency at the beginning of the twentieth century to cultural autonomy and sovereignty at the century's end. Equally importantly, these novels expose the instability of 'the medieval' itself. Far from simply being arbitrary, instrumental or anachronistic misreadings of medieval culture, Nora's and Cecily's differing Arthurianisms reveal the extent to which, as Stephanie Trigg has argued, the medieval period is 'realisable, even "real", only in subsequent attempts to recreate and rewrite it'.[6] In arguing this, I want to underline a point increasingly stressed by scholars of medievalism: that a comprehensive understanding of the Middle Ages must renounce what David Greetham has described as Schadenfreude[7] toward so-called medievalist 'misreadings' and extend its reach to encompass creative, popular, post-medieval and non-European reinventions of the medieval past.[8]

'Dolorous Death and Departing': Nostalgia and Loss in Anderson's Fictions

Before interpreting the cultural significance of Nora's and Cecily's Arthurianism, it is important to understand its personal significance; for these heroines are alike not just in what they read but also why they read it. Of central importance to each novel is the theme of personal loss, in particular the loss of parents and family. In *Tirra Lirra* Nora, long-divorced and childless, returns from London after the death of her only remaining family member, her sister Grace. Settling again into her childhood home she re-examines her lost loved ones and, more importantly, what she regards as the 'vile wastage' of her adult life, which has led to the loss of her creative girlhood self. In *Wattle Birds* Cecily, an only child, has returned from a year abroad to find not only that her mother Christina has died while she was away, but — even more painful and inexplicable — that Christina 'let me go away without telling me she was dying, and let me stay away till it was over' (20–21). Trapped in a cycle of

---

[6] Stephanie Trigg, review of *The Year's Work in Medievalism: 1995*, ed. by James Gallant (vol. 10 [1999]; Holland, MI: Studies in Medievalism, 2000), in *Prolepsis* http://www.uni-tuebingen.de/uni/nes/prolepsis/01_06_tri.html

[7] David Greetham, 'Romancing the Text, Medievalising the Book', in *Medievalism in the Modern World: Essays in Honour of Leslie J. Workman*, ed. by Richard Utz and T. A. Shippey (Turnhout: Brepols, 2000), p. 430.

[8] The breadth of recent formulations of 'the medieval' is most fully reflected in Utz and Shippey's call for a 'new paradigm of medievalism as inclusive of any and all previous attempts at rewriting and/or rethinking the medieval past', *Medievalism in the Modern World*, p. 5.

uncomprehending grief, and unconvinced by the platitudes offered by others, she is driven finally to seek an explanation for her mother's behaviour from the father who abandoned them both before she was born. As unexpected as it might seem, Camelot is the locus of both women's quests for understanding in the face of loss. Furthermore, these heroines are also to some degree alike in their shared motives and the way they read, or indeed misread. Neither of their readings of the Arthurian legends is what it initially seems, even to Cecily and Nora themselves. Rather, as each novel unfolds the manifest purpose for dwelling on these legends is peeled back, revealing a deep yearning to end a debilitating private pain.

It dawns on Nora early in her reminiscences that her girlhood preoccupation with Camelot provided her with an escape from the 'raw gentility' of Brisbane. The frenzied artistic pursuits of her youth — reading and writing poetry and 'bejewelled' prose, making embroideries and clothes and 'drawings of [...] thin ladies and gentlemen in medieval garments' (19) — were, she admits, all ways of transforming her 'backward and unworldly' home so it would 'match that region of my mind, Camelot' (15). Yet despite recalling her adolescent obsession with Tennyson, she cannot account for why she has continued to be haunted by fragments from his depiction of Sir Lancelot in 'The Lady of Shalott':

> [a]t intervals all through my life [...] there has flashed on my inner vision the step of a horse, the nod of a plume, and those times I have been filled for a moment with strange chaotic grief. (23)

No amount of even the most intricate self-examination can disclose the particular resonance of these images or the 'choking grief' that accompanies them. It is only on the novel's final page that, in a flash of involuntary memory, she uncovers the early childhood incident that explains the deep personal significance she has attached to Tennyson's words:

> out of a moment of groping, of intense confusion, comes the step of a horse, the nod of a plume, come the plumed heads of the curbed horses at my father's funeral. (202)

Nested in her recollection of Tennyson's Lancelot is a longing for her dead father, and an echo of the 'excessive' grief (148) she experienced at his death but has long since repressed.

This ending has been dismissed by some critics as a pop-Freudian anti-climax that reduces Nora's complex self-estrangement to a banal family romance.[9] What this criticism overlooks, however, is that Nora's father has fused with Sir Lancelot in her unconscious not simply because he is a lost infantile love-object, or even simply because Lancelot obscurely evokes his funeral. Rather, we learn early on that it is in one of her father's books that Nora first encounters this, her favourite poem — a crucial experience for a girl whose life-world is one of literary romantic fantasies. Her dead father is not just an absent male, but a cherished fellow-reader of

---

[9] Barry, *Fabricating the Self*, p. 82.

poetry in a world where Nora encounters few such. Her loss of him, a loss profound enough to warrant absolute repression into old age, is the loss of a kindred spirit and an ally who could have defended her against the resentful derision of those around her.

Cecily similarly seeks to understand her loss of comradeship through tracing the labyrinthine betrayals in Malory's Arthuriad. In a splintering reminiscent of the break-up of the Round Table, her closest relationships have reached a point of imperceptible yet inexorable fracture. She realizes that her oldest friendship, in which she and her friend Katie were loyal 'like Arthur's knights' (142),[10] has run its course, and that camaraderie has waned within the fellowship of friends with whom she travelled the previous year. She even hints that her formerly intimate relationship with her partner Wil might be coming adrift, such that by the end of the novel she declares 'I foresee no end to the things I won't tell [him]' (192). However, if she is drawn to Malory's narrative for its charting of breakdown, she also takes heart from its conclusion: for just as on 'The Day of Destiny' Arthur is taken to Avalon 'to hele me of my grevous wounde',[11] so too Cecily's own day of destiny, when she meets her father and half-siblings, brings her into a new realm that promises love and completion.

Cecily's central, and more deeply personal, motive for reading Malory is less immediately apparent, even to herself. As a protagonist who is more self-conscious than Nora but hardly more self-aware, she admits to no personal motive, mentioning only that she is reading the *Morte Darthur* with the intention of preparing an essay for her final exams. Her argument for this essay focuses on how Malory makes Arthur's character 'more and more modern' throughout his text, tracing in particular how 'after the first section, Arthur is the only central figure whose fate is not changed by the intervention of magic' (25–26). In the three-day period covered by the narrative, her familiar red-covered Vinaver edition is her constant companion, which she mines selectively 'with a piece of card and a mechanical mind' (134) for fodder to support her argument. In the course of this reading, she does encounter exceptions to her argument, such as the episode when Arthur is rescued from Lady Anowrie by the 'subtle crafts' of the Lady of the Lake. To these she responds with a determination to absorb anomalies into her argument, saying '[o]ne instance of magic does not disprove a theory' (139).

As her exam preparation proceeds, however, it gradually becomes clear that beneath this apparently dispassionate analysis of Arthur's agency lies Cecily's deeper struggle to come to terms with her own agency in the face of crippling loss. A year after being informed of her mother's death she is regarded, in the words of

---

[10] Jessica Anderson, *One of the Wattle Birds* (Ringwood: Penguin, 1994). All further references are to this edition.

[11] *Malory: Works*, ed. by Eugène Vinaver, 2nd edn (Oxford: Oxford University Press, 1971), p. 716, l. 25.

her estranged father, as 'that most fortunate of human creatures, a healthy young person with an adequate intelligence and a small private income' (168). Relatives and friends, even the sympathetic Wil, all consider that enough time has elapsed for her to have reconciled herself to her mother's decision, and to have embraced her independence. Yet despite her desperation to comply, she finds she cannot. Unlike Nora, who must dredge her father out of the depths of her unconscious, Cecily is all too aware of the wound caused by her mother's death. Furthermore, her confusion over Christina's inexplicable exclusion of her makes her feel she has lost all sense of who her mother was. Her obsessive sifting of memories emerges from her conviction that she will only be capable of independent agency when she can find the true explanation of her mother's behaviour.

The significance of Arthur's immunity from magic to Cecily's quest for autonomy will be elaborated further into my argument. For now what is vital is that Cecily learns to apply her method of reading Malory to her interpretation of her loss. On day two of the narrative she is liberated when she realizes that the 'essentially rubbery' nature of Malory's tale — its fluctuating dialectic between supernatural and human agency — allows her to accommodate exceptions into her rigid, 'neat' argument (96). This discovery prepares her for another which is more profound: that the best way of understanding her mother is not to seek a single truth that will explain her, but, more simply, 'an answer' (179) that will embrace Christina's flawed complexity and make reconciliation possible.

'She Has a Lovely Face': Arthurian Identifications

The point on which these heroines differ most conspicuously is the Arthurian character with whom they identify or are identified. Nora's central identification is with Tennyson's Lady of Shalott. Cecily, on the other hand, identifies with Malory's Arthur. This discrepancy proves significant at a number of levels. In order to understand this fully, it is necessary to examine the impact of these differing approaches on the gendered identities of the two heroines. In so doing, we can see the ways in that Anderson uses Arthurianism to trace her female characters' paths to self-acceptance and self-determination.

Long before she detects the ghost of her father in Tennyson's Lancelot, Nora begins to recall the particular appeal that 'The Lady of Shalott' held for her as a girl. Quoting a stanza many decades later, she surmises:

> Many readings must have been necessary to drive it into my mind so that I still retain it, because I was — am — a person of undisciplined mind, and in spite of the passion I had for poetry, I could seldom hold more than a few consecutive lines in my head (13).

What she never fully acknowledges is the extent to which her own fate can be identified with that of the Lady. Nevertheless, this is the central structuring principle of Anderson's text, and becomes apparent in repeated, if sometimes oblique, allusions throughout her story. Tennyson's poem is in fact an indispensable intertext to Anderson's novel, illuminating its events and motifs, and adding a tragic gravity to Nora's already moving narrative.

At the most intimate level, Nora's sexual infatuations echo the Lady's doomed passion for Lancelot. To begin with, as a teenage aesthete she focuses her nascent erotic energies not on the local youths but on Lancelot himself, cherishing his presence in the 'Camelot' she has built from early childhood. This displaced desire is revisited with subtlety throughout the novel as we trace Nora's series of abortive and illicit fascinations with men whose dark hair is reminiscent of Lancelot's 'coal black curls'. The most clearly recalled of these is the Byronic John Porteous, to whom she is instantly drawn, and of whom her husband Colin is but a fair-haired shadow. The Lancelot-type appears most powerfully, however, and most unexpectedly, in the form of Arch Cust, the pubescent neighbour with whom Nora had a humiliating quasi-erotic encounter as a young woman. Although Nora presumes her rigorous repression of this event is due to embarrassment over Arch's youth, we recognize the real reason when she mentions a crucial physical detail:

> His black curls had been cut off long ago, but I was familiar with the whorls that remained, and in a moment of dazed tender silence I set my cheek against his head to trace on my skin the base of those absent curls (137).

Indeed, Arch's appeal is such that even when he himself is forgotten, his ghost is resurrected fifteen years later in the form of the unnamed American with whom Nora has a brief shipboard romance. And of course lurking behind all of these Lancelot-surrogates is her father, the primal love for whom even Tennyson's knight is a replacement.

Anderson's identification of Nora with the Lady of Shalott also carries a broader significance that emerges out of Nora's recognition of her socio-historical conditions. As Ros Haynes and others have shown, in this identification we see Nora, like the Lady, embodying the dilemma of the woman artist in a repressive society. Born at the turn of the century into a still-Victorian society, Nora is subject to codes of femininity that strongly discourage her from developing her obvious artistic abilities into an adult vocation. Living through the Great Depression and two world wars — unarguable incursions of the Real — her artistry is regarded as a luxury that she must sacrifice or turn into something useful like cakes or curtains. Thus while we can never quite discern the mysterious curse which prevents Tennyson's Lady from looking directly at the world, we are left in no doubt that the 'curse' which, in Ros Haynes's words, 'determines [Nora's] behaviour and punishes relentlessly any deviation from the permitted pattern'[12] is patriarchal society. Caught between creating art out of 'the compression of a secret life' (184) or plunging into a

---

[12] Ros Haynes, 'Art as Reflection in Jessica Anderson's *Tirra Lirra by the River*', p. 318.

world which will destroy or domesticate her artistic vocation, Nora, like the Lady, is caught in an impasse.

It is mainly through images that Anderson suggests the parallel between the two. First of all, Nora's Queenslander house, raised on stilts, is reminiscent of the 'four gray towers' inhabited by the Lady. Within her suburban tower, Nora, like the Lady with her mirror, views the world at one remove, visualizing lush miniature landscapes through 'distortions in the cheap thick glass' of her window (12). Finally, the embroideries she creates as a girl recall the 'magic web' woven by the Lady. This parallel becomes more insistent when we consider that just as the Lady's tapestries are destroyed by direct contact with life,[13] so Nora's marriage to the boorish Colin Porteous, which occasions her move away from Brisbane, leads her to abandon her embroidery for dress making, a more conventional channel for female creativity. Her subsequent job making theatre costumes allows her more satisfaction, but only brings her into a subordinate proximity with the creativity of others.

Unlike Tennyson's female artist *manqué*, Nora's contact with reality does not condemn her to death; in fact the only non-conformist woman who suffers this fate is Dorothy Rainbow, whose surrender to domestic conformity drives her to murder and suicide. But as an old woman, studying with amazement the excellence of her early embroideries, Nora does ponder the question of what marvels she might have created had she remained at home and kept her secret aesthetic world. She comes to acknowledge this again when she contemplates the beauty of the tropical garden created by her late sister Grace, whom she had always deemed insensible to aesthetics. In many respects Nora's final gesture, narrating her life, can be seen as a cognitive equivalent of Grace's use of compost to create her garden, for it is a creative act in which she does not 'make' but 'find', taking the 'vile wastage' of her life and recycling it into something productive and meaningful. It is here that her fate most sharply diverges from the Lady of Shalott's: although she is not granted the Lady's beauteous death, growing instead into 'an old woman with [...] hands like bunches of sticks' (142), Anderson's gift to her of a reflective old age is arguably more generous and certainly more optimistic.

Although Elaine of Astolat, an earlier version of the Lady of Shalott, appears in Malory's *Morte Darthur*, she is at no point mentioned by Cecily, whose desire to identify with Arthur is absolute. Despite this, Cecily, like Nora, never overtly proclaims her affinity with Arthur; we are simply told that she has had an abiding scholarly interest in his character:

---

[13] In her unpublished essay 'A Magic Web: Cloth and Literature', Dorothy Jones interestingly observes that 'Tennyson's line 'the web flew wide and free' suggests liberation rather than destruction' (13) of the Lady's tapestry. Anderson appears to have adhered to the more conventional interpretation of this moment as the death of the Lady's artistry.

In this notebook are all my notes on Malory [...] the interest in Arthur was there from the start, and is continuous and accumulative, as if he were always my choice, but hidden from myself. (142)

As mentioned earlier, however, Cecily's preoccupation with Malory's hero, far from being scholarly, is inseparable from her understanding of her own character and circumstances. Specifically, Cecily's wish to demonstrate that Arthur's 'fate is not changed by the intervention of magic' reflects her desire to determine her own fate. Given her situation, her concern with this issue is not without reason. The confusion that already plagues her over her mother's reclusive death is exacerbated by a clause in Christina's will which stipulates that Cecily can only inherit when she marries — a truly troubling proviso given Christina's own defiant single motherhood. Because Cecily, unlike Nora, has grown up with the freedoms won by the women's movement, being faced with the knowledge that her future has been controlled by her mother is especially limiting to her sense of autonomy. It is unsurprising, then, to find that in her reading of Malory she is drawn to the figure of Arthur, who is described as Emperor 'by dignity of his own hands' (26) — a phrase which Cecily finds 'promising' and which she repeats in her description of his actions. That her own sense of autonomy depends on verifying Arthur's is revealed by the fact that when recounting her reading process she repeatedly collapses personal pronouns, so that any threat to his human agency also threatens both her theory and her self-perception. Thus when she comes across an episode where she suspects Arthur might be in 'danger' of receiving supernatural assistance, she says 'here, in North Wales, in the Forest Perilous, I am in dangerous territory' (135).

Arthur's unique exemption from supernatural intervention resonates for Cecily at several levels. This has most obviously to do with her feelings about her mother; for Cecily's rational disposition notwithstanding, it is clear she feels Christina is exerting a kind of supernatural control over her from the grave. At the most concrete level, the 'marriage clause' in her will equates Christina with a sorceress, her invisible influence directly determining her daughter's marital choices and financial future. At an emotional level, her unexplained reclusive death equates her with a remote goddess, her silence provoking obsessive speculation from her baffled daughter, whose grieving process is thereby stymied. Cecily also feels her path to resolution to be obstructed by those whose well-wishing but facile explanations constitute attempts to intervene in, and lay to rest, her pursuit of an explanation that will satisfy her craving for truth. Her world has become a hostile one in which all her friends and relatives keep 'putting up guards' (7) when she seeks answers about her mother, leaving her at the mercy of the nagging doubts that beseige her, 'like one of those raggedy birds trying to feed her remorseless young' (21).

The image of the raggedy bird is only one of several negative representations of maternity offered by Cecily throughout the novel. Because of her resentment toward Christina she has become jaundiced toward not only marriage but motherhood, which she presents in quasi-feminist terms: 'I see so little point in maternity that I can't imagine why anyone wants children' (16). Taking this into account, it is perhaps not incidental that she identifies with a distinctly masculine model of personal sovereignty. This active identification with the *Morte Darthur*'s male hero is worth investigating. It is not surprising that Cecily, with her feminist-influenced sensibilities, is not susceptible to the masochistic pathos embodied in Malory's Elaine of Astolat, or to the amorous caprice embodied in his Guinevere. Nevertheless, there are other female characters in the text whose ability to control the course of events might have provided Cecily with a model of female empowerment. Her comment that 'The Lady of the Lake and Morgan le Fay are both at large, and either can work their magic in one line' (26) reflects her awareness of the power, whether evil or benevolent, wielded by a number of Malory's women. The problem with these female characters, however, is that the supernatural basis of their power makes them unappealing to Cecily, who is desperate not to conjure away her curiosity with platitudes but to satisfy it by plausible explanation. Moreover, although she never makes a direct comparison, her wariness of their unbidden intervention in Arthur's affairs parallels her offence at her mother's posthumous interference in her life. Her comment that 'women of former times [...] seem to me to have been a sneaky lot' (81), while aimed at no-one in particular, places her mother within an obsolete tradition of feminine mendacity stretching back to Malory's mythic sorceresses. It is a mark of Cecily's youth that despite her broadly feminist outlook she, unlike Nora, appears to have little understanding of the limited scope offered 'women of former times', real and fictional, for the exercise of legitimate power. In any case, she has come to see autonomy, the exercise of one's power without resorting to subterfuge, not just as a human ideal, but as a masculine prerogative embodied by Arthur.

However, even as Cecily pursues masculine autonomy, the novel's narrative logic self-consciously works against this pursuit; for as her journey to understanding gains momentum, it is increasingly punctuated by quasi-magical interventions. The most important of these is the fortuitous phone call Cecily receives from her Aunt Gail, informing her of her father's phone number just at the moment Cecily is contemplating visiting him. Although Cecily continues to tell herself that her visit to her father is completely random, she realizes that Aunt Gail's 'subtle crafts' (141) have divined her need and led her to her father, who does in fact shed light on her mother's behaviour. By referring to Gail's 'subtle crafts' Cecily self-consciously narrates this incident as an echo of one she has just read in the *Morte Darthur* when, in the Forest Perilous, 'the Lady of the Lake, that friendly sorceress [...] divines Arthur's danger by her subtle crafts, and [...] warns Tristan of the king's peril' (136). As Cecily approaches her destination, Gail's intervention is compounded by that of a young surfer, whom Cecily calls 'a great magician' (147), who arranges for her to be transported up the steep hill to her father's house. By the time she has arrived, she has given herself over to the magical nature of the event, whispering a password 'arrivo' to herself before entering the forest perilous of lantana that surrounds the house. Despite the awkwardness of the meeting, Cecily finally finds in her estranged father someone who will refrain from platitude and subject Christina's action to unsentimental appraisal.

Cecily's father Vernon explains Christina's behaviour as 'high-handedness', a capacity to allow her needs to overcome her scruples, describing how she, his mistress, had furtively conceived Cecily knowing he wanted no more children. It is when we learn of this that we understand the significance of Cecily revising 'all but the first of the [*Morte Darthur*] Tales' (26), a detail mentioned apparently incidentally. Her selective revision of Arthur's life is an unconscious echo of her resistance to examining the opening chapter of her own life, as reflected in her refusal to know her father. For readers familiar with the early chapters of the *Morte Darthur*, the conditions of Cecily's conception are uncannily like Arthur's: Christina's cunning fulfilment of her own needs by conceiving Cecily against Vernon's wishes is reminiscent of Uther Pendragon's siring of Arthur by Igrayne through subterfuge. It is the avoidance of this chapter in her life that delays Cecily's understanding of her mother; for it is only when she finally meets her father, and understands that Christina was simultaneously capable of love and selfishness, that she can gain a sobering but liberating perspective on her mother's death. The fact that Cecily finds some peace by surrendering herself to the guidance of others means that just as her theory of Arthur's character must 'absorb [...] one or more instances of magic intervention', so her insistence on her own autonomy can now be modified. Thus the masculinist model of autonomous agency upheld throughout the novel is ultimately questioned, and by the end there is a sense not of tragic isolation, but of the possibility of new community for Cecily.

'That Region of my Mind': Cultural Legacy and Sovereignty

As discussed earlier, a considerable amount has been written about the ways in which the Lady of Shalott's fate reflects Nora's own artistic career and the loss of her father. But to focus only on the personal romantic quest does not, I believe, adequately address the important cultural implications of Nora's choice of Tennyson's poem as the vehicle for her romantic self-identification. Indeed, both Nora's and Cecily's pursuit of self-acceptance is inseparable from the larger quest for cultural sovereignty that is central to both novels. Their recognition, and indeed perpetuation, of the mythic power of Tennyson's and Malory's texts is central not only to their introspective quests but also to the way in which they view their antipodean environments. It is on this point that the two heroines differ strongly, in ways that directly reflect the changes in the Australian scene.

The cultural implications of Nora's and Cecily's readings of Arthurian legend are suggested by the versions of the tales they prefer. Elaine Barry notes the significance of this distinction, saying 'the intellectually sophisticated and confident Cecily reads Malory in the original, where Nora, a victim of the Victorian values that still determined gender roles in the Brisbane of her girlhood, reads Tennyson's Victorian rendering of him'.[14] Barry emphasizes the issue of female emancipation here, in a statement that reinforces my earlier point about the gender assumptions underlying Nora's and Cecily's respective identifications with Elaine and Arthur. However, Barry's point is problematic in that it uncritically privileges scholarly over amateur reading, and academic mastery over appreciation, and medieval over medievalist texts, thereby reinforcing a hierarchy which, as David Hult points out, has been understood in manifestly gendered terms, with the 'feminine' amateur approach being regarded as inferior.[15] Rather than privileging Cecily's reading for its 'authenticity' or 'masculine' qualities, I wish instead to draw out what the two reading practices reflect of the cultural context in which they live, focusing in particular on their respective understandings of Australia as a colonial — and later postcolonial — nation.

There are some strong interpretations, such as those offered by Glenn Thomas and Alrene Sykes,[16] which do connect Nora's devotion to Tennyson to her cultural status, arguing that his poem offers a landscape that is ideal to a colonized subject. However, a limitation of these accounts is that they do not situate Nora's individual devotion fully enough within the broader context of imperialist medievalism in general and Arthurianism in particular. A brief excursus into this phenomenon is necessary to provide some insight into the established cultural and ideological discourses that underpin and inform Nora's and Cecily's personal interpretations of Arthurian legend.

As a result of increased attention over the past two decades, we have come to better understand the many ways in which fantasies of the medieval period have been instrumentalized to provide a range of imagined pasts for modern culture. Far from being the dispassionate expression of interest in the pre-modern past, medievalism in its many forms has been central to the formulation of cultural, political, and national identities in Europe and Britain.[17] Harking back to ancient local myths and languages has allowed these modern states to create nationalistic narratives which have fostered, and justified, their sense of their own cultural

---

[14] Barry, *Fabricating the Self*, p. 168.

[15] David Hult, 'Gaston Paris and the Invention of Courtly Love', in *Medievalism and the Modernist Temper*, ed. by R. Howard Bloch and Stephen G. Nichols (Baltimore: Johns Hopkins University Press, 1996), p. 211.

[16] Glenn Thomas, 'Post-Colonial Interrogations', *Social Alternatives*, 12 (1993), 8–11; Sykes, 'Jessica Anderson: Arrivals and Places', pp. 62–68.

[17] Of the numerous texts by medieval scholars, see R. Howard Bloch, 'Naturalism, Nationalism, Medievalism', *Romanic Review*, 76 (1985), 341–60; *Medievalism and the Modernist Temper*, ed. by Bloch and Nichols; 'National Identity and the Politics of Publishing the Troubadours', in *Medievalism and the Modernist Temper*, pp. 57–94; Hans Ulrich Gumbrecht, '"Un souffle d'Allemagne ayant passé": Friedrich Diez, Gaston Paris, and the Genesis of National Philologies' *Romance Philology*, 40 (1986), 1–37; and the numerous volumes of *Studies in Medievalism* devoted to national medievalisms.

antiquity and glory — a function especially crucial for imperial powers looking to mark their primacy vis-à-vis the colonized territories. In this respect, the Arthurian legends have been vital for providing Britain with mythic models for gender, nation, and, crucially, empire.[18] Tennyson's work, for instance, is widely regarded as offering a historical vision of England as Camelot in which, to quote Ian McGuire 'the Arthurian ideal [is] the ideal of Britain and Empire'.[19]

Less is known about how this kind of Anglocentric Arthurianism has contributed to the formation of Australian identity and national consciousness. However, when we turn our gaze to the early colonies we find educators, poets, and others drawing on Arthurian legend as a vehicle for expressing their experiences and their outlook in an unfamiliar environment. In some instances, the Arthurian legends provide a buffer that distances the colonial subject from the antipodean locale, as in Adam Lindsay Gordon's 'The Rhyme of Joyous Garde'. The content of Gordon's poem — the aged and remorseful Lancelot recounting his betrayal of Arthur — imparts no clue as to the poet's Australian context, highlighting rather his devotion to English Arthurian poets Swinburne and Tennyson. While in a broader sense the Arthurianism of 'Joyous Garde' is conventionally Victorian, it is nevertheless striking to find it in the collection *Bush Ballads and Galloping Rhymes* (1870), alongside 'The Sick Stockrider', 'Wolf and Hound', and 'From the Wreck', with their direct horseback view of the Australian bush. It is equally striking to find fellow-poet Henry Kendall, author of 'The Muse of Australia' and *Leaves from an Australian Forest*, depart from his local themes and take up an Arthurian motif in his memorial ode to Gordon. Here Kendall likens Gordon to the departed king, while he himself becomes Sir Bedevere bidding farewell:

> I stand to-day as lone as he who saw
> At nightfall, through the glimmering moony mist,
> The last of Arthur on the wailing mere,
> And strained in vain to hear the going voice.[20]

Elsewhere, however, we see a determined attempt to produce a vision of Camelot modelled on life in the colonies. The mid-nineteenth-century speeches of John

---

[18] These studies include Mark Girouard, *The Return to Camelot: Chivalry and the English Gentleman* (New Haven: Yale University Press, 1981); Debra N. Mancoff *The Arthurian Revival in Victorian Art* (New York: Garland, 1990); *King Arthur's Modern Return*, ed. by Debra N. Mancoff (New York: Garland, 1998).

[19] Ian McGuire, 'Epistemology and Empire in Idylls of the King', *Victorian Poetry*, 30 (1992), 389. See also Victor Kiernan, 'Tennyson, King Arthur, and Imperialism', in *Culture, Ideology, and Politics: Essays for Eric Hobsbawn*, ed. by Raphael Samuel and Gareth Stedman Jones (London: Routledge and Kegan Paul, 1982), pp. 126–48.

[20] 'The Late Mr A. L. Gordon: In Memoriam', in *Henry Kendall: Poetry, Prose & Selected Correspondence*, ed. by Michael Ackland (St Lucia: University of Queensland Press, 1993), pp. 88–89.

Woolley, Australia's first professor, are a pertinent example of this. In his 1860 lecture on the first four *Idylls of the King*, Woolley presents Tennyson's characters, with their sorrows and struggles, as typological forerunners of modern-day Australians:

> Enid, Elaine, and Arthur [...] Geraint, Launcelot, Vivien, and Guinevere [...] [e]ach has a separate and living type, familiar to our daily observation, suffering, repenting, in the nineteenth century, and the unpoetical streets of Sydney, just as they did long ages ago in the wild forests of Devon, or the romantic castle of Astolat, in the glittering hall of Camelot, or the cloistered cell of Almesbury.[21]

He goes on throughout this lengthy lecture to develop an elaborate and idiosyncratic reading of the *Idylls* in which the collapse of Camelot functions as a cautionary tale pointing to the potential pitfalls of colonial life. As I have discussed elsewhere, in Woolley's singular reading Arthur becomes an autocratic colonial administrator, with Guinevere as his indolent and delinquent subject, while Elaine becomes emblematic of the dissatisfied and transient colonial who yearns to leave. Woolley's most inspired 'colonializing' of Tennyson is, however, arguably found in his adaptation of the knight Geraint, who in the professor's reading becomes a typical hard-headed Sydney businessman, while his wife Enid epitomizes for Woolley the ideal of unquestioning colonial stoicism.[22] What is most vital about Woolley's Arthurianism for the purposes of this discussion is that, unlike the examples discussed above, it makes sense of the Arthurian world through the lens of life in the Australian colonies.

Having briefly outlined the mixed heritage of early Australian Arthurianism, we can now consider the ways in which Nora's and Cecily's reading practices emerge out of, and modify, this larger tradition.

Nora's alienation from her Brisbane environs, fuelled by her piecemeal consumption of romantic literature, has bred in her from her earliest years a determined disavowal of her physical surroundings, as we see in her recollection of her frequent walks through her neighbourhood:

> Often I used to walk by the river, the real river half a mile from the house. It was broad, brown, and strong, and as I walked beside it I hardly saw it, and never used it as a location for my dreams. (13)

Dreaming of Tennyson's river, her own is invisible to her. Before leaving this area as an adult, she spends her girlhood selectively reconstituting (or, in her own words,

---

[21] John Woolley, Lecture 9, 'The Idylls of the King', in *Lectures Delivered in Australia* (Cambridge: Macmillan, 1862), pp. 390–91.

[22] An extended discussion of this can be found in Louise D'Arcens, 'Antipodean Idylls: An Early Australian Translation of Tennyson's Medievalism', in *Postcolonial Moves, Medieval to Modern*, ed. by Patricia Ingham and Michelle R. Warren (New York: Palgrave, 2003), pp. 237–56.

'distorting') her prosaic hometown into the 'green, wet, romantic' (12) Arthurian landscape of her childhood books. The extent of her disavowal is captured in the pathos of Nora's self-styled romanticism:

> I was in love with beauty. I carried my pale face, my dropped flag of ashen hair, my abstract eyes, my damp concealed body, along the rough roads and streets [...] of a raw but genteel town. (16)

Among the standard attributes of the pre-Raphaelite muse, the jarring detail of a perspiring, damp body reintroduces Nora's subtropical environs and reinforces the uncomfortable extent of her denial. This aestheticizing capacity for denial, which earns her scorn (and the derisive pseudo-courtly moniker of 'Lady Muck'), continues throughout her life in Australia. She admits in old age that at times it bordered on delusional; of her move to Sydney as a young woman, she says 'Sydney [...] stood proxy for Camelot, in a substitution forced on me by what little commonsense I had' (25). At other times, however, it is this very capacity which has preserved her sanity in circumstances of entrapment and poverty:

> In whatever circumstances I have found myself, I have always managed to devise a little area [...] that was not too ugly. At times it was a whole room, but at others it may have been only a corner with a handsome chair, or a table and a vase of flowers. (27–28)

As Anderson herself has noted, Nora is 'partly ruined and partly made by romantic notions'.[23] Moreover, as is subtly indicated by a conversation between the aged Nora and her neighbours Jack and Betty Cust, it was early twentieth-century Queensland that provided the soil out of which Nora's youthful Europhilia sprang. Recalling their parents' planting of larkspurs, hollyhocks, columbines, and other non-indigenous plants, the Custs, whose own garden is a subtropical triumph, conclude of Nora's generation 'the old people fought the place' (199). Nora's power of distortion, then, far from working against her environment, can be seen to be simply a more conspicuous and personalized example of the unacknowledged Euro-centric nostalgia that went on everywhere in her colonial context.

It is true that Nora never openly recognizes her romanticism as a legacy of colonialism or cultural imperialism. However, an unconscious acknowledgment of the impact of colonization on her identity is detectable in the telling image she uses to represent her memory:

> for some years now I have likened [my memory] to a globe suspended in my head [...] it is miraculously suspended and will spin in response either to a deliberate turn or an accidental flick. The deliberate turns are meant to keep it in a soothing half-spin with certain chosen parts to the light [...] I have become so expert at this, so watchful and quick, that there is always a nether side to my globe. (36)

---

[23] 'Jessica Anderson: Interview', in Ray Willbanks, *Speaking Volumes: Australian Writers and their Work* (Ringwood: Penguin, 1992), p. 22.

At the most obvious level this image seems the logical expression of Nora's life, the two halves of which were lived in Australia and England. However, Nora admits that of the 'multitude of images' she carefully guards on the 'nether side' of her memory, all are drawn from her life in Australia. Thus at the level of Nora's individual colonized psyche, Australia has become the dark side of the planet, her life there either repressed or, in the case of those parts kept on the light side, diminished into self-deprecating comedy to entertain her friends in London. At a broader level her caricature of her own life in Australia is a belittling of colonial life itself, which she represents as petty, provincial, and absurd. This globe, with its many-faceted surface, functions as yet another mediating 'glass' through which Nora, like the Lady of Shalott, views her life at one remove, its Australian aspect being refracted through not only her personal concerns but also the imperialist expectations she has imbibed since her childhood.

Cultural nostalgia is complicated, however, both in this novel and in *Wattle Birds*. This tendency is noted by Barry who, comparing Anderson's novels to those of Henry James, comments 'if James is ambivalent about the abstract value of Europe, Jessica Anderson is even more so'.[24] In *Tirra Lirra*, Nora's early inchoate Anglophilia, in which England is the font of life and culture, appears at first to be actualized by her falling pregnant on the way to London, and then amplified by the new-found sense of freedom she feels when she leaves Sydney. On arrival in London, however, she undergoes an abortion and goes on to experience loneliness and celibacy, chronic bronchitis, a failed face-lift, and suicidal despair, settling finally into a companionship that is reassuring but also brittle and ultimately claustrophobic. As she recovers from pneumonia the aged Nora comes to admit that her 'edited' caricature of Australian life was disingenuous and self-serving, and thus in need of revision. When this revision is completed, her globe of memory exists in 'free spin, with no obscure side' (201). She also comes to recognize the possibilities for beauty and artistry in the seemingly prosaic antipodean setting, in her admiration for Grace's lush garden and the quiet dignity of Betty Cust. Her final state of self-knowledge is, in fact, achieved through establishing contact for the first time with her surroundings, in particular the neglected Brisbane River of her girlhood. Unable to locate the actual river in the tangle of suburbia that has grown up around it, she revisits her memories and finds, submerged beneath her fantasy of Tennyson's river '[f]lowing down to Camelot', a recollection of its singular beauty:

> I believe I have found the river — the real river I disregarded on my first walks and failed to find on my last — because never before have I seen its scoured-out creeks nor known that the shadows of its brown water are lavender at evening. (201)

Stripped of its medievalist veneer, her environment can reassert its claim to her affections and she, in turn, can finally feel at home. In one of the novel's most delicate ironies, it is through contemplating the river's shadows, with their distinct

---

[24] Barry, 'The Expatriate Vision of Jessica Anderson', p. 9.

Australian palette, that Nora finally differentiates her own world from the 'shadows' created by her distorting cultural glass. This hard-won recognition of 'the real river' is, finally, paralleled by her involuntary discovery of her father behind the fetishized figure of Lancelot: both are discoveries of her true love-objects, which have existed all along in humble Brisbane. This affects a decisive reversal in Nora's medievalism, as the Victorian Anglophilia of her youth is replaced by what can be described as an emerging postcolonial medievalism, in which formerly cherished medieval tropes are enlivened and valued only insofar as they correspond to her newly-beloved local environment. She now loves Camelot only because it reminds her of Brisbane.

Nora's budding sensibility reaches its corollary in Cecily's postmodern Australian interpretation of Camelot. There can be no doubt that the academic approach to Malory's Arthuriad adopted by Cecily is, as Barry suggests, an index of her education and her emancipation relative to the young Nora. What I wish to explore, however, is how the version of the tales and the reading strategy favoured by Cecily also reflect the cultural framework in which she lives. Barry's claim that 'Malory offers [Cecily] that reassurance of universal experience that is part of the appeal of imaginative literature' does not adequately account for the specific pertinence of this text for Cecily as a cultural subject. A more productive approach must consider how Cecily's contemporary urban Australian context, a context characterized by a heightened and reflexive consciousness of the effects of cultural hegemony, intersects with her interest in the anatomy of power, agency, and subjectivity within Malory's text.

The Anglocentric, colonial anxiety that underpins the Brisbane of Nora's girlhood is absent from *Wattle Birds*. Anderson is intent (indeed at times somewhat heavy-handed) in her rendering of Sydney's altered cultural demography: this is a multicultural, Pacific city where Anglo-Asian couples are formed, migrant families flourish, and the characters eat at a restaurant that is 'Sydneyan with an Italian accent and Asian undertones' (98). It is, moreover, postcolonial, in the sense that the submerged imperial ideology that underpins young Nora's Brisbane been replaced by a social milieu in which characters are free to express overt concern about the politics of cultural domination as they have been manifested in Australian society. From jokes about the influence of 'inherited British militarism' on the Australian male character (12), to incidental comments about the dispossession of indigenous Australians (45) and Australia's complicity in the Indonesian occupation of East Timor (186), there is a generalized awareness amongst the novel's educated and professional characters of the ill-effects of colonialism in Australia and the Pacific region. Lest her portrait of Sydney seem too utopian, however, Anderson does question the romanticism and superficiality occasionally underpinning the city's self-congratulatory cosmopolitanism. This is most pointed in an episode where Cecily's precociously fashion-conscious cousins have decided to reclaim the original 'i' in 'Ambrussi' not out of any desire to de-Anglicize their Italian surname but because they feel it has 'panache'. The fact that they are children might suggest that Australian multiculturalism is still, to some extent, in its infancy.

It is only recently that Cecily has become interested in the workings of power and agency in 'this tale which less than three years ago could send me into whirls of romantic fantasy' (134). It is unclear from this comment whether her previous contact with the Arthurian legends is through Malory; however, one suspects not, given that while reading Malory, Cecily is gently disparaging of her former predilection for romantic literature. When recounting her and her cousin Gene's adolescent fantasies of 'living in rich simplicity', she adds wryly 'Yes, we had been reading Mum's copy of *Walden*' (108). While Nora at nineteen is still firmly ensconced in her pre-Raphaelite dreams, Cecily at the same age has, nostalgic pangs notwithstanding, come to regard her former Arthurian fantasies as a mark of personal and cultural naivety. This is, of course, attributable in part to her university education; however it is also due to the fact that Cecily, a beneficiary of the age of air travel, has experienced European culture first hand, and has found it to be hidebound and forbidding in spite of its (significantly autumnal) beauty. The fantasies of her adolescence have been dashed by an ugly face-to-face encounter with her mother's family in Lucca, who reject her because of her illegitimacy. In this respect her more matured, postcolonial view of Europe is the outcome of a cultural opportunity denied the young Nora, whose Anglophilic reveries are kept intact by the constriction of movement that prevented many Australians of her time from travelling.

Cecily does not read the *Morte Darthur* because it feeds a nostalgic fantasy of the European past that rescues her from a culturally void contemporary context. Rather, as she states, her interest in Arthur is based on her sense that his freedom from magical intervention makes him precisely a 'modern' character (25). While she concedes that 'modern' for Malory means fifteenth-century, her emphasis on Arthur's modernity establishes him as a model not only for contemporary individual subjecthood, as discussed earlier, but also for sovereign nationhood, embodying its ideal of self-determination. In terms of the novel's setting, he could be emblematic of a vision of postcolonial nationhood in which Australia as a sovereign state is free to conduct its own affairs unimpeded by imperial interference or expectations. The fact, however, that Arthur ultimately profits from benevolent intervention tempers any isolationism that might attend this vision, and makes him emblematic of a culturally complex polity like the multicultural Australia presented in the novel.

Up until the final stages of *Wattle Birds*, Nora's romantic projection of Camelot onto her Brisbane backyard has been replaced by Cecily's de-romanticized topography of Sydney, 'where no dragon has ever been seen rolling in on the surf [...] [and] where no knight in armour has ever trod' (138). Far from disavowing or attempting to medievalize her immediate surroundings, Cecily revels in the promising warmth of the city in early summer, noting the colours and scents of jacarandas, flame trees, tristania, and lantana. If anything, it is nature that masters her: her only attempt at surfing results in 'the Pacific Ocean [...] trying to batter its way into every orifice in my head' (143). To a reader familiar with Sydney, Cecily's urban topography, with its references to bus numbers, suburbs, street names, and landmarks, is accurate and evocative, although Anderson occasionally verges toward touristic panegyric in her celebration of 'the harbour [...] glittering all silent and silver and blue' (31) and the 'deep thrilling oceanic embrace' (144) of Sydney's beach suburbs.

It may seem that Cecily is simply inverting Nora's romanticism, expunging any hint of the medieval from her Pacific locale. By the end of the novel, however, it is clear that Cecily, unlike Nora, does not have to renounce her attachment to the Arthurian world in order to occupy her own. After she has relinquished her obsession with autonomy and accepted her Aunt Gail's intervention, her father's coastal suburb of Coogee is transformed into a chivalric beachscape complete with surfers in 'beautiful knee-length armour [...] black and glistening and stabbed and banded with bright electrical colour' (144) who gallantly transport Cecily up the steep slopes of the suburb's main street, Arden Street. It is through surrendering herself to this outside influence or 'craft' that Cecily is able to reach the knowledge she has been seeking throughout the novel. Thus Cecily achieves a synthesis in which Arthur is modernized while Sydney is medievalized, transformed into a space where fate and human agency effortlessly coincide.

Through Anderson's two very different heroines, then, we gain an insight into the complexity of medievalism, and most specifically Arthurianism, as a vehicle for psychic repression, denial, and hopelessly idealistic quests — and for self-knowledge, familial unity, and emotional renewal. Its workings are deceptive: it seems to draw these women away from themselves only to return them to their deepest, and seemingly most irretrievable, loves; and it is this that makes their futures possible. While Tennyson's Lady and Malory's Arthur exit their tales dead or grievously wounded, thwarted by their tragic fates, Nora and Cecily have learned from them and are left at the end of their stories contemplating a future, however brief, of self-reliance and simplicity.

These heroines' evolving relationship to the medieval period is, furthermore, not just an index of their personal development, but also traces Australia's halting path from immature or 'adolescent' colonial dependency to the mature cultural sovereignty of the late twentieth century. When read as companion texts, the trajectory that can be discerned across these two novels begins with medievalist discourse organizing the Australian cultural space and concludes with the attainment of a far more dialogic relationship between pre-modern Europe and the postmodern Australia that interprets it. And it is in offering this trajectory that Anderson is arguably tendering her most pressing hermeneutic point for our consideration. For we can read these novels as her notion of an ideal form of medievalism for the postcolonial, multicultural polity that Australia has become. Through her heroines' stories Anderson calls for an Australian medievalism that replaces the redundant imperative to recreate the European past with the freedom to creatively integrate this past into the hybrid reality of the present 'where no knight in armour has ever trod'. The paradoxical but ingenious truth of this medievalism is that it is only when the medieval world is located within the contemporary cultural landscape that its 'infinite expansion' becomes truly possible.

Australian 'Everymans': Post-Medieval Spiritual Adventurers

MARGARET ROGERSON

O ut there in cyberspace, the newest frontier for adventurers, 'everyman' can be virtually anyone we want him to be. Search the internet and you will find thousands of 'Everyman' sites offering almost anything from on-line pornography, to restaurants, folk clubs, bookshops and publications of various kinds, and scholarly editions of the medieval morality play, *Everyman*, whose central character has inscribed his name on posterity.[1]

The word 'everyman' derives from a dramatic fiction appropriated from a Dutch original by an anonymous English writer at around the year 1500. *Everyman* takes the audience into the mind of a dying man as he struggles to reconcile his shortcomings in his preparations to face the supreme judge. This is a religious play, a spiritual adventure that unfolds inside Everyman's head, a journey through the landscape of the mind, told in terms of the Christian beliefs of the period. In common with the general 'Last Judgement' at the end of all time in the medieval mystery play cycles, the outcome of Everyman's trial hinges on the defendant's good deeds, his record of generosity towards his fellow humans. The biblical Mysteries of the York, Chester, Wakefield, and N-Town cycles all conclude with a Last Judgement episode in which the souls of the dead are saved or damned according to their performance or non-performance of the Acts of Corporal Mercy — feeding the hungry, giving drink to the thirsty, sheltering the homeless, clothing the naked, giving comfort to the sick, and visiting those in prison — private acts of social welfare in a pre-welfare state. Everyman learns to recognize that he must trust in his good deeds rather than his worldly goods, and he converts these goods into good

---

[1] For an on-line edition, see http://www.luminarium.org/medlit/everyman.htm. For a print edition in modernized spelling see A. C. Cawley, *Everyman and Medieval Miracle Plays* (London: Dent, 1956). All quotations are from this edition.

deeds by making a will in which half his wealth goes to 'there it ought to be' (l. 702) and the other to 'alms' for the relief of the poor (l. 699).

In common with other medieval moralities, the action of *Everyman* is expressed through an allegory in which the protagonist, a universal rather than a particularized figure, interacts with personified abstractions. When Death summons him to appear in the celestial court, Everyman seeks companions for his final journey. He reaches first for the tangible supports of the outside world, Goods, Fellowship, Cousin and Kindred; then for his own physical and mental attributes, Beauty, Strength, Discretion, and Five Wits, those props that he assumed would always be there for him; and finally for the only things that in the Christian cosmology of the play can help him find peace: the self-Knowledge of where he stands in the universe, the emotional release of Confession, and the assurance that Good Deeds will go with him into the grave to stand witness in his defence and bridge his passage to the other side in heaven.

In the twentieth and early twenty-first centuries, *Everyman* has rarely been seen on stage and its reading audience has been confined largely to the academy. Nonetheless, in spite of this limited first-hand knowledge of the play, the term 'everyman' has passed into common parlance and the medieval notion of the universality of human experience has impacted on modern culture. In spite of its origins in a Christian spiritual context, the 'everyman' concept is now much more generally applicable. It can appear in contexts where it operates within a non-Christian ontology and where it has no relation to spirituality of any kind.

The absorption of the word into English language consciousness was given a significant boost by the founding of the Everyman Library series by J. M. Dent in 1906. Both the hardback and the paperback volumes in the series blazon the words of Knowledge from the play — 'Everyman, I will go with thee, and be thy guide' (522) — as an encouragement to readers. *Everyman*'s rise to fame, however, was initially launched in London in 1901 by William Poel, an eccentric theatrical entre-preneur, who was 'bent on redeeming the theater by means of the classics'.[2] Poel's production of the play was a landmark occasion in English theatre history because, for the first time since censorship regulations were established at the end of the sixteenth century, a director dared to represent God on the public stage. This set in motion the revival of medieval religious theatre in England and established *Everyman* as the 'classic' medieval morality play.

The *Oxford English Dictionary* defines 'Everyman' as 'the ordinary or typical human being', yet paradoxically, many of those to whom the word is applied are far from 'ordinary or typical'. American presidential hopeful, Al Gore, for example, was described by his wife, Tipper, in the lead-up to the year 2000 election as 'a general everyman slob'.[3] This may have been good press, designed to appeal to the mass of

---

[2] Robert Potter, *The English Morality Play: Origins, History and Influence of a Dramatic Tradition* (London: Routledge, 1975), p. 1.

[3] Reported by Sandra Sobieraj, 'Gore at ease: an "everyman slob" whose mind never rests',

'ordinary' voters, but even though he was the loser in that election, it is extremely doubtful that Mr Gore, his wife, or his press secretary would have believed for one moment that the presidential hopeful was 'ordinary or typical'. The same will be claimed in this essay for the 'everyman' figures in the Australian-authored fictions to be discussed here: The Man in Dulcie Deamer's morality play *Easter* (1933); Stephen Heriot in Randolph Stow's novel *To the Islands* (1958, rev. edn 1981); and Harley Savage, Douglas Cheeseman and Felicity Porcelline in Kate Grenville's Orange Prize-winning work, *The Idea of Perfection* (1999). Like the medieval 'Everyman', who has more than proven his extra-ordinariness by living on for over half a millennium as a household name, these modern Australian 'everymans' are no ordinary spiritual adventurers.

Each of the major texts and authors I have chosen as case studies here represents a different type of medievalism. While they all take us into the landscapes of the mind, Deamer was attracted to the form of the medieval morality play as a medium for expressing religious narratives and moral truths; Stow responded to *Everyman* as a specific literary source; and Grenville engaged in a more indirect form of medievalism as she explored various types of imperfection. In their very differences these texts demonstrate the timelessness of the 'everyman' concept and its applicability in the post-medieval context. The landscape of the mind can be 'anyplace' and is as comfortable in the arid northwest or the sleepy country towns of the world's oldest continent as it was in the Europe of the Middle Ages.

Everyman and the Australian Theatre

After the unexpected success of Poel's 1901 production in London, *Everyman* was seen in other capitals around the world. The first recorded production in Australia was in the Melbourne Town Hall in October 1905, directed by J. C. Williamson.[4] The first performance had caused, in the words of the advertisement for the second, a 'profound sensation', and the play, 'one of the most telling sermons ever formed', was 'marvellously impressive'.[5] Whatever audiences felt about this dramatized sermon in 1905, *Everyman* went on to have an impact on Australian amateur theatre in the early twentieth century, both as a choice for production, and as an inspiration for new plays written in imitation of medieval models.

In line with the situation in Britain, performances of modern religious plays and medieval 'revival' productions in the first half of the twentieth century were more common in Australia in amateur theatre circles than they were on the professional stage. Christian drama groups were, of course, especially drawn to them. In the

---

http://www.abilene2000.com/elec./gorease1029.html, accessed 29 October 2000.

[4] *The Age* (Melbourne), 25 October 1905.

[5] *The Age*, 28 October 1905.

1940s, for example, *Everyman* was a favourite with an association of Catholic women, the Grail Group, whose medievalism is reflected in their name and in their educational and dramatic activities. In Melbourne the Grail established six-month-long residential 'Quest' courses for young women in which each participant embarked on a spiritual quest to discover 'her future role' in society.[6] The medievalism encouraged in these courses, with their obvious heroic, Arthurian frame of reference, was considered to be an imitation of a lifestyle long past and in some cases this even went so far as the wearing of Tudor-style costume. Besides enacting their own 'medieval' theatre, Quest participants took part in Grail productions in Melbourne, and *Everyman* was presented regularly in the early 1940s.[7]

The Sydney branch of the Grail performed *Everyman* in the Town Hall in 1943 and in the Great Hall of Sydney University in the following year.[8] The *Sydney Morning Herald* reviewer for the 1944 production conceded that although the play was not likely to engage the masses, it nevertheless 'captured and contained something of the soul of man and the eternal pursuit of happiness that belongs to all ages'.[9]

Among other Grail productions in the Sydney University Great Hall were *The Vision of Hope* in 1940 and *The Royal Road to the Holy Cross* in 1941. *The Vision of Hope* was 'a medieval-style satire on despair in Australia in the 1920s and 1930s', specially written for the Grail and 'modelled on the old morality plays such as *Everyman*'.[10] According to the publicity for *The Royal Road*, the play was intended to present the 'Catholic solution of the problem of suffering' and, in order to reflect the 'group spirit' of wartime, the 1941 production had 'no individual parts'. Rather, groups of actors worked 'together in verse-speaking, singing, and rhythmic inter-pretation'.[11] The 1943 *Everyman* employed the same group technique with a large cast recreating the spiritual adventure of the representative individual.[12]

Dulcie Deamer: 'Easter' (1933)

Interest in medieval plays and the *Everyman*-style moral play was not confined to specifically Christian theatre groups. In 1930, for example, the Nativity play from

---

[6] Sally Kennedy, *Faith and Feminism: Catholic Women's Struggles for Self-Expression* (Sydney: St Patrick's College, 1985), p. 190.

[7] Kennedy, *Faith and Feminism*, p. 196.

[8] *Sydney Morning Herald*, 15 October 1943; Kennedy, *Faith and Feminism*, p. 218.

[9] *Sydney Morning Herald*, 7 October 1944.

[10] Kennedy, *Faith and Feminism*, p. 196; *The Union Recorder* (The University of Sydney), 1 August 1940.

[11] *The Union Recorder*, 2 October 1941.

[12] *Sydney Morning Herald*, 15 October 1943.

the Coventry Mystery Play cycle was presented in Sydney by The Community Players at their little theatre in Darlinghurst.[13] In 1931, the same group performed the Crucifixion play from the Wakefield Mysteries. In accordance with good manners and decorum, the cross in this production was 'supposed to be behind the curtains, and hidden from the audience [...] and the voice of Our Lord was heard from behind the scenes'.[14] As was the rule in England, Christ could be heard but not seen on the stage.

In 1933 there was a production at the Savoy Theatre in Sydney of Hugh Benson's 'Christ-less' Passion play, *The Upper Room*, in which the events of the Trial of Christ, the Scourging, and the Road to Calvary were relayed to the audience through the dialogue of the disciples, who were observing them from the windows of the room of the Last Supper.[15] *The Upper Room* was by a foreign playwright, but local writers also contributed to the revitalization of the medieval religious theatrical forms in Australia.

One Sydney writer who adopted the medieval theatrical mode in 1933 was Dulcie Deamer, a 'flapper and pioneer journalist'.[16] Deamer wrote plays, novels, short stories and poetry for a popular audience and has many claims to fame as an individualist and as a member of the Sydney avant-garde of the 1920s and 30s. She had a habit of 'performing the splits and belly-dancing at parties' and is remembered for her wearing of a revealing cavewoman outfit to the Artists' Ball in 1923.[17] In 1925 she was crowned as 'Queen of Bohemia' at Theo's Club in Campbell Street.[18]

Flamboyant in so many ways, Deamer was straightforward in her faith, described in her autobiography as a 'basic Christianity' through which she '*looked forward* to death as the "next adventure"'.[19] This was a notion that appeared over and over in her writings and it has overtones of at least one of the moral lessons of *Everyman*, that is, that death is a new beginning to be embraced rather than feared. Both her published and unpublished work reveals an intense interest in the spiritual, sometimes expressed in Christian terms with unnamed, and hence universalized protagonists experiencing visions of religious icons, sometimes expressed as a general enthusiasm for other worlds and the paranormal.[20]

---

[13] *Sydney Morning Herald*, 16 December 1930.

[14] *Sydney Morning Herald*, 1 April 1931.

[15] *Sydney Morning Herald*, 5 April 1933.

[16] Alison Alexander, *A Wealth of Women: Australian Women's Lives from 1788 to the Present* (Sydney: Duffy and Snellgrove, 2001), p. 126.

[17] Peter Kirkpatrick, *The Sea Coast of Bohemia: Literary Life in Sydney's Roaring Twenties* (St Lucia: University of Queensland Press, 1992), pp. 162, 183.

[18] Kirkpatrick, *The Sea Coast of Bohemia*, p. 179.

[19] *The Queen of Bohemia: The Autobiography of Dulcie Deamer*, ed. by Peter Kirkpatrick (St Lucia: University of Queensland Press, 1998), p. 72.

[20] For a list of Deamer's works see *The Queen of Bohemia*, pp. 175–77. Kirkpatrick omits

Deamer can be regarded as a 'medievalist' in that she was attracted to medieval-style tales and, in common with medieval writers, utilized biblical settings. In her novel, *Revelation* (1921), for example, she features a 'Jewish boy, David, who lives only for the coming of the Messiah' and after his death, is 'restored to life by Christ, who happens to be passing by', and in *The Devil's Saint* (1924) she tells a tale of 'medieval witchcraft'.[21] In *Revelation*, the links with the popular miracle stories of the Middle Ages are clear, as are the religious overtones even in the love scene that precedes the death of the hero:

> It was evident that he held himself in check with difficulty — like a rider fighting with an unschooled horse.
>
> 'I — I worship you!'
>
> Astarte shivered slightly, for the night had become colder, and the supple satin stuff that sheathed her loosely slipped from her shoulders, and so downward, lying about her feet [...] She looked at him without any coquetry, but with a sort of breathless, childlike anticipation, for she wanted his kisses and she felt, instinctively, that she was irresistible.
>
> 'Oh, God! ... You are a miracle!'[22]

Peter Kirkpatrick argues that Deamer's 'attraction to the remote past was a means of enabling her to talk more freely about sexual desire — especially women's desire — at a suitably "pagan" distance, away from the inhibiting moral conventions of the early twentieth century'.[23] This may well be true of the *Revelation* passage quoted above and of many of her writings, but a different case can be made for her attraction to the *Everyman* model in the four morality plays performed at the Tom Thumb Theatre in 1933.[24] In this instance the attraction of the morality genre was that it offered Deamer a platform from which to 'talk more freely' about Christian spirituality away from the 'inhibiting' conventions of modern theatre, especially the convention that prevented God from appearing as a character in the action. Deamer broke free of this convention in *Easter*, but she used the morality play form to disguise her daring.

Dennis Carroll notes that Deamer's four one-acters contributed to the 'symbolist and expressionist drama in the 1930s' and that the characters are 'personified abstractions' with the 'religious message [...] patterned on *Everyman*'.[25] The four

---

reference to the Dulcie Deamer Collection in Fisher Library at the University of Sydney, which contains thirty-eight typescripts of short stories, novels and a play.

[21] Kirkpatrick, *Sea Coast of Bohemia*, pp. 163, 164.

[22] Quoted in Kirkpatrick, *Sea Coast of Bohemia*, p. 164.

[23] Kirkpatrick, *Sea Coast of Bohemia*, p. 165.

[24] *Sydney Morning Herald*, 31 July 1933.

[25] Dennis Carroll in *Companion to Theatre in Australia*, ed. by Philip Parsons with

plays, *In the Mind of a Child*, *In the Soul of a Man*, *Easter*, and *In the Heart of a Woman*, all were set, like the medieval *Everyman*, inside the human consciousness.[26] The *Herald* reviewer in 1933 wondered, however, whether *Easter* really belonged 'strictly within the category of a morality play'.[27] This intuition was entirely correct, for what Deamer did in *Easter* was to combine the medieval Mystery Play model with the classic morality play to produce a hybrid form.

The first three of Deamer's 'morality' plays certainly fit the *Everyman* pattern of allegory. *In the Mind of a Child* presents the imaginary scene in the Child's head, set in a pirate's cave. The Hero (the Child) is dressed as a pirate with the slightly incongruous addition of a policeman's cap, and Conscience, dressed as a schoolmaster, is asleep. With the aid of the Spirit of Adventure, the Hero lands himself in trouble as he shows off to Mary Next-Door by trying to light the bath-heater. He has to be rescued by Uncle John and Mother. Moral: 'Sonny, wait till Mother comes home before you take the matches and go into the bath-room' (p. 10). Sound advice, but scarcely of cosmic proportions!

In the Soul of a Man is a more grown-up morality and also has clear links with the Fall of Lucifer episode in the medieval Mystery Play tradition. Greed and Fear strive for the right to occupy the throne that is placed centre stage. Fear dances wildly with his mistresses Lust and Pride but eventually sinks onto the throne:

> FEAR. (*Speaking gaspingly, and like a person in delirium.*) Fire — red against the sky ..... blackened buildings ..... churches turned into brothels ..... What have I done? ..... I — am — God? (*His eyes close; his body goes limp.*) (p. 11)

This is an allegory of a world that has turned away from God, where mob violence has taken over as a daemonic force of destruction. It is a Fall in which Fear has taken the ascendant in the Soul of the Man and tries to usurp the place of God. The child, Simplicity, prays for God to 'send someone to be Master of this House, so that Thy Will may be done on earth as it is in Heaven. Amen' (p. 12). The Master, an 'everyman' figure, with Generosity on his right hand, sets Simplicity above them both in a perfect world where there are 'no mysteries; there's only God talking to us in everything — and we're learning His language' (p. 13). Deamer's 'basic Christianity' shows through here and the world is put to rights by the mastering of the enticements to turn away from God and the acceptance of an unquestioning childlike faith.

Victoria Chance (Sydney: Currency Press and Cambridge University Press, 1995), p. 188.

[26] The plays were published in typescript by the Australian Theatrical Society, North Bondi, *c.* 1933. *Easter* was also published in a collection edited by William Moore and T. Inglis Moore, *Best Australian One-Act Plays* (Sydney: Angus & Robertson, 1937), pp. 13–25. All quotations from *Easter* are from this edition; those from the other plays are from the typescripts.

[27] *Sydney Morning Herald*, 31 July 1933.

In the Heart of a Woman is subtitled 'A Christmas Morality Play' and it lives up to this name by presenting a message about the Nativity. The scene is a 'dimly-seen interior of an Oriental Inn' with 'a doorway opening into the night without, and another leading down into the crypt of the sub-conscious' (p. 1). Intellect, Indulgence and Vanity, all female characters, inhabit the Inn and Pity is with them, presenting herself as an image of the Virgin Mary in both attitude and costume. She is 'enveloped in full, flowing, white Madonna-draperies', kneeling 'with hands crossed on her breast' (p. 2). Pity, it unfolds, has admitted a male Intruder, who is ejected while she is banished to the 'cavern-stable of the sub-conscious' to 'sleep on straw between the dumb ox of obedience, and patience — that foolish ass' (p. 4).

Just in case the audience has not understood this as an allegory of the Nativity, Intellect says loudly 'THERE IS NO ROOM FOR YOU IN THIS INN' and Pity claims that she has had a 'message from an angel' that 'a great miracle may soon be made manifest' (p. 5). The miracle is the birth of Love, the child of Pity; and all the other characters, including The Intruder, the 'everyman' figure, who returns as a guest of Love, assume suitable attitudes of reverence to present a Nativity tableau. This is both an allegorical Nativity and an allegory of one of the medieval Acts of Corporal Mercy, sheltering the homeless, one of the 'good deeds' required of the citizens of the Middle Ages as a down-payment on their passage to heaven. There are, then, echoes of the medieval *Everyman*, but the medieval generic model has been used to explore the meaning of the Nativity. *Easter* takes this method even further.

Easter begins as an allegory set 'in the brain of a Man just dead', which 'wears the semblance of a garden'; there is a suggestion of a 'chapel, or tomb' and there is a 'black door, which is closed' (p. 15). The allegorical abstractions might be taken initially to represent aspects of the selfhood of the dead Man: Love, Memory, Wisdom and Skill. Like *Everyman*'s Beauty, Love, who opens Deamer's play is female, and clearly not without the sexual allure of other females in this author's work:

(*She is a young woman whose long, dishevelled hair, unbound, hangs loose. She wears a trailing, semi-low-cut gown of rose-colour, with a gold girdle. It has been beautiful, but is rent, and torn down from one shoulder ...*)

LOVE. Master! Master! You're not dead — you're only sleeping! Don't be deaf to me — I can't bear it! (p. 15)

Her outlandish expressions of grief are unlike anything in *Everyman*, where Beauty and Strength, Discretion and Five Wits, physical attributes of the central protagonist, all desert him in a notably pragmatic fashion. When Wisdom, 'a grave, elderly man' tries to comfort Love, she attempts to rally, but is unable to collect herself:

WISDOM. He was our light — our leader; the centre and meaning of our world. It was from him I gained all the knowledge that is mine. And this is the end.

LOVE (*with a cry*). There *could* not be such an end! I am not wise, and I suffer — but I believe!

WISDOM. In what? Did he not endure agony and call on God, and then fall silent? Were we not all witnesses — you and I and the others? Did not we, his followers, suffer in sympathy, aware with him of the racked limbs, the cold sweat, the desolation, and the final, nameless pang? (pp. 16–17)

By now, it should be clear to the audience that the 'Master', the dead 'Man' is no ordinary 'everyman'. If the play was strictly an imitation of *Everyman*, we would expect that the Master would be there lamenting that his followers had left him, not the other way round. Yet the clues to unravelling this are clear enough and there are more to come.

When Memory, 'a sweet, ageing woman in a dark dress' (p. 17), comes to comfort Love, the recollection of the Nativity comes into focus along with the bread and wine of the Last Supper:

there's bread and wine, and laughter and work, and darkness and light ... And angels that come to us at night, when the stars are crowns on the heads of invisible kings who bring gold and frankincense, and myrrh. (p. 18)

The pattern of a biblical allegory emerges. Love is clearly Mary Magdalene and Memory is Mary the mother of Christ.

Death, a policeman, and his assistant, Decadence, enter and evict the other characters from the garden, but Love sneaks back, only to be accosted by the 'leering' Decadence, who gives the piece a distinctly Australian tone with his 'Strike me lucky!' (p. 24). As Love struggles against the unwelcome advances of Decadence, rescue arrives:

(*The closed door opens and golden light, like the light of morning, streams through it. In the doorway stands* THE MAN. *He is neither young nor old, and his face is one of radiant nobility. White, shroud-like wrappings fall to his feet, leaving his arms bare and free.*)

DECADENCE (*turning towards the light*). Oh! (*In abject terror*) God! (pp. 24–25)

The Man has come to lead Love, Memory, Wisdom and Skill 'into the Kingdom, the Power and the Glory'. The Man is the risen Christ. The play is not a morality play, it is a post-Resurrection Passion play in which Christ meets his followers and leads them into heaven. By disguising her Christ as 'The Man' in a play that looks superficially like a modern *Everyman*, Deamer has been able to present the deity on the stage. The agonies of the Passion are presented second hand, as they are in Hugh Benson's *The Upper Room*, but Deamer breaks with convention and brings Christ into view to be seen as well as heard in the triumphal finale.[28]

---

[28] The censor in Britain, ever watchful to prevent the Holy Family from appearing on stage, was sometimes confused by allegory and failed to discern breaches of stage etiquette. In the

Randolph Stow: 'To the Islands' (1958, rev. edn 1981)

Randoph Stow's medievalism exhibits itself in a number of his works including two set in Britain: *The Girl Green as Elderflower* (1980) and *The Suburbs of Hell* (1984). In the earlier of these two novels, the translation and retelling of twelfth-century otherworldly tales in the frame of the story of a man trying to come to terms with his life during a period of convalescence in Suffolk brings pagan spirituality to bear on the twentieth-century present. There is an element of the 'everyman' complex here as Crispin Clare, whose ancestor of the same name lies in the local graveyard, lives through the old stories 'from midwinter to midsummer, from cold to warmth, from death to new life'.[29] What unites the medieval stories with his own is that the central characters of the old tales suffer the same plight as Clare himself, making all stories the same story and making Clare an 'everyman'.

The Suburbs of Hell has been described by Anthony Hassall as an 'unusual combination of a naturalistic "whodunit" with a moral tale about the visitations of death'.[30] Stow himself regarded it as 'a modern version of *The Pardoner's Tale*'.[31] Chaucer's Pardoner tells a tale of greed and murder and the plague-like contagion of death, a tale that can readily be linked to *Everyman*. The moral of Stow's novel, as Hassall suggests, is 'that no man is secure from sudden and inexplicable death, and that we should therefore so live that we are always ready to die'.[32] *Everyman*, in which the protagonist is not an old man on his deathbed but a man of indeterminate age, apparently in the prime of life, offers the same advice.

Stow's earlier novel, *To the Islands*, presents the spiritual adventures of an 'everyman' in an Australian setting. Murder, as in *The Suburbs of Hell*, and the need to gain self-Knowledge, as in *The Girl Green as Elderflower,* are central to this novel. The main protagonist undertakes a literal journey towards death through what he initially perceives as a wild and desolate countryside and a spiritual journey towards acceptance of the past, and of individual and universal human failings. In the introduction to the revised edition of the novel, Stow notes that there are many

---

case of Alice Buckton's *Eager Heart*, for example, the Holy Family was able to come and go as they pleased under the cover of the allegorical framework of the play in 1904. See Gerald Weales, *Religion in Modern English Drama* (Philadelphia: University of Pennsylvania Press, 1961), p. 98 and Laurence Houseman, *The Unexpected Years* (Indianapolis: Bobbs-Merrill, 1936), p. 212.

[29] Anthony J. Hassall, *Strange Country: A Study of Randolph Stow*, rev. edn (St Lucia: University of Queensland Press, 1990), p. 150.

[30] Hassall, *Strange Country*, p. 165.

[31] Quoted in Hassall, *Strange Country*, p. 165.

[32] Hassall, *Strange Country*, p. 166.

literary 'influences', including *Everyman* that 'had been assimilated over some years'.[33]

Stow's 'everyman' is Stephen Heriot, the administrator of an Aboriginal mission in the north-west of Australia, a tired old man, who has lost both wife and offspring — his own and his adopted children — and, he fears, his faith in God and his love of humanity. Heriot's thoughts are fixed on death from the beginning of the novel. He looks forward to his own escape from this life in terms of Aboriginal spirituality rather than the Christianity that has been his life's work, but finds himself nervous of it at the same time. Speaking to one of the elderly Aboriginal men on the mission he jokes that he will go 'to the islands' before him, clumsily breaking the decorum of silence surrounding the Aboriginal beliefs about the next life:

> Oh, that I am such a fool, cried Heriot inwardly, such a fool. To mention death, the islands of the dead, here, to him. Oh God, let him not die now, let me not have killed him.
>
> [...]
>
> Galumbu was turned to stone. (p. 19)

Heriot's fears of being a murderer take on a more definite form when he thinks that he has fatally wounded Rex, the man he holds responsible for the death of his Aboriginal 'daughter', Esther. Heriot is both guilty 'murderer' and innocent 'everyman'. Rex does not die, but Heriot is afraid of his own anger that caused him to cast the stone at his fellow man, one of his Aboriginal 'children'. His sin of Anger is no more than that of any person torn between love and the anguish that can lead to hatred, but to him, Anger is more to be feared than Death.

Murder is a recurring motif in the novel. Other white workers on the mission speak of it with Justin, the Aboriginal man who subsequently goes into the unknown with Heriot:

> [Gunn] '[...] What happens when a man murders someone'?
>
> Justin shifted uneasily. 'How do you mean?'
>
> 'Where does he go? Does he run away?'
>
> 'He goes to other country,' Justin said, 'that way,' pointing north. 'Lost man's country. He stay in that country.' (p. 25)

Heriot's journey is both the flight of a murderer into 'lost man's country', and a deliberate acceptance of his proper trajectory 'to the islands' of the dead. This country is understood by the Aborigines in the novel, from the old men to the young boy, Normie, as a place of physical and spiritual loneliness:

---

[33] Randolph Stow, *To the Islands* (Melbourne: Minerva, 1997), p. xi. All quotations are from this imprint.

[Normie] 'All hill and rock there […] Only old people go there …] He real lonely, all that country.'

'I know,' Gunn said meditatively […] 'No sense in being lonely, is there?' (p. 35)

Unlike his medieval counterpart, this 'everyman' does not seek companionship, even though he eventually accepts it and acknowledges Justin as his 'Good Deeds':

Justin said, with perfect deference: 'I got to come, brother.'

[…]

'Listen,' said Heriot in a choking voice, 'I'll get to the hills tonight and I'm going no farther. There's nothing you can do, I don't want you or need you. Or your food or blankets. I need nothing at all.'

[…]

'Brother' —

They stared hungrily at one another. 'Yes?'

'If you go along with me, I go with you, always.'

[…]

'Welcome, my Good Deeds,' whispered Heriot. (p. 47)

Everyman, is not the only literary reference here. There are reflections of the biblical Ruth refusing to allow the aged Naomi to journey to her people alone (Ruth 1. 16–18). Justin is not a guide for Heriot, since his knowledge of the 'lost country' is little better than Heriot's own, but his presence prolongs Heriot's life as he feeds and cares for him: '"Damn you, damn you, damn you," whispered Heriot to the sky. "You do me wrong, you do me wrong to take me out of the grave."' (p. 60)

At the end of the novel, the 'everyman' in Heriot recognizes what the companionship of Justin has meant to him: '"Ah, Justin", said Heriot, turning away, "you're my good deeds, my salvation from myself …"' (p. 123)

The delaying of death by means of the literal journey, as in the medieval play, has allowed for the allegorical journey to take Heriot to a destination that is not 'the islands' but a place marked out on the internal landscape of his soul: '"My soul", he whispered, over the sea-surge, "my soul is a strange country".' (p. 126) The journey has not been to any literal dying ground, either in the Christian or the Aboriginal cosmology, it has been a spiritual adventure to self-Knowledge.

Like Everyman, Heriot makes confessions on the journey as he speaks to Justin and to the two old white men, Rusty and Sam, who also confess to murder. Heriot learns that he is not alone in his predicament in being, or at least thinking himself a murderer, and he muses on murder, the first murder of Cain by Abel, the more recent murders of the Onmalmeri massacre, all murders of which Heriot, as 'everyman', finds himself guilty.

In the medieval play, Everyman puts on the garment of sorrow and does penance. Heriot can also be seen to enact sorrow and penance as he travels further away from the mission. As in *Everyman*, a spiritual forgiveness is enacted in the novel when Rex, the supposed murder victim, insists on joining the search party for Heriot. Heriot himself acknowledges that Rex is not dead by giving Justin his watch, knife and rifle to hand over to Rex as a token of love. Like Everyman making his will, Heriot has made some restitution and accepted that he has done all he can to prepare himself for whatever is to come. This 'everyman' is no ordinary man; he is Lear with his near mad wanderings and he is Christ in his acceptance of the burden of the sins of humanity.

Kate Grenville: 'The Idea of Perfection' (1999)

Kate Grenville has used the medieval 'everyman' motif in more than one of her novels, but her medievalism, unlike that of Stow, is unselfconscious. In *Joan Makes History* (1988), the central figure, in her many manifestations, is present and active at great moments in white Australian history: Cook's arrival in Australia in 1770; the opening of Federal Parliament in 1901; and at other great moments for white Australians in between. The Joans present a story of Australian nationhood in which Joan is 'everyJoan', she is 'every woman who has ever drawn breath [...] a woman as plain as a plate, and devoid of bust, a grandmother you would pass on the street without a glance'.[34] Joan is both convict, white settler and part-Aboriginal woman; she is the daughter of European migrants, who struggle to learn English; and she is even, for a time, disguised as a man (Jack).

Lilian's Story (1985) also reflects the pattern of a medieval morality play, but in this case it is not *Everyman* that we can see in the mirror, rather it is one of the other, more typical English morality plays. While *Everyman* remains the most well known of its genre and the most accessible for modern audiences, the majority of the surviving morality plays do not deal with the last moments of the protagonist's life but show him over a long period of growth struggling to resolve an inclination to lead a blameless and socially generous life against the blandishments of evil. Grenville admits to the influence of Shakespeare's *Tempest* in her writing of this novel, declaring that it is 'full of lines from *The Tempest*. "Every third thought shall be my grave" and "I would fain die a dry death" — they're just wonderful lines.'[35] Shakespeare's lines are, in their turn, echoes of the medieval view of dying, and so Grenville can be seen to have inherited the Middle Ages second hand. Lilian ends

---

[34] Kate Grenville, *Joan Makes History* (St Lucia: University of Queensland Press, 1988), p. 5.

[35] Kate Grenville and Sue Woolfe, *Making Stories: How Ten Australian Novels were Written* (Sydney: Allen & Unwin, 1993), p. 98.

her journey of self understanding not with death, but with an acceptance that death, when it comes, is not something that she is afraid of: 'The story of all our lives is the story forward to death [...] *Drive on, George*, I cried at him. *I am ready for whatever comes next.*'[36]

In *The Idea of Perfection*, more than one central figure is seen coming to terms with the self and as in the medieval morality genre, where the names of the abstract figures enunciate an interpretation of the character, names are significant in this novel. Harley Savage, christened 'Pixie', renounces her first given name because it does not fit her brown largeness and plainness or the 'dangerous streak', which she sees as responsible for the suicide of her third husband and the difficulties of her children. In the spirit of self-loathing, she takes the name of a dead male from her family, a name that implies, apart from someone other than herself, the virility and power associated with the legendary 'Harley Davidson' motorcycle, and the violence of a 'Savage'. She is an 'everyman' by virtue of denying her own identity and the taking on of that of others. Harley seeks a perfection in imperfection, as signified by her quilts, deliberately fashioned with light and dark browns. The light and dark combination is, of course, what every quiltmaker knows makes the design work, and metaphorically it signifies the combination of good and evil, strong and weak in the human condition. Quilt tradition also says that there should be a flaw in every quilt to avoid giving offence to God by creating something that is perfect (p. 114). An accomplished seamstress, Harley takes this imperfection to extremes by excessively engineering corners that do not meet and decorating the finished quilt with ungainly stitching. Her idea of perfection is to strive for the imperfect, yet in this very striving, she is not reconciled with the imperfections in herself until the end of the novel.

Douglas Cheeseman likewise is a homely individual, who does not have a name of his own but is named after his father, a heroic figure who cannot be lived up to. 'Douglas' implies a doughtiness that this engineer with a professionally unfortunate fear of heights is self-consciously aware he does not have, and 'Cheese-man', is a family name that must have caused many an unpleasant moment in the school playground. We are taken into the landscapes of the mind of both Douglas and Harley. They think through their encounter in the run-down country town about to lose its historic bridge and forge an emotional bridge that exemplifies the epigraph of the novel: 'An arch is two weaknesses which together make a strength' (Leonardo da Vinci).

It is through the 'everyman' instinct to perform acts of human charity towards one another that these two central figures, an unlikely pair for a love story, begin to form an affection that may be the saving of them both. Harley performs the first 'good deed' when she rescues the transfixed Douglas from a mob of cows. Later, tempted to drown in the waters of the local swimming hole, which can be seen as analogous

---

[36] Kate Grenville, *Lilian's Story* (Sydney: Allen & Unwin, 1985), pp. 210–11.

to the medieval Everyman's baptism, she realizes that she cannot implicate Douglas, the last person to see her, in her death. She sees him as an 'everyman' like herself and does not wish to burden him with the murderer's guilt she still feels over the suicide of her husband. Douglas seals the arch of the bridge between them when he overcomes his vertigo to rescue her ugly brown quilt from the fire in the building next to his hotel. None of these are mighty feats, yet they are made highly significant in the context of the interior journeys observed in the text.

Felicity Porcelline is also allegorically named. Her life, in which her sexual fantasies have an unfortunate habit of becoming real, is scarcely felicitous, especially in its effects on her husband and their son, and so she is as much at odds with her given name as are Douglas and (Pixie) Harley. She is, however, very much in tune with meanings and associations of her surname. She is spiritually as brittle as fine china in her obsession with her own personal appearance and although we see her wandering in the landscape of her mind, she is left still wandering and unresolved at the end of the novel, having neither allowed herself to acknowledge her weakness nor placed herself so as to be able to come to terms with it.

While Felicity is painfully aware of her prettiness, Harley and Douglas are painfully aware of their plainness like 'everyJoan' and Lilian. They are ordinary people, not much noticed by others in the fiction, yet they are extraordinary in their journeys of the mind to find self-assurance. It is because Grenville sends them on journeys that they appear in the novel as extraordinary 'everymans'. The strength that is formed between Harley and Douglas has nothing to do with religion of any kind, yet it represents a way of thinking about how to live in this world in relation to other members of the human race that has its own spirituality.

Conclusions

The early twentieth-century productions of *Everyman* struck audiences with their religious aura and their distinctly medieval look. The 1901 production by William Poel, founder of the Elizabethan Stage Society, established this particular version of medievalism in line with the society's avowed interest in replicating the imagined original staging conventions of early theatre. Although he did not subscribe to the play's religiosity, Poel was concerned to be faithful to this aspect of its original conception as well as avoid reprimand from the stage censor. In one respect, however, he departed from English medieval stage conventions, which demanded all male casts, by selecting a woman to play the title role.[37] Poel was not making a stand

---

[37] This was a favourite eccentricity of Poel's, who also elected to cast women as male heroes in productions of Shakespeare and other early dramatists. See Robert Speaight, *William Poel and the Elizabethan Revival* (London: Heinemann, 1954), pp. 101, 126–27, 130, 146–47, 178, 196, 233.

for political correctness before its time, but the nature of the 'everyman' concept is such that anyone — including women — can play the title role.

The casting of black actor Joseph Mydell, who rose naked from his bath as Everyman for the Royal Shakespeare Company's 1996 modern dress production at The Other Place, did make a deliberate political statement. 'Everyman' need not be white and Anglo-Saxon anymore than 'he' needs to be gendered male. But such a statement is from a mindset that would have seemed odd when Poel's elegantly attired female Everyman sauntered across the courtyard of the Charterhouse in London in 1901.

The Royal Shakespeare's *Everyman*, in common with many late twentieth-century productions of the play, was presented on a bare stage. This bare stage technique has the effect of giving the action a non-specific locality that can then be transformed imaginatively by the audience into any place they wish. Non-specificity was one of the stated aims of the directors in 1996, who decided against medieval costume because they feared it would be 'alienating' and would suggest that the play 'belonged in that age, whereas from the start (they) felt it to be a story that belonged to any age and culture in spite of its Christianity'. [38]

But, perhaps because of this very universality, a specific location for *Everyman* can also have a highly desirable effect for some audiences. In 1992 a promenade production at an American college took its participants on a mile-long tour of the campus. The director made pointed use of the local setting with, for example, the scene with Goods played in the 'yard of the college's Physical Plant Department' to emphasize the 'ugliness of a life focused on the material'.[39] Costuming and casting also capitalized on local reference, with Strength represented by a muscular actor in a Los Angeles Raiders jacket and Discretion 'appropriately played by the college registrar in tweed suit and clipboard'. This specificity was enhanced and balanced by attempts at universality through the outdoor promenade itself with its potential for blurring the physical distance between audience and action, and through 'references to Asian and Native American religion […] while Everyman's confession was turned into a ritual reminiscent of the Japanese tea ceremony'.[40]

Processes similar to those that can be observed in modern productions of *Everyman* also operate in the examples of Australian medievalism considered as case studies in this essay, particularly the novels of Stow and Grenville. Whereas Deamer's plays attempt to replicate the psychological 'anywhere' of the old morality

---

[38] Kathryn Hunter, 'Making Meaning', in *Moral Mysteries: Essays to Accompany a Season of Medieval Drama at The Other Place* ed. by David Jays (Stratford: Royal Shakespeare Theatre, 1997), p. 82.

[39] Peter H. Greenfield, 'A Processional *Everyman* at St Martin's College, Olympia, WA, April 16–18, 23–25, 1992', *Research Opportunities in Renaissance Drama*, 32 (1993), 151–54 (p. 152).

[40] Greenfield, 'A Processional *Everyman*', p. 153.

play tradition, the more recent novels discussed in detail here present us with a more distinctively Australian form of medievalism. In Stow's *To the Islands*, Anglo-medievalism coalesces with what might be termed 'dreamtime-ism'. Heriot's pilgrimage towards death and exploration of white guilt is converted into an attempted exercise in aboriginality by the title of the novel itself. The protagonist's physical and emotional projection takes him closer to the acceptance of the end and the afterlife as it is understood by the culture of Justin and Galumbu than it does towards a Christian formulation of heaven. The spirituality expressed in the novel strives towards a universality that is broader than that which can be enclosed within the version of English Roman Catholic Christian spirituality expressed in the medieval analogue. The text makes the point that spirituality has its own universality regardless of the gulfs opened up by creed, time, race or place. Yet despite the universality suggested by the novel, Heriot remains an eccentric individual, as do all the post-medieval spiritual adventurers considered in this essay, just as the place within the mind that he reaches is undeniably an eccentrically Australian place.

Grenville's *Idea of Perfection* presents a non-religious form of spirituality that is also genderless in that both the central male and female protagonists experience a similar journey towards self-knowledge and self-acceptance. In what is so often referred to as a 'secular' age, these are the heroes 'Australia had to have'.[41] Yet despite the fact that their journeys are not expressed in the terms of any formal set of religious beliefs, they represent a spirituality that is still recognizable as a psychological adventure. Their brownness/colourlessness/-plainness is something onto which anyone can write their own fictional personality and the country town setting where their adventures as aliens from the city take place is one where anyone can feel at home, at least, like Harley and Douglas, as aliens.

'Everyman' transports well. (S)he is creedless, timeless and genderless, and because (s)he is also placeless, can be inscribed on any location as if it were a *terra nullius*.[42] Yet the *terra nullius* itself, as in the instance of the 1992 American college production of the play, has the potential of writing something of its own identity back onto the 'everyman' concept. It can use the concept to explore its own specificity and offer that exploration as a further proof of the universality of the central motif. The Australian 'everymans' considered here can be seen as interrogating and defining a local culture. Heriot, for example, blends his Anglo-Christianity with the Aboriginal belief system, and Harley and Douglas come to terms with themselves as misfits or underachievers within the set of expectations which they imagine their Australian society imposes on them. Equally, all these spiritual adventurers grapple with issues that transcend national boundaries and defy enclosure within timeframes confined by the individual imagination.

---

[41] This colourful phrase was given local currency by Paul Keating's defence as Federal Treasurer in November 1990, of the 'recession that Australia had to have'. See Edna Carew, *Paul Keating: Prime Minister* (Sydney: Allen & Unwin, 1992), pp. 283–84.

[42] See the essay by Jenna Mead in this volume, p. 111.

Medievalism and Memory Work: Archer's Folly and the Gothic Revival Pile

JENNA MEAD

A s the essays in this volume show, medievalism is diffused broadly across mainstream Australian culture, in a range of forms; from early public and domestic architecture, literary and non-literary texts, and right through to contemporary practices in media as diverse as film and computer software.[1] Mainstream Australian culture shares this phenomenon with other post-industrial Western cultures and particularly those with a colonial past that provides a sub-structural link to Britain. As in other postcolonial cultures — India, Canada, New Zealand — medievalism in Australia is an 'effect': the medievalism of Britain, with its tracery of links to similar European cultural forms, appears not as an authentic origin or proof of an immemorial past but rather as a distinctive kind of memory.

This chapter draws medievalism into a purposive and analytical relationship with memory. This is a potentially complex argument and I present it here in a necessarily simplified form. It is potentially complex because of the variety of cultural forms in which medievalism and its sometimes stylish partner, Gothic, are manifested; and it is simplified here in that I focus on only two such manifestations: an architectural feature in the Tasmanian Midlands and an academic discipline practised in some Australian universities. They represent two distinct and circumscribed but, as I will argue, adjacent aspects in mainstream Australian culture; neither makes any claim to speak for 'ordinary Australians' or even 'all Australians', as a popular political

[1] I am grateful to Tony Stagg for research on this essay, to Julia Davis for expert legal advice, and to Mrs Maree Mills of 'Panshangar' who gave me permission to visit the property and was generous in sharing her knowledge with me. My thanks to Ken Ruthven who read an earlier draft: Stephanie Trigg, and the anonymous reader for this volume who also read earlier drafts. My argument here had its beginning in a casual remark in an essay by John Frow for which I am also grateful.

shibboleth has it. The claim I make on their behalf is that they are aspects of public culture in Australia and, as such, each is open to public scrutiny and evaluation; as a corollary, each carries a kind of meaning or value that is publicly conferred. The colonial architecture of the Tasmanian Midlands and the discipline of medieval literary studies practised in Australian universities (usually, the more established ones) both have some valency within what has been called the public imaginary.

A further methodological complexity to any argument about medievalism in Australia is that the specificity of any local manifestation is blurred by the simple fact of medievalism's global economic, historical and cultural range, and the competing specificities of other local medievalisms, in India, New Zealand, or Tasmania, for example. There is a kind of triangulation in play here between the global and the different versions of the local. Or, as Umberto Eco puts it, '[s]ince the Middle Ages have always been messed up in order to meet the vital requirements of different periods, it was impossible for them to be always messed up in the same way'.[2] These different pressures are apt to strain in contrary directions: while the global necessarily reaches for the summary statement developed out of macro-analysis, the local, also necessarily, conducts a different kind of analysis on a small, precise scale. The methodological ideal of a general principle adduced from the data, an exemplary instance and a reliable set of proscriptive rules is unequal to the particular cultural terms and phenomena under scrutiny; medievalism has no single, unified, methodological core.[3] Hence — as these essays demonstrate — the need for critical discourses that make visible the micro-narratives analyzing medievalisms in Australia while also acknowledging the pervasiveness of medievalism's global reach.

In responding to this need, I will use the term 'afterlife' to describe medievalism's circulation in a small part of Australia's public imaginary.[4] I want to draw attention to the ways in which the (re)use of aspects, fragments, and discourses of medieval culture in a post-medieval present produces an afterlife for that particular medievalism, asserting and breaking a link between medieval past and contemporaneous present. It is this afterlife that asserts the importance of 'the medieval' in mainstream Australian culture despite geographical distance, temporal discontinuity, and historical alienation. Two consequences follow logically: 'medievalism has to do with the *use* of the Middle Ages'; it is instrumental, selective,

---

[2] 'Dreaming of the Middle Ages', *Travels in Hyperreality. Essays*, trans. by William Weaver (San Diego: Harcourt, Brace, Jovanovich, 1986), p. 68.

[3] Richard Utz, 'Resistance to (The New) Medievalism? Comparative Deliberations on (National) Philology, *Mediävalismus*, *Mittelalter-Rezeption* in Germany and North America', in *The Future of the Middle Ages and the Renaissance*, ed. by Roger Dahood (Turnhout: Brepols, 1988), pp. 151–70.

[4] *Victorian Afterlife: Postmodern Culture Rewrites the Nineteenth Century*, ed. by John Kucich and Dianne F. Sadoff (Minneapolis: University of Minnesota Press, 2000).

political; never quite suppressing the untidy politics of its use (emphasis added).[5] Furthermore, medievalism initiates a reciprocal process: it 'is the process of *creating the Middle Ages*' (emphasis added); on this count too medievalism is partial, heterogeneous, inconsistent.[6] My argument here is both interpretively and ideologically charged because it challenges the certainty of received historical opinion, on the one hand, and the supposed neutrality of academic inquiry, on the other. A further challenge is that this kind of argument deliberately eschews the boundary between history and literary studies by drawing attention to the historicity of literary studies and the literariness of historical documents. My argument assumes that what is lodged in the memory of a culture — what I have called its public imaginary — is what is regarded as valuable by that culture and thus, properly, open to challenge and revaluation. Memory is not only part of history but has its own history.

But let me be clear that what follows is simply a reading; in order to draw medievalism and memory together into an argument I offer a reading of two of medievalism's afterlives. My first sifts together two medieval towers and the sparse and ephemeral historical documents pertaining to one moment in the history of those towers; my second reads three documents in what might be called the history of literary studies in Australia and, more narrowly, that history as it focuses on medieval literary studies. For all that readers might want robust argument, solid proof and sensible conclusion, texts, I think, 'are rarely candid'; they are 'unable to tell us all they know — everything about their antecedence, their suppression and evasions, the uses and appropriations to which are, or will be, exposed'.[7] The question my argument frames is this: what are the meanings exposed by these two afterlives of medievalism?

In 1880, Joseph Archer Esq. instructed W. T. Bell to prepare a public auction of his property 'Panshanger' to be held in Charles Street, Launceston, Tasmania, on Wednesday 1 December. The pamphlet, published and distributed prior to the sale, was printed at the Launceston *Examiner* office and contained descriptions of the house, properties and effects; it also quoted two earlier newspaper features on Archer's properties, 'Panshanger', Burlington and Fairfield:

> This delightful residence, the property of MR. JOSEPH ARCHER, is situated to the south-east of the town of Longford, and about eight miles distant. It is surrounded by

---

[5] Britton J. Harwood, 'The Political Use of Chaucer in Twentieth-Century America', in *Medievalism in the Modern World: Essays in Honour of Leslie J. Workman*, ed. by Richard Utz and Tom Shippey (Turnhout: Brepols, 1998), p. 391.

[6] Leslie J. Workman, quoted by Richard Utz and Tom Shippey, 'Medievalism in the Modern World: Introductory Perspectives', in *Medievalism in the Modern World*, p. 5.

[7] Paul Strohm, 'Introduction', *Theory and the Premodern Text* (Minneapolis and London: University of Minnesota Press, 2000), p. xii.

park-like scenery, and presents a strikingly English and finished appearance [...] while in places the ground is carpeted with sweet violets, which, when in flower in the spring time, form, with lilies of the valley, honeysuckle, lilacs, laburnums, hawthorns, sloes, and other flowering shrubs, such a combination of beauty and fragrance as would be difficult to find elsewhere out of old England [...] Water is raised from the river by a pump, worked by horse-power, to the top of an ornamental tower, from whence an extensive view is obtained, and which can be seen from a great distance rising above the green foliage of the trees [...].

The Archers, being originally from Hertfordshire, have given names of various residences in that county, such as Panshanger (the seat of Earl Cowper), to the estates of which they have become possessed in the new country of their adoption, thus affording evidence that the love of home never departs from the heart of the true Briton.[8]

Joseph Archer had inherited the properties from an uncle of the same name who had established himself on two thousand acres in the Longford-Cressy area in the early 1820s. The first Joseph Archer and his brothers had become wealthy squatters: by 1831 Joseph alone valued his estates and stock at over thirty-two thousand pounds, with large property holdings in the Tasmanian Midlands and significant political influence through holding public office.[9] Archer built a mansion on his property, before 1835, in what is usually described as a classical style that was 'the epitome of Georgian architecture (derived from early Greek and Roman forms)'.[10] There is some uncertainty as to who designed the house and its associated buildings — Archer himself or his architect, John Alexander Jackson; or whether, perhaps, he 'procured the plans during a visit to Europe in 1829'.[11] An account of 'Panshanger' published in the *Mercury*, 20 October 1883, describes the house as 'the simplest Grecian style'; the front 'is rigidly classical' and 'in the middle of the upper part of the lawn is a fountain supplied from tanks in the top of the square battlemented tower'.[12] Elsewhere the water tower is described as having a 'castellated parapet'.[13]

---

[8] *Particulars and Description of the Valuable and Desirable Estates of Panshanger, Burlington and Fairfield* [Launceston: n. pub. [1880]), pp. 7–8, quoting 'Panshanger' and 'Horticulture in Tasmania', *The Leader* (Melbourne), 27 March 1875. I am grateful to Tony Marshall of the State Library of Tasmania for this reference.

[9] 'Archer, Joseph', by G. T. Stilwell, *Australian Dictionary of Biography*, gen. ed. Douglas Pike, vol. 1, 1788–1850, section editors A. G. L. Shaw and C. M. H. Clark (Melbourne: Melbourne University Press, 1966; London: Cambridge University Press), p. 24. See also Neil Chick, *The Archers of Van Diemen's Land: A History of Pioneer Pastoral Families*, artwork Miriam Chick, cadastral data, David Archer (Lenah Valley: Pedigree Press, 1991), pp. 110–16.

[10] E. Graeme Robertson and Edith N. Craig, *Early Houses of Northern Tasmania: An Historical and Architectural Survey*, vol. 1 (Melbourne: Georgian House, 1964), p. 156.

[11] Chick, *The Archers*, p. 112; compare Robertson and Craig, *Early Houses*, p. 156.

[12] Quoted in Robertson and Craig, *Early Houses*, p. 156.

The tower with its medieval aspect, provided by its shape and precise crenellation, rises above dense, leafy foliage and a meandering river in Emily Bowring's 1859 sketch 'Willows at Panshanger' now held in the Allport Library and Museum of Fine Arts (see Fig. 1).[14]

The later Archer found himself in financial difficulties and, while the properties were not sold at this auction, they passed out of the Archer family in 1908.[15] Bell's pamphlet includes another item reprinted from a contemporary newspaper:

Of all Anglo-Colonial estates I have visited in Tasmania Panshanger is the most English. The scenery is made up of wood, water, and mountains, green paddocks, cultivated cornfields, lovely gardens, and gravelled walks; also weeping willows bending gracefully over the stream, which murmurs —

Men may come, and men may go,
But I go on for ever [*sic*].[16]

This thin little pamphlet, now discoloured and frail in texture, combines the genres of real estate catalogue and newspaper feature. It is a suggestive set of texts that articulates not simply a descriptive account of the properties for sale but also some indication of its meanings and associations for Archer's contemporaries. The language of the description recalls the pastoral diction of early Romantic nature poetry with the rhetorical figure of the onomasticon detailing the horticulture of the country garden. The tower is 'ornamental' pointing to the guiding hand of cultivation shaping both the natural ('water') and the utilitarian ('horse-power') to pleasing and polite effect. The elemental 'wood, water, and mountains' combine with the cultivated 'green paddocks, lovely gardens, and gravelled walks' in a scene almost unique to England ('difficult to find' elsewhere). The flowers and bushes 'carpet' the ground in springtime. The 'extensive view' and 'great distance' suggest a painterly perspective that arranges the 'park-like scenery' into the pleasant prospect reproduced in both William Thomas Lyttleton's coloured lithograph (1835) and another of Emily Bowring's sketches (also 1859).

'Panshanger' is 'delightful' precisely because of its 'strikingly English and finished appearance'; it is superlative, 'the most English' 'of all Anglo-Colonial estates' the writer has visited — manifesting the civility and gentility of the Archer family's social aspirations, the underpinning of their economic success, and their national character. There is an Englishness twice removed here: 'Anglo' is the term for English used usually in imperial contexts; 'colonial' underlines the remoteness

---

[13] *The Heritage of Tasmania: The Illustrated Register of the National Estate* (Melbourne: Macmillan, 1983), p. 132.

[14] Image available at http://www.images.statelibrary.tas.gov.au.

[15] '"Panshanger" was bought by The Honourable Edward David Mills, of Brisbane for Col. Charles Mills, ancestor of the present owner.' Chick, *The Archers*, p. 196.

[16] 'A Tour through Tasmania', reprinted from *The Tribune* (Hobart, 1877).

from the imperial centre. A sense of duty — that quintessential colonial and English quality — prevails here: the property has a 'finished appearance': a 'consummate, perfect, accomplished' (*OED*) effect that implies devotion to a nostalgic vision, the application of muscular labour, and no want of liberal expenditure. In the person of the Archers, the pamphlet asserts, the reader can be reassured that the inheritors of Hertfordshire have recognized the need for continuity 'in the new country of their adoption' and, thus, have marked the landscape with the place names of their original home. In the Archer family, as demonstrated by their property and wealth, readers have the 'evidence' of a single trait that guarantees 'the heart of the true Briton': 'love of home'.

Fig. 1 Emily Bowring, 'Panshanger', *Sketchbook of Tasmanian Scenes*, c. 1859.

'Panshanger' is a synecdoche for Englishness — suasive by means of its allusion to Romantic nature poetry but also powerful through its element of surprise: it has a 'strikingly English appearance' that evokes the memory of familiar scenes 'at home'. There is a familiarity and timelessness here too for the scene presented by 'Panshanger' recalls 'old England' though located in a new and strange setting. The couplet from Tennyson's 'The Brook' coalesces these connotations of continuity, duty, home, and national character by invoking the figure of England's poet laureate, Alfred Lord Tennyson, the Prince Consort's favourite and the mythologist of English imperial prowess (an ode on the death of Wellington appeared in 1852 and 'The Charge of the Light Brigade' in 1854). Tennyson's couplet works as a tagline: the 'weeping willows' manifesting a trace of melancholy, at the loss of home, to strengthen the conviction that 'I', the personification of Englishness, 'go on forever'.

This is language that reveals much: it is the diction of the popular press and commercial enterprise, an admixture of sensational appeal with a keen sense of offering an exciting business opportunity. Similar expressions of popular taste appear in other Tasmanian country houses, public buildings and architectural decoration, as they do elsewhere in Australia. To a large extent, this is generic diction in that it is the conventional language of the medium: note the appeal to class markers in the allusion to 'the seat of Earl Cowper' in Hertfordshire where Joseph Archer's father owned and operated a mill.[17] But that same conventionality should not blind us to the layering of affect and acumen that prevents the language becoming flaccid or effete. For the lasting impression here is that of mastery: this is the language of the successful colonial enterprise that has tamed the native soil, reduced indigenous barbarities and (re)produced a convincing version of England. The measure of this success is the complete absence of any alternative discourse: neither gum tree nor hot sun, brutal landform nor cacophonous birdsong, strange flora nor outlandish fauna appears here. These are the 'other' tropes of colonial Tasmania familiar from, for example, popular sensational novels of the mid- to late nineteenth-century such as Oliné Keese's *The Broad Arrow; or, Passages from the Life of Maida Gwynnham, a Lifer* (London 1859, Hobart 1860) or Marcus Clarke's *His Natural Life* (serialized 1870–72). Instead, time-honoured Englishness displaces newly-found exotica. 'Panshanger' with its parapet tower is both a memorial to 'old England' — hence the melancholy of remembrance (as a memoration)[18] — and the interlocking of loss and desire, 'the love of home [that] never departs from the heart of the true Briton'.

But the afterlife of Archer's battlemented tower does not end with Bell's catalogue, for Archer had not been content with just one 'tower glimpsed through the trees'[19] and on an adjoining property called Burlington he had commissioned a truly remarkable structure. In 1957, Michael Sharland, the early and influential cultural historian of Tasmanian landscapes, visited Burlington to see 'Archer's Folly', a dovecot, now known as a pigeon tower,[20]

which takes the form of a tower some 60' high, adorned with battlemented crest and a curious inverted roof that matches its ancient architecture. It is, one could say, a veritable fowl castle, very definitely elevated from the status of an ordinary fowlhouse,

---

[17] Chick, *The Archers*, p. 113.

[18] John Frow, *Time and Commodity Culture: Essays in Cultural Theory and Post-Modernity* (Oxford: Clarendon Press, 1997), p. 229.

[19] Stilwell 'Joseph Archer', p. 24.

[20] See, for example, *Heritage of Tasmania*, p. 131.

and the way it was fitted out showed that the owner not only made a feature of his poultry but also took considerable pride in accommodating them adequately.[21]

In Sharland's vision of the Tasmanian Midlands, Archer's 'medieval tower',[22] situated on the south bank of the picturesque Macquarie River, has an historical valency but he can also appreciate the possibly parodic ripple produced by the conjunction of its elements:

> One would never find so dignified a 'fowlhouse' now. Its mellow colours — brown and red and rain-stained grey — are typical of age, and this is emphasised by the prolific growth of ancient lichen on the walls. Disused and empty and scarred by decay, it nevertheless forms a striking feature in the lush meadows along the river that mirrors its weathered masonry and the blue range of the Western Tiers behind. There are buildings as old as this, but few have remained for more than a century free from the devastating touch of those who would convert them to the requirements of modern times.[23]

In the absence of surviving architectural plans or a diary with entries recording his hopes and plans, it is difficult to know what Archer thought he was doing with his two towers on either side of the river. Does a 'fowlhouse' dressed up as a medieval castle suggest some ancestral sense of humour, or is this Gothic such as we might see almost anywhere in Australia? This second medieval tower — referred to simply as 'an ornamental tower' that is part of Lot 2 in Bell's catalogue,[24] absent from some pictures of the property such as Bowring's 'Willows' sketch, while displacing the water tower in others such as Lyttleton's coloured lithograph — complicates Archer's medievalism. Sharland's perhaps droll account nevertheless retains the intimate connection between property and person, evidenced in Bell's catalogue, whereby the fowl house shows us the man: demonstrating 'that the owner not only made a feature of his poultry but also took considerable pride in accommodating them adequately'. This tower is unambiguously medieval: 'a veritable fowl castle' with 'ancient architecture' and 'battlemented crest'; its 'weathered masonry and the blue range of the Great Western Tiers behind' suggesting the ruin that is a typical detail of the Gothic.

For Sharland there is not only a sense of vastness preserved in Archer's Folly but also of modernity resisted: the tower survives despite 'the devastating touch' and 'requirements of modern times'. Sharland's tone is delicate here — ironic, nostalgic,

---

[21] Michael Sharland, *Stones of a Century* (Hobart: Oldham, Beddome & Meredith, 1957), p. 45.

[22] Michael Sharland, *Oddity and Elegance* (Hobart: Fullers Bookshop, 1966), p. 76. See, for example, Joan Kerr and James Broadbent, *Gothick Taste in the Colony of New South Wales* (Sydney: The David Ells Press in association with the Elizabeth Bay House Trust, 1980).

[23] Sharland, *Stones of a Century*, p. 45.

[24] Bell, *Particulars and Description*, pp. 12–13.

pragmatic. There is a genuine affection for the 'fowl castle' and a sense of relief at finding something '[d]isused and empty and scarred by decay' whose 'mellow colours' are 'typical of age'. That relief derives, in part, from Sharland's having found what he has been searching for: not only do the Midlands 'hold more objects of historical and romantic interest' than elsewhere in Tasmania but, more importantly, they 'are yielding these links with old times, with our domestic history, our folk lore and legend'.[25] Age, ruin, lichen-covered stonework — these are all palpable traces of continuity. '[O]ur links with old times' are tangible; 'our folk lore and legend' are not new; they are 'old'. Archer's medievalism shifts from being a metaphor for Englishness transported to 'the new country of [his] adoption' to an historical one standing for 'our folk lore and legend'. In Sharland's medievalism, the afterlife of Archer's Folly provides the conditions for a cultural history that shares the desire for Englishness evident in Bell's catalogue. But it does so with a self-consciousness typical of 1950s Anglophile Australia — basking in the afterglow of the newly-crowned Queen Elizabeth's Royal Visit in 1954, vehemently debating the existence of a national literature and caught up in what would later be called 'the cultural cringe' that denigrated anything 'Australian'. The sign of this conflicted relationship between identity and Englishness for Sharland is that in his medievalism the event of colonial transposition is occluded: the medieval tower stands for '*our* domestic history, *our* folk lore and legend' (emphasis added). If, in the afterlife documented by Bell's catalogue, 'Panshanger' and its towers 'remember' an English cultural genealogy by memorializing the desire for that genealogy, then for Sharland that same afterlife makes possible the act of forgetting the intervening act of severance separating Tasmania from that originary Englishness.

Thirty years later, the afterlife of medievalism in Tasmania still intrigued Australian cultural analysts. Gathering together traces of medievalism, extremity and intensity, and inflecting them with a sense of insouciant parody, Jim Davidson characterized Tasmania — 'an island of high latitude, of mountains, lakes, mists, clouds and rain; of wastes of awesome scenery, tempestuously mocking the homely allusions made by the early settlers' — as 'our own little gothic repository'.[26] Davidson's Gothicism, spotted with references to 'feudalism', 'Merrie England' (p. 307), and 'the Old Country' (p. 311), foregrounds what Sharland's medievalism had sought to deny, namely, the rupture between past and present, colony and centre, communal tradition and fragmentary modernity. Tasmanian Gothic

> proves to be a synthesising vision, since it can accommodate disjunctions between past and present, even thriving on them, settling them down in a common landscape [...]

---

[25] Sharland, *Oddity and Elegance*, p. 76.

[26] Jim Davidson, 'Tasmanian Gothic', *Meanjin*, 48 (1989), 307–24 (p. 310). For a critique of Davidson's underpinning of Romanticism, see Amanda Lohrey, 'The Greens: A New Perspective', in *The Rest of the World is Watching*, ed. by Cassandra Pybus and Richard Flanagan (Chippendale: Pan, 1990), pp. 89–100.

the slaughtered Aborigines, the downtrodden convicts, and hunted species like the diminutive Tasmanian Emu and the gothically named Tasmanian Tiger. The colony was cradled in excess, grew up with the constraints of intricacy in landscape and social arrangements, and today delights in odd juxtapositions. Thus, while it may sometimes seem to sustain neo-Georgian notions of gentility, it also has a wonderful way of sabotaging them. (p. 310)

Here this afterlife of medievalism moves into another register. In Davidson's backward glance from late twentieth-century cultural commentary to eighteenth-century Gothic, it is a literary trope that provides the 'synthesising vision' he wants to see; that same trope provides Davidson with both a metaphysical and affective discourse for Tasmania. The generic Gothic's over-investment in sublime landscape, hyperbolic sensation and, thus, a subject's emotional equanimity gives Davidson a way of mapping the atmospherics of the Apple Isle and the people who call it home. It is the extremity of Tasmania that calls for 'gothic intensity' (p. 311); 'it is the low-keyed gothic of the grotesque that remains in evidence today' (p. 318); 'Tasmanian gothic does not mean merely picturesqueness, or a pleasing aesthetic treatment of past sorrows, but also a great deal of continuing pain, muddle, and a sense of defeat' (p. 312).

The Gothic provides Davidson with a psychopathology that he uses to read a series of literary works (chiefly novels and a biography) and a recent film that chronicle Tasmanian life. Commenting on Peter Conrad's memoir *Down Home: Revisiting Tasmania* (1988), Davidson argues that 'part of the island's gothic character [...] arises from the fact that the past, whether acknowledged or not, is constantly intercessed with the present' (p. 318). In the afterlife that is Davidson's Gothic, with its recurrent medieval details such as David Herbert's 'late flowering of medieval sculpture' in the social grotesques on the Ross bridge, the past insists on being remembered: the repressed insists on returning. The work of memory is distorted by the past's refusal to remain past and thus, in some way, manageable, however disturbing the memory. It is this distortion that is rendered in Davidson's Gothic as the past — the cruelties of the convict system, the genocide of indigenous peoples, the extinction of native animals, the enervating depression of economic decline, the poisonous parochialism — irrupting into and juxtaposing itself with an ongoing present trying to imagine a future.

Whilst, in the case of *Down Home*, the specific point of opposition to Tasmania is the metropolitan centre of Oxford, it is Conrad's identity as Tasmanian, rather than a putative Englishness, that is at stake. In this afterlife, Davidson's Gothic medievalism is a therapeutic discourse: like the 'synthesising vision' into which he sees the Tasmanian cultural landscape resolve its extremities of climate, topography, and history, Conrad is finally 'cured' of his 'adolescent rage to invent myself' (p. 319). Mimicking the gestures of his parents, unconsciously as he realizes, and seated between them like some medieval grotesquery, Conrad resigns himself to remembering what he used to be and discovers, on his return to England, that 'Tasmania had even infiltrated the literary scenery of England: "from where else had

I derived my liking for Celtic faerylands and Gothic bogs?"' (p. 319). At this moment, Conrad's memory of Tasmania and his recognition of it in the English landscape deconstructs the binary opposition between Englishness and Tasmanian identity that has been played out in the (re)use of aspects, fragments and discourses of medievalism's afterlife I have been reading. Tasmania has moved from the rude colonial periphery to appropriate the centre of the familial heartland that Bell's sale catalogue had called 'home'; 'another England'[27] has come to displace the original England, reconstructing that original in the image of Conrad's own home.

Writing about memory, Freud comments that

> our memories — not excepting those which are most deeply stamped on our minds — are in themselves unconscious. They can be made conscious; but there can be no doubt that they can produce all their effects while in an unconscious condition. What we describe as our 'character' is based on the memory-traces of our impression; and, moreover, the impressions which have had the greatest effect on us — those of our earliest youth — are precisely the ones which scarcely ever become conscious.[28]

This is suggestive at the rhetorical rather than the scientific level: it's not, I think, that the afterlife of medievalism I have been tracing may be subject to the empirical stages of dreaming that Freud is hypothesizing. Rather, this afterlife, in its producing of medieval effects, its reuse of fragments or traces of the cultures of the Middle Ages, its 'messed up' quality (as Eco called it), iterates, in different and heterogeneous ways, that passing from unconscious into conscious manifestation that Freud sees as the *point* of memory. How such memories enter the unconscious is a separate intriguing question but not the one I confront here. My focus is on that moment at which the various medievalisms at work here, from Archer's twin towers and Bell's catalogue, through Sharland's cultural history and Davidson's cultural generics, to Conrad's memoir, stage a series of anxieties about 'our "character" [that] is based on the memory-traces of our impression'. It is the afterlife of medievalism that provides the means — the discourses, images, concrete objects, the passing of time, the movement in place — for the dynamic negotiation of those anxieties about 'character' that change from, in Archer's towers, that 'form of melancholia caused by prolonged absence from one's country or home' (*OED*) we call 'nostalgia' to Conrad's witty and insightful realization that in travelling back to the Home country what he recognized was the meaningfulness of his own home country.

While Peter Conrad's memoir uses a strategy and achieves a realization that we have come to recognize through postcolonial theory — as the imperial relation of colony to centre is deconstructed to disclose new power relations — the language of

---

[27] Stilwell, 'Joseph Archer', p. 24.

[28] Sigmund Freud, 'Psychology of the Dream Processes', *The Interpretation of Dreams*, trans. by James Strachey [*Standard Edition*, vols IV–V] (New York: Avon Books, 1965), p. 578.

Down Home owes nothing to this mode of analysis. For complex and half-submerged reasons, this is one of the suppressions or evasions, as Paul Strohm terms them, of Conrad's text; perhaps because, in Conrad's lexicon, the notion of irony — rather than ideology — helps nuance the intricacies of his relationship to Oxford and Englishness. Conrad's memoir is a personal document that enters the public domain through its genre and the act of publication whereby private work becomes public text. It aims to represent a private self to a public audience and it shares this permeable boundary between public and private with those other texts I have been reading. Similarly, Bell's sale catalogue is printed and distributed to advertise a public sale by invoking private witnesses; Sharland's cultural history is built incrementally out of his own personal experiences of the Tasmanian Midlands to form a public expression of community genealogy; Davidson's cultural generics is sifted together out of his own readings of novels, memoir and film to fill what he perceives is a gap in the public's perception of things Tasmanian. But the strategy of address in these texts — their use of an individual voice positioned as or close to a first-person speaker — makes it difficult for them to use what has become the powerful language of analysis for postcolonial questions of nation, identity, and memory. In Australian contexts, the language of postcolonial critique is usually, and rightly, reserved for indigenous black speakers; it is not available to white settler speakers.

Where public institutions are under scrutiny, however, the situation changes. I want to turn now to another afterlife of medievalism to offer a reading of its relationship to memory that discloses a different set of meanings. In 1960, in an essay called 'Medievalism and Australian Culture',[29] John Gilchrist, a historian, articulated an attitude that had circulated as axiomatic in mainstream Australian culture and its public institutions. Gilchrist's polemical claims for medievalism may produce something of a shock some forty-five years later and I am quoting his essay here not to suggest that his view was universal but rather that its articulation is typical. This is the language of a particular aspect of educated, middle-to-upper class Australian culture during the period after Australia's participation in the Korean War (1950–53) and before its collaboration with the US in the Vietnam War (1962–71). The essay is shadowed too by the Cold War in which Australia is co-opted by means of its Anglo-American and Anglo-European affiliations. It comes from a period marked by post-Second World War migration, which was mainly British and European, and prior to the migration from Asia and the Middle East that began in the 1970s. The particular version of the Middle Ages it constructs — a conservative Catholic Middle Ages given the hegemonic dominance by the Church as the primary socio-economic, political and cultural force — coincides with a sectarian politics in which the muscular White Anglo-Saxon Protestant mainstream was played off

---

[29] John Gilchrist, 'Medievalism and Australian Culture', *Twentieth Century*, 14 (1960), 293–301.

against a vehement Catholic (mainly Irish-Catholic) minority in public and private sectors of Australian cultural and political life.

Gilchrist aims to intervene in a cultural debate underway during the late 1950s about the relevance of medieval history (his own discipline), the dominance of modern history (posited as the opposing discipline of history available to be taught but actually a figure for modernity) and a recent 'complaint' about 'the "invasion" of Australia with American culture on the one hand and the continued reliance of this country on the conservative British culture on the other' (p. 295).

> In a country located geographically in Asia but whose culture is European-based, it is equally necessary to possess a knowledge of European history as of Far Eastern [...] Asiatic studies have a place in Australian universities and, by implication, in its culture, but to argue that because Australia's nearest neighbour is Indonesia, therefore the schools ought to teach Indonesian and drop French and German shows little knowledge of the historical and psychological bases of the Australian education system.

> Thus medieval studies in this country could have a different value and effect from that which would generally be imagined, not necessarily from their subject matter but because their presence indicates a change in attitude, almost an intellectual revolution among those responsible for planning the education of the nation. It would indicate a desire to deal with the feeling of rootlessness that characterizes Australian society, and would mark a change among those who believe that intellectual humanism, and liberalism, is the only habit of thought worth cultivating. (p. 296)

This essay only barely conceals its anxiety about race by conceding Australia's geographical location before hastening to invoke a hierarchy whereby 'Asiatic studies' 'have a place in Australian universities' but are a distant second to European languages because of 'the historical and psychological bases of the Australian education system'. This is an argument about origin that draws on the historical facts of white settlement that are (apparently) beyond contention combined with a sense of conviction and rightness — 'psychological bases' — that shape the education system forming the nation's citizens. Nominating Australia as a 'European' culture, Gilchrist claims a genealogical descent from that source and its cultural heritage that not only *is* right but *feels* right. 'It must also be remembered that Australia is essentially European in origin and therefore has its roots in the Middle Ages as much as, say England, France, or Germany' (p. 293). Australians, Gilchrist argues, need to remember who they really are. Further, since medieval studies are the guarantee of Australia's 'European-based' culture, medievalism is a purposive and instrumental, rather than abstract, knowledge that has political and cultural agendas. It is used to teach what Gilchrist calls 'the Australian' (p. 296) to think and feel — to remember — 'his' heritage, his identity, and his Europeanness. Medievalism, then, identifies 'the Australian' as European, white and male and it is with the appearance here of the gendered subject that medievalism is drawn into a (now familiar) struggle that threatens to ambush the main argument. The strategic move to assert genealogy and heritage implies the corresponding need for the policing of those racial boundaries and the preservation of those bloodlines. There is, as Australian readers will recognize, a covert threat of miscegenation for which the essay is unable to find a discourse and reaches, instead, for the language traditionally associated with genealogy — that of 'roots' and family trees. Thus the malaise of 'rootlessness' that an education system based on the heritage of Catholic Europe and Reformation England will cure by preventing Australia from taking root in and engendering close ties with non-Christian (i.e. non-white) Asia. In this afterlife, medievalism is deployed as overtly political in its use and essentially definitive of Australian culture; it is a medievalism that depends upon and mobilizes (race) memory.

While Gilchrist's argument urges Australians to remember their European heritage and consequent identity, it depends upon an act of forgetting that, until 1993, underpinned Australia's formation as a nation state and, very precisely, the question of what the nation's heritage might be. The events of British/European invasion and colonization do not trouble Gilchrist's account of Australia's history nor, at least in this essay, its education system. But there is a trace of anxiety produced by this act of forgetting or repression which, in the intervening years between Gilchrist's essay and the three relevant legal decisions (*Mabo v Queensland* 1986, *Mabo v Queensland 2* 1993, and *Native Title Act* 1993), became a defining aspect of Australia's national identity and brought the easy assumption of Australia's European heritage into question. In establishing the circumstances for his polemic, Gilchrist refers to his hearing of the 'complaint' that Australia has recently experienced an 'invasion' of American culture. It is this word 'invasion' with its sense of 'infringement by intrusion', 'encroachment upon the property, rights, privacy', and 'incursion with armed force' (*OED*) that recalls the legal fiction of *terra nullius* — the eighteenth-century presumption, following Roman law, of Australia's being an unoccupied land, that the acquisition of sovereignty over the country was legitimate and thus the rights of any traditional owners were extinguished[30] — that enabled the other, far more significant, invasion of Australia by British forces to the lasting detriment of its indigenous peoples. The point is not to castigate Gilchrist's essay for its ignorance of legal argument that had not yet occurred but rather to draw attention to the un-self-conscious and naturalized way in which his claims on memory are made and to understand that Gilchrist's medievalism is not, as he feared, irrelevant to the work of Australian universities in forming the nation's cultural heritage. Instead, this same medievalism, with its recall of European heritage and its idealization of that historical period as exemplary in 'teaching' the lessons of the past occupies a privileged position in terms of cultural and national formation by forgetting — repressing — the 'facts' of Australia's national history. In this afterlife, medievalism, practised as an academic discipline

---

[30] See entry under 'Mabo', Garth Netheim, *Oxford Companion to the High Court of Australia*, ed. by Tony Blackshield, Michael Coper, and George Williams (Oxford: Oxford University Press, 2001), pp. 446–48.

but also shaping the education system, becomes a powerful conservative, anti-modernist and anti-liberal force that does not operate serendipitously but rather, as Gilchrist's argument makes clear, as a purposive, deliberate and cogent program. It performs what we might call, by analogy with Freud's account of the processes by which dream thoughts are censored and manifested in dream content, memory work[31] and aims to manage national anxiety and psychic conflict.

The urgent need to critique the ideological régime such as that discernible in Gilchrist's collaboration of the political conservatism of medievalism's afterlife and its colonial project guides the argument of Leigh Dale's study *The English Men: Professing Literature in Australian Universities.*[32] I am less concerned with the detailed history Dale provides of the formation of the discipline of English in Australia — fascinating and compelling though that material is — than with the discursive possibilities initiated by Dale's study. *The English Men* is an account of disciplinary history but its terms are situated squarely by the acknowledgement that Australia is a postcolonial nation and its public institutions, in this case its universities, are formed by this historical datum. 'Poetry, politics and Englishness' is its opening phrase and the study aims 'to contextualize the well-documented interpellation of the colonial and postcolonial reader through and by literary texts, by describing and analyzing the protocols of the institutions in which those readings have been given a forceful and lasting legitimacy' (p. 5). Drawing on scholarly accounts of both the 'social mission' of English formalized by Matthew Arnold (Baldick) and postcolonial critics of the academy (Viswanathan and others) Dale seeks to write 'not a "history" in the conventional sense: the aim is not to reconstruct personality or event so much as it is to read critical and institutional texts within the *contexts and conditions of their own making*' (emphasis added) (p. 7). So, the postcolonial analytical frame is structural rather than superficial, axiomatic rather than optional: it is the condition of Australia's having been a colony and now confronting its own postcolonial cultural formation that shape Dale's terms of analysis. Thus, in the context of Australia's postcolonial status, Dale describes the 'long-held affiliation to cultural and intellectual regimes of Englishness' she sees as formative in the academic discipline of English in Australia, as hegemonic. At the same time — and here is the intelligent reach of Dale's analysis — 'hegemony involves the *minutiae* of daily life: our language and our bodies brought into conformity with institutional expectations' (p. 6). The result is a nuanced reading of the history of English in Australian universities, responsive to the Arnoldian project that saw English as a means of inculcating imperial values, colonial citizenship and

---

[31] Freud, *The Interpretation of Dreams*, Part IV, pp. 311–546 and Sigmund Freud, *Introductory Lectures on Psychoanalysis*, vol. 1, trans. by James Strachey, ed. by James Strachey and Angela Richards (Harmondsworth: Penguin, 1973), especially Lecture 11, 'The Dream-Work', pp. 204–18.

[32] Leigh Dale, *The English Men: Professing English in Australian Universities* (Toowoomba: Association for the Study of Australian Literature, 1995).

class allegiance, the radical destabilizing of authority that was consequent on attempts to pursue that project in the Australian context, and the often conflicted subjectivities produced by the uncertain success of that same colonial project, as it was overtaken by Australia's often uncertain and fraught reformulation as a postcolonial nation.

If we accept Dale's argument for the foundational importance of postcolonial critique as a mode of historicizing the formation and practice of knowledge in Australia[33] then the question arises as to what a postcolonial medievalism might look like? Bruce Holsinger, writing in the US journal *Speculum*, argues that '[p]ostcolonial studies has had an explicit and self-acknowledged presence in medieval studies for nearly a decade now'.[34] Holsinger deconstructs the apparent opposition between postcolonial theory (as a critique of modernity) and medieval studies (as the study of the premodern): a commonplace in arguments against the use of theory in a traditionally empirical discipline. He does this by uncovering the theoretical and methodological debt to medievalism owed by perhaps the most powerful of the anti-imperialist historians, the Subaltern Studies group. His argument uses an illuminating set of examples from both *Subaltern Studies*, the journal initiated in 1981 by the group around Ranajit Guha, Partha Chatterjee, and others, and the seminal critique of the group's work, 'Subaltern Studies: Deconstructing Historiography', published in *Subaltern Studies* by Gayatri Spivak in 1985. For Holsinger, this relationship between postcolonial theory and medieval studies is exemplary: 'the group's writings thus lay out a historiographical project which, if admittedly partial, remains nevertheless rich in comparativist heuristics for a postcolonial medievalism' (p. 1209). It is the Subaltern Studies group's engagement with medieval studies — their borrowing of theories, methodologies and arguments from medievalists, especially the *Annales* school — that enables them to identify 'the subaltern' that underpins their critique of coloniality. Far from medieval studies practising theory belatedly and 'from the margins', 'the work of the Subaltern Studies group [which] has engendered some of postcolonial theory's most urgent conflicts, keywords, and historical reclamations over the last twenty years' (p. 1209) has proceeded from the medievalism that lies deep at its centre.

Having mapped a genealogy of postcolonial medievalism Holsinger then turns his attention to the often highly trained and highly successful medievalists hidden in the careers of such theorists as Mikhail Bakhtin, Umberto Eco, Julia Kristeva, and Hans Robert Jauss, Hegel in the *Lectures on the History of Philosophy*, Max Weber's dissertation and first book, Martin Heidegger's *Habilitationsschrift*, French avant-

---

[33] For an alternative argument, see Louise D'Arcens, 'Europe in the Antipodes: Australian Medieval Studies', *Studies in Medievalism*, 10 (1998), 13–40.

[34] Bruce Holsinger, 'Medieval Studies, Postcolonial Studies and the Genealogies of Critique', *Speculum*, 77 (2002), 1195–1227 (p. 1207). Holsinger also uses 'postcolonial medievalism', *passim*.

gardists before and after World War II such as Georges Bataille, Jacques Lacan (*The Ethics of Psychoanalysis*, Lecture 7), later work by Jacques Derrida, Jean-François Lyotard, and so on. Holsinger's argument is that in 'forgetting' these intellectual genealogies, '[w]e risk forgetting the vital historical role that our methods and disciplines have played in the elaboration of the critical languages that have in turn transformed the human sciences over the last several decades. We forget these particular histories at our own, considerable cost' (p. 1225). This argument owes little to the strategy of identifying the subaltern but a great deal to another deconstructive move characteristic of the Subaltern Studies group, in particular, and postcolonial theory, in general: the decentring of the metropolitan, the marginalizing of the centre, the 'provincialising of Europe' or, in this case, the medievalizing of 'theory'. This is a radical defamiliarization of the history of theory — at least from the point of view of medievalists — that might enable a rethinking of disciplinary relations, if not disciplinary boundaries.

The point I want to draw attention to is that the afterlife of Holsinger's medievalism is mobilized by an act of memory: one that is supplementary to and thus destabilizes traditional histories of the human sciences by remembering that medievalism is central, not marginal, to the intellectual formation of some of its most powerful practitioners. This is a postcolonial medievalism that calls for another kind of disciplinary history — one that 'remembers' what has been forgotten and, on the basis of that memory, reshapes the traditional history from which medieval studies is a rigorously empirical and only belatedly theoretical discipline energized by '"modes of self-marginalisation" that [it] eternally enjoys perpetrating against itself' (p. 1198) into one that can imagine 'anti-imperialist historiographies' (p. 1227). Memory has a strategic role here; as does its reciprocal act of forgetting which operates less as omission ('to omit or neglect through inadvertence', *OED*) and more as 'determined by an unconscious purpose'.[35] Forgetting its implication in the development of postcolonial theory enables medieval studies to remain hermetically sealed in, for instance, an afterlife of anti-modernist antiquarianism. Holsinger's argument puts pressure not only on the different taxonomies of memory and history but also on the relationship between memory and history; a relationship that has a history of antagonism but that has recently undergone significant change and from which memory has emerged as 'a subject in its own right [...] [raised] to the status of a historical agent'.[36]

And it is as an historical agent that I want to conclude by reading the work of memory in one final example of this second afterlife of medievalism in Australia — the 'Preface' to David Matthews's book *The Making of Middle English, 1765–1910*,

---

[35] Freud, *Interpretation of Dreams*, p. 202.

[36] Kerwin Lee Klein, 'On the Emergence of *Memory* in Historical Discourse', *Representations*, 69 (2000), 127–50 (p. 136).

published 1999.[37] Here the distinction between private and public texts circulating in
the public domain is, if not erased, then made faint since Matthews's 'Preface',
while being written in the first person, precedes and thus frames his disciplinary
history of Middle English as an academic discourse. A preface is the 'introduction to
a literary work, usually explaining its subject, purpose, scope, and method' (*OED*)
and thus has generic links to the medieval and scholastic form of the academic
prologue or *accessus*[38] and here the 'Preface' takes over from the *accessus* the
function of identifying the author. As Alistair Minnis understands the trope, naming
the author of a work (the 'efficient cause') is of primary importance because
'authentic statements — statements which can be attributed to a named authority —
are more worthy of diligent attention and to be committed to memory' (p. 9) and, in
all three kinds of academic prologues or *accessus*, the *nominem auctoris* followed
the introduction to the work's title and sometimes included a short *vita auctoris*.
What is at stake here, in medieval literary theory, is the issue of the authority
claimed by or attributed to an author — the measure of which is whether the author's
text is sufficiently valuable to be repeated by being remembered. Identity, the
authority to speak and memory are each played out in Matthews's 'Preface' but here
the work of memory is not that of storage and retrieval by the systematic procedure
of memory[39] that underpin medieval academic learning but instead another kind of
memory work in which forgetting is 'an integral principal' and 'memory has the
orderliness and the teleological drive of narrative. Its relation to the past is not that of
truth but desire'.[40] Matthews's study of academic medievalism begins in this way:

> Working through *Sir Gawain and the Green Knight* some years ago as undergraduates
> at the University of Adelaide, South Australia, a fellow student and I came to the line
> 'Towres telded bytwene, trochet ful þik'. George Turner, leading the seminar, stopped
> us and asked us where the nearest example of such an architectural feature might be
> found. The question left us both perplexed. Not only did we not know the answer, the
> question itself seemed obscure. There are no medieval castles in Australia; the text was
> not about the things we knew, and its very otherness was the reason we had gone onto
> the advanced course in Middle English. What was the nearest bit of England, where
> such things are to be found? Was that what we were being asked? Altogether the
> question seemed to be one of those tricks in which the literature and history of the Old
> World abound. The answer to the question seemed to be sneakily unstraightforward,
> and the person who answered it likely to be caught, just like Gawain. We kept quiet.

---

[37] David Matthews, *The Making of Middle English, 1765–1910* (Minneapolis: University
of Minnesota Press, 1999).

[38] A. J. Minnis, *Medieval Theory of Authorship: Scholastic Literary Attitudes in the Later
Middle Ages* (London: Scholar Press, 1984).

[39] See Mary Carruthers, *The Book of Memory: A Study of Memory in Medieval Culture*,
Cambridge Studies in Medieval Literature, 10 (Cambridge: Cambridge University Press,
1990).

[40] Frow, *Time and Commodity Culture*, p. 229.

The answer was that the nearest *towre ful þik* was 'about two hundred yards away, on top of the Mitchell Building, a Gothic revival pile then serving as the university's main administration block' (p. ix).

The language casts Matthews's memory of himself and his fellow student as two knights-errant confronting a riddle, posed by a sage, that impedes their progress but that, if solved, will take them one step forward toward whichever grail it is that they seek. Perplexity, obscurity, otherness, the 'sneakily un-straightforward' are the 'tricks [...] of the Old World' that serve as obstacles to these two students, trying hard not to be 'caught'/ 'kaʒt'[41] — like Gawain — as they search for the answer on their quest in the New World. If Gawain's dilemma is the conflict between his own desire, 'for gode of hymseluen',[42] and the obligation to honour his 'trawþe'[43] then what is being learned here in the architectural detail of a Gothic revival pile that is, surely, over-determined?[44]

The narrative that memory work produces in Matthews's medievalism recalls a loss and mourning that are familiar: '[m]y education led me, as it happened at a very early age, to an appreciation of medieval literature, but even that deep appreciation could not smooth over the rift that seemed to divide me from this culture deriving from elsewhere' (p. x). This is the colonial melancholia inspired by Joseph Archer's two towers; just as it recalls the affective relationship between literature and 'the *minutiae* of daily life' to which the lives of *The English Men* drew our attention. Likewise, Matthews's claim that his book 'comes from the margins' where 'the story [of Middle English] becomes visible' (p. x) rehearses Bruce Holsinger's deconstructive reversal of margin and centre and the result is a coherent narrative to account for the history of a British Middle English being written by an Australian for a US publisher. But the desire which this text is unable to speak, the *telos* toward which this narrative moves exposes the question that is at stake here: not, where is the nearest *towre ful þik* but what 'trawþe' authorizes Matthews to speak at all? This anxiety is answered by the shortest and simplest sentence in the text. 'We kept quiet' (p. ix). This is a fraught moment marked by silence — unlike Peter Conrad's eloquent and enabling Tasmanian gothicism. Neither Matthews nor his companion remembers the neo-Gothic pile just two hundred yards away; each has forgotten that quintessential Englishness for which such architecture is iconic in the Australian imaginary and which Michael Sharland worked so assiduously to remember. The

---

[41] 'And syþen karp with my knyʒt þat I kaʒt haue', *Sir Gawain and the Green Knight*, ed. by J. R. R. Tolkien and E. V. Gordon, 2nd edn rev. by Norman Davis (Oxford: Clarendon Press, 1967, 1972), p. 34, l. 1225.

[42] 'ʒet laft he not þe lace, þe ladiez gifte, / þat forgat not Gawayn for gode of hymseluen.' *Sir Gawain* ll, 2030–31.

[43] 'For I schal stonde þe a strok, and start no more / Til þyn ax haue me hitte: haf here my trawþe.' *Sir Gawain* ll. 2286–87.

[44] For this particular use of 'over-determined' see Freud, *Interpretation of Dreams*, p. 318.

effect of memory work has been to bring to consciousness a rupture between the un-self-conscious certainty of John Gilchrist's traditional role for medievalism in Australian culture and the now self-conscious contemporary meanings of such a medievalism. So Matthews's quest is to find an authorized speaking position since the substitution of medieval heritage for invasion history as the foundational narrative of national identity and subject formation is no longer tenable and the consequent need is for an anti-imperial historiography. The afterlife of medievalism, in other words, provides a discourse — albeit a conflicted discourse — which stages this negotiation between official history and collective memory, national identity and subject formation, public imaginary and private self, and here, between teacher and student. It is the persistence of this discourse, the manifest usefulness of medievalism, and the iteration of its afterlife that teaches us that such memory work speaks to questions of the meaningfulness in authority and identity that, for the historiographies of postcolonial Australia at least, remain both contested and urgent.

Medievalism as Heritage:
Australian Children's Books

VALERIE KRIPS

> There are two distinctive features of the mythology of the antique [...] that need to be
> pointed out: the nostalgia for origins and the obsession with authenticity.
>
> Jean Baudrillard

In the eighteenth and nineteenth centuries nostalgia was treated as a disease.[1] It certainly seemed to affect the Brontë sisters particularly badly, though there is no evidence that they sought medical help for their condition. Today we are more likely to think slightly fondly of the idea: there's a kind of pleasant sadness associated with its longing; we can afford its tinge of regret, since we know it won't kill us. Some nostalgia is perhaps useful, reminding us of kinder times and places, and providing an impetus for action in the present. Whether nostalgia about origins is useful or not is, however, an open question. Perhaps it depends upon how our origin is understood, and why we long for it. Whether for good or bad, a longing for origins seems to have taken a firm grip upon Australia's consciousness in the early twenty-first century, and its most apparent form is heritage.

Many critics have written about the astonishing and rapid acceleration of interest in heritage in the West in the late twentieth century. The heritage they have in mind is as pervasive as it is compendious: anything goes, it seems. Much of the work on heritage to date has taken a European country as its focus. Most begins from the idea that Europeans, from the eighteenth century on, slowly lost touch with their past as economic, social, and scientific changes caused a break with earlier, and sometimes very ancient, traditions of thought and behaviour. The heritage movements in

---

[1] David Lowenthal, *The Past Is a Foreign Country* (Cambridge: Cambridge University Press, 1985), pp. 10–11.

European countries tend to try to reconnect to the bits of the past that seem worth remembrance. That is, heritage wants us to remember the past, not to subject it to the critical analysis called history. The Australian situation is similar, with one important distinction.

Australians inhabit an ancient continent, as they are continually reminded, one which has been lived in for many thousands of years. Yet as a nation Australia is relatively young, and all of its past as a nation is historical, that is, is recorded; we can afford to be obsessed with authenticity, the 'truth' of the record. Within that record lie facts that are unpalatable, as must surely be the case with nations everywhere. Australia's peculiarity is that its past is both capable of authentication and lies very close to its present. The past tells the story of conquest, though it is spoken of more generally as settlement. With settlement and conquest came the displacement of the indigenous population. This is a past whose presence is still felt. Indeed, it has become something of a focus for the nation, as national 'Sorry' days indicate. Is this the story we tell ourselves about our country? Is this what Australian heritage must represent?

Clearly it does not. Australian heritage is not so much concerned with reconnection to the past as it is to construct a sense of the past that is fruitful for the present. Its purpose is to give depth and meaning to an everyday life which has become detached from its anchoring in the past. Understood in this way, the sorry story of Aboriginal displacement cannot express the whole of the Australian heritage, any more than the dark days of Port Arthur give a complete account of the penal colonies. The story of settlement and conquest is understood to be part of a greater heritage, one which looks in part beyond the historical landfall of Captain Cook and the later convict settlement at Botany Bay, important as they are to our sense of history. Australian heritage also includes the dreamtime, a mythology that defies European colonization, and reminds settlers of their difference. Reconciling this heritage with the other, imported, European ones, is a complex matter. However, we live in a period of reconciliation, and in a climate of opinion which is perhaps more capable of enabling a synthesis than any other in modernity. The way in which this synthesis is undertaken is the underlying topic of this chapter, through its focus on cultural artefacts that, perhaps more than any others, are contingent. These are childhood, and books written for children.

While childhood is generally overlooked as a topic for heritage studies, it remains one of the most potent of all our cultural links to the past. Childhood is both a fact and an idea, a cultural construction within which actual childhoods are lived. Our notions of childhood are based upon evidence, hope, and imagination, all tinged with nostalgia, a longing for home, for what we remember. Childhood is the home we all acknowledge, even as we move around geographically in unprecedented ways. It represents a past that we like to think of as sunny and happy, as Edenic. This holds true even if our particular version of it did not meet these criteria: such is our present day expectation of childhood, and one that we do everything we can to assure. The narratives that surround the idea of childhood are, thus, a complex mix of reality and imagination, of mythology and fact.

One of the best ways of revealing our current concepts of childhood is to study the books that enshrine it. Such books inevitably bear within them traces of the kinds of history we currently avow, that is, representations that, in some way or another, attempt to show the past as it really was, to paraphrase Leopold von Ranke's famous remark. However, children's books must always also reveal another history. In that version, the past is represented as we would have liked it to be. This is a history in which individual childhoods, including our own, meet our culture's figurations and expectations. Within all books written for children these two pasts, that of history and that of the child as remembered and figured by the adult, coexist. The reconciliation between these two pasts effected by the children's book is made within the frameworks of other, different cultural givens, and is profoundly influenced by them, as many studies have shown. In a cultural moment such as ours, when the past and how to deal with it has become a topic of importance, books written for children respond in a particularly acute way as a result of their underlying assumptions, which, in their complex relationship to history, look forward to the child and back to the past. These are assumptions that combine fact and fiction, or mythology and history, as does childhood itself. The fictional child, like the living child, effects culture's reconciliation of past and present. And it does so, presently, as part of heritage.

The adult's memory of childhood, which must always be incomplete, is censored, as all memories are. This is a censorship applied by culture itself, as it tells us what our childhood should have been like, and by our own unconscious, which protects us from harmful unworked-through material. Some books for children address this fraught but vital material: fairytales do so, as they rehearse some of childhood's most haunting fears and actualities. So too do many contemporary picture books. A good example is the American writer Maurice Sendak's famous picture book *Where the Wild Things Are*. His is a story about hating one's mother, and the terror that attends such feelings. In it, a little boy is told he is a 'wild thing' and sent to his room. The room becomes a forest, and soon, with the abrupt change of scenery reminiscent of dreams, he is with the Wild Things themselves: dear monsters, with great toothy smiles. After being crowned king, the little boy returns home, to find his supper waiting. His wildness, which includes hating his mother for reprimanding him, has been safely navigated.

Not all children's books address fears so directly, however, particularly when they are written for older children, those who read to themselves. In children's novels we are more likely to see the fears of the culture in general approached, fears which the child frequently faces, and sometimes faces down, on the adult's behalf. The child is capable of this because it has come to represent the self. It hasn't always done so. The history of childhood is one in which, from the fifteenth century on, a steadily growing sense of the importance of the individual has played a vital part. Equally, an awareness of the importance of the child as the centrepiece of the family grew. The development of the *Bildungsroman*, the story of a life beginning with childhood, bears witness to the new consciousness, as does the introduction of publishing explicitly for children, both developments of the eighteenth century. As stories about a shared past became increasingly difficult to tell in the face of social and economic change, the child was positioned as representative of the newly important 'self', which was increasingly a 'lost self' as Carolyn Steedman has recently argued.[2] Meanwhile it was also slowly coming to symbolize a past of lost innocence, a prelapsarian state to which both Rousseau's *Emile* and Goethe's *Wilhelm Meister* pay homage.

That lost self is historical: the past of childhood can never be recovered. Childhood understood thus came readily to symbolize at some level the past that lay within history's story, as well as the story of the self. The past of childhood is an unrecoverable state at the core of the individual, and lies too at the core of the family and, by implication, the nation. The child is thus profoundly historical. It represents the past in the clearest of ways, but also indicates that history is about a past that is over, and cannot be revisited. Yet that past resides within the individual as a living force, as Freud was to show so powerfully. The great flowering of children's books in the nineteenth and early twentieth centuries plays out and plays upon this coexistence: we need only consider Lewis Carroll's *Alice in Wonderland*, Kenneth Grahame's *Wind in the Willows* and, most profoundly, J. M. Barrie's *Peter Pan* to glimpse the power of this coexistence. All these writers dwell upon childhood with profound nostalgia, even as they reflect upon their culture's changing mores and demands. But although none of the child or animal characters are imagined as growing up and leaving childhood behind, they do not enter the past. Going back in time, while certainly not restricted to contemporary writing, plays a greater role today than it has ever done. We send child characters back, and they go for us.

One of the best-known Australian books of recent decades, Ruth Park's magical *Playing Beatie Bow* (1980) takes its protagonist Abigail back in time literally, to Victorian Sydney. Abigail slips back in time through a well-established literary device as an object from the past becomes her conduit. However, apart from the connection established by the conduit (a lace collar) the past and present are resolutely differentiated from each other. Abigail learns personally from the past which she visited, but cannot establish a broader connection; nor, indeed, might she want to do so. The Rocks as Park describes them, although lively and fascinating, are also dark, dirty, noisy and dangerous: a far cry from heritage's reconstructions of them. In effect, then, Abigail's time travel confirms, rather than breaks down, the lack of connection between past and present. In this sense, this is a pre-heritage novel.

More recently, Australian writers for children have turned to a fantastic time which, to use a phrase coined by Patrick Wright, 'trafficks in history'.[3] The 'traffick'

---

[2] Carolyn Steedman, *Strange Dislocations: Childhood and the Idea of Human Interiority 1780–1930* (Cambridge, MA: Harvard University Press, 1995).

[3] Patrick Wright, *On Living in an Old Country* (London: Verso, 1985). His Chapter 2 is

Wright was thinking about included a tendency to set chronology aside, and to represent the past as 'historical'. Sovereign Hill in Victoria presents an example of 'trafficking', as it brings together houses, shops, and mining facilities so as to present the ten years (roughly 1851–61) when Ballarat was the centre of goldmining. 'It's just like stepping back in time', its website declares: except, of course, you can't, speaking literally, and to imagine that you can undermines the duration of history itself. From a strictly historical point of view, therefore, what is represented is ahistorical, that is, it does not provide a strictly evidential account of a mining town's development and context, but shows it as arrested, caught in a time which is 'present now' to the visitors.

The 'trafficking' undertaken by three recent Australian children's books is similarly ahistorical, even though each employs themes which hark back to medieval Europe: knights and feudalism, crusades and romance all make their appearance. The young people who appear as protagonists do not go back in time, but rather find themselves in the nebulousness of what I will call heritage time, which is, as found in Sovereign Hill, time out of time. Two of the novels are fantasies, the third a realist novel with an historical setting. But, like heritage itself, the past as represented in each novel is in the service of present concerns.

Isobelle Carmody's *Darkfall* (1997) takes its readers to what seems to be a missing aspect of Australia. Her novel begins in biblical tone: 'In the Beginning was the Void, filled with the madness of the Unmade and the spirit of Chaos. But all things struggle towards Harmony and Form and so there came from the Void, a song, and this was the Song of Making.'[4] This is a quotation from the Legendsong, the creation myth and prophecy of Keltor, Carmody's imagined world. Keltor and our world are brought together by eighteen-year-old Australian twins, Ember and Glynn. Soon after the reader's introduction to the girls Glynn goes for a swim. She swims to the horizon, rests and floats, looking up at the silvering moon, when, surprised by a current of icy water, she imagines a shark where there is none, and cramps. She sinks. When she comes to her senses she is in a strange ship, and is surrounded by even stranger people. She is paralyzed and speechless, but she is thinking in a familiar vernacular. However her new companions tend to lapse into a different form of English: an island is only a 'scantling' away; had Glynn not been picked up by the ship she would have been 'eaten ere now'. We are in the world of romance, remote from the everyday. And romance speaks in archaic tones, at least in Carmody's version of it.

This is not enough to suggest that Carmody's vision is medieval. However, in the Legendsong's obvious reference to the great Judeo-Christian story of Genesis, the novel's picture of a complex society bounded by guilds, and the delineation of otherness as that which is dreadful because it is sufficiently like the known to offer a

---

entitled 'Trafficking in History'.

   [4] Isobelle Carmody, *Darkfall* (Ringwood: Penguin, 1997), p. 1.

realistic threat to it, we recognize familiar medieval themes. In this romance we can expect the antagonist to be eventually recognized and drawn back into the unity of the world; evil then becomes a baleful element, a sorcery, existing outside inter-personal relations, yet influencing them.

Carmody's other world is reached through a portal in the sea. The suggestions of the return to a former state, to the undifferentiated world of the womb, is apparent; equally clear is the proposal that this other world, connected to ours in obscure ways, must be reconnected to ours if either world is to prosper. Carmody's use of archaic language emphasizes the idea that a healing reconnection demands a return, as does Keltor's pre-industrial, pre-technical society. However, Keltor is scarcely primitive, either in its political formations, its social hierarchies, or its provisions for living, even though the latter go without explanation. What Carmody is at pains to explain, and what she requires the reader to understand as distinctive from the real world, are the features that make Keltor unique. Healers in Keltor do their work largely through the force of their inner capabilities, aided by the judicious use of herbs and potions. Mariners sail the dangerous seas by communing with them and the creatures that inhabit the sea; Soulweavers establish and protect those they serve, fulfilling the functions of counsellors and analysts; Windwalkers fly without the assistance of engines. In Keltor individuals, their gifts, and the material world operate in harmony, a harmony disrupted only because Keltor's creation myth includes a fall. Our world, or people from our world, it seems, have the power to redeem that fall. The presumption must be that our world, too, will be healed by this redemption.

Darkfall's themes, in which magic and mystery affect events, and in which supra-human beings exist side-by-side with the quotidian, are thoroughly medieval in tone. In reaching back to a European past it seems that Carmody is repudiating the Australian past, replacing it with one that can have little connection to a continent sublimely ignorant of it. But the medievalism here is otherworldly, not historical at all; its themes are its vitality, not its basis in history. This medievalism is the past brought into the present, a past which cannot be pinned down to real historical periodization, but which can imaginatively extend even to the complex and contradictory past of Australia. In the possibility which exists for Keltor, Carmody paints the picture of a reconciliation, the kind of coming together and erasure of the past which is found in many heritage representations of Australia's past.

We can think of the Aboriginal exhibit in the new Melbourne Museum in which past differences are exposed and explained within a framework (the museum itself) that can encompass, and thus dissolve them. The Melbourne Museum has become a keeping place for Aboriginals; they bring to it sacred objects so that they may rest safely. Housed within the walls of the museum, these objects join the other relics found there, objects from the settler past, and from that of other colonized peoples. The museum holds them all together, offering them to the visitor as part and parcel of what it is to be Australian. Outside the confining and comforting walls of the museum this complex heritage is seldom so securely brought together. Instead, the possibility of a future in which the gap between Australia's two origin stories can be closed remains a hoped-for goal, rather than an accomplished fact. The potential of its possibility exists in the activities surrounding the national 'Sorry' day, in the increasing interest in, and dignifying of, Aboriginal stories and myths, and in the understandings that the Aboriginals, too, were migrants. Thus we all become strangers in the land in which we yet hope to make a home to enfold us all.

The time of heritage is not real, historical time, but is a set of signs or indices of time. Heritage delights in a historicalness that is, to quote Jean Baudrillard, 'a refusal of history masked by an exaltation of the signs of history: history simultaneously invoked and denied.'[5] Such an exaltation runs through Dave Luckett's *A Dark Winter* (1998). His book relates the struggle to overcome a troubled past, and to replace it with a kinder, more inclusive world. All the world's current inhabitants must remake themselves if the desired end is to be achieved. In the tortuous process long-established monuments and institutions must be destroyed. Less complex in structure than Carmody's novel, yet narrated with subtle irony, Luckett's novel takes up romance themes, in particular those of chivalry and derring-do. However, while the action of the book refers to a code from the medieval past, it remains steadfastly twentieth-century in its outlook, preconceptions and narrative style. Luckett's protagonist and narrator, William Parkin, is squire to a knight who will set out to fight the Dark.

Like Carmody's *Darkfall*, Luckett's novel is the first in a proposed trilogy of which, so far, we cannot know the end. His medievalism is more securely pictured than Carmody's. The frontispiece shows knights and armour, accurately detailing each piece of the cumbersome apparel. In his imaginary world aristocrats and their armies are pitted against each other, but more importantly against a foe brought into being by a great mage, who can bring the dead back into the fight, and oppose wraiths to human armies. The book ends as a great fortress, once thought to be the greatest defence against the dark, is torn down: it nurtured an evil, a controlling force, within its fastness. Even as Luckett's medievalism is more powerfully drawn, it does not allow a direct historical connection. His is a world in which a mother figure presides in gentle and all encompassing love, even though she exists in a realm which is not yet part of the everyday world in which the characters exist. Nor is she a great lady: 'She was sitting on the bank of the brook just by the wall, dabbling her toes in the water, a country lass in soft faded homespun. I nodded as she looked up and smiled at me. And then I saw Her eyes, and I knew, and I snatched my cap off and stepped back, dropping to one knee.'[6]

The mages gain their power from *mana*, an ore found deep within the earth, which has the power to destroy as much as it may also be used to heal. Should it be mined at all? Who should mine it, who make use of it? It is by using *mana* that the

---

[5] Jean Baudrillard, *The System of Objects*, trans. by James Benedict (London: Verso, 1996), p. 74.

[6] Dave Luckett, *A Dark Winter* (Norwood : Omnibus Books, 1998), p. 323.

mages can bring back the dead, deploy wraiths, implant horrors in the mind. There are no traditional owners of the land from which the *mana* is plucked, but there are people who, living actually in the earth, are immune from its influence. For them the *mana* is part of their environment, rather than an expendable asset. This is not to suggest that Luckett imagines a romantic alliance of these people with the earth, but the work so far suggests the potential coming together of those who once thought of themselves as the guardians of the world, and these others, who live within it. Luckett indicates his debt to J. R. R. Tolkien in an author's note. Tolkien attempted to produce a peculiarly British myth, albeit one which was an amalgamation of many European traditional themes. Luckett's novel speaks the themes of displacement and dismemberment, of an essential conflict over the land, and authority over it, which responds powerfully to questions that presently beset Australia; whether or not he will yet produce an Australian myth remains to be seen.

Rather than instituting a sense of history as chronological and incomplete, and of historical understanding as available for reconceptualization and revision, heritage representations tend to present history as 'ready for exhibition as "the past"', as Wright puts it.[7] While Catherine Jinks's *Pagan's Crusade* concerns itself directly with history, it does so in heritage terms. It is not an historical novel in the strict sense, that is, it does not, in Georg Lukács's terms, provide the stage upon which a great figure, a 'subject of history', can approach.[8] Instead it is historical 'only as regards [… its …] purely external choice of theme and costume. Not only the psychology of the characters, but the manners depicted are entirely those of the writers' own day.'[9] Since Jinks does not attempt to present the mind of a medieval squire as essentially different from the mind of a present-day youngster, the reader is prevented from imagining the past as radically unlike the present.

Narrated by Pagan, an Arab Christian, Jinks's book tells the story of the young Arab's adventures, opening in twelfth-century Jerusalem. Pagan is also a squire, and while his story is set within an actual historical period, and includes accounts of recorded events, there is no recourse to archaic language. 'If I was a brigand, I wouldn't be boiling out my brains in this sun. I'd have my feet up in some nice, cool cave, with a jug of lime juice and a damp cloth over my eyes.'[10] Pagan's story is exciting and interesting, particularly in its depiction of the unlikely pairing of an aristocratic French knight and an Arab squire. This relationship fares better than the crusade, and manages to establish the kind of coexistence to which the crusades were

---

[7] Wright, *On Living in an Old Country*, p. 78.

[8] Lukács still provides the most instructive and detailed account of the genre, and it is in the light of his understandings that this point should be understood: Georg Lukács, *The Historical Novel* (Lincoln: University of Nebraska Press, 1983).

[9] Lukács, *The Historical Novel*, p. 19.

[10] Catherine Jinks, *Pagan's Crusade* (Rydalmere: Hodder Headline, 1994), p. 28.

so singularly opposed. At the end of the book, Pagan and his knight have left the Holy Land, and are returning to France.

Jinks's setting, the 'purely external' historical twelfth century, reminds us of the way in which historical settings can reveal much about the present in which they are written. Of interest to Jinks are those themes that are found repeatedly in contemporary children's novels set in the present. The revelation of Pagan's youthful character, and an account of his desire to enter the adult world, without yet being fully prepared to do so, are among the book's most constant concerns. While the action of the text is interesting in itself, it is a backdrop to this greater (in this book's view) adventure, that of coming to understand the adult world, and to survive in it. In this sense, Pagan is a modern boy undergoing his apprenticeship in a time and place that, although seemingly historical, is in fact as fantastic as anything that Carmody and Luckett imagine. Jinks's twelfth century is out of time: its interest for us lies in its medievalism.

To remark that Australia did not know the medieval period is to state the obvious, yet it is part of the past of one of the origin stories of Australia. The convicts who came to these shores, unwittingly and unwillingly, were inheritors of a European past. In all three novels discussed here, that past has taken on a mythological status. It is a past perfectly fit for heritage themes, since heritage mimics some of the attitudes to the past that the medieval historical period itself owned. Lee Patterson explains the medieval attitude to history in a way which illuminates our own stories: 'the past is rendered not as a process that has its own temporality but as a storehouse of disconnected and timeless *exempla* that assume authority precisely because they are no longer timebound [...] the medieval historical consciousness [... is...] always at issue, at times emerging towards an authentic apprehension of temporality and periodization, at other times retreating under the pressure of various ideologies toward reification and idolization.'[11]

Authenticating the past, when that past is problematic, is something of a problem. Patterson reminds us that medieval history was by no means opposed to the idea of including mythology within its narratives. However, our own determination to place our stories of the past within an evidential framework prevents us from incorporating the purely metaphoric from our understandings. But heritage has no such difficulty; in its system of representing the past, the metaphoric is not only welcome, but pervasive and persuasive. This does not mean that heritage is oblivious to the need to produce an authentic account — far from it. History takes issue with heritage because of its system of authentication, not its determination to provide it.

When heritage writes the history of Australia, it need not be restrained by all of history's difficult demands. It can, in a way that history so far cannot, gesture towards a reconciliation of the two origin stories precisely because it is not bound by

---

[11] Lee Patterson, *Negotiating the Past: The Historical Understanding of Medieval Literature* (Madison: University of Wisconsin Press, 1967), p. 206.

history's form of authenticity. What heritage can show is the past as we would like it to have been, as well as what it was. That liking should not be dismissed out of hand as mere fiction or fantasy. Instead, it can offer a way of resolving the otherwise unresolvable, as myths, and indeed medieval romance, undertook to do. In the ways in which the three children's novels I have discussed take up their task, we can see some of the possibilities of resolution offered by heritage. In moving to a past time that actually excludes Australian history, these works take their reader into a sphere that is partly historical, partly mythological. In this realm the possibilities of reconciliation can be sketched. Their solution is utopian, as were the solutions of medieval romance. The existence of these romance novels for children can be understood as a symptom of social and historical change and, indeed, of desire for change. To the extent that heritage is their vehicle, we can conclude that, for all its problems, heritage may be one way forward to a new understanding of our relation to older preconceptions, and their eventual overcoming by newer, more inclusive, ways of thinking of ourselves as Australian.

Part II

Gothic Landscapes and Medieval Communities

Passing through Customs:
William Dampier's Medieval Baggage

GERALDINE BARNES AND ADRIAN MITCHELL

If William Dampier is known at all these days, it is for his scathing dismissal, in *A New Voyage Round the World* (1697) and *A Voyage to New Holland* (1703/1709), of the unprepossessing natives of north-west New Holland and their even more unprepossessing habitat.[1] In terms of English historical geography he was, in the late seventeenth century, master mariner of the Southern Seas. In terms of English literary history, he was on the ship that marooned Alexander Selkirk, a.k.a. Robinson Crusoe; and also aboard the ship that subsequently picked him up again. In the history of English travel narrative, Dampier was writing at the point where travel as fiction and travel as fact diverge, his voyages to the coast of New Holland momentarily parting the veil which shrouded inexact ideas of a Southern Continent.[2] Dampier's stance is that of a plain-speaking witness of remarkable things in out-of-the-way places, a prototype of the new natural philosopher. But his notorious description of the natives of New Holland, which set the pattern for the entire orientation of European attitudes to both the land and its indigenous people, arises from a point of view as much attuned to medieval as to early modern thought. This was, after all, a time when sailors might still be apprehensive about falling off the edge of the world: 'Many were well pleased with the Voyage; but some thought, such was their Ignorance, that he [Captain Swan]

---

[1] *A New Voyage Round the World,* intro. by Albert Gray (London: Adam and Charles Black, 1937); and *A Voyage to New Holland*, ed. by James A. Williamson (London: Argonaut Press, 1939).

[2] 'The voyages that began to replace fiction with fact, speculation with experience, were those of Dampier [...].' W. T. James, 'Nostalgia for Paradise: *Terra Australis* in the Seventeenth Century', in *Australia and the European Imagination*, ed. by Ian Donaldson (Canberra: Australian National University, Humanities Research Centre, 1982), p. 81.

would carry them out of the World' (*A New Voyage*, pp. 191–92), says Dampier of his shipmates' anxiety about sailing from Mexico to the East Indies.

Scientifically and culturally, Dampier stands midway between medieval lore and modern empirical investigation. The authorial Prefaces of *A New Voyage* (*NV*) and *A Voyage to New Holland* (*VNH*) align them with the scientific aims and methodology of the Royal Society, which, in its instructions to travellers, had extended the daily recording of distance and bearing required of navigators in the Tudor period to a broader sphere of firsthand geographical, meteorological, and ethnographic reporting.[3] Intellectually, technologically, and imaginatively, however, the late seventeenth century was still connected with the Middle Ages and the Renaissance. Although the 'new' science had attempted to break with the medieval reverence for textual authority, by asserting the new authority of empirical observation, adhesions of the pre-modern remained in popular and high culture. Milton, for example, projected an epic on the Matter of Britain; Bunyan read *Beves of Hamtoun* as a child; Samuel Pepys had two chapbook versions of *Guy of Warwick*, and prose versions of other medieval romances remained in circulation. A list of the sights of London in 1611 has among its attractions Guy's sword and Merlin's cave.[4] And emerging doubts about its veracity notwithstanding, at least seven printings of *The Voyages & Travels of Sir John Mandevile, Knight* appeared between 1618 and 1696. Mandeville's tomb is mentioned with only a hint of scepticism about its authenticity in a letter to the *Philosophical Transactions* (1702–03) by a traveller to Liège: '[...] whose Epitaph is also at *St Albans* with us, which may be hard to be reconcil'd'.[5]

Dampier's construction of a first-person narrative persona might be read, simultaneously, as implicit commentary on medieval and Renaissance travel writing and as a more deliberate manoeuvre to take up the assumed superiority of firsthand observation over untested authority. In the case, for example, of the cannibalism widely reported by Mandeville, and accepted as true of the Caribs by Ralegh and other voyagers to the West Indies, Dampier is confident in the authority of his own experience — 'I speak as to the Compass of my own Knowledge' (*NV*, p. 325) — and refutes the claim altogether. The compass of Dampier's own knowledge does not extend so far in practice, however. Unlike the report by another member of his buccaneering company, Lionel Wafer, of his actual experiences with the natives of the Panama Isthmus,[6] Dampier's unsupported generalizations about the New

---

[3] See Mary Fuller, *Voyages in Print: English Travel to America, 1576–1624* (Cambridge: Cambridge University Press, 1995), pp. 2–7.

[4] See Margaret Spufford, *Small Books and Pleasant Histories* (Cambridge: Cambridge University Press, 1981), pp. 7–8, 224–37; Richard Altick, *The Shows of London* (Cambridge, MA: Belknap, 1978), pp. 7–8.

[5] 'An Extract of a Letter [...] Giving an Account of [...]. Sir Jo. Mandevil's Tomb at Leige[...]', *Philosophical Transactions*, 23 (1702–03), 1418.

[6] *New Voyage and Description of the Isthmus of America by Lionel Wafer*, ed. by L. E. Elliott Joyce (Oxford: Hakluyt Society, 1804).

Hollanders and their customs construct the racial Other at a remove, more in line with Mandeville than with the burgeoning interest in anthropology.[7] Contrary to his own statements of method and intent, Dampier's narratives reveal a slippage between medieval and modern modes of reporting.

Even as he dismisses medieval superstition and embraces the Royal Society's principles of travelogue, Dampier carries a detectable residue of the unpacked imaginary in his cultural baggage. He perpetuates, for example, ancient travel myths of zoological monstrosity. And although he represents himself as an eyewitness observer, there are occasions when, like Mandeville, he ventures into the realm of speculative possibility to recount that which he has been told rather than that which he has seen.[8] For example, he reports the existence in Brazil of 'the *Amphisboena*, or Two-headed Snake' (*VNH*, p. 53). This, he initially indicates, he has not seen but only heard about: 'Tis said to be blind, tho it has two small Specks in each Head like Eyes: But whether it sees or not I cannot tell' (*VNH*, p. 53). But then it seems that he has also seen one. He cannot, he says, vouch for its two heads, 'for one I had was cut short at one end' (p. 54). It is to be hoped he did not pay too much for his specimen. He repeats the Spanish view that the avocado 'inclines to lust' (*NV*, p. 144), and the natives of Central America claim that alligators' cods are the best remedy for ague. 'I would have tried it', he writes (*NV*, p. 178), but presumably the experiment was hampered by an unreliable supply of alligators.

Dampier's contemplation of the route from the Cape of Good Hope across the Indian Ocean to New Holland is coloured by elements of ancient cosmographical belief in a magnetic mountain in the sound between India and the Southern Continent, which drew ships built with iron nails to their destruction.[9] Mandeville had situated similarly treacherous magnetic rocks off Prester John's far-eastern island of Pentexoire:

> [...] where are many Rocks of a stone that is called Adamant, the which of his own kind draweth to him all manner of Iron, and therefore there may be no Ships that have iron nails pass, but it draweth them to it [...]. (Chapter 86) [10]

It may not be an entirely accidental formulation, given the location, that the Reverend Fletcher's account of Drake's voyage round the world, published in 1628, recounts how the *Golden Hind*, run aground on a rock just south of the Spice

---

[7] On this subject, see Margaret T. Hodgen, *Early Anthropology in the Sixteenth and Seventeenth Centuries* (Philadelphia: University of Pennsylvania Press, 1964).

[8] See, for example, Christian K. Zacher, *Curiosity and Pilgrimage* (Baltimore and London: Johns Hopkins University Press, 1976), pp. 143–44.

[9] See Rudolf Simek, *Heaven and Earth in the Middle Ages* (Woodbridge: Boydell, 1996), pp. 40, 138, n. 11.

[10] Quotations are from *The Voyages and Travels of Sir John Mandevile, Knight* (London, 1677).

Islands, was held fast in 'Adamantine bonds in a most narrow prison'.[11] Dampier echoes this kind of lore when he notes that ships keep foundering off the New Holland coast: 'the *Dutch* call that part of this Coast the Land of *Indraught,* (as if it magnetically drew Ships too fast to it)' (*NV*, p. 200).

Mandeville had implicitly embraced the role of *curiosus*.[12] Dampier explicitly claims, in a marginal note to the manuscript version of *NV (*BL Sloane 3236) but not in the final published version, that his impetus to travel was curiosity rather than profit: 'I came into these seas this second time more to Endulge my cureosity then to gett wealth' (fol. 128ʳ).[13] *Curiositas,* that 'morally excessive and suspect interest in observing the world, seeking novel experiences, or acquiring knowledge for its own sake',[14] had been considered inimical to the pursuit of Christian *sapientia* in the Middle Ages. Ranulf Higden's *Polychronicon,* for example, was critical of novelty- and profit-driven curious English travellers, who 'konneth betre wynne and gete newe than kepe her own heritage'.[15]

By the late seventeenth century, the negative connotations of 'curiosity' were being contested by the notion of curiosity as a beneficent spur to scientific knowledge. Thomas Herbert employed the term in the intrepid spirit of empirical investigation in *Some Years Travels* (London, 1677): 'In curiosity I put some of the wood into my mouth and chewed it [...] for half an hour my mouth was inflamed as if I had taken so much Vitriol' (p. 382). Nevertheless, although curiosity had become a virtue in 'scientific' circles, travel was an ambiguous scientific pursuit, and curiosity as its motivation retained its medieval sense as a reprehensible desire for novelty well into the seventeenth century. As Joseph Hall put it in *Quo vadis? A Censure of Trauell* (London, 1617):

> The priuate contentment of a mans owne heart in the view of forraine things, is but a better name of an humorous curiosity. If a man yeelde to runne after his appetite and his eye [...] after many idle excursions, [he] shall lie downe weary, but vnsatisfied. (pp. 20–21)

Such 'humorous curiosity' would, Hall declared, lead to nothing but the recounting of unreliable travellers' tales (p. 37). In the pseudo-confessional admission that his motivation was to 'indulge' his curiosity, Dampier implicates

---

[11] *The World Encompassed by Sir Francis Drake* (London: Hakluyt Society, 1854), p. 153.

[12] See Zacher, *Curiosity and Pilgrimage,* Chapter 6.

[13] On the manuscript and printed versions of *NV,* see Philip Edwards, *The Story of the Voyage: Sea-Narratives in Eighteenth-Century England* (Cambridge: Cambridge University Press, 1994), pp. 17–46; Glyndwr Williams, *The Great South Sea. English Voyages and Encounters 1570–1750* (New Haven: Yale University Press, 1997), pp. 112–14.

[14] Zacher, *Curiosity and Pilgrimage,* p. 4.

[15] *Polychronicon,* ed. by Churchill Babington, Rolls Series, 41 (London, Longmans Green, 1869), II, p. 169.

himself in the ranks of Hall's idle excursionists and underlines his borderline position between medieval and modern ways of measuring the world.

Renaissance voyages of discovery had uncovered the New World, but when Dampier sailed into the waters of New Holland he was entering a region — the Southern Continent or *Terra Australis Incognita*, that landmass stretching south of Africa across to South America — whose very existence had been debated in the Middle Ages and yet which, even after the voyages of Magellan and Drake, still persisted in the European imagination. One influential construction of the Southern Continent was the mid-sixteenth-century invention by Dieppe mapmakers of Java la Grande, a land southeast of Sumatra with a marginal resemblance to the north coast of Australia and furnished with neo-Sumatran images of lush vegetation, thatched houses, elephants, exotic birds, and cannibalistic *cynocephali* (dog-headed men).[16]

Seventeenth-century cosmographers typically allowed the world its four quarters: Europe, Asia, Africa, America. Some acknowledged a fifth: the South Land or *Terra Australis Incognita*. The new New World, in seventeenth-century literature, was frequently a utopian destination.[17] Richard Brome's *The Antipodes* (1638) construes a satirical Land of Cockayne. For some, *Terra Australis Incognita* held out a renewed prospect of the existence of the earthly paradise: in the early years of the seventeenth century, Ferdinand de Quirós thought that he had found such a place, which he named *Austrialia del Espiritu Santo*, in the islands now known as Vanuatu. By the century's end, classical, medieval, and Renaissance cartographical and geographical tradition still resonated in the concept of *Terra Australis Incognita*. Even though Magellan and Drake had disproved it once and for all, seventeenth-century geographers continued to point out the error of Augustine's doctrine of the uninhabited Antipodes[18] ('there is no reason to believe that such men exist [...]').[19] In some medieval maps deriving from the geographical theory of Macrobius, according to which the equatorial Torrid Zone was a ragingly hot and uninhabitable wasteland, the 'Antipodes' appear as a region at the bottom of the world, either uninhabited or occupied by monstrous races.[20] More's *Utopia* (1516) demonstrates a familiarity with that correlation between climatic zone and degrees of humanity:

---

[16] See Helen Wallis, 'Java la Grande: The Enigma of the Dieppe Maps', in *Terra Australis to Australia*, ed. by Glyndwr Williams and Alan Frost (Melbourne: Oxford University Press 1988), pp. 39–81.

[17] See, for example, James, 'Nostalgia for Paradise', pp. 59–85.

[18] For example, Nathanael Carpenter, *Geography Delineated Forth in Two Books* (Oxford, 1625), p. 230.

[19] Augustine, *The City of God Against the Pagans*, ed. and trans. by R. W. Dyson (Cambridge: Cambridge University Press, 1998), p. 710. On this debate, see Valerie Flint, 'Monsters and the Antipodes in the Early Middle Ages and Enlightenment', *Viator*, 15 (1984), 65–80; Simek, *Heaven and Earth*, pp. 48–55.

[20] See further, John Block Friedman, *The Monstrous Races in Medieval Art and Thought* (Cambridge, MA: Harvard University Press, 1981), pp. 39–50.

[...] under the equator and on both sides of the line nearly as far as the sun's orbit extends there lie waste deserts, scorched with continual heat. A gloomy and dismal region looms in all directions without cultivation or attractiveness, inhabited by wild beasts and snakes or, indeed, men no less savage and harmful than are the beasts. But when you have gone a little farther, the country gradually assumes a milder aspect, the climate is less fierce, the ground is covered with a pleasant green herbage, and the nature of living creatures becomes less wild.[21]

The classical notion of the vastness of the territory extending below Africa and America prevailed in Renaissance cartography, where the distinguishing characteristic of the southern hemisphere is that so much is overscaled. Maps from the second quarter of the sixteenth century consistently represent the unknown continent as in disproportionate size to North America. Mercator's world map of 1569, Ortelius's of 1570, and several others printed between 1502 and 1700 name an area of *Terra Australis* as *Psittacorum regio* ('Region of Parrots'): 'thus spoken of by the Portuguese', says the legend on Ortelius's map, 'on account of the incredible size of those birds there'.[22] The seventeenth-century Oxford geographer, Peter Heylyn, identifies the *Psittacorum terra* in the same location.[23] It is consistent with the elusive nature of antipodean evidence that the word 'incredible' should be set down so firmly. For a moment's reflection confirms that indeed, the southern hemisphere is inhabited by extremely large birds (emus and ostriches, condors, albatrosses and dodos) and in this instance, very large parrots. The Pacific Ocean itself is the vast unknown, the silent sea of Coleridge's ancient mariner and his equally extraordinary albatross.

Sixteenth- and seventeenth-century travel narratives, real and imaginary, maintained the assumption of the massive in and about *Terra Australis*. This was the zone of the oversized. Magellan's alleged giants of Patagonia were not dismissed as altogether fanciful by *The World Encompassed by Sir Francis Drake*: Magellan, it says, 'was not altogether deceived, in naming of them Giants; for they generally differ from the common sort of men, both in stature, bignesse, and strength of body' (p. 28). When Drake shoots an aggressive Patagonian, it is the narration that becomes overscaled; the characteristic Elizabethan hyperbole is itself the excess: 'his cry [...] was so hideous and horrible a roar, as if ten bulls had joined together'

---

[21] *The Complete Works of St. Thomas More*, ed. by Edward Surtz, S.J. and J. H. Hexter (New Haven: Yale University Press, 1965), IV, *Utopia*, Book I, p. 53: 5–11.

[22] For Ortelius's map, see *Terra Australis to Australis*, ed. by Williams and Frost, plates 1.5 and 1.6. 'The white-tailed black cockatoo is found only in Australia and is one of the largest parrots in the world [...] with a range extending for some 700km from Cape Leeuwin to north of Geraldton', Donald and Molly Trounson, *Australian Birds Simply Classified*, 4th edn (Frenchs Forest: David, 1998), p. 72.

[23] Peter Heylyn, *Cosmographie in Four Books, Containing the Chorographie and Historie of the Whole World* (London, 1666), p. 1091.

(p. 27). Abel Tasman reported what he took to be evidence of giants in Tasmania in 1642. His landing party

> [...] had seen two trees [...] which trees bore notches [...] forming a kind of steps to enable persons to get up the trees [...] fully 5 feet apart, so that our men concluded that the natives here must be of very tall stature, or must be in possession of some sort of artifice for getting up the said trees [...] So there can be no doubt there must be men here of extraordinary stature.[24]

The griffin-like 'bird-monsters' in Gabriel Foigny's *La Terre Australe connue* (1676; translated 1693), are beasts of an amazing and extraordinary size. They 'seemed to be a species of horse, but with a pointed head and clawed hooves [...] I believe they were feathered and had wings'.[25]

The distinctions between real and imaginary discovery narrative remained blurred in the early seventeenth century. Medieval fiction merges iconically with presumptive Renaissance fact by making no distinction in kind between the voyages of Mandeville and of Drake in the shared title page format of *The Voyages & Travels of Sir John Mandevile, Knight* [...] *Together with many and strange Marvels*[26] and *The Voyages & Travels Of that Renowned Captain, Sir Francis Drake* [...] *giving a perfect Relation of his Strange-Adventures* [...] *His Descriptions of Monsters, and Monstrous People* (1652). Attributed to his love for the royal lady, Eleanor, Mandeville's voyages were taken to an artful level of fiction and figured in the rhetoric of chivalric romance in Books 11 and 12 of William Warner's verse history, *Albions England* (1586), where they are interleaved with those of the sixteenth-century explorers, Stephen Borough, Chancellor, Jenkinson, and Willoughby. *Terra Australis Incognita* becomes a destination for knights errant in the second (1657) and subsequent editions of Heylyn's *Cosmographie* [...] *Containing the Chorographie and Historie of the Whole World* (although a large part of that world remained *Incognita*), a digest of universal history and geography first published in 1652, with a largely facetious *Appendix* [...] *Endeavouring a Discovery of the Unknown Parts of the World*. Here Heylyn devises an image of *Terra Australis Incognita* grounded in the metaphor of chivalry, as he proposes to undertake an imaginary voyage to the Southern Continent — 'And here we are upon a new and strange *adventure*, which no *Knight Errant* ever undertook before' (p. 1089) — the assumed location of the fantastic lands of utopian and chivalric literature, including the ship-wrecking Isle of Adamants in *Huon of Bordeaux*.

---

[24] *Sources of Australian History*, ed. by M. Clark (London: Oxford University Press, 1957), pp. 15, 17.

[25] Gabriel de Foigny, *The Southen Land, Known*, trans. by David Fausett (Syracuse: Syracuse University Press, 1993), pp. 28, 29.

[26] As printed in 1625, 1639, 1657, 1670, 1677, 1684, 1696.

Unlike Mandeville's travels in *Albions England*, however, the impetus for Heylyn's jocose voyage to *Terra Australis Incognita* is not love but material reward. Knightly ideals are replaced by the terminology of greed and privateering:

> Certain it is that here is a large field enough for Covetousness, Ambition, or desire of glory [...] enough to satisfie the greatest and most hungry appetite of Empire, Wealth, and Worldly pleasures; besides the *Gallantry* and merit of so brave an Action [...] I will try my fortune, and without troubling the Vice-Roys of *Peru*, and *Mexico*, or taking out *Commission* [in the mode of the privateer's Letter of Marque] for a new Discovery, will make a search into this *Terra Australis* [...]. (pp. 1091, 1093)

The real-life 'romance of navigation'[27] is driven by profit rather than honour. Its most successful English exponent is Francis Drake, 'that adventurous and valiant Worthy',[28] constructed in the popular imagination of the seventeenth century as an exemplary national hero — perhaps the last of the Matter of England — to rival Guy of Warwick.

The figuring of exploratory travel as chivalric narrative and the attempted re-inscription of Drake shape the framework of *NV*.[29] Seventeenth-century privateers — loose companies of mariners attached to commanders of their choice, licensed by the crown to attack enemy shipping, but often guilty of downright piracy — might themselves be seen as an unholy brotherhood of knights aberrant, for whom buccaneering is commensurate with *aventure*. 'It was', says Dampier early in the narrative, 'resolved to march by Land over the Isthmus of *Darien*, upon some new Adventures in the *South-Seas*' (*NV*, p. 8). He represents himself and his companions as hardy swashbucklers, 'all inured to hot Climates, hardened by many Fatigues, and in general, daring Men' (*NV*, p. 240). In narrative detail, though, *NV* is perhaps less 'on the verge of romance', as Albert Gray suggests (*NV*, p. xiii), and more a distorted reflection of it. Although the actions of the buccaneers constitute romance's familiar raw material of voyages to dangerous and exotic destinations, encounters with princes and potentates, and the fabulous wealth of distant kingdoms, its material rewards are never realized. A series of get-rich scenarios — fantasies of power and of a fortune in gold, cloves, and ambergris — are enacted only in conjecture. The most ambitious of these are, as he calls them, the 'Golden Dreams' of Peru, where he and his company could, he says, have mined gold and become lords of the coast, if only their captains had had the resolve (*NV*, p. 114).

---

[27] Jonathan Lamb, *Preserving the Self in the South Seas, 1680–1840* (Chicago: University of Chicago Press, 2001), Chapter 2.

[28] *Sir Francis Drake Revived* [...] (London, 1653), A3.

[29] On links between chivalric and exploration narrative from the fourteenth to the early seventeenth century, see Peter Burke, 'Chivalry in the New World', in *Chivalry in the Renaissance*, ed. by Sydney Anglo (Woodbridge: Boydell, 1990), pp. 253–262; Jennifer F. Goodman, *Chivalry and Exploration 1298–1630* (Woodbridge: Boydell, 1998).

Drake was prompted not by curiosity, or new discoveries, but by 'trade', or plunder, the profit motif in one guise or another; and by a passionate nationalistic Protestantism, the fervour of which is not to be underestimated either in his own case or in the construction of him as agent for a providential care for England — the Matter of England as new Writ. Discovery was not much of his concern; his quest was for new routes to known or reported riches. Dampier likewise is restrained about the novelty value of his travels, for in retracing Drake's route he seemed more intent on reliving that greatness. Dampier's actual returns were not Drake's horde but the supercargo of his own specimens and adventures.

The point of convergence for Mandeville, Drake, and Dampier — the place where the riches of the East met the glamour of chivalry, within the orbit of the legendary Java la Grande and at the furthest reach of Mandeville's geographic imagination — are the Spice Islands. Just off the northern coast of Java la Grande in Guillaume le Testu's *Cosmographie universelle* (1555) are the *Illes des grifons*. Hermann Moll's map in *VNH* of Dampier's track to New Britain shows a 'Bird Island', in a comparable location southeast of the Banda Isles, and which Dampier was unable to identify positively from his charts. What R. V. Tooley tentatively designates as 'the first printed map of Australia', a 1593 illustration of New Guinea and the Solomon Islands by the Dutch mapmaker Cornelius de Jode, shows a landmass with an archer, a griffin, a lion, and a serpent in its lower half.[30] The griffin is curious. It is consonant with a range of significance, particularly concerning the legendary wealth of *Terra Australis*. From as early as Persian times the griffin was a guardian of treasure. Mandeville saw 'Stories of Knights, and Battels' inscribed on the gold-plated walls of the magnificent palace of the king of Java (Chapter 56). The king of Ternate met Drake's envoys attired in gold and precious stones, and the *Golden Hind* departed loaded with tons of cloves. Here, where Drake and the Dutch sought untold treasures of spices and gold, the image of a griffin — widely used in European heraldry from the fifteenth century[31] — trampling a serpent on the standard of the sultan of Celebes prompted an admiring description from Dampier in which the blazon leaps into narrative life in the register of medieval romance:

> There was a large white Silk Flag at the Head of the Mast, edged round with a deep red for about two or three Inches broad, and in the middle there was neatly drawn a Green Griffon, trampling on a winged Serpent, that seemed to struggle to get up, and threatened his Adversary with open Mouth, and with a long Sting that was ready to be darted into his Legs. (*NV*, p. 306)

Coincidentally, a griffin tramples all over the mainsail of the woodcut on the title page of all the seventeenth-century printings of Mandeville. A griffin likewise

---

[30] R. V. Tooley, *The Mapping of Australia* (London: Holland Press, 1979), p. 55 and Plate 27.

[31] Goodman, *Chivalry and Exploration*, p. 76.

appears below the mainsail on the title page emblem of *Sir Francis Drake Revived* (1626). Here we read of it in the testimony of early modern investigative thought. Reading confirms experience; life imitates art. All that Dampier managed to acquire in the Spice Islands, however, despite a Quixotic scheme to repatriate a tattooed native, Jeoly — alleged to be the exiled and enslaved heir to a tiny gold- and clove-rich island off Mindanao — was a half-share in that 'painted prince' (*NV*, p. 347).

NV, reworked from the journal which he kept rolled up and sealed in a length of bamboo throughout his twelve-year buccaneering career, is an account of a *seriatim* circumnavigation of the globe. Dampier's later (1699) exploratory voyage to New Holland, sponsored by the admiralty and endorsed by the Royal Society, seemed to offer the prospect of a treasure haul on a par with Drake's and a landscape as idyllic as that reported by de Quirós and published in a petition to the King of Spain (translated 1617):

> It is a fat and a fertile land [...] The Country aboundeth in wood [...] there are spatious & goodly plaines [...] at the dawning of the day you shal heare from a wood [...] a sweet and various harmony of a thousand birdes of all sorts [...] no Fleas, Cater-pillers, or Gnats.[32]

Dampier refers to that expedition, in correspondence with the admiralty and in *VNH*, in terms that parallel Heylyn's aims for his knightly excursion to *Terra Australis Incognita*:

> [...] as there is no larger Tract of Land hitherto undiscovered yn ye *Terra Australia* [...] 'tis reasonable to conceive yt so great a part of the World is not without very valluable commodities to incourage ye Discovery [...]'. (undated letter to the Admiralty)

> This large and hitherto almost unknown Tract of Land is situated so very advantageously in the richest Climates of the World, the *Torrid* and *Temperate Zones*; having in it especially all the Advantages of the *Torrid Zone*, as being known to reach from the *Equator* [...] that in coasting round it [...] I could not but hope to meet with some fruitful Lands, Continent or Islands, or both, productive of any of the rich Fruits, Drugs, or Spices, (perhaps Minerals also, &c.) that are in the other Parts of the *Torrid Zone*, under equal Parallels of Latitude. (*VNH*, p. 122)

These buoyant expectations were, however, to be utterly deflated. The apparent unseaworthiness of Dampier's ship (the *Roebuck*) and the frustratingly unremitting unproductivity of the promising interface between the Torrid and Temperate Zones — 'among so many Islands, we might have found some Sort of rich Mineral, or Ambergreece, it being a good Latitude for both these' (*VNH*, p. 96), he writes of the rocky Dampier Archipelago, off the Pilbara coast of Western Australia — prompted him to curtail exploration southeast of New Guinea and head back to England. Some

---

[32] Ferdinand de Qvir, *Terra Australis Incognita* (Amsterdam: Da Capo Press, 1970), pp. 11, 15, 17, 22.

two hundred and seventy years later, the port of Dampier was to be established in that same latitude, to ship the heavily magnetic iron ore riches from the Pilbara. What Dampier encountered on both his visits to that stretch of *Terra Australis* that the Dutch had named New Holland was not the promised land but something more akin to earlier traditions of the desolate Torrid Zone.

Traces of the medieval notion of the uninhabitable Antipodes — or inhabited only by debased and monstrous people — shaped Dampier's response to a forlorn and dismal coast, north of the Tropic of Capricorn, on his first visit. The bays of present-day King Sound and the tip of the peninsula between Broome and Derby proved a barren and inaccessible landscape, with no groundwater found, where fish were scarce, the grass was thin, and the disappointing trees had no fruit or berries. This is a landscape described entirely in negative or negating terms, a landscape to be avoided. It is, predominantly, a 'land of flies' — the very antithesis of de Quirós's gnat-free, paradisical *Austrialia del Espiritu Santo* — 'they being so troublesome here, that no fanning will keep them from coming to one's Face; and without the Assistance of both Hands to keep them of, they will creep into ones Nostrils; and Mouth too, if the Lips are not shut very close' (*NV*, p. 312). Animal life is otherwise evident only *in absentia*: — as it was for Tasman in Tasmania ('they had observed certain footprints of animals, not unlike those of a tiger's claws', he reports).[33] So Dampier testifies: 'We saw no sort of Animal, nor any Track of Beast, but once' (*NV*, p. 312). The nature of evidence itself, in this exceptional quarter of the world, is marked not just by the exaggerated and the monstrous but, as it were, by the negative monstrous. Just as *Terra Australis Incognita* is an idea affirmed by its evasiveness, a myth disclosed by geographical incursions that proved nothing, so the absence of presence seemed to confirm mythical reality. The incredible is, as it turns out, the true manifest.

This is perhaps what *terra nullius* comes to mean, that it resists being known. The people of this place fitted no acknowledged ethnographic scale; they eluded the measure of humankind that the seventeenth century inherited from the Middle Ages and the Renaissance.[34] They wanted nothing that Dampier had to offer, dismissed him with '*Pooh, Pooh, Pooh*' (*VNH*, p. 102) and went away. When, a century later, English ships reached the east coast of New Holland, the natives paid no heed; and in turn, disappeared from the pages of white Australian history. The New Hollanders, being inscrutable, became invisible to the European gaze. In that resistance, *terra nullius* may ultimately be identified as a medieval signature.

Such animal life forms as were actually encountered on Dampier's second visit to New Holland, an approximately fifteen-hundred-kilometre coastal trip from Shark Bay to Broome, are grotesque. The bobtail lizard — rank, frightening, ugly — has

---

[33] Clark, *Sources of Australian History*, p. 16.

[34] See Hodgen, *Early Anthropology*, pp. 358–82.

(shades of the fabled Amphisbaena!) what at first appears to be a head at each end and, with extended antipodean perversity, four forelegs:

> [...] they had a Stump of a Tail, which appeared like another Head; but not really such, being without Mouth or Eyes: Yet this Creature seem'd, by this Means, to have a Head at each End; and [...] the legs, also, seemed all four of them to be forelegs, being all alike in shape and length, and seemingly the joints and bendings to be made as if they were to go indifferently either head or tail foremost. They were speckled black and yellow like toads, and had scales or knobs on their backs like those of crocodiles [...] the Body when opened hath a very unsavory Smell. I did never see such ugly Creatures any where but here. (*VNH*, p. 86).

For the extraordinarily omnivorous Dampier, the lizard's monstrousness is ultimately defined by its unpalatability:

> Tho' I have eaten of Snakes, Crocodiles and Allegators, and many Creatures that look frightfully enough [...] yet I think my Stomach would scarce have serv'd to venture upon these *N. Holland* Guano's, both the Looks and the Smell of them being so offensive.

There is evidence of unnervingly oversized animal life, too: the unidentifiable tracks that he saw in *NV* were 'as big as [those of] a great Mastiff dog' (p. 312). On the second voyage, the contents of a shark's maw, almost certainly a dugong, are identified as the remnants of a 'Hippopotomus' (*VNH*, p. 87). The blatant question-ability of this assertion is unparalleled in Dampier's writing. He refers to the dugong in *NV* as the 'manatee' or 'Sea-Cow' (p. 32) and says he has seen it in New Holland. The two descriptions of the hippopotamus in his *Voyages to Campeachy* (1699) are carefully differentiated from his account of the manatee.[35] Dampier can be assumed to know the difference between a hippopotamus and a dugong. It appears, then, that while he might have been surprised at what was inside the shark, he was not totally surprised to find such evidence in this part of the world. After all, the maps of Java la Grande had been populated with large and intercontinental fauna,[36] and otherwise accurate mappings of New Holland, like Danckerts's of 1690 and Coronelli's of 1696, had shown elephants rampaging around Kakadu.[37] Dampier appears here to be attempting to convey his sense of both the fabulous bigness and monstrousness of the southern latitudes.

Couched, like the rest of his account of New Holland in *NV*, almost entirely in negative rhetoric, the hyperbole and allegations of behavioural eccentricity in the famous description of its natives betray traces of medieval concepts of the antipodes. Lacking the civilized attributes of houses, boats, clothes, fishing tackle and religion,

---

[35] *Dampier's Voyages*, ed. by John Masefield (London: Richards, 1906), II, 203.

[36] See Wilma George, *Animals and Maps* (London: Secker and Warburg, 1969), pp. 175–78.

[37] Tooley, *The Mapping of Australia*, Plates 135 and 136.

the full-fledged humanity of these 'poor Creatures' (pp. 314, 315, 316) — 'the miserablest People in the World' (p. 312) — seems, like that of the people of Tarkonet in Mandeville's *Voyages and Travels*, 'where all men are as Beasts, for they are unreasonable, and they dwell in Caves, for they have not Wit to make Houses' (Chapter 60), open to doubt. Setting aside their 'Humane Shape', says Dampier, they 'differ but little from Brutes'. Their custom of half-closing their eyes to keep out the flies —

> they being so troublesome here [...] that from their Infancy being thus annoyed with these Insects, they do never open their Eyes as other People: And therefore they cannot see far, unless they hold up their Heads, as if they were looking at somewhat over them — (*NV*, p. 312)

which, it is implied, induces near blindness ('they had such bad Eyes, that they could not see us till we came close to them', *NV*, p. 316), is the sort of behavioural aberrance which, as much as physical deformity, categorizes the monstrous races.[38] In what reads like a rare glimmer of rhetorical wit, Dampier reverses the monstrous roles to figure himself and his company, in the view of the New Hollanders, as fearsome cannibals: 'Some of the Women, and such People as could not go from us, lay still by a Fire, making a doleful noise, as if we had been coming to devour them' (*NV*, pp. 314–15).

Some of Dampier's reported customs of the people of New Holland are no more than unsupported generalizations in the Mandevillian mode. The sensational claim that their eyes are never fully open from infancy, for example, sits oddly with his insistent indifference to other potentially immediately verifiable practices, such as the explanation for their missing front teeth ('whether they draw them out, I know not', *NV*, p. 313), marriage customs ('[w]hether they cohabit one Man to one Woman, or promiscuously, I know not', *NV*, p. 313), and method of making fire ('How they get their Fire I know not', *NV*, p. 314). His revulsion makes him unlikely to have been witness to their gustatory habits, which he relates with a tinge of sentiment at odds with the otherwise disparaging tone of this account and his studiously objective reportage elsewhere: 'be it little or much that they get, every one has his part, as well the young and tender, the old and feeble, who are not able to go abroad, as the strong and lusty' (*NV*, pp. 314–15). Dampier's uncharacteristic syntactical balancing here is reminiscent of the repetition and antithesis which often underline the recitation of strange customs in Mandeville's *Voyages and Travels*, as, for example, in Lamory (Sumatra), where

> [...] there is no woman married, but women are all common there [...]. Also the land is all common [...] for that one man hath now this year, another man hath the next year [...] And thither do Marchants bring children for to sell, and those that are fat they eat, but those that be lean they keep till they be fat [...]. (Chapter 60)

---

[38] See Friedman, *The Monstrous Races*, p. 1; *Simek, Heaven and Earth*, p. 93.

Clearly embellished for the published version of *NV*, this is essentially 'bookish' monstrousness. The flies, the half-closed eyelids, speculation about 'promiscuity', and a comparison with the Hottentots ('The *Hodmadods* [...] though a nasty People, yet for Wealth are Gentlemen to these', p. 312) are absent from the manuscript. In declaring the inhabitants of New Holland inferior even to the Hottentots, whom other writers in the late seventeenth century had relegated to the bottom of the racial ladder — 'the Most beastlike of all the Souls of Men with whom our Travellers are well acquainted', according to William Petty (1623–87);[39] 'the very Reverse of Human Kind [...] if there is any medium between a Rational animal and a Beast, the Hotantot lays fairest claim to the Species', in the opinion of John Ovington (1696)[40] — Dampier puts them and their blighted landscape at a further remove from human civilization, indeed from humanity itself, and propels them into the ranks of the monstrous races.

Medieval notions of racial monstrousness extended into the Enlightenment. Linnaeus classified the Hottentots — along with Patagonians (the natives of New Holland are absent from his ethnographical classification) — as a species of *Homo monstrosus* in his *System of Nature* (1735), subscribing, as Margaret Hodgen remarks, 'to the reality of fabulous, monstrous men. He was subservient to un-examined medieval ideas'.[41] Without opening it up to formal inspection, Dampier, too, carries the baggage of medieval thought in his report of New Holland and its non-people.

In so comprehensively dispelling the seventeenth century's utopian imaginings of *Terra Australis* after the high hopes of his second trip, Dampier surrendered any prospect of fame or fortune through his attempted romance of navigation. 'His voyage to New Holland [...] has no great matter of new discovery', say the Church-ills of *VNH* in 1704.[42] And, with supreme irony, the very negativity of his account seems to have made it, at least to one writer, as suspect as the travellers' tales of monstrous men and exotic wonders which Heylyn had derided in his *Cosmographie*. In Edmund Bohun's revised version of the *Cosmographe* [...] *Improv'd. with an Historical Continuation to the Present Time* (1702), the west coast of New Holland appears, accurately drawn, on one of five new maps, but although prefaced by a new *Advertisement to the Reader*, Heylyn's *Appendix* remains unchanged. Despite the favourable reception of *NV*, the voyages of Dampier are not acknowledged there. Negative reports of the 'South Continent' were, in Bohun's opinion, merely the product of mercantile rivalry:

---

[39] Cited Hodgen, *Early Anthropology*, p. 422.

[40] Cited Hodgen, *Early Anthropology*, p. 422.

[41] *Early Anthropology*, pp. 426; 430, n. 49.

[42] 'The Whole History of Navigation', in *The Works of John Locke* (London: Tegg, 1923), vol. 10, p. 50.

Thus the *Dutch East-India* Company having found [...] the parts of the South Continent over against the Islands of the *East-Indies*, would never suffer [...] them to be any further discovered or discoursed of, for fear the States of *Holland* should Erect a new Company [...] and take from them some part of their profit: And the same humour without doubt possessed our *East-India* and *African* Companys, and kept from endeavouring a perfect discovery of this South Continent, and also from giving any good account of that which they Accidentally met with. (p. 1126)

It was to be seventy years before Cook and Banks were to view the natives of the east coast of 'New Holland,' with preconceptions filtered through the quasi-medieval mindset of Dampier, and almost another two hundred after that before the humanity of the Aborigines was to become a legal fact in the Commonwealth of Australia.

Rebuilding the Middle Ages: Medievalism in Australian Architecture

SARAH RANDLES

In 1995, *HQ Magazine*, a popular, glossy magazine, published an article on the Sydney branch of the medieval recreation group, the Society for Creative Anachronism (SCA).[1] Photographs accompanying the article portrayed members of the society, dressed in medieval costumes, posed against a backdrop of the nineteenth-century Gothic Revival buildings of the University of Sydney's main quadrangle.[2] Clearly the recreationists and the *HQ Magazine* photographer felt that the sandstone buildings with their crenellations, cloisters and gargoyles were an appropriate setting for the SCA's performative medievalism.

Australian interpretations of the European Middle Ages, whether inbuilt, material form, or performed in other ways, are separated from their source material by hundreds of years and thousands of miles. Yet medievalism — the imitation, reproduction or evocation of the European Middle Ages — is a prevalent theme in the Australian built environment, evident in many of our most prominent and venerable buildings, whether they are designed for public, commercial, institutional or residential use. In a landscape sometimes strikingly dissimilar from Europe in its climate and topography, there is no scarcity of examples of medieval structural forms, as well as buildings not necessarily medieval in overall design or structure but decorated with spires and turrets, mullions and crenellations, gargoyles and grotesques, stained glass and carved stone, all evoking the distant European past.

[1] I am grateful to the archivists at St Mary's Cathedral Archives, the University of Sydney Archives and the ANZ Group Archives for their assistance in locating primary source material for this paper. I am also indebted to Sigmund Jorgensen for taking the time to answer my questions about the history of Montsalvat, and to Dr Victoria Emery for providing transport and accommodation during my research trip to Melbourne.

[2] 'They Love the Knight Life', *HQ Magazine* (Sept/Oct, 1995), pp. 60–65.

Although Australia's indigenous history stretches back thousands of years, the oldest buildings of the European settlement are scarcely more than two hundred years old, yet they are a much more visible and tangible version of an historical past for many Australians.

While the SCA deliberately sets out to recreate an idealized and sanitized version of the Middle Ages, the relationship between the medievalism of Australian buildings and the medieval past is rarely articulated with such a high level of self-consciousness. None of the buildings discussed in this essay was built in a deliberate attempt to recreate a medieval building. Nor were they designed as sites for performative medievalism, although some have been used for this purpose. Rather, medieval architecture has been used as a source from which the designers borrow, sometimes systematically, sometimes less so, in order to evoke particular associations. This medieval idiom often becomes symbolic of such conservative qualities as continuity, stability, wealth, religious authority, and tradition, but it also has the potential to highlight points of difference between emerging Australian institutions and the traditions from which they were derived. To interpret the functions of medievalism in Australian architecture, it is necessary to position these buildings firmly in their historical and social contexts.

The time period covered by the buildings in this essay coincides with the progression of Australia from precarious convict settlement through the prosperity of the later colonial era, to the post-Federation and Depression eras. Accordingly, medievalism in Australian architecture covers a range of styles. The earliest buildings in the Australian colonies to incorporate medieval features, from around 1800, were those in the Gothick style. Gothick architecture was essentially Romantic, concerned more with borrowing individual elements such as pointed windows or decorated stonework from medieval sources than with structural forms or aesthetic principles.[3] From the 1840s in Australia, Gothick gave way to the Gothic Revival (also known as nineteenth-century Gothic, or simply Gothic), a style based on closer examination of medieval models, and a concern for authenticity in overall design.[4] Medievalism also persisted in Australian architecture beyond the decline of the Gothic Revival, giving rise to features less easily classified, but still referring to the medieval in recognizable ways.

In some ways the use of medieval idiom in Australian buildings is hardly surprising: Australia's colonies were founded and developed at a time when first the Gothick, and later the Gothic Revival were the fashionable forms of architecture, and these spread with British colonization to the furthest reaches of the Empire. But these were not the only choices for building styles, and Australian medievalism

---

[3] Joan Kerr and James Broadbent, *Gothick Taste in the Colony of New South Wales* (Sydney: David Ells Press, in association with the Elizabeth Bay House Trust, 1980), p. 8.

[4] Brian Andrews, *Australian Gothic: The Gothic Revival in Australian Architecture from the 1840s to the 1950s* (Melbourne: Miegunyah Press and Melbourne University Press, 2001), p. 7.

differs in significant ways from British medievalism, though it has its roots in the same traditions, and was sometimes adopted for similar reasons. Australian medievalist buildings are rarely replicas of medieval buildings; it is also rare for an Australian building to copy an eighteenth- or nineteenth-century medievalist design. Even when European designs were re-used in Australian contexts, they were often subtly modified to fit the situation, climate, materials and especially the purpose of their new settings. The physical settings of these structures, and the social, demographic and cultural concerns of the communities for which they were built make it impossible to interpret Australian medievalist buildings in the same way as British ones.

Nor were the ideologies that underpinned the design of neo-medieval buildings in Australia the same as those influencing similar buildings in England and in America, for example. The demographics and institutions of the new country differed markedly from the old, and the colonial builders and designers were conscious both of the traditions to which they considered themselves heirs and of the emerging positions of the colonies in the British Empire. Later designers show a greater sensitivity to the local environment, and their buildings come to reflect elements of Australian identity and emerging nationhood.

This essay examines the motivations for and the effects of choosing medievalism as a stylistic idiom in Australian buildings, highlighting the way these motivations and effects, purpose, and reception have changed over time. I will focus on the medievalism of four Australian buildings, using them as representative case studies: St Mary's Catholic Cathedral in Sydney; the main buildings of the University of Sydney; the ANZ Bank at the corner of Queen and Collins Streets in Melbourne; and the various buildings of the artists' colony of Montsalvat at Eltham in Victoria.[5] These buildings are well known to Australians, and feature significantly in the popular imagination as 'medieval'. Each of them is in fact a collection of buildings, constructed over time, sometimes supplanting earlier versions, sometimes accumulating additional structures, and sometimes absorbing other buildings intended for different purposes. Together they span a long period of Australian architecture, starting with the Gothick in the 1820s and progressing through the various stages of the Victorian Gothic Revival, and beyond. As a group they also represent a range of public and private, religious and secular, commercial and residential uses. Each is still used primarily for the purpose for which it was built and each has been listed with either a state or national heritage body, indicating their significance to the history of Australian architecture. Each of these buildings is, however, an individual creation, and although some of them contain elements representative of particular styles, purposes or chronological periods, or have had a lasting influence on the architectural styles used subsequently for buildings of a

---

[5] The earliest of the St Mary's churches is treated by Kerr and Broadbent; Andrews provides brief discussions of St Mary's Cathedral and the ANZ Bank.

similar purpose, each also occupies a unique position in the history of Australian architecture.

St Mary's Cathedral

St Mary's Cathedral as it exists today is not the first version of that building to stand on its present site. In 1820 Father Joseph Therry, the first Catholic priest to be legally appointed in the colony of New South Wales, began to raise funds for a Catholic chapel in Sydney. The chapel was to cater for the Catholic population of the colony: about half of these were convicts, and the rest, with very few exceptions, were ex-convict 'ticket-of-leave' men and women.[6] They were nearly all Irish, and nearly all poor. Therry was given financial and moral support by Governor Lachlan Macquarie, a fact which was to be crucial in the development of St Mary's, particularly when we remember that Catholicism was viewed with a great deal of suspicion by the English authorities at the time. On 29 October 1821 Governor Macquarie laid the foundation stone of the church, at the site at the north-eastern corner of Hyde Park where the present cathedral stands. Although this is now one of Sydney's more commanding sites, at the time the land was granted to the church it was on the margins of the township.

The size and the form of the church were matters for contention. Originally the convict architect Francis Greenway was employed to design the church, and a pencil and ink sketch from 1821 shows his design for a simple, box-like form in Gothick style, with pointed window arches and small crenellated turrets.[7] Greenway worked on the assumption that it would be best to build a simple building that could be added to later as money allowed. Father Therry, however, had a much grander plan. He had always envisaged that the church would eventually be a cathedral, as his sketch, entitled 'rough outline of intended cathedral', indicates.[8] Therry had no architectural training, but made up for it with a great deal of enthusiasm, particularly for pointed windows, and a desire that the cathedral should be, above all, as large as possible. In 1821 the total population of Sydney and its surrounding districts was only 12,079[9] and Greenway is recorded as saying that 'any one must be mad who would suppose that the Catholics of Sydney would require such a large building for the next hundred years at least'.[10]

---

[6] R. W. Harden, 'Old St Mary's 1821–1865', in *St Mary's Cathedral, Sydney, 1821–1971*, ed. by Patrick O'Farrell (Sydney: Devonshire Press, 1971), p. 1.

[7] Kerr and Broadbent, *Gothick Taste*, pp. 56–57.

[8] Kerr and Broadbent, *Gothick Taste*, pp. 56–57.

[9] Cited by J. P. McGuanne, *Old St Mary's, Sydney* (Sydney: Ford, 1915), p. 6.

[10] Columbus Fitzpatrick in 1865, quoted by O'Farrell, *St Mary's Cathedral*, p. 39.

Greenway resigned as architect in 1823, and although some elements of his design survived, it was Therry's cruciform design that was eventually built — a large stone building, recognizably medieval in structure, with pointed windows and crenellated turrets. By 1840 Therry's confidence was vindicated, and St Mary's was already overcrowded.[11]

In 1835 the church became a cathedral with the arrival of Bishop John Bede Polding. Polding made it a priority to make the church into a building worthy of its new status, and asked A. W. N. Pugin, the celebrated Gothic Revival architect, to provide designs for extensions to Therry's building. Pugin designed a costly and ornate structure, complete with stone carvings, a slate roof, stained glass windows and a temporary bell-tower to house the cathedral's bells.

On 29 June 1865, Therry's church and Polding's extensions were destroyed by fire. The cathedral was uninsured, and so once again money had to be raised for its replacement. This time Polding engaged the architect William Wilkinson Wardell, who had already gained a substantial reputation for his Gothic Revival designs in England before emigrating to Australia in 1858. Wardell lived and worked in Melbourne, and the latest version of St Mary's, like its predecessor, was designed from a distance.[12] Wardell was not constrained as Pugin had been by any previously existing building, and he designed a pure Gothic Revival building, combining elements of French and English medieval churches, especially from Chartres cathedral.[13] The St Mary's Cathedral website claims it to be 'the last Gothic Cathedral to be built in the world'.[14]

The cost of the new cathedral was to be enormous, as Wardell had warned Polding,[15] and would be the subject of a great deal of criticism, a recurring theme in the building of Gothic Revival buildings in Australia, since the Gothic style was necessarily expensive. Polding set forth his reasons for building in such a costly medieval style:

> A building is to be completed, which shall express to all beholders the store that the men of Australia set upon a due outward expression of their religion. The works of God in the material world, show forth something of His eternal majesty and wisdom: the works of human art and science, in their application to the building and ornament of principal churches, must be taken, are naturally taken, to express our ideas of the nobleness and dignity of the faith which is to lead men's souls back again to God.

---

[11] Kerr and Broadbent, *Gothick Taste*, p. 125.

[12] Cash, *As Perfect as Possible: The Gothic Bank of Collins Street* (Melbourne: Historic Buildings Council, Victoria, 1989), p. 7.

[13] O'Farrell, *St Mary's Cathedral,* p. 74.

[14] http://www.sydney.catholic.org.au/html/stmarycathedral/getmarried.htm, accessed 17 May 2001.

[15] Ursula M. de Jong, *William Wilkinson Wardell: His Life and Work: 1823–1899* (Clayton: Monash University, 1984), p. 45. The projected cost was more than £300,000.

[...] It is a stately protest against the practice of the world in dedicating everything that is costly, and spacious and exquisite, to the service of Mammon, or to the gratification of luxury.[16]

Wardell's approach to cost can be seen in the similar advice he gave to the council of St John's College at the University of Sydney:

> You are about to build not for this generation only, nor for the next, but for those who will exist in centuries yet far removed from us; and you have with an admirable zeal proposed a work which will vie with the noblest of those edifices that bless and grace the soil of the old countries — But at present your means do not correspond to the full extent of your wishes. [...] What you do now do well — even if the funds at your immediate disposal require it to be less in quantity than your generosity intended.[17]

The advice was also applied to St Mary's Cathedral. Building was periodically suspended while further funds were raised, and it was not until 2000 that the spires designed by Wardell were completed, enabled by a matching five million dollar grant from the New South Wales state government and accompanied by spirited public debate.[18]

Fig. 2. Old St Mary's Cathedral: Lithograph by Robert Russell, 1836.

---

[16] Pastoral letter of Archbishop Polding, Feast of St Joseph, 1862, quoted in O'Farrell, *St Mary's Cathedral*, p. 105.

[17] De Jong, *William Wilkinson Wardell*, p. 31.

[18] *Sydney Morning Herald*, 27 November 1996, p. 5; 24 April 2000; 23 June 2000 and letters pages around these dates.

Father Therry and Bishop Polding each had a vision for a thriving Catholic community, large enough to warrant a cathedral, and occupying a position of status within the colony. Building a large, Gothic cathedral (or, rather, several of them) not only reflected their vision, but also helped to realize it. As the medieval idiom of all the versions of St Mary's provided a link to the past, it also evoked the sense of an unbroken religious tradition, while the opulence and cost of the buildings helped to give Catholicism a position in the mainstream of Australian society very different from that which it had occupied in Britain. C. J. Duffy was later to write:

> From the beginning, Australian Catholic Church buildings proclaimed a challenge which was an irritant to the society of the time: Their apparent presumption was all the more offensive because of their evident appeal to the Catholic people. These people were a minority of inferior social and economic status, yet in their choice of location and grandiose design of their churches they sought to overshadow any rivals. They wrote their message plainly enough on the horizon for all to see that their inferiority in the lands from which they had come was to be a thing of the past.[19]

St Mary's can also be read as part of the Irish struggle against British colonialism, even as it participated in the colonization of the new country. Pugin was explicit about the colonizing purpose of his designs for Australian churches; colonizing, in this case, not for Britain, but for Catholicism:

> more than one Bishop has departed across the ocean to the antipodes, carrying the seeds of Christian design to grow and flourish in the New World, and soon the solemn chancels and cross-crowned spires will arise, the last object which the mariner will behold on the shores of the Pacific till their venerable originals greet his glad view on England's shores.[20]

This colonization was not limited to religion, however. Old St Mary's was depicted in a lithograph in 1836 [see Fig. 2]. No other building of comparable size is visible, and the small, simple buildings in the foreground — the school and the presbytery — provide a marked contrast. The group of Aboriginal people in the foreground gives the only indication that the church is in Australia, rather than a remote part of Britain. Dressed in European clothing, but barefoot, and with one of them carrying a long spear, they look away from the church towards the viewer. The picture provides a graphic representation of colonization: the indigenous owners of the land have been dispossessed and supplanted by a culture whose buildings embody the past of another country.

St Mary's Cathedral in its various incarnations highlights a number of significant aspects of the use of medievalism in Australia. In the early days of the penal settlement, it represented a form of colonialism in which the indigenous past was

---

[19] C. J. Duffy, 'The Ethos of St. Mary's', in O'Farrell, *St Mary's Cathedral*, p. 39.

[20] A. W. N. Pugin, 'Catholic Church Architecture', Letter to the Editor, *Tablet*, vol. 9, no. 435, 2 September 1848, p. 563, quoted Andrews, *Australian Gothic*, p. 69.

literally displaced by the past of the colonizing country, in an attempt to provide continuity with selected traditions. It also represented a hope for a portion of the community which had itself also been forcibly displaced and dispossessed, that in the new country it might transcend poverty and marginalization to occupy a position of wealth, power and status. This came to pass as the cathedral grew in size and grandeur, and St Mary's Cathedral itself set a standard to which other churches, both Protestant and Catholic, could aspire.

The University of Sydney

Similar themes of costliness, desire for grandeur, appeals to tradition and colonialism can be found in the secular neo-medieval buildings of the University of Sydney, the first university in Australia. The choice of Gothic Revival style was not a foregone conclusion, however. The building committee was initially motivated by pragmatism, suggesting in its report of November 1853, an Elizabethan style of architecture for two reasons:

> 1st. From the peculiarity of this Style of Architecture, inasmuch as a Building constructed in accordance with it admits of indefinite extension without impairing its general effect as a whole.

> 2nd. That for the Buildings in this Style bricks may be employed, stone being alone used for the Mullions [...] and circumstances of great importance, stone being only procurable at a distance from the site of the proposed buildings; whereas the clay soil of which it consists is peculiarly well adapted for Brick.

On 28 April 1854, the senate of the university wrote to Edmund Thomas Blacket, the Colonial Architect, informing him of their decision regarding the style of the buildings, and requesting that he undertake the commission to design them.[21] But Blacket had his own ideas about a suitable style for the new university, less constrained by practicality than those of the building committee. In the university archives is an undated page of notes in Blacket's hand, possibly a draft for a speech:

> In building an University therefore, in the 19th Century, one has a difficulty at the outset which never troubled the founders of those ancient seats of learning which it is our ambition to imitate. We have to determine which of all architectural styles shall be taken, whether in fact the new Building shall be Gothic or Roman or Greek, a strange question to arise, certainly, but still requiring an answer.

> In this perplexity it is gratifying to consider that there is one great peculiarity that overrides all others — that leaves the question of Architectural beauty or comparative perfection untouched — that avoids the real or supposed requirements of the climate of the colony — that evades all objections & defies all contradictions — I mean the

---

[21] University of Sydney Archives, Blacket Papers.

fitness of association — It is impossible for an Englishman to think of an University without thinking of Mediaeval Architecture — We cannot entertain the most visionary idea of study or learning without associating in some way or other the forms and peculiarities of the Gothic Style.[22]

Blacket originally agreed with the senate's desire that he build in bricks made from the clay available on the university site, but he later discovered these bricks would be too light in colour to provide the contrast with the stone he thought necessary to the Elizabethan style.[23]

The senate accepted Blacket's recommendation, and his revised estimate of £148,000, more than £18,000 above his estimate for the cost of building in brick.[24] In the light of Blacket's undated notes and known fondness for the medieval style, it seems at least possible that he had intended to build in the earlier style from the beginning.

In choosing a Gothic Revival style for its buildings, Blacket and the senate of the university were deliberately evoking an association between the new university and the medieval universities of Oxford and Cambridge. The associative relationship is explicit in the university's motto: *sidere mens eadem mutato* ('the constellations having changed, the mind remains the same'), and the coat of arms, an amalgam of elements of those of Oxford and Cambridge. Blacket's Great Hall features two windows depicting the founders of the Oxford and Cambridge colleges, and the university's arms are displayed in stonework amongst those of other British and European universities.

Several aspects of the university buildings were borrowed with little modification from existing English buildings, particularly the roof of the Great Hall that was modelled self-consciously on Westminster Hall, 'down — or up — to the angels'.[25] Joan Kerr has demonstrated that Blacket relied heavily in his plans for the Sydney University buildings on design books featuring detailed drawings of elements of medieval architecture.[26] In 1925, Leslie Wilkinson, the university architect, modelled the western face of the western tower of the main quadrangle on the entry to Jesus College, Cambridge.[27] The buildings were modified in one important respect, however. From its beginning, the University of Sydney was intended to be a 'non-sectarian [...] teaching institution, founded and endowed by the State to impart

---

[22] University of Sydney Archives, Blacket Papers.

[23] University of Sydney Archives, Letters Received 1851–55, Blacket to Registrar, 17 January 1855.

[24] Clifford Turney, Ursula Bygott and Peter Chippendale, *Australia's First: A History of the University of Sydney, Volume 1 1850–1939* (Sydney: Hale and Iremonger, 1991), p. 102.

[25] Bertha McKenzie, *Stained Glass and Stone: The Gothic Buildings of the University of Sydney* (Sydney: University of Sydney, 1989), p. 29.

[26] *University of Sydney News*, 29 September 1981, p. 203.

[27] McKenzie, *Stained Glass and Stone*, p. 137.

secular instruction [...]'[28], and consequently the religious imagery of its predecessors and model was removed or replaced with secular references. The side windows in the Great Hall depict not saints but British luminaries of the Arts and Sciences throughout history, and the angels on the ceiling serve no religious function, but are used to represent the medieval trivium and quadrivium. On the outside of the main quadrangle there are a number of empty niches in the stonework, faithfully copying those designed for statues of saints in the medieval buildings, though remaining unfilled in this secular context.

Like St Mary's Cathedral, the main buildings at Sydney University represented a wider vision for the colony of New South Wales as well as for the university community. Blacket's desire for grand-scale Gothic buildings was matched by Sir Charles Nicholson's sense as provost of the university that it should be 'an ancient and influential symbol of the established order'.[29] F. L. C. Merewether, an original fellow of the senate and subsequently vice-chancellor, earned himself the nickname 'Futurity' for his insistence on building not for the contemporary requirements, but for the future needs of the university.[30]

Fig. 3. The University of Sydney buildings, including the Great Hall (on the right), now the eastern side of the main quadrangle, *c.* 1887.

---

[28] Turney, Bygott and Chippendale, *Australia's First*, p. 92.

[29] Turney, Bygott and Chippendale, *Australia's First*, p. 110.

[30] Quoted in McKenzie, *Stained Glass and Stone*, p. 11.

Although the university buildings are now in the inner suburbs of Sydney, like St Mary's Cathedral they were originally built on land on the margins of the city. Early photographs show the grand Gothic buildings on this higher ground, surrounded by cow paddocks [see Fig. 3]. Loyalty to Queen and Empire was demonstrated by the liberal use of the royal monogram in the Great Hall and the Royal Window that depicts selected English and Scottish monarchs from King Alfred to Queen Victoria. The heraldic devices used to represent the colony's governors and the chancellors and fellows of the university suggest a continuity with medieval aristocratic traditions of patronage. The university (then comprised of the Great Hall and the eastern section of what is now the main quadrangle) remained the largest building in the colony until 1862[31] while MacLaurin Hall (see Fig. 4) also vied for prominence on the basis of size: 'only one other roof in the world is of larger span than this, Westminster Hall being 68 ft. wide [...]'.[32]

The ornateness of the buildings was criticized on the grounds of both cost and aesthetics,[33] but the public response at the time of the completion of the Great Hall was almost entirely favourable and indicated that the buildings and the university itself had been appropriated into the public domain as a 'permanent monument of our liberality, taste, and skill'.[34] In later years, however, cost meant that parts of the original design, including the cloisters for the northern and western sides of the quadrangle, which were designed by Wilkinson to incorporate elements from Brasenose and Wadham Colleges in Oxford, were never completed, and the university resorted to cheaper, more functional building styles.

The medievalism of the University of Sydney's Gothic Revival buildings, like that of St Mary's Cathedral, manages to be both forward- and backward-looking. On the one hand it positions the university as the latest inheritor of a tradition of scholarship stretching back to the Middle Ages; on the other it presents a challenge to those older institutions of learning, in its vision of the Colony of New South Wales as capable of supporting a university of similar eminence.

In the same way that St Mary's Cathedral set a pattern for church architecture in Australia, the decision to use a medieval idiom for the University of Sydney buildings had a far-reaching effect on university architecture in Australia, with the result that the nation's oldest and some of its most prestigious universities are known as the 'sandstone seven', while medievalist architecture, rightly or wrongly, has become synonymous with traditional academic prestige.

---

[31] University of Sydney, *Guide for Visitors* (single page leaflet).

[32] 'The Fisher Library', *Lone Hand*, October 1909, p. 698. MacLaurin Hall is fifty feet wide.

[33] McKenzie, *Stained Glass and Stone*, p. 14.

[34] *The Empire* (Sydney), 19 July 1859, quoted in Turney, Bygott and Chippendale, *Australia's First*, p. 104. See other quotations from Sydney newspapers also cited by Turney and others.

Fig. 4. MacLaurin Hall, University of Sydney, then the Fisher Library, 1909.

The ANZ Bank, Collins Street, Melbourne

Cost was not a restricting factor in the building commonly known as the 'Gothic Bank', on the corner of Queen and Collins Streets in central Melbourne, one of relatively few Gothic Revival commercial buildings in Australia.[35] It was designed by William Wardell, and built between 1883 and 1887 as the Australian head-quarters of the English, Scottish, and Australian (ES&A) Bank, at the behest of the general manager, Sir George Verdon. Now the ANZ Bank, the building was expanded between 1921 and 1926 to incorporate the Melbourne Safe Deposit and Stock Exchange buildings, designed by William Pitt, and built between 1889 and 1891, in what Andrews calls 'boom-style Gothic'.[36]

Andrews describes the bank as being 'in a restrained, scholarly and — by that time — rather archaic Decorated idiom' with 'clean and uncluttered lines'.[37] The restraint is only apparent when this building is compared to others in the Gothic Revival style, since the bank now stands in stark contrast to the plain office

[35] Andrews, *Australian Gothic*, p. 23.

[36] Andrews, *Australian Gothic*, p. 25.

[37] Andrews, *Australian Gothic*, pp. 24–25.

buildings of the surrounding Central Business District. The exterior is built of the same Pyrmont sandstone as Sydney University, and features logia, arched windows, and a corner turret, Verdon's addition to Wardell's original design. In the *Illustrated Australian News* article which reported the selection of Wardell's design for the bank, it was described as 'English of the fourteenth century',[38] but it actually owes more to Venetian Gothic design, being, as Robin Boyd put it, 'probably the most Italian-looking thing in Australia until the espresso bars of the 1950s'.[39] The interior of the banking chamber incorporates painted cast iron columns, decorated with metalwork flowers at their heads. Its painted ceiling features roses, thistles and waratahs, emblems of the three countries represented in the bank's title; and heraldic devices representing these countries and the cities in which the bank had offices. Information leaflets currently displayed in the banking chamber claim that the ceiling incorporates enough gold leaf to run an inch-wide ribbon around the equator. Around the walls is a painted frieze of heraldic lions. The floor was originally laid with Minton tiles, but is now covered with carpet. The counters and partitions are made of Australian blackwood, carved with linenfold and quatrefoil patterns and polished to a high sheen.

Fig. 5. The English, Scottish, and Australian 'Gothic' Bank, Melbourne, *c.* 1920, with the Stock Exchange building to the right.

---

[38] *Illustrated Australian News*, 3 October 1883.

[39] Robin Boyd, *The Australian Ugliness*, rev. edn (Ringwood: Penguin, 1960; in association with Cheshire, 1968), p. 63.

The Stock Exchange and Safety Deposit buildings could not, in contrast to the bank, be called restrained by any definition of that word. Andrews describes the façade of the Stock Exchange building as 'smothered in tracery, diaper work, leadlight, clustered shafts, pinnacles, buttresses, gargoyles and all the unfettered minutiae of the Gothic lexicon [...]'.[40] Inside the Stock Exchange building is the exchange hall, known soon after its completion as the Cathedral Room for its vaulting, arches, blind tracery and foliated capitals and corbels, all executed in white limestone, and appropriating the vocabulary of medieval religious architecture to a secular and commercial purpose. It was not forgotten that the magnificence of these buildings rested on the extraordinary wealth produced from the Victorian gold mines: the 'saints' of the stained glass windows in the Stock Exchange are a digger panning for gold, and an allegorical figure of labour, represented as a bare-breasted woman. The overall effect is one of astonishing magnificence and extravagance. In the words of Charles Hegan, the director sent by the London branch of the ES&A Bank to investigate the rising costs of the building: 'nothing has been spared — time, trouble, or money — to make the building inside and out as perfect as possible'.[41]

It appears from the archives that Sir George Verdon was just as determined as Therry and Blacket to realize his designs and he deserves to share the credit for the eventual form of the Gothic Bank with Wardell. The relationship between the general manager and the architect was sometimes fraught, as Wardell's terse letter to Verdon in response to his request to replace arches with horizontal lintels shows:

> Having thus placed before you what as Architect of the building I know is the proper treatment, I am perfectly conscious that it rests with you as the Proprietor, to say what should be done, and I will carry out what you order, but I am satisfied that if you accept the straight line in that position you will regret it as soon as the ceiling is finished.[42]

Miles Lewis suggests that Verdon's suggestions derived from his copy of Viollet-le-Duc's *Dictionnaire*, a pattern-book of medieval design, 'with which he seems to have battered the reluctant head of his architect'.[43]

It is hard to credit Verdon with the altruistic concern for the future that informed the planning for St Mary's Cathedral and Sydney University, but he certainly wanted to build an enduring monument, and saw the opportunity to prove a point to Britain on behalf of the colonies and their inheritance and fulfilment of older traditions:

---

[40] Andrews, *Australian Gothic*, p. 25.

[41] Letter from Charles Hegan to Chairman, Court of Directors, ES&A Bank, 30 November 1887. ANZ Group Archives, E284/3/2 Letterbook.

[42] Wardell to Verdon, 19 May 1884, Mitchell Library, MS 10/1, copy held in ANZ Group Archives. Wardell won that battle.

[43] Miles Lewis, 'The Definitive Gothic', *Australian Book Review*, July 2001, p. 53.

we, having nothing to undo can, if we will, make the last page of their history the first of our own, and complete to its finished perfection the temple of which they have but laid the solid foundation.[44]

The ES&A bank was not publicly funded and so did not generate the same levels of public interest in its costs as St Mary's Cathedral and the University of Sydney had done, but the bank's directors in London were sufficiently concerned about rising costs to send Charles Hegan to investigate. Even Wardell, not generally known for his penny-pinching, attempted to restrain Verdon's excesses, suggesting that the linenfold panelling on the doors might be omitted from the manager's residence. He found, however, that the panels had already been sent for carving.[45] Hegan appears to have been won over by Verdon, and although the archives do not record the bank's response to his report, it seems likely that they were unable to do anything about Verdon's *fait accompli*.

In hindsight the Gothic Bank, and even more the adjacent Stock Exchange and Safe Deposit buildings, seem like *fin-de-siècle* decadence, the last monuments to the prosperity of the gold rush before the depression of the 1890s. They were among the last buildings to be started in Gothic Revival style in Australia, although many others were completed later. The Gothic Bank has had an enduring popularity: in 1987, Victorian readers of the *Age* newspaper voted the Gothic Bank their favourite building.[46] Like the other buildings discussed in this essay, it is now a tourist attraction:

> Tourists regularly tramp through here, necks craning, eyes agog. This is the way banking should be — all oak, brass and refinement. Frankly, an Autoteller just doesn't feel the same.[47]

If the medievalism of St Mary's Cathedral and the University of Sydney suggested that the colonies had the potential to rival the old country, in the Gothic Bank the ornate and opulent medievalism could be seen as staking a claim for colonial superiority, and unrivalled wealth and splendour of its cities, as the Australian colonies moved towards Federation in the later decades of the nineteenth century. The choice of a native timber for the copious linenfold panelling in the banking chamber indicated an acceptance of Australian raw materials that, with the exception of stone, was rare in early medievalist buildings. Similarly, the use of an Italianate style for the bank suggested that the designers and architects were now willing to look beyond Britain for their design sources, although the confidence that this might exhibit is belied by the persistent description of the Gothic Bank as English in contemporary sources.

---

[44] Cash, *As Perfect as Possible*, p. 8.

[45] Cash, *As Perfect as Possible*, p. 15.

[46] Cash, *As Perfect as Possible*, p. 24.

[47] *Herald* (Melbourne), 21 May 1987.

Montsalvat

The artists' colony of Montsalvat provides, in many respects, a stark contrast to the examples of nineteenth-century medievalism discussed above, but it also represents a continuation and further development of some of the elements of earlier Australian medievalism. Montsalvat was built well after the fashion for Gothic Revival architecture was over, and its medievalist style represents a very different kind of aesthetic or political choice. Montsalvat also differs from the other buildings discussed in this essay, in that it was designed as a private rather than a public space, albeit communal in use. However, from 1963, in an attempt to defray the costs of running the colony, Montsalvat was opened to the public as an arts centre and tourist attraction while still providing accommodation and working space for artists.

Fig. 6. The Great Hall at Montsalvat, showing the large windows salvaged from Wilson Hall.

Montsalvat was founded in 1934 by the artist and architect Justus Jorgensen, in what is now the outer Melbourne suburb of Eltham, then a rural township, as a retreat from the city. Jorgensen was an unconventional and charismatic personality, with a reputation as a 'ratbag'. Both the architecture of Montsalvat, in its defiance of 'every canon of artistic criticism', and the libertarian lifestyles of the colony's members 'blew a resonant raspberry' at suburban values.[48]

Jorgensen had been inspired by the mud-brick and pisé buildings he had seen in the south of France and realized that the local soil could be used for earth building. The first buildings at Montsalvat were built in a French provincial style, and are not particularly medieval in design. However, Jorgensen's friendship with Jim Whelan, who as 'Whelan the Wrecker' was responsible for demolishing many of Melbourne's by then deeply unfashionable Gothic Revival buildings, meant that the artists' colony acquired many salvaged items, including the large Gothic stone window frames from the University of Melbourne's Wilson Hall after it was destroyed by fire. According to Sigmund Jorgensen, the current trustee of Montsalvat, Justus Jorgensen's desire to create a stylistically consistent effect, using the Wilson Hall windows, together with the accidental discovery on the site of mudstone suitable for building, led to the decision to build the Great Hall as a large, three-story structure in a medieval idiom.[49] The members of the colony then proceeded to add a bell tower, carved gargoyles and grotesques, and made leadlight windows from recycled photographic plates. Betty Roland, a sometime member of the Montsalvat colony, described the result as 'improbable, incongruous, majestic', asking rhetorically, 'Who but Jorgensen would have planted a piece of medieval Europe in the Australian bush?'[50] The view of Montsalvat as improbable reflects a change in public attitudes in Australia since the nineteenth century, since the idea of a medieval manor house in the bushland is, if anything, rather less improbable than a medieval cathedral on the marginal land at the edge of a convict settlement, or a medieval university in the middle of a cow paddock.

The Great Hall set a stylistic precedent, and later buildings on the site, including a number of timber-framed buildings and the bluestone chapel completed in 1975 by Horry Judd, show elements of medieval form and decoration, such as pointed windows and castellated caps on the walls.[51] It is hard to classify the architecture at Montsalvat as representative of any particular medieval style, however. The combination of recycled materials from a wide variety of different sources (local stone, earth and timber), and original designs by the artists who formed the colony have been melded together to produce a whole which is entirely unique, while still recognizably medievalist. Built during the Depression, Montsalvat provides a stark contrast to the hugely expensive Gothic buildings of the nineteenth century while incorporating elements from them in a series of elaborate architectural quotations.

---

[48] *The Age* (Melbourne), 24 May 1975, p. 12.

[49] Boyd, *The Australian Ugliness*, p. 244; Betty Roland, *The Eye of the Beholder* (Sydney: Hale and Iremonger, 1984), p. 45.

[50] Roland, *The Eye of the Beholder*, p. 157.

[51] See the guide booklet, *Montsalvat* [n.p., n.d.], p. 13.

As with the other buildings, individual vision was important in the selection of a medieval idiom. The strength of Jorgensen's personality can be judged by his ability to convince the members of his community to work towards the realization of his dream. He likened himself to a child building sandcastles:

> you've seen children on the seashore building little sand castles; you'll find one boy, another girl and other people coming along and helping them, bringing along a bit of stick, sand, buckets of water and buckets of sand, and you'll find that there's one little fellow that is directing it all. Now I seemed to be the person who was directing it and I had a lot of individuals trying to help me build this thing because in some way or another I fascinated them, or made them feel what a fascinating thing it is to build.[52]

The labour required to build Montsalvat was donated by the members of the colony, as was much of the money for those materials that were purchased.

The model for Montsalvat, in a broad sense, is the medieval manor, and there is no doubt that Jorgensen adopted a feudal approach, maintaining responsibility for all the building work, which was done to his direction, and instituting communal dinners in the Great Hall at which he presided. Montsalvat's medievalism was essentially subversive, in contrast to the appeals to tradition and heritage of the nineteenth-century institutional buildings. As lord of his manor, Jorgensen could maintain an alternative centre of power, separate from civic or religious authority. Jorgensen's dream for Montsalvat, named after the home of the Holy Grail, was essentially utopian, reminiscent of William Morris's vision of communities of medieval artisans.

Montsalvat has only an indirect relationship with the historical Middle Ages, being based not on any real medieval building, nor even selected parts of them. Its references are, instead, to the nineteenth-century Gothic, and to a fictive medievalism, based as much on literary and artistic perceptions of the Middle Ages as on historical architecture. The ahistorical nature of Montsalvat is acknowledged in the derisive nicknames that have been given to it: 'Jorgy's Camelot' and 'Disneyland on the Yarra', but these names also betray a view that Montsalvat's medievalism is one that yearns towards a fictional rather than a historical Middle Ages.[53] In Montsalvat's plundering of various representations of the Middle Ages without care for historical accuracy or stylistic consistency, Australian medievalism had come full circle to resemble that of the early colonial Gothick style, dependent on allusion rather than authenticity for its effect.

The medievalism of Montsalvat differs from that of the nineteenth-century buildings discussed above. Built after the nation-defining events of Federation and World War I, Montsalvat participates only indirectly in the discourse of colonialism.

---

[52] Justus Jorgensen, interview with Hazel de Berg, Melbourne, 4 December 1965, National Library of Australia, MS Oral DeB 166.

[53] Keith Dunstan, *Ratbags* (Melbourne: Sun Books) 1980, p. 240. Philip Adams also uses the terms 'Camelot' and 'Disneyland' (*The Age*, 24 May 1975, p. 12).

Where those buildings respond to external, British institutions — the Catholic Church, the Universities of Oxford and Cambridge and the London headquarters of the ES&A Bank respectively — Montsalvat has no such 'parent' institution to embrace or challenge. In its use of local materials, naturalistic representations of Australian flora, its modest scale, and its incorporation of discarded elements of the Gothic Revival Montsalvat presents both an awareness of a European heritage and an Australian identity.

The Middle Ages through the Australian Looking Glass

Andrews asks whether there was an identifiably Australian Gothic style, and concludes that at least 'ecclesiastical Gothic, buttressed by the powerful influence of Associationism, remained resolutely British in its buildings', but that '[o]utside the conservative confines of church patronage some of the later offshoots of the Gothic Revival found fertile soil for brief if marvellously nationalistic growth'.[54] While Gothic style itself may not have had a distinct Australian version, it is possible to trace the development of an Australian character in the wider field of medievalism in the built environment.

Early in the history of the Australian colonies, architects strove to design buildings that could give the impression that they had been plucked entire from their English settings and transported. Buildings were often designed from a distance with no sense of the landscape in which they were to be built, and the widespread use of design books meant that architects in Australia could cobble together their designs entirely from pre-existing elements of buildings that they might never have seen. The patternbook approach meant that there were, at least initially, few concessions made to the Australian landscape, climate or conditions. This changed as the nineteenth century wore on: by the time Wardell designed St Mary's Cathedral, he was sufficiently aware of Australian conditions to reduce the amount of glassed windows from his models, in order to avoid making the interior of the cathedral too bright or too hot.[55] He also insisted that the English manufacturers of the windows, Messrs Hardman Brothers & Company, use much deeper colours in the glass than they would usually do in order to compensate for the stronger Australian light.[56]

Such overt nationalism as there was in Australian medievalist buildings was mostly limited to minor symbolism in the form of native flora and fauna, but this

---

[54] Andrews, *Australian Gothic*, p. 133. Andrews invokes 'Associationism' to refer to the way in which Australian Gothic buildings relied for their effect on their audiences' familiarity with and nostalgia for the buildings and artefacts of the 'old country'.

[55] O'Farrell, *St Mary's Cathedral*, pp. 75–76.

[56] O'Farrell, *St Mary's Cathedral*, p. 79.

symbolism was pervasive, and appears rather earlier than Andrews suggests.[57] St Mary's Cathedral features waratahs around the western portal, and the same flowers appear in the ceiling of the Gothic Bank. The University of Sydney has grotesques in the forms of a wallaby, kangaroo and kookaburra, placed alongside the mythical beasts of medieval tradition. Both the doors of the Stock Exchange building and the window labels of the Great Hall at Montsalvat are decorated with gumnuts and gum leaves, but whereas in the earlier building these are arranged into Gothic quatrefoils, at Montsalvat they have a more naturalistic form.

There was an initial reluctance to work with local materials, perhaps due in part to their unfamiliarity to artisans. Where they are used, it is often with a sense that they are somehow inferior. Some Australian materials were used in Pugin's extensions of St Mary's Cathedral; the pillars supporting the groined vaulting were made of ironbark, but they were clad with imported cedar, suggesting that the native wood had not yet gained acceptance.[58] Later, however, this reluctance disappeared: Kenneth Binns, writing about the new MacLaurin Hall, takes pride in the use of Australian cedar for its ceiling,[59] and Montsalvat is entirely constructed from local materials.

A parallel can be drawn between the increasingly Australian nature of the medievalism of these buildings, and the ways in which they have used medievalism in various guises to express the changing relationship between Australia as settlement, colony and nation, and both the European past and Britain as a colonial power. From Father Therry's earliest design, St Mary's Cathedral was the expression of a desire for Catholicism in the new settlement to be part of the continuing tradition of the medieval Church, but also of a desire for a changed social and economic status for Catholics. Similarly the University of Sydney used a medieval idiom to share in the tradition and status of the medieval university, but it also represented the ambitions of the Colony for similar prestige of its own. The Italianate grandeur and costliness of the Gothic Bank made a claim, not just for colonial equality but supremacy; but it was in Montsalvat, built using a medievalism based rather on a fictional Middle Ages than on the elements of existing medieval architecture, that medievalism was used to express a postcolonial and independent identity.

In each of these four buildings, the medieval idiom is used to evoke an ideal, a perfected or utopian view of the Middle Ages. St Mary's Cathedral represents an idealized church, in which medieval Catholicism was untainted by Reformation; the University of Sydney presents an ideal antipodean university, rivalling the ancient centres of learning, but free from sectarian strife; the Gothic Bank, by using medievalism as a vehicle for splendour and magnificence, manages to create a sense

---

[57] Andrews, *Australian Gothic*, p. 133.

[58] O'Farrell, *St Mary's Cathedral*, p. 16.

[59] 'The Fisher Library', *Lone Hand*, October 1909, p. 698.

of 'banking as it ought to be'; and Montsalvat uses the ideal of the medieval manor to create a utopian society where artists can work and live outside the strictures of conventional society. This sense of idealism means that Australians have been more comfortable with medievalism in certain buildings than others. Andrews points out that there was 'relative acceptance of the Gothic style for a range of types of building in Australia', but in most cases the use of the medieval idiom was limited to buildings which had a clear religious, moral or civic function – churches, hospitals, schools, funeral parlours, post-offices and the like.[60] When medievalism moved beyond this axis the public could become quite uneasy about it. At a commemorative dinner for the opening of the Stock Exchange building on 26 June 1891, one of the guests, Sir Frederick Sargood, commented that he felt as if he were 'entering a cathedral, for its architecture was hardly in keeping with a place where mundane matters were dealt with'.[61] The equation of medievalism and religion in the public eye is persistent, as borne out by the 1971 headline of an article dealing with the opening of Montsalvat to the public: 'Why Mammon Came to Montsalvat'. The article claims that some locals 'see the new commercialism as a betrayal of Montsalvat's old crusading idealism'.[62] In 1986 Keith Dunstan wrote:

> Almost as saintly in appearance [as St Patrick's Cathedral] is the ANZ, originally the ES&A Bank [...]. You keep looking round for the altar so that you can pray and you think the show, the atmosphere of theatre, would be helped with a dash of incense.[63]

In Australia, and in other parts of the world outside Europe, medievalist buildings fill a different imaginative space than they might in Europe. Here such buildings do not stand alongside the real medieval buildings which inspired them, and against which they must be measured. Stewart Brand, in *How Buildings Learn*, suggests that the most important factor in whether a building is liked is its age, or at least its perceived age: 'Apparently the older a building gets, the more we have respect and affection for its evident maturity. [...] Age is so valued in America it is far more often fake than real'.[64]

The appearance of great age was also appreciated in Australia. Dr Roger Oldfield commented on old St Mary's in 1828:

---

[60] Andrews, *Australian Gothic*, p. 11.

[61] Information board in the Stock Exchange building.

[62] *Bulletin*, 8 May 1971, pp. 44–45.

[63] *The Age* (Good Weekend Supplement), 7 November 1986, p. 45.

[64] Stewart Brand, *How Buildings Learn: What Happens After They're Built*, rev. edn (London: Phoenix Illustrated, 1997), p. 10.

The Gothic edifice, though a plain structure, is a surprising piece of work, standing where it does. [...] yet the whole has a fine effect, and by moonlight, but that the stone is fresh, you might fancy it is some old abbey.[65]

For many Australians, these buildings represent their first, and often only, encounters not only with the spatial and decorative principles of medievalism, but with the Middle Ages themselves. Even professional medievalists must encounter medieval art and architecture primarily through the media of photographs, film and the internet, with perhaps only the occasional luxury of visiting the original works, while the more accessible and tangible medievalist buildings and spaces in which Australians might work or study, worship, bank, or re-create medieval battles have a direct influence on the ways in which they approach and construct the historical Middle Ages.

Each of the buildings discussed in this essay participates in some way in a performative medievalism. In the case of St Mary's Cathedral this is most obviously the daily celebration of the liturgy, in an unbroken (although not unchanging) tradition from the historical Middle Ages. Similarly, Sydney University conducts the ritual of graduation, where academics and graduands wear medieval caps, hoods and gowns. The electronic banking which is carried out in Wardell's Gothic Bank is radically different from the banking of the Middle Ages, but the 'cathedral room' of the Stock Exchange building is now used as a gallery and performance space, which occasionally hosts performances of early music. Montsalvat derives a significant part of its income from its role as a wedding and reception centre, and is frequently a venue for weddings with a medieval theme. It has also been the site for several 'Renaissance Fairs', and, like the spaces around the Sydney University buildings, is a popular site for the activities of medieval re-enactment and recreation groups, as well as for musical and dramatic performances.[66]

These buildings also help to define the Middle Ages for Australians, but in so doing they participate in the transformation of that period from a historical category to a nostalgic fantasy. This is perhaps not surprising if we consider fantasy as history without place, or occupying a place that is entirely imagined. Since the European churches, castles, universities and manor houses to which Australia's neo-medieval buildings refer exist for many Australians only in their imaginations, there is no need for the buildings to represent accurately any aspect of medieval architecture to fill the conceptual position of the medieval built environment.

Medievalism in Australia is necessarily a form of colonialism, a way of claiming the new land for the purposes, ideals and peoples of the old. By modifying the

---

[65] *South Asian Register*, 1828, p. 328, quoted Kerr and Broadbent, *Gothick Taste*, p. 6.

[66] Surprisingly, St Mary's Cathedral has also been a site for secular historical recreation: the first use of Wardell's unfinished (and unconsecrated) building was for the month long 'Ye Fayre of Ye Olden Tyme' which opened on Easter Monday, 1882. O'Farrell, *St Mary's Cathedral*, p. 14. The fair was very loosely Elizabethan in concept.

landscape and by erecting structures which appear (at least from a distance) to be many centuries old, the European settlers of Australia were constructing a false past for themselves, as they failed to acknowledge the real past of the continent they had colonized. But in the post-colonial era the effectiveness of Association waned, together with Australians' knowledge of and nostalgia for the landscape and built environment of Europe. The medievalist buildings discussed in this essay, and others like them, become representative, not of 'home', but of the Middle Ages themselves, shaping Australians' perception of the historical period and of medieval architecture. In this way, they participate in a kind of reverse colonization, in which the medieval past is claimed for Australia, and the Middle Ages are rebuilt in the image of Australian medievalism.

The Daughters of the Court: Women's Medievalism in Nineteenth-Century Melbourne

VICTORIA EMERY

In September 1892 in an elaborate ceremony in the Russell Street Hall, Melbourne, the Countess of Hopetoun[1] gave her vice-regal blessing to a recently formed women's organization, the Order of the Daughters of the Court, graciously accepting the position of patroness or 'Grand Dame' to the order:

> The 'Grand Dame' shall be met at the carriage door by the High Chatelains, the Chatelains being drawn up in two lines between which the 'Grand Dame' will pass and be received at the door of the Hall by the High Dame and Dames of all Coteries, who will then form a procession two and two and procede [sic] the Grand Dame and High Dame into the Hall, the Chatelains following.[2]

The details of this ceremony describe a complex structure of members and officers — dames, chatelains, companions and chancellors — whose relationships and functions were established and expressed through a language of hierarchy and mutual service which drew explicitly on the imagery of religious communities and a poetic understanding of the Middle Ages. According to the order's journal, this language was based on the 'Old "Courts of Chivalry," "Love" or "Courtesy".'[3] It

---

[1] The Countess of Hopetoun was the wife of the governor of Victoria. Her husband, the seventh Earl of Hopetoun, had served as a lord in waiting to Queen Victoria and was later to be the first governor-general of the Commonwealth of Australia. *Dictionary of National Biography: The Concise Dictionary*, Part II, 1901–50 (Oxford: Oxford University Press, 1961), pp. 218–19.

[2] '1892/Investment of Dames and Others/Order of the Day. Sept: 22nd' (manuscript sheet, unsigned), *Daughters of the Court Scrapbook*, 'Daughters of the Court', Australian Manuscripts Collection, State Library of Victoria, MS 11537.

[3] 'History of the Order of the Daughters of the Court', *The Court: A Journal of the Order of the Daughters of the Court, and for Women*, 1 (1894), 2–3 (p. 2).

was chosen for its inclusiveness, to enable the order to attract as wide a following as possible.[4] Their apparently humble programme — 'To form an Order of women who shall undertake to speak ill of none, and to cultivate the spirit of helpfulness'[5] — was set in place by a group of women who possessed energy, ambition, and not inconsiderable social clout. It was undertaken at a time when university education and the learned professions were opening to women, when women's suffrage, married women's property and related issues were on the political agenda; and it was undertaken in the language of literary medievalism.

How are we to understand the Daughters of the Court, and their intentions? This essay interrogates the surviving evidence, and attempts to understand the daughters in their social, political and cultural context. In particular, it asks what meanings we may attach to an appropriation of the language of medievalism in the setting of a late colonial capital in the final decade of the nineteenth century. In interpreting the 'medievalism' of the daughters, we must also interrogate their relationships with each other and with the broader social and political setting in which they acted. What led these women to unite? What possibilities were realized by framing their activities and relationships in an idealized vision of the medieval past?

If we are to consider this as a form of medievalism, it is a type that has received little consideration up to now. In *The Shock of Medievalism*, Kathleen Biddick draws a line between the 'new academic medievalists of the nineteenth century' and the 'popular studies of medieval culture' against which they defined themselves.[6] In terms of this divide, the daughters' medievalism was of the least scientific sort. Their ideas were derived from the contemporary literature of the day — the novels of Walter Scott, the poetry of Alfred, Lord Tennyson, and most directly, from John Ruskin's essay 'Of Queens' Gardens'. However, it would be misleading to consider them primarily as promoting a vision of the medieval past. The Order of the Daughters of the Court was not involved, either directly, or indirectly with the debate on medieval studies. Their concerns were social and political rather than historical or literary. Their use and interest in this language had little to do with medieval studies, and everything to do with their vision of social and political change.

The terminology which is expressed through the order's constitution, its journal, *The Court*, and the available commentary which has survived, is testimony to the intricate interconnections between language, authority and politics in this period. Inspired by a desire to do good in the world but constrained by a limited or overly-politicized definition of womanhood, the daughters harnessed the language of medievalism to create a space and a method for positive social change. In doing so,

---

[4] The major sources for information on the daughters are their journal, *The Court*, published quarterly between 1894 and 1899 and the *Daughters Scrapbook* held at the State Library of Victoria.

[5] Constitution of the Order of the Daughters of the Court, *Daughters Scrapbook*.

[6] Kathleen Biddick, *The Shock of Medievalism* (Durham: Duke University Press, 1998), p. 1.

they appealed to ideas which had common currency in the literature of the period, and which were considered uncontroversial, even conventional. The terminology of dames, chancellors, high courts and courtesy, with their deliberate religious and historical connotations, combined with an emphasis on interpersonal relationship and personal behaviour to present a resolutely non-threatening façade to public scrutiny.

Accordingly, this paper does not identify a projection of medieval culture into the politics of late colonial Melbourne, but rather a social reform project that co-opted the language of medieval romance, known through contemporary or near-contemporary writings. I seek to identify not what was medieval in the programme which the daughters promoted, but rather, what was called 'medieval', why it was useful to call it so, and what effect it might have had on the arguments into which it was introduced.

On one level, the order was one among hundreds of clubs and societies in Melbourne whose members sought 'self-improvement' in various ways. Some were solely philanthropic, some educational but most involved both social and charitable or cultural activities. They were organized around religious affiliation, social grouping, language or profession; and their numbers bear witness to their enthusiasm.[7] In addition to the 'Rule' of the order quoted above, the daughters could choose secondary activities for their coteries (branches) and they took part in the spectrum of cultural and charitable activities that were common to the ladies' organizations of the time. The members read, studied, sang or played music, sketched, sewed for charity, provided entertainments and raised funds for churches. Yet the daughters, with their dames, chatelaines and companions, their coteries and courts, their Rule and their ambitions for an international membership, shared wider aspirations than rational recreation, and a conviction of the possibilities for social change.

In observing their Rule, and in their creation of a network of women pledged to 'positive helpful action', the daughters sought to harness the widely discussed 'influence' of women to a systematic programme of moral and spiritual improvement. The programme was intended to be open to all women, in every sphere of activity:

> Women have plenty to do, be they studying for the wider fields of work that have been recently opened to them — be they mothers of families in the busy home — or be they girls in school, or in the house, or in business, pursuing their quiet duties — or even if they be the so-called 'idle' women of fashion [...] In all this work, of whatever kind,

---

[7] So far I have been able to trace more than one hundred and twenty clubs or branches in Victoria (both of men and women, though rarely both together) which took part in activities which can be loosely related to reading, music, arts or cultured leisure in the period between the mid-1880s and the early 1900s. See my 'Reading and After: Literary Community, Identity and Practice in Melbourne c. 1886–1910' (unpublished doctoral thesis, University of Melbourne, 1999), Section 3 and Appendix 3.1.

women and girls must be, and always are influencing those about them in some way or other.[8]

Despite this ambition for universal inclusion, the programme was clearly based on an elite, and to some extent ambivalent, understanding of womanhood. The moral authority of the lady, the authoritative and historically based culture of anglophone letters, and the culture of conventional social action and observance formed the frameworks within which this programme was to operate. The daughters and the medieval language and symbolism that they employed represent an attempt to fuse these elements into a structure that would allow a proactive posture for women who remained outside the formal politics of the 'Woman Movement'.

The 'History of the Order' that appeared in the first issue of the journal *The Court* presents the language of the order as almost self-evident. It was seen, not as historically or culturally specific, but rather as accessible and inclusive, specifically broad enough to include members who were of other faiths than Christianity. '[T]here are others whom we rejoice to have with us in the observance of the Rule, who could not unite if the pledge were less wide.'[9] I have not been able to establish the identity of these ladies, but given the period and the milieu they might well have included Jews, Unitarians and followers of various spiritualist philosophies:

> All were anxious to avoid anything that could narrow the Order, it being desired to make it wide enough in name and title to embrace all. The Old 'Courts of Chivalry,' 'Love,' or 'Courtesy' suggested that the 'Daughters of the Court' would be suitable as it was desired to begin a Court of Gentle Helpfulness and Courteous Truth.[10]

The 'medieval' titles given to office holders were intended to fit with the 'Court' of the title. The star and pearl were chosen for the badge 'with the idea of purity and gentleness belonging to the pearl and of cheer and guidance to the star'. The pearl has a long history as a symbol of purity or chastity in Christian iconography, and the 'guidance' of the star recalls the star of Bethlehem, yet it seems unlikely that these associations were overlooked, so much as subsumed. The daughters' confidence in the ubiquity of these symbols points to a form of universalization through which the 'medieval' as a category had become historically decontextualized and non-specific; in effect, mythologized. Through this process, social and cultural forms and symbolism which were associated with the 'medieval' took on an ideal rather than historical meaning, emphasizing order, harmony and chivalry. Uprooted from their historical setting, these 'medieval' forms were available to be reinvented or appropriated in ways that made sense to the social, political and religious life of the nineteenth century. In this case the 'Courts of Chivalry' and other paraphernalia of the mythological Middle Ages take their place in a constellation of higher values to

---

[8] Quote is from an address by Louisa Bevan, 'The New Order', extract from *The Herald* (Melbourne), 28 March 1891, pasted in to the *Daughters Scrapbook*.

[9] 'History of the Order'.

[10] 'History of the Order'.

which reference is made when needed. They co-exist with such abstractions as Music, Art, Truth, Nature and Literature as repositories of positive social value.

The overlap of historical, cultural and religious contexts are clear in the names which the daughters chose for their coteries. Amidst the coteries of St Catherine (nursing), St Cecilia (music), the White Cross (nursing) and Fairie, were echoes of the classics, in Muses ([needle]work and reading) and Euterpe (music, [needle]work and entertainments for Mission Halls); and of Shakespeare (reading, music, needlework). Music was represented by Mozart ('study of music', and to 'give what pleasure we can to others') and Beethoven (music). Flowers were popular — Clematis, Snowdrop, Pansy, Jessamine, Carnation, Myrtle, White Violet and Waratah (a rare native inclusion). Quasi-religious names abound — Willing Daughters, Happy Family, Ministering Children, Golden Rule, Busy Bee, Willing Workers — while some refer specifically to nature: Sunbeam, Star, Cobalt and Cosmos. Others relate more directly to the order, such as Pearl. Only a few were local in reference: in addition to Waratah, there is also Southern Cross and Narre Warren.

Self-definition, performance and public visibility were important aspects of the life of any club, even when it was a 'private' affair. Much of the significance of association lay in the collective production of an identity, which was displayed to the public, to an audience of friends and neighbours, or to carefully selected invited guests. Whatever form a club took, it created its corporate identity with great care and an eye for its audience. The contemporary Melbourne Beefsteak Club, for example, kept its membership to fifteen (later twenty-one) and its activities were based around dinner and an after-dinner address. The 'Master', who gave the speech, performed both for the club and for an invited guest, usually chosen from Melbourne's literary or artistic circles. The speeches, heavily larded with quotation, allusion, and reference, were a deliberate display of the 'right' background among junior members of Melbourne's professional elite.[11] In a different social context, the Ormond Elocution and Dramatic Society, recruiting its members from the elocution classes run by Reverend Macully at the Melbourne Working Men's College, ran its evening gatherings as a series of recitations from members, followed by critique from the floor. The members of the club were enthusiastic and successful competitors in the public 'literary' competitions of the time.[12] The Order of the Daughters of the Court deliberately deployed language and forms of organization that appealed to historical frameworks of religious orders (the 'Order', the 'Rule'), or medieval forms of organization ('Courts' and 'Coteries' governed by 'Dames' and 'Chatelains') or of the language of approved personal conduct ('gentle helpfulness and courteous truth').

---

[11] The Recorder [J. F. Deegan], *Chronicles of the Melbourne Beefsteak Club* (Melbourne: McKinlay, 1890).

[12] *Literary Societies' Monthly Gazette*, December 1890, p. 4.

In a social context in which public action by women was frequently the subject of criticism or ridicule, the daughters' self-presentation was crucial, and the surviving commentary suggests that even so simple a programme as theirs could not be assumed to be uncontroversial:

> It is, of course, too much to expect that the Order will meet with a very sympathetic reception from critics of the opposite sex. It must run the gauntlet as other organisations among women have done before it. But its promoters probably find encouragement in the success achieved by those societies of women that have already been subjected to man's criticism. The Primrose League in the old country, the Austral Salon in this colony, have shown what women can do in the way of successful organisations, whether men applaud or sneer at their efforts.[13]

This writer, although clearly sympathetic, was somewhat at a loss for a model with which to compare the new society. The Primrose League, a league of women supporting conservative politics in England, used similar terminology — dames, councillors and habitations — while the Austral Salon was an organization of professional women in Melbourne. The general tone of this article is defensive, an attempt to argue that there is 'nothing objectionable about either the aims or the methods of the "Daughters of the Court"' and the (anonymous) writer notes that it is intended 'to inculcate the principles of respect for authority and of ready compliance with healthful discipline'. The other commentary which appears in the *Daughters Scrapbook* — from the *The Daily Telegraph* — concentrates almost entirely on the subject of malicious gossip but compares the order to the masons on the basis of their sign.[14] The 'History of the Order' takes a determinedly philosophical view:

> We were questioned, laughed at and commended by various people as well as by the Press, for all of which we were sincerely grateful, as we felt sure that if once our rule and order were understood, sympathy would be aroused, and that even if we did not enlist all in our Court, the influence could not help being useful.[15]

Despite the mildness of the daughters' programme, any discussion of women's affairs at this period was likely to raise anxieties about the social order and the possible effect on women of any activities outside the home. When the women of New Zealand achieved the vote in 1893, an article entitled 'A Leap in the Dark' had this to say of the 'experiment':

> We shall watch it with an open mind, and should it not result in dethroning women in society, in dissipating that gentle respect for her which all but the worst men entertain,

---

[13] 'The New Order', *Daughters Scrapbook*.

[14] 'Ladies Column', *The Daily Telegraph* (Melbourne), 4 April 1891, *Daughters Scrapbook*.

[15] 'History of the Order'.

and in depriving her characteristic virtues of their bloom, then we shall become converts to woman's rights in the political sense.[16]

The daughters, with their sights set on the broadest possible membership, were bound to steer clear of the openly controversial, whatever their private sympathies.

Although the founders were keen to avoid public controversy, it is clear that convention would not have been invoked for its own sake. Neither the convenor of the first meeting nor the early members were strangers to the movement for women's rights, nor the controversy that accompanied it:

> On Oct. 24, 1890, a meeting was held, convened by Dr. Bevan, consisting of ten ladies, most of whom were University students, to consider the desirability of starting some society or order which should help women to realize the great and wide-spread influence which they cannot help exercising, and by checking idle and ill-natured gossip and encouraging unselfish helpful action to raise the tone of society and tend to a higher ideal of life.[17]

Dr Llewelyn Bevan, the popular Welsh-born minister of the Collins Street Independent Church, had a history of involvement in cultural and self-improvement activities on three continents, and was known for his support of women's suffrage and women's rights. Having commenced his ministry in London, where he studied literature and was involved in the early growth of the Working Men's College, he spent a number of years in New York, then returned to England for a time before taking up the 'calling' to Melbourne. In all of this he was accompanied by his wife and biographer, Louisa Bevan, who was to become high dame and chief proselytizer for the order.[18]

The 'History' also asserts the common nineteenth-century belief in the moral authority and responsibility of women:

> It was felt that in the rapidly advancing condition of society, and the changed and still changing position of women, it would be well to keep in remembrance the fact that woman's queenship involved responsibility as well as honour, and that the two great powers entrusted to her are speech and personal influence.[19]

---

[16] *The Advocate* (Melbourne), 16 September 1893, p. 6.

[17] 'History of the Order'.

[18] Louisa Jane Bevan, *The Life and Reminiscences of Llewelyn David Bevan, LlB, DD* (Melbourne: Wyatt and Watt, 1920). Regrettably for the historian interested in Louisa Bevan, this auto/biography (the first part of the book is comprised of Llewelyn Bevan's dictated reminiscences, the latter half, Louisa Bevan's writings after his death) deals almost exclusively with his ministry and the churchmen of interest with whom he was involved. His wedding day is mentioned as the most important of his life, but his wife is almost invisible in the book, and his children are unnamed and unnumbered. Social interactions are almost invisible, even with people who, on the external evidence, were important in his life.

[19] 'History of the Order'.

The 'queenship' of women invokes John Ruskin's essay 'Of Queens' Gardens', the most direct source for the daughters' rhetoric, if not for their programme. The relationship between the order and Ruskin's work is a complex one, which will be discussed below. The 'History' provides further pointers to the rhetorical and authoritative framework on which the founders of the order based their efforts. The references to Dr Bevan (a clergyman) and the university in the first paragraph are followed by a discussion of the 'influence' of women, the 'Courts of Chivalry', 'Love', or 'Courtesy', the countess, and other eminent persons, the geographical spread of the order, and the hope of further international expansion. In the language of association of the period, these aspects seek to identify the order with sources of authority and validity. Acceptance by church and university; the common understanding of the moral superiority and responsibility of women; social acceptance by the highest-ranking lady of the colony; and the use of international (imperial) connection: all these features assert firm claims to moral and spiritual value.

In terms of its membership, and in the light of its own rhetoric, the order straddled a number of lines of social connection and activity, but its heart lay in the Protestant intelligentsia of Melbourne. Neil Gunson's *Australian Dictionary of Biography* entry for Dr Bevan adds the following note on Mrs Bevan:

> Louisa Bevan shared her husband's intellectual and musical interests, wrote and illustrated poems and hymns which were occasionally published, and at 60 learned Greek and Sanskrit in order to assist him.[20]

It is likely that the original group out of which the order grew, was the Young Ladies' Reading Society which had been associated with the Independent Church:

> One of the societies connected with the Church and under the Doctor's guidance was 'The Young Ladies' Reading Society,' which held quarterly meetings at the Doctor's house. The members studied, under the Doctor's direction, Bacon's Essays, 'Paradise Lost,' Dante's 'Divine Comedy,' and many other classics. Once a quarter the Doctor gave the society a lecture on Shakespeare's plays. This society had some most gifted members, and was a real intellectual inspiration for many years. We owed much to our secretary, Dr. Emily Mary Page Stone, who was one of the first band of University women who won the right to, and succeeded in gaining, their degrees. They were a courageous and hard-working set of girls, who, with some adverse criticism and

---

[20] *Australian Dictionary of Biography*, vol. 7 (Melbourne: Melbourne University Press, 1979), p. 284. Gunson also notes the foundation of the daughters and that they were later renamed 'Friends in Council'. As the title 'Daughters of the Court' was in use at least as late as 1904, when Lady Northcote (wife of the third Governor-General) was invested as grand dame, this may indicate that the order continued well into the new century (*The Home Journal*, 1 April 1904, p. 4).

difficulty, gained what since those days, many have entered into with ease and as a matter of course. [21]

Dr Stone was a cousin of Dr Constance Stone who had been Melbourne's first female doctor (American educated, at a period when women could not study medicine in Australia). She and Dr Clara Stone, one of Melbourne's first two women medical graduates, were among the ten women doctors who set up an outpatients clinic in the Welsh Church Hall, the success of which led to the establishment of the Queen Victoria Hospital.[22] Dr E. Mary P. Stone is also listed as high chancellor of the order (i.e. Chancellor of the High Court) in the first issue of *The Court*.[23] These were intelligent, able women, not averse to challenging convention. The choices they made were unlikely to be those of timidity.

The significance of John Ruskin for the order is both personal and general. Ruskin was one of the eminent lecturers at the London Working Men's College during the young Llewelyn Bevan's involvement with the institution, though whether there was any more direct relationship is unknown.[24] Ruskin was one of an older generation of European, mainly British, writers, whose views helped to form the orthodox understanding of books and reading in the anglophone world, and specifically in the Australian colonies. In this belief system books encapsulated both the thought and the character of the author and influenced the reader for good or ill, in the same way that good or bad companions were supposed to. Books and the literary order which they symbolized had the potential to transform the reader, to 'place him in contact with the best society in every period of history; with the wisest, the wittiest — with the tenderest, the bravest, and the purest characters who have adorned humanity. You make him a denizen of all nations; a contemporary of all ages'.[25] This view of reading also encouraged a hierarchy of literature both historical and generic. The older the book the more worthy, with the Greek and Roman classics at the pinnacle, while poetry, history and biography far outweighed fiction. Books were to be read both for information and for moral reinforcement, with an eye to augmenting knowledge (facts) but also to absorbing moral improvement, through understanding heroic attitude and action. Ruskin's praise and encouragement of the

---

[21] Bevan, *Life and Reminiscences*, p. 181.

[22] See Farley Kelly, *Degrees of Liberation: A Short History of Women in the University of Melbourne*, The Women Graduates Centenary Committee (Melbourne: University of Melbourne, 1985), p. 19. See pp. 14–20 for the experience of the early women medical students in general.

[23] List of Office Bearers, *The Court*, October 1894, p. 3.

[24] Bevan, *Life and Reminiscences*, p. 103.

[25] Sir John Herschel, 'Address to Subscribers of the Windsor and Eton Public Library and Reading Room, January 29, 1833', quoted in Charles Long, *The Aim and Method of the Reading Lesson: A Lecture Delivered Before the Melbourne Educational Centre, University Extension, Session 1903* (London: Macmillan, 1910), p. vi.

'queen woman' called on just this combination of the historical and the heroic. Bringing together the language of chivalry with far-reaching demands for action and moral leadership, he created a template for noble action, by and for women. The pivotal passage of his essay 'Of Queens' Gardens', was quoted by Louisa Bevan in her address to the daughters' Lady Day gathering in 1891.

> Your fancy may be pleased with the thought of being noble, and attended by a train of vassals. Be it so. You cannot be too noble and your train of vassals cannot be too great, but see that it consists of those whom you serve and aid, not of those who serve you, and that the multitude which surrounds you is of those whom you have comforted and helped. The highest duty is open to you if you will accept it [...] Queens to your lovers, to your husbands and children, and queens to the wide-world which ever bows to the sceptre of womanhood. It is for you to check injustice, misery and suffering, not by taking the man's place, by fighting or declaiming, but by so living that the paths where you step are strewn with the flowers of patience gentleness and truth.[26]

Ruskin used the conventional language of ladyhood explicitly to challenge women to action beyond the home and family: in fact he condemned as 'idle and careless queens' women who limited themselves to a purely domestic metier. He demanded social service, but from a position of privilege. He also argued for the effectiveness of individual action. As Mark Girouard puts it:

> Service for Ruskin was closely bound up with the ideals of chivalry; he adjured the upper classes of his own day to retain 'the ancient and eternal purpose of knighthood, to subdue the wicked and aid the weak'. Like Maurice and Carlyle, although he was passionately concerned about the condition of the working classes, he was very far from being a democrat; he believed in a ruling class, but wanted it to be so altruistic, noble, and free from self-interest that people would freely accept its rule.[27]

This attitude of service, extended to women, offered a template in which women could assert their power without stepping beyond the boundaries of ladyhood. This form of feminine service was only a step away from a female-*gendered* chivalry. Women were duty bound to protect the morally weak and if not to subdue the wicked, at least by precept and example render them socially unacceptable.

In choosing Ruskin, the daughters also took on some of the ambiguity of his view of women as both powerful and potentially dangerous, and this may have something to do with the emphasis that the daughters continued to place on the taming of 'idle

---

[26] Ruskin, 'Of Queens' Gardens' quoted by the high dame in her address to the order, 25 March 1891, *The Herald*, 28 March 1891, *Daughters Scrapbook*. I have reproduced the abridged passage as presented in the newspaper. Some phrases vary from the original. It is notable that the daughters, despite their Protestant religious background, adopted Lady Day (25 March), the feast of the Annunciation, as a major festival for the society.

[27] Mark Girouard, *The Return to Camelot: Chivalry and the English Gentleman* (New Haven: Yale University Press, 1981), p. 250. The quote is from Ruskin, *Fors clavigera*.

and ill-natured gossip'. It is clear, though, that like any other externally derived social impulse, this reading of Ruskin was filtered through local relationship, convention and circumstance. His language was acceptable to them because it transformed the privileged yet circumscribed social conception of 'ladyhood' that was a standard of the period. In the words of an essay quoted in *Australian Etiquette:*

> From the lady there exhales a subtle magnetism. Unconsciously she encircles herself with an atmosphere of unruffled strength, which, to those who come into it, gives confidence and repose. Within her influence the diffident grow self-possessed, the impudent are checked, the inconsiderate are admonished; even the rude are constrained to be mannerly, and the refined are perfected [...] The finest and most characteristic acts of a lady involve a spiritual ascension, a growing out of herself. In her being and bearing, patience, generosity, benignity are the graces that give shape to the virtues of truthfulness.[28]

This discourse of 'ladyhood' intersected with other discourses about Australian women, most notably about the attributes and possibilities of the 'Australian girl', usually by comparison with her European or American counterparts:

> The Australian girl is not a sentimental being. All her sympathies appear to be with the present. She is *fin-de-siecle* [...] as far as circumstances permit, but she is at a disadvantage as compared with her foreign cousins. She is, unfortunately, too far removed from the great centres of art and literature, or even fashion, to be quite 'up to date,' so to speak; but she loses no opportunity for improvement, for she is ambitious, and wishes to excel.[29]

While the lady and the girl inhabited subtly different social (and class) environments, this discourse within the advice literature suggests the contested nature of even the conventional parameters for female behaviour as the twentieth century approached. That the order chose the older, more established (and class bound) form suggests that they saw their programme, despite its relationship with an increase in women's rights, as somehow more congruent with a personal vision of social progress.

Ruskin's discourse of 'queens' spoke both to popular conceptions of medieval chivalry and to the demands for personal moral excellence which were common to religious and social reform movements of the period. By utilizing Ruskin's language of rule by service, and by couching their activities in the language of courts and coteries, dames and scribes, the daughters brought together aspects of proto-

---

[28] Calvert [no further reference], quoted in *Australian Etiquette, or the Rules and Usages of the Best Society in the Australasian Colonies, together with their Sports, Pastimes, Games, and Amusements* (Melbourne: People's Publishing Company, 1885; facsimile edition, Knoxfield: Dent, 1980), p. 28.

[29] 'The Australian Girl', by M. G. in *The Catholic Magazine*, 3 (1890), p. 35.

feminism,[30] moral/social improvement, and the conventions of literature and performance in the language of the 'medieval'. The daughters' vision of a worldwide sisterhood of women sworn to 'Gentle Helpfulness and Courteous Truth' was nothing less than an attempt to create a model of heroic action which could be undertaken by women, without infringing the boundaries of 'ladyhood', a code of belief and personal behaviour on which rested a great deal both for the individual and her family. In taking on Ruskin's definition of the two great 'powers' of women, 'speech and personal influence' and forming them into a programme for social renewal, the daughters sought to broaden this understanding of the queenship of women into the context of Australian society. The establishment and spread of the order in its early years suggests that the combination had considerable appeal at least within the sections of society at which the message was primarily directed.

Having begun at the nexus of the Independent Church and the University of Melbourne, the coteries of the daughters spread out along the lines of geographical and social contiguity, following the lines of connection between churches and educated women. The 'Daughters of St Catherine' coterie listed Miss Marie McKee at the Alfred Hospital, Prahran, as scribe while the chancellors were Miss Amelia Chinn and Miss Agnes Dale of Geelong Hospital. The 'White Cross' coterie operated from the Homeopathic Hospital in St Kilda Road. The 'Ministering Children of the King' and the 'Marguerite' or 'Margarita' coterie were girls' coteries, and had ties to churches with missionary endeavours:

> The Coterie of the Ministering Children of the King have held meetings regularly every Saturday excepting during the school holiday and have together with the Margarita Coterie made a variety of fancy articles and dressed a number of dolls some of which have gone to India and some are going to China with Miss Halley.[31]

The 'Cosmos' and 'White Heather' coteries were based at the Presbyterian Ladies' College, at that time the major centre of academic secondary education for girls.[32] Geographically the coteries spread first among the suburbs of the inner city and then further afield — the scrapbook preserved at the State Library of Victoria includes letters from East St Kilda, Ormond College, Narre Warren, St Kilda Road, North Melbourne, Armadale, Fitzroy, Elsternwick, Jolimont, Windsor and Stawell. (Of this list only Narre Warren and Stawell are country centres; the remainder are city or suburban locations.) Personal connections remained important in the creation of new coteries. At the investment ceremony in October 1892 Mrs Clarke, 'the

---

[30] I use the term to indicate women who were interested in the position and possibilities for women, but were not necessarily involved in formal political action. While it is likely that some daughters were directly involved in the women's rights movement of the time, it is clear that the organization went to some lengths to avoid being associated with such action.

[31] 'Report from the Ministering Children Coterie', handwritten report, dated 10 September 1891, in *Daughters Scrapbook*.

[32] 'Report of Coteries', *The Court*, October 1894, p. 7.

originator of the Christian Endeavour movement' was accepted into the society as were the Misses Spicer from England. (James Spicer, resident in London, had been a major influence in recruiting Dr Bevan to Melbourne.) The spread of the daughters to other colonies was due largely to Mrs Bevan as high dame, who used her travels to Queensland, New South Wales, South Australia, Western Australia and Tasmania with her minister husband as an opportunity to spread another gospel.

Fig. 7. Cover of the Constitution, Daughters of the Court Scrapbook, 'Daughters of the Court', Australian Manuscripts Collection, State Library of Victoria, MS 11537,

Co-opting existing social networks was both a strength and a weakness of the order, and one it shared with many other organizations of the period. It is characteristic of the cultural associations of the time to recruit within existing networks, reinforcing relationships and creating new opportunities for connection between people in socially and culturally appropriate positions. By corollary, organizations tended to remain within similar social spheres, acting on congruent social and behavioural assumptions.

When the journal *The Court: A Journal of the Order of the Daughters of the Court and for Women* was launched, the order had been established for four years, and had enjoyed considerable success. Based on the listing of coteries and single members the membership may have been as high as six hundred though it is likely it was substantially less. There were members in all of the Australian colonies, India, England and America.[33] The journal seems to have been the first women's political journal to be published in Victoria.[34] It identified itself with women, and without taking a stance on specific issues, offered its pages for discussion of issues of social and political change:

> this organization has come into existence at a time when all questions affecting women are very prominent. It is impossible for the Daughters of the Court to ignore these subjects. They come up for discussion in every social circle [...] Our Magazine must therefore deal with these subjects. It will be a woman's journal. While holding an independent position upon all of these topics, as for example, the franchise, professional education, dress reform, temperance and Christian work, identifying itself with no society or organisation which may deal with any of these questions, it will yet open its pages for the most free and unbiassed [sic] expressions of opinion, [35]

The membership was both willing and able to take part in discussion of these burning (women's) political issues of the time, yet the focus of the order itself was consistently on the relationships between individuals, and on the difference which personal action might make in society.

The internal organization of the order echoed the emphasis in its public representation on the importance of personal influence and relationship and the ties of support between members. Its hierarchy was based partly on an implied meritocracy, and partly on the length of involvement with the order. The order was organized according to an elaborate constitution, in which the structure of semi-autonomous coteries and their relations to the court and the high court are set out in some detail. As with other aspects of the daughters' public representation, the cover of the constitution pamphlet preserved a conventional image of womanhood (see Fig. 7).

This constitution, which the order published as a self-contained pamphlet, first defines the object of the order:

> To form an Order of women who shall undertake to speak ill of none, and to cultivate the spirit of helpfulness, endeavouring to do at least one helpful deed every day.

---

[33] The opening issue of the journal gives the names of 39 coteries, which could have up to ten members each, as well as listing 216 members not in coteries (including 35 in England, 101 in India, and 1 in America), and nine children. If all of the coteries had a full complement this would make 615 members. It is unlikely that they did, and the numbers of active members could well have been much lower, but this is still impressive. 'Names of Coteries', *The Court*, October 1894, p. 4.

[34] The more widely known, *Australian Woman's Sphere*, edited by Vida Goldstein, was founded in 1900.

[35] 'Ourselves', *The Court*, October 1894, p. 1.

This statement is followed immediately by a statement of the relationship of members to each other:

> Members shall enter into a mutual compact for the above object, and shall wear a distinguishing badge, and shall be known to one another by a sign. (Constitution)

The three grades of members are designated by the formation to which they belong: a coterie, a court or the high court. Ten members make a coterie, ten representatives of coteries make a court, representatives of the courts, along with the order's founding members, constitute the high court. The officers of each group of any level are a dame, scribe, chancellor, two chatelaines and two companions. The dame, scribe and chancellor act, respectively, as president, secretary, and treasurer for the group, while the companions 'sit as supporters of the Dame', and the chatelaines are 'Stewards or Messengers' at her command, 'and specially to introduce and present new members on their election'. The constitution states specifically:

> The Members of the Order shall be designated Daughters, and in transacting the business of the Order the official names shall always be employed.

The high court has authority to establish coteries and courts by writ, and to approve the 'special objects' of each coterie. All coteries report to the high court. Questions of discipline are left to the coterie, with appeal to the high court available if a difficulty arises which cannot be settled internally. The main point of this 'discipline' appears to centre upon whether members are observing the Rule. It is notable in this designation of the relations among members that there is very little in the constitution to govern the daughters' relations with the outside world. The order operates within its own (safe) social space, which, though allied to the world beyond, and drawing authority through it, yet functions separately within its own terms.

The order, then, became a space in which the daughters could seek an alternative vision of the world and their relationship to it. They could explore the notions of the personal and relational power of womanhood and erect a structure of ideal relationship based on mutual support and critique. Bearing in mind this idea of the order as a 'safe space' in which to explore variant notions of power, it is instructive to turn once more to the 'investment' of Lady Hopetoun. The patronage of the countess, the highest ranking lady in the colony, and a member of the British nobility, was a considerable social coup, yet nowhere in the 'Investment of Dames and Others' document is Lady Hopetoun named: she is designated the grand dame throughout. Although the focus of the ceremony (both literally and symbolically) is the grand dame, the document claims that it is the 'Dames and Others' who are being invested. The ceremony, rather than installing the patroness, brings the whole order notionally under the hand and authority of the supreme 'lady' of the colony. In fact, the document records no names. True to the constitution, the high dame, dames, chatelains, youngest member, and others are designated only by their relationships within the order:

The Regalia of the High Court will then be handed to the Grand Dame who will present each Officier [*sic*] with her distinguishing badge.

The Coteries will then approach the Dais in the order of their creation being summoned by the High Dame and each Dame will be invested by the Grand Dame with the collar, the regalia of the other officers and daughters being handed to them by the corresponding officers of the High Court.

The Grand Dame will then invest the High Dame with her collar.

The High Dame will present the Grand Dame with the thanks of the order for the service which she has accorded them, and beg her acceptance of a bouquet of flowers fastened by the badge of the Order to be preserved as a momento [*sic*] of the occasion.

The entire assembly will then rise at the request of the High Dame and repeat aloud the rule of the Order.

This ceremony wove together elements of religious and civic ceremony and the rites of the 'at home' or 'conversazione'. Processions, 'songs', readings, and recitation, the order of precedence, the installation of the highest ranking lady at the centre of attention, the constitution of the occasion by act and word, operate within a series of contexts designed to give due weight and solemnity to the occasion. The new grand dame took all symbols of office (collars for the dames, wands for the chatelains) into her own hands and redistributed them, recreating all 'officiers' of the order by her personal authority. According to a later report, during this ceremony 'her ladyship [...] decorated between fifty and sixty ladies, and shook hands with the oldest member of the Order'.[36] Within the ceremony the group identity, and the identity within the group was asserted on multiple levels. With its emphasis on ceremony, regalia, order, titles and hierarchy, the 'general court' can be seen as an idealized performance of relationships of patronage and deference. The gracious lady at the centre of the ceremony performs a 'service' for her clients by agreeing to be their nominal leader, and is thanked at the end of the ceremony, with a bouquet of flowers fastened with the badge of the order, a pearl and star. Yet these idealized relations exist in a social and conceptual space that is separate from daily life, and entered only by women who have undertaken to live out the Rule of the order. Both the empowerment of the members within their space and the limits of the space itself are clear within the ceremony.

One way of interpreting the daughters and their activities is to see them as performing an understanding of an idealized cultured and literary world. The medieval framework within which they fashioned their activities was a strategic deployment of an available literary form, rather than a reflection of any historical intent. The language of the medieval was used as a touchstone of the values to which

---

[36] 'History of the Order'.

they appealed, but both the medievalism of the club and its emphasis on form and relationship create a space and an idiom within which to construct a vision of the heroic feminine. The values which were identified with the 'Old "Courts of Chivalry," "Love" or "Courtesy"' were assigned for reasons other than any direct connection with the Middle Ages, but they are not random assignments of positive value. The language of the order fulfilled specific political and rhetorical requirements for the daughters as they formulated their central values. These included the separateness of the order from daily life, the valorization of personal behaviour, even in ordinary circumstances and the extension of an idea of chivalry (the protection of the weak by the strong) to the moral realm where women could be and often were considered to be the superior sex.

The daughters responded to the tensions in women's changing social and political roles, in a context in which opportunities for women were opening up, but where the conventional behaviour expected of them remained highly restrictive. For women with a sense of moral mission, this created a radical disjunction between what they perceived as their duty in the world and the means at their disposal to achieve it. The activities and language of the daughters may be seen as a response to these conflicts, an attempt, not necessarily successful, to re-think the boundaries of civic virtue, and to find a language in which chivalry could be gendered female, without reference to external status. The language in which such a vision could be articulated derived on the one side from the traditions of religious orders and sodalities, while on the other it connected with what was already becoming known as the 'shrieking sisterhood' of supporters of female suffrage, who were to become the leading voice of Australian feminism in the opening years of the new century.

The 'medieval' voice of the court was a borrowed idiom, sufficiently distant from contemporary life to encompass a series of new relationships, in which personal and social reform could be couched in ways that neither infringed the boundaries of ladyhood nor forced a confrontation with the political process. The limits of such an approach are obvious, though its achievements, in the personal and professional lives of the daughters, are impossible to quantify. The Daughters of the Court remind us that in a variety of guises, and to a variety of political ends, the language of medievalism can be a powerful focus for personal and social idealism.

'A Place of Horror and Vast Solitude': Medieval Monasticism and the Australian Landscape

MEGAN CASSIDY-WELCH

All human beings — and monks and nuns are no exception — live, choose and act in a particular cultural universe. Any change in this cultural world causes changes of behavior, due to the change in one's general perception of reality. The mass media of social communication have created a 'cultural industry', that is, they produce symbols, values and meanings which change the way we see ourselves and how we relate to ourselves, to others, to the Other and to other things.[1]

The Abbot General of the Cistercians, in his general letter to the order in 1999, spoke of the ways in which cultures create worlds charged with meaning for themselves and for others.[2] Familiar to cultural historians and those interested in the practices of medievalism might be the Abbot General's recognition of the historicity of cultural production and experience, together with the reflexive nature of representation and recognition. The production of cultural meaning is dynamic and complex. The articulation of personal and group identities through performative

---

[1] 'Todos los seres humanos — y los monjes y monjas no somos excepción — vivimos, decidimos y actuamos desde un determinado universo cultural. Y todo cambio en el universo cultural genera a su vez cambios de conducta debido a cambios de percepción de la realidad. Los medios de comunicación social han creado una "industria cultural": comercian símbolos, valores y sentidos que alteran las formas de percibirnos y de relacionarnos con nosotros mismos, con los otros, con el Otro y con lo otro (las cosas)'. Abbot General's letter to the order, 1999, online at: http://www.ocso.org/ag-let-99-esp.htm, accessed 4 April 2002.

[2] 'O.C.S.O.' abbreviates the official name of the Trappists: 'Order of Cistercians of the Strict Observance'.

practices of social behaviour, the ongoing construction and reworking of the past itself and the creation and representation of material and imagined space are all parts of such production. This is especially evident in the various practices of 'medievalism', which not only explore the historicity of 'the medieval', but which also consider the ways in which the medieval past is imagined, appropriated, mythologized and used in the popular and academic cultures of the contemporary west. In 'wallowing in the question of its origins',[3] medieval studies thus confronts cultural history. Any consideration of medievalism must attend to the questions raised by those cultural historians who have insisted on the importance of the production of meaning, who argue that the imaginary and the real are more closely related than the dichotomy would suggest, and who see the historical character of discursive production as central to any reading of the past.

These general claims might be teased out by looking closely at one specific culture which is located in the world of contemporary Australia, but which has its historical origins in the monastic culture of the European Middle Ages: the Cistercian abbey of Tarrawarra, a twentieth-century foundation at Yarra Glen in Victoria. This monastic foundation raises a number of questions about the intersection of medieval and modern cultures and the ways in which the Australian landscape can accommodate the cultural practices of the European past. How does a twenty-first century monastery imagine, reflect and express the medieval past to which it is so indebted? To what extent does the practice of everyday life at Tarrawarra acknowledge 'the medieval', if at all? In approaching these questions, I am suggesting that cultural practice itself — whether asserted through text or performance — demonstrates fluidity of meaning, rather than meaning's immutability, and that the symbiosis of medieval and modern in contemporary Australian monastic culture provides one excellent example of the interplay between the past and present; between cultural representation and cultural production; and between 'medievalism' and Australian identity.

Tarrawarra Abbey

Tarrawarra abbey was founded in 1954 from the mother house of Mount St Joseph abbey, Roscrea in Ireland, the same year that Southern Star abbey was founded in New Zealand, near Palmerston North. The site of Tarrawarra lies in the fertile Upper Yarra Valley, where vineyards and farmland mark the end of the suburban sprawl that now stretches past Lilydale in Melbourne's east. The Upper Yarra Valley had been inhabited by white settlers since 1837, when the Ryrie brothers (originally from Scotland) established a homestead at Yering, and then a pastoral run called 'View Hill' two years later. View Hill pastoral run spanned twelve thousand acres of land

---

[3] R. Howard Bloch and Stephen G. Nichols, introduction to *Medievalism and the Modernist Temper* (Baltimore: Johns Hopkins University Press, 1996), p. 2.

north of the Yarra river, between what is now Yarra Glen and Healesville. This region was also known as Tarrawarra. The existing large homestead building at the centre of the present monastic site of Tarrawarra abbey was built by David Syme at the beginning of the twentieth century as a wedding gift for his daughter Lucie.[4] The property with its generous acreage was chosen as the site for a monastic foundation by the abbot of Mount St Joseph, who is said to have toured the district looking for a suitable site and upon seeing Tarrawarra instinctively 'knew' that this was a spiritual space. According to Father Michael Casey, prior of Tarrawarra, the area around Tarrawarra was, in the 1950s, a strongly Protestant area, its inhabitants potentially averse to selling the old homestead to a Catholic monastic order. The Cistercians had to purchase the site through an agent without the vendors knowing exactly who was going to move in.[5] The site is also meaningful to the indigenous inhabitants of the area: there is a canoe tree and a fireplace on the site from the pre-colonization period and a tree which is said to be particularly sacred to the Aboriginal people of the Upper Yarra Valley still standing on the property.

The building currently at the centre of the monastic site is a late Victorian timber structure with many alterations and additions. Nonetheless, elements of a standard monastic plan are in evidence, particularly in the broad regulation of public and private space. The homestead building serves as the public face of the monastery, with its guest rooms, main foyer, parlour and gift shop. The eastern end of the building is adjoined by the abbey church, recently renovated. Behind the homestead building are the inaccessible or private areas of the monastery: the monks' rooms, the cloister, the refectory and so on. There is still some hint of medieval delineation of space in that the cloister demarcates various zones within the monastic precinct, although it is not quadrangular.[6] Covered walkways zigzag across the cloister between the original house and the rest of the claustral buildings: unlike medieval cloister arcades, these walkways are not enclosed. Glimpses of the hills and surrounding landscapes may be caught through the open cloister walks, which means that the walled-up feeling of some of the medieval sites is avoided. Nonetheless, a sense of enclosure persists in the separation of the monastic part of the site from the site accessible to visitors, and although possums and other local fauna wander at will around the cloister due to the absence of an enclosed cloister wall, the openness of

---

[4] See Maxime Palmer, *Tarrawarra: 130 Years on a Victorian Property* (Melbourne: The Hawthorn Press, 1967) for some rather sketchy background on the pre-monastic history of the site.

[5] Interview with Michael Casey, 6 April 2001. I would like to thank Michael Casey for his time and assistance in answering my questions about Tarrawarra.

[6] For the medieval cloister see *inter alia*, W. Horn, 'On the Origins of the Medieval Cloister', *Gesta*, 12 (1973), 13–52; Roberta Gilchrist, 'Community and Self: Perceptions and Uses of Space in Medieval Monasteries', *Scottish Archaeological Review*, 6 (1989), 55–64.

the cloister does not undermine the ultimate resolution of what we might see as open and closed space.[7]

It is worth noting that although Tarrawarra is a male monastic community, the principles of spatial delineation are not gendered. Rather, space is regulated according to a broader secular/monastic divide. Non-monastic men and women cannot enter the cloister: secular men were originally able to visit this area of the precinct, but it was decided that the segregation of lay and monastic should not be articulated along gender lines.[8] Many of the other barriers that construct spatial boundaries within the precinct are symbolic. Feeling that it was inappropriate to erect 'Keep Out' signs, it was decided to encourage rather than enforce segregation. Curtains rather than locked doors are used within the homestead building to indicate to guests that they ought not to cross certain points, for instance. This is in keeping with the policies of other monastic houses, according to Casey, who told me of one French abbey where signs depicting silhouettes of monks with their hoods pulled up are dotted around the precinct to denote that only monks can be in certain places. At Tarrawarra, the guest-house occupies six rooms in the original building and a small heritage-listed cottage elsewhere on the site. The community does not run organized retreats, but is welcoming to guests.

Building work, itself a feature of the medieval histories of European Cistercian houses, continues at Tarrawarra. In recent years for instance, the abbey church has been completely remodelled. It is a light and airy space, retaining a stylistic simplicity often said to be at the heart of medieval Cistercian architecture. Although the church is fairly traditional in layout, with a central nave and separate entrance and seating for guests, it is an intimate interior that in many ways reflects its immediate location. The church certainly incorporates what we might call vernacular elements into its design and ornament. The altar and altar furniture, for instance, are made from the remains of cypress trees burned in the Ash Wednesday bushfires of 1983 and the organ comes from a now disbanded convent at Chadstone. Light in the church comes partly from the stained glass windows behind the altar that were installed in the old church building and were the work of a Czech-Australian artist, Miloslav (sometimes known as Dismas) Zika during the late 1950s.[9] These windows, together with a portrait of Our Lady of Tarrawarra in the main aisle of the church, are the only obviously colourful decorative elements within the church space: the rest of the glass in the building is clear. The portrait was commissioned from a local artist: it depicts Mary as a mature woman, holding a book and standing in front of the view out across the valley from the main building (with the railway line painted out for aesthetic reasons). A similarly modern wooden crucifix hangs behind the altar. There are choir stalls on either side of the central aisle in the traditional design,

---

[7] Robert Venturi, *Complexity and Contradiction in Architecture*, 2nd edn (New York: Museum of Modern Art, 1977).

[8] Interview with Michael Casey, 16 April 2001.

[9] Personal correspondence with the artist's son, Charles Zika, 1 June 2001.

but there are computerized hymn-boards and a computerized lighting system that will vary the light according to the time of day. At vigils, for instance, there is just enough light to see but not so much that the community would forget that the office was taking place at 4am. The church space is quiet, as one would expect, but not silent, and the sound of birds outside can be heard within the building.

For medieval Cistercians, the monastic landscape provided opportunities to describe the monastic enterprise itself. The early twelfth-century monastery of Clairvaux, for example, lay 'in terra deserta, in loco horroris et vastae solitudinis' ('a desert land, a place of horror and vast solitude'), according to St Bernard's biographer, William of St Thierry,[10] who like other Cistercian commentators stressed the importance of monastic solitude, silence and removal from the secular world. At the same time, medieval Cistercian writers were able to talk about their monasteries in paradisal terms: Meaux abbey in Yorkshire, for example, was equated with a heavenly garden, where lilies of the valley and roses grow and where the scent of cinnamon, myrrh and other spices sweetens the air.[11] For medieval Cistercians, the transcendent qualities of monastic life could be at times discursively tempered by the language of bleakness. The monastery was the gateway to heaven, but it was also a desert and a prison; this 'spirituality of light' could also speak of ontological shadows. As I have argued elsewhere, medieval Cistercians crafted a carefully enunciated discourse on space, in which the relationship between enclosure and freedom could be expressed.[12] Do we find the same uses of spatial discourse at Tarrawarra?

The abbey at Tarrawarra certainly mirrors some of the basic spatial principles that medieval Cistercians found so important. The regulation of material space itself in the demarcation of the site into monastic and non-monastic areas, together with the siting of the monastery outside the urban centre of Melbourne are two fundamental echoes of early monastic treatment of space.[13] Furthermore, the general organization of the built environment of the monastery would not be unfamiliar to the twelfth- and thirteenth-century monks in the order's period of greatest expansion, although the fabric of Tarrawarra's construction is local and contemporary. Indebtedness to or

---

[10] *Vita Prima, PL* 185, col. 241, quoting Deuteronomy 32. 10.

[11] Jean Leclercq, 'Lettres de vocation à la vie monastique', *Analecta Monastica: Textes et études sur la vie des moines au moyen âge*, 3rd series, ed. by M. M. Lebreton, J. Leclercq, and C. H. Talbot, Studia Anselmiana, fasc. 37 (Rome: Herder, 1955), pp. 169–82 (p. 178). 'Hic fragrat odor inaestimabilis suavitatis, hic redolent flores rosarum et lilia convallium [...] cinnamon et balsamum, myrrha et aloe [...]'.

[12] Megan Cassidy-Welch, 'Incarceration and Liberation: Prisons in the Cistercian Monastery', *Viator*, 32 (2001), 1–35.

[13] For the earliest statutes of the Cistercian Order giving directions for the foundation of new communities, see *Les Plus anciens textes de Cîteaux: sources, textes et notes historiques*, ed. by J. De La Croix Bouton and J. B. Van Damme, Cîteaux. Commentarii cistercienses: Studia et documenta, 2 (Achel: Abbaye cistercienne, 1974).

acknowledgement of the medieval past may also be found in the naming of the monks' rooms at Tarrawarra. Fontenay and Rievaulx are two examples of twelfth-century Cistercian foundations that are memorialized as the names of two 'cells'.

More fundamental, however, is the representation of landscape and space at Tarrawarra. Although there has been no formal foundation history yet written of the abbey,[14] the site itself is frequently represented as spiritually meaningful in oral and written narratives describing the beginnings of the community. It is often reported that during his tour of the Yarra Valley to find a suitable site for a Cistercian foundation, the abbot of Roscrea (then Dom Camillus Claffe) came across the site of Tarrawarra and 'uttered the immortal words: "Stop! This is the property for an [a]bbey!"'.[15] Father Kevin O'Farrell writes in his account of the abbey's history that 'on this very first day the abbot felt deep in his heart that this was the spot chosen by God, and he never altered this conviction; this was how Tarrawarra was found'.[16] Medieval narratives of abbatial foundations describe a similar air of predestination in chronicle accounts of the selection and development of sites. Fountains abbey, according to its early thirteenth-century historian was always 'holy ground',[17] as was Rievaulx abbey in Yorkshire, in the eyes of its precentor.[18] When the foundation history of Kirkstall abbey was composed in the early thirteenth century, its author was also careful to describe the geographical site as a traditional *locus amoenus*, a spiritually resonant landscape appropriate for a new foundation.[19]

Tarrawarra's land itself is also reported as having been difficult to subdue: farming the cattle which initially provided the abbey with its main source of income was extremely laborious and even hazardous, with snakes on the river flats and so on. The success of the foundation, according to O'Farrell, was due not only to the perseverance of the founders, but also to the *terra sancta* of Tarrawarra itself. He reflects:

---

[14] Although a lengthy account of the abbey's foundation has been written by and published electronically. See Fr Kevin O'Farrell, O.C.S.O, *Our Lady of Tarrawarra Abbey: Its Story and Spirit. The First Forty Years: A Short Account, 1954–1994*, online at, http://members.tripod.co.uk/jloughnan/far00.htm. Accessed 4 April 2002.

[15] John Hamilton, 'Sanctuary for the Soul', *Herald Sun* (Melbourne), 1 June 1996, *Weekend*, p. 4.

[16] See http://members.tripod.co.uk/jloughnan/farch4.htm, accessed 4 April 2002.

[17] *Memorials of the Abbey of St. Mary of Fountains*, ed. by J. R. Walbran, Surtees Society, 42, 67, and 130 (London: Andrews, 1863–1918) [hereafter *Mem. F.*], p. 76.

[18] A. Wilmart, 'Les Mélanges de Matthieu, préchantre de Rievaulx au début du XIIIe siècle', *Revue Bénédictine*, 52 (1940), 15–84 (p. 74).

[19] See *Fundacio Abbathie de Kyrkestall*, ed. and trans. by E. Kitson Clark, Miscellanea. Publications of the Thoresby Society, 4 (Leeds: Thoresby Society, 1893), pp. 173–208 (p. 177).

taken in all the whole place is quite simple and ordinary. Yet there hangs over the whole place a mysterious aura of grace: the very air seems to be permeated with the presence of Our Lady, in her role of a gentle yet strong mother, loving and welcoming.[20]

Early difficulties and eventual stability are frequently the paradigms within which medieval monastic historians fashioned their narratives, too. The monks of Fountains abbey were forced to sleep under the shelter of an elm tree in the mid-twelfth century, according the monk who wrote their foundation history, while the monks of Kirkstall had to move sites a number of times before they finally settled permanently.[21]

Such discursive debts in the representation of the space of this modern monastery may easily be related to the narrative practices of the Cistercian past, while the few examples I have given here give us some insight into the ways that language can be used and read to forge links between the past and the present. From the perspective of Australian medievalism we might also acknowledge the ways in which medieval narrative techniques reappear in the informal oral and written histories of Tarrawarra. The appropriation of medieval frameworks of self-representation is one way in which modern Cistercians situate themselves in a longer spiritual history that transcends the localization of the abbey's immediate physical environment and acknowledges (however implicitly) the European historical foundations of the Yarra Valley community. The representation of this monastic site as both difficult, especially in terms of farming, and at the same time spiritually rich, situates the abbey's material environment within a longer history of monastic representational practice.

Performing Medieval Monasticism

'Once you get over the fancy dress, life here is very very ordinary', remarked one member of the Tarrawarra community.[22] The temporal discipline of the monastic day continues to be structured around the singing of the Divine Office, some of whose chants were composed within the community.[23] The day begins at 4am with vigils and ends at 8pm with compline. In between, the monks sing lauds at 5.30am, terce at 8am, sext at 11.15am, none at 1.40pm and vespers at 6pm. Between dawn and the third hour is often a time for private prayer, as was the case in the thirteenth century, when a book for novices recommended this hour as a time for the novice to be fully

---

[20] See http://members.tripod.co.uk/jloughnan/far00.htm, accessed 4 April 2002.

[21] *Mem. F.*, pp. 34–35; *Fundacio Abbathie de Kyrkestall*, pp. 173–208.

[22] Brother Steele, O.C.S.O., quoted in Hamilton, '*Sanctuary for the Soul*', p. 5.

[23] *Benedictine Pathways: Benedictines in Australia and New Zealand* (New Norcia: The Benedictine Union of Australia and New Zealand, 2000), p. 36.

alone with God.[24] Manual labour and self-sufficiency are also important at Tarra-warra. The community now operates a Eucharist-bread distributing business rather than the dairy business of previous years that provided the monastery with its regular income, but the monks also still run a herd of beef cattle that brings in two cheques per annum. Other manual work depends on the skill of the individual. Some members of the community cook, others sew, mend fences, and complete basic maintenance on the buildings and around the property. Study and writing also count as manual work. The monks still wear habits and scapulars for the offices, although at other times of the day, whilst working, they wear non-monastic dress.

Daily life in the monastery reflects the basic principles of the *Rule of St Benedict*, itself still considered the foundational monastic treatise guiding life at Tarrawarra.[25] There are some liturgical distinctions between members of the community: lay brothers, for instance, are not bound to attend all the monastic offices. It is worth noting that there are still some lay brothers at Tarrawarra, but the abbey is not receiving any more, on the basis of a broader decision made by the order's general chapter. Whereas twelfth- and thirteenth-century lay brothers were distinguished from choir monks on the basis of literacy levels and class and undertook most of the heavy manual work in a monastery, the lay brothers at Tarrawarra are not distinct from the rest of the community in terms of class or educational status.

Hospitality continues to be an important element of monastic life at Tarrawarra as I have mentioned previously. The presence of guests and occasionally the families of members of the community ensures that familial and social interaction can occur on the site of the abbey itself. For two weeks of the year, monks may leave the monastery to spend time with their families. More generally, the community is involved with the locality of the Upper Yarra Valley: the monks go into Yarra Glen every day to pick up their mail, and they are certainly known to the local community. They use the local doctor, for instance, and they used to donate blood *en masse*. The local schools and members of the community assisted in the regeneration of the natural environment at Tarrawarra, where an extensive program of replanting indigenous flora has taken place. Some members of the community are frequent travellers: Michael Casey himself, as a scholar and as someone who has undertaken a number of senior administrative duties both within the abbey and the order, attends conferences and meetings nationally and internationally. The community at Tarrawarra is thus 'closed' only in the sense that space within the monastery is off limits to non-monastic visitors. Although the abbey is quiet, it is also a place of great activity.

---

[24] E. Mikkers, 'Un *Speculum Novitii* inédit d'Etienne de Sallai', *Collectanea Ordinis Cisterciensis Reformatorum*, 8 (1946), 17–68 (p. 64).

[25] *Benedictine Pathways*, p. 36. Tarrawarra is a member of the Benedictine Union of Australia and New Zealand, an association of religious institutes following the Rule of St Benedict.

Novices are few, and the process of joining the Tarrawarra community is long. After a potential recruit has expressed interest in joining the abbey, he then spends some time there, getting to know the community and reflecting on his own life. This might take a year or two. The novice master then invites the applicant to live at the abbey for a month, at the end of which the applicant makes a formal written application to enter the community as a postulant. A postulant will ultimately enter the novitiate after six months, and remain there for two years. A further three years pass during which time temporary vows are made, and at the end of this period the formal vows of profession are made. As during the twelfth and thirteenth centuries, the novice is distinguished from the rest of the community by dress: one highly visible way in which boundaries are created between the abbey and the world without. Medieval Cistercian novices were known for being voluntary members of the community: the order rejected the common Benedictine practice of receiving oblates and it was understood that the instance of apostasy would be lower were novices to be adults.[26]

As in the medieval novitiate, the period of transition for a new monk at Tarrawarra is also a time of learning. The twelfth-century biographer of Aelred of Rievaulx described the novitiate as a testing place, where 'a novice finds it so hard to stamp out the old and endure the present and take precaution against future vices'.[27] The novice master at Tarrawarra, Michael Casey, told me that in his view, novice does not mean 'no vice', and that the popular vision of men who choose to become monks as being 'pure as the driven snow' is erroneous. Casey reflected on a universal tendency to the repression of vice, saying that part of the purpose of the novitiate is to allow an individual's vices to emerge and to be dealt with. Although the psychological principles behind this view may, to the twenty-first century reader, sound indebted to Freudian discourses on repression, Casey also pointed out that such matters were addressed by John Cassian and Evagrius. Part of the novice's 'training' in this regard is thus an expression of what Casey described as the Cistercian 'spirituality of light', and an element of the process by which a monk may 'shed the outer man' to work towards union with God.

I have outlined some of the features of daily life at Tarrawarra in order to make a more general point about the performance of monastic culture in this modern abbey. Some of the outward trappings of life at Tarrawarra that are redolent of medieval practice, such as dress, the training of novices and a strict liturgical structure, are also ways in which the community distinguishes itself from non-monastic religious cultures, and indeed secular culture in general. As anthropologists have long understood, the creation of boundaries, both material and imagined, is one way in which cultures demarcate and articulate their own identity, and imagine the identity

---

[26] On apostasy see Christopher Harper-Bill, 'Monastic Apostasy in Late Medieval England', *Journal of Ecclesiastical History*, 32 (1981), 1–18.

[27] *The Life of Ailred of Rievaulx by Walter Daniel*, ed. and trans. by F. M. Powicke (Edinburgh: Nelson, 1950), p. 17.

of others. Distinguishing one community from others by means of dress or ritual serves to reinforce that community's own identity. This was true for medieval Cistercians, too. Recent scholarship on Cistercian culture has stressed the tension that existed between monastic ideas of withdrawal from the world and medieval Cistercian involvement with the secular world. Nonetheless, it has been recognized that this tension was negotiated by the creation of a particularly Cistercian culture, which drew on monks' individual and collective experiences to enable the order to 'reject society's norms [yet] still share with the surrounding society ingrained ideas and customs'.[28] Thus, while Cistercian writing (spiritual, historical and even legislative) continued to affirm the basic principles of enclosure, solitude, stability and withdrawal from the world throughout the thirteenth century, the practice of everyday life was more accommodating than one might expect.[29]

At Tarrawarra, boundaries are also clearly delineated by practice, and although fundamental monastic principles articulated in the *Rule of St Benedict* are observed (such as chastity and obedience, and the renunciation of personal property), the monks of this abbey certainly retain a place in the non-monastic world. This may be seen in minor ways (using the post office), or in more theoretical ways. The O.C.S.O. website, for instance, stresses that Cistercian monks have an important role in contemporary society:

> The postmodern world is far from being uniform or consistent, but there is in it a deep need for transcending what is visible, a thirst for both mysticism and community, a desire for divine union. The search for God appears in the different ways of going beyond oneself: social service, a sense of mystery, silent prayer as an integral part of human life. This is where Cistercian life becomes surprisingly meaningful for the world, since its spirituality emphasizes union of the human person with God and with others in the transforming mystery of Christ.[30]

The medieval past is thus understood to be important in this context in that it provides a model for guidance and witness. In 1998, a program of studies called *Exordium: A Program of Reflection and Study on the Values of the Cistercian Reform* was developed and offered to all Cistercian communities, which reinforced the importance of the order's medieval heritage. This course, which was taken in ten monthly units over the year of the nine hundredth anniversary of the founding of the first Cistercian monastery of Cîteaux, was a systematic reflection on the founders and founding texts of the Cistercian Order.[31] New translations of some of the *Carta caritatis* and other seminal documents were made available, and the order's website

---

[28] Martha Newman, *The Boundaries of Charity: Cistercian Culture and Ecclesiastical Reform 1098–1180* (Stanford: Stanford University Press, 1996), p. 5.

[29] Thus St Bernard and Aelred of Rievaulx were travellers, as were many of the lay brothers, who dealt with the commerce of the monasteries at markets and fairs, for instance.

[30] See http://www.ocso.org/net/faq-eng.htm, accessed 4 April 2002.

[31] See http://www.ocso.org/net/exord-en.htm, accessed 4 April 2002.

provided an historical overview of the early years of the order. This program had a number of spiritual aims for both individual monks and for the order as a whole. In the context of medievalism, however, the program provides an example of the sort of historical trajectory that has been fashioned between medieval past and postmodern present. The more obvious elements of medieval practice that may be observed in the performance of everyday life at Tarrawarra are only a small part of the more general indebtedness of today's community to the principles of its initial reforming impulse, the textual traditions of its ancestors and the meaningful dialogue that can still exist between historical and contemporary monastic practice.

Space, Solitude and Redemption

The performance of monasticism, the representation of space and acknowledgment of the long history of the Cistercian Order tells us that the Tarrawarra monks are indebted to the medieval past. But are they also indebted to the Australian present? Michael Casey indicated that there are certainly cultural differences between the practice of monasticism here and in other non-European countries. He cited the example of India where the caste system is so entrenched in the non-monastic world that the monastic world cannot help being influenced by the same sorts of spoken and unspoken societal divisions. Casey told me, too, of the importance in Africa of family and kinship cultures being carried over into the monastic realm: there have been cases (not in the Cistercian Order) where people in charge of the monastery's finances have given away money to their families, as familial obligations are not understood to end when a family member 'renounces' the secular world to become a monk.[32]

If there is anything particularly Australian about Tarrawarra, Casey suggested that it might be found in the egalitarianism of their community. The monks do not address each other by title (such as Father), but by given name. In a recent Benedictine publication, however, Casey questioned the value of seeking something called 'Australianness' in monastic practice, arguing that defining either 'Australian' or 'Benedictine' (or Cistercian, it might be added) is in some ways a fruitless task, given the myriad different expressions that may be found of each. The subjective experience of being 'Australian' or the subjective experience of being 'Benedictine' does not rest on easily defined and totalizing categories of identity or identification. Rather, both cultures need to be understood as fluid, mutable and historically time bound if one is to acknowledge the subjectivity of belonging to, representing or claiming a culture. Casey suggests, nonetheless, that monasticism generally might be perceived as counter-cultural in some ways and that being a monk is at odds with the

---

[32] Within the community at Tarrawarra, resources are to be shared. For instance, each member of the monastic community has the right to 1/25 of the community car.

'lives of ordinary Australians', especially in 'the intensity and discipline required by the Rule of St Benedict'.[33]

Another reading of the relationship between monastic practice and Australian culture connects the white Australian past with the growth of the abbey at Tarrawarra:

> In the very short term of its white colonisation, our country's story has been a complex one, with very differing groups contributing to its development, as we know so well. All these [...] form an integral part of our heritage [...] These are the people who tilled the land, discovered its mineral wealth, built its towns, cities and ports. They pushed roads, railways and communication links across vast plains and through deserts and mountains. As well they built schools and hospitals, places of worship and places of recreation, and a thousand other services [...] In the truest sense, we at Tarrawarra are heirs of all these people who have prepared the way for us. In another sense their life work has reached a certain phase of fulfillment in the foundation of this abbey. It is significant to hear of how from the early years of the Church in this land, bishops longed and petitioned for the coming of Cistercian monks.[34]

The relationship between 'brave pioneers' and the foundation and growth of Tarrawarra situates the abbey within a progressivist history of white colonization, hinting at a longer historical drama in which indigenous Australians play but a peripheral role. Such narratives of Australian history have long been questioned. Most recently, historian Henry Reynolds in *Why Weren't We Told?* exposed and traced the creation of a particular form of Australian historical writing and teaching, in which violence, resistance and conflict were often written out of narrative and syllabus in favour of a (single) neat and palatable tale of individual bravery, white fortitude and national 'development'.[35] Accepting the notion of the civilizing propensity of Christianity in such narratives is often central in such a national story, and, as is clear from the above quotation, remains an enduring motif in the articulation of a particular historical vision.

White histories of the Tarrawarra region also fail to address the reality of nineteenth-century colonizing or 'settlement' practices. Such practices involved dispossession throughout Australia, and the Upper Yarra Valley's indigenous inhabitants (the Wurundjeri people) were not isolated from the violence that marked the activities of the 'overlanders' and other settlers. In 1840, while the Ryrie brothers were expanding their sheep farming run in the region, the commissioner of Crown Lands, Henry Gisborne, wrote to Governor La Trobe, stating that 'the natives' had acquired firearms and had fired on a white settler on Ryrie's station near Tarrawarra. The alleged culprit, 'Jackie Jackie', was arrested by Gisborne and his troopers and

---

[33] *Benedictine Pathways*, p. 6.

[34] At http://members.tripod.co.uk/jloughnan/farch10.htm, accessed 4 April 2002.

[35] Henry Reynolds, *Why Weren't We Told?: A Personal Search for the Truth About Our History* (Ringwood: Viking, 1999).

incarcerated: 'Jackie Jackie [...] is a very tall, powerful man and made a desperate resistance', remarked the commissioner. Other indigenous men tried to fight off the troopers with spears and muskets.[36] The presence of armed black men on their land alarmed Ryrie and neighbouring settlers. One of them wrote to the Governor La Trobe, complaining 'there are now encamped in my paddock on the Yarra Yarra [...] two to three hundred blacks [who] threatened to burn the huts [...] the blacks had from twenty to thirty guns and muskets [...] The blacks have not committed any outrage, but of course the men are frightened and are not willing to go out alone'. The black protestors were eventually removed by mounted police.[37]

More recent events in the indigenous history of Tarrawarra and its surrounds are also absent from the abbey's representation of its relationship with the land it occupies. In 1863, Coranderrk Aboriginal station was established on 2300 acres of Ryrie's station near Healesville with two aims: to create a self-sufficient farming community which the indigenous people who were housed there could manage, and to function as a place where 'neglected' children and infirm adults from other regions could be relocated. The fourth report of the Coranderrk board in 1863 stated with surprise that 'it was found that the blacks are reluctant to give up their children'.[38] Nonetheless, children from as far away as the Wimmera in Western Victoria were eventually brought to the station where they lived in dormitories with other infants and adolescents. Families also occupied Coranderrk. *'Bringing Them Home'*, the 1997 document which made public to many white Australians the reality of these children's experiences and which did so much to publicize 'the stolen generation' specifically named Coranderrk as one of the many places where Aboriginal children were taken after forced removal from their parents.[39] Coranderrk station had a chequered history. For the first ten years of its foundation, it was very successfully farmed and the hop-growing business that the residents had established turned a tidy profit. When this was realized, the Victorian Aboriginal Protection Board began to appropriate the profits and over a ten-year period attempted to reclaim the now valuable land. A vocal and assertive Aboriginal protest movement grew at the station, and despite a catastrophic measles outbreak in 1875 which killed

---

[36] *Historical Records of Australia. Volume 2B; Aborigines and Protectors 1838–1839*, ed. by Michael Cannon (Melbourne: Victoria Government Printing Office, 1981–88), pp. 729–31 (letter from Gisborne to La Trobe, 15 January 1840).

[37] *Historical Records*, ed. by Cannon, p. 732 (letter from Armyne Bolden to La Trobe, 2 May 1840).

[38] Cited in Aldo Massola, *Coranderrk: A History of the Aboriginal Station* (Kilmore: Lowden Publishing, 1975), p. 17.

[39] National Inquiry into the Separation of Aboriginal and Torres Strait Islander Children from their Families (Commissioner: Ronald Wilson), *'Bringing Them Home': Report of the National Inquiry into the Separation of Aboriginal and Torres Strait Islander Children from their Families*, Part 2.4: Sydney (Sydney: Human Rights and Equal Opportunity Commission, 1997).

thirty-one of the one hundred and fifty residents, a Royal Commission two years later upheld the residents' petition that the station remain self-supporting. In 1886, however, the Victorian Aborigines Act was passed, stating that only 'full-blood' Aborigines could remain on Aboriginal reserves. Half the population of Coranderrk was deported. By the beginning of twentieth century, the station had lost half its land. In 1944, ten years before the foundation of Tarrawarra abbey, the last of the original residents died.[40]

These events are not part of the abbey's current historical identity, which imagines the Australianness of Tarrawarra through a white Yarra Valley landscape. Aboriginal dispossession, regional complicity in the forced removal of Aboriginal children from their families and the history of vigorous Aboriginal resistance, first against the presence of white settlers and later against white interference with farming, are all crucial parts of the history of the Upper Yarra Valley which have not been incorporated into the history of Tarrawarra abbey. Instead, the community's self-representation privileges its medieval past and its recent white past, using a cultural vocabulary that talks of colonization as part of the triumph of pastoralization. The wilderness landscape in this vocabulary evokes an Australian landscape of emptiness and possibility, a landscape we find in old epic narratives of Australian history. For Manning Clark, for instance, the unforgiving vastness of Australia was the stage on which his vision of the tragedy of the coming of the Europeans was performed: the hapless explorer Robert O'Hara Burke tottered through the endless heat of the desert unable to escape his own 'fatal flaw' just as much as he was unable to escape the vertiginous prospect of infinite space between Melbourne and his goal of the Gulf of Carpentaria.[41] For Patrick White, the figure of Voss, 'so vast and ugly' was 'fascinated by the prospect of desert places', those places of 'perfect abstraction'.[42] Australian painter Arthur Boyd, too, in the words of Clark himself, had 'a vision of the Australian landscape, of trees, of plains of desolation, of a vast sky in which there lived a fragile beauty [...]'.[43] Space, solitude and redemption — these qualities have all played their part in creating visions of past and present in the uncertain and anxious worlds of Australian identity and cultural expression.

---

[40] For a recent resume of Coranderrk, see Inga Clendinnen's Boyer Lecture for Radio National, 'Inside the Contact Zone', broadcast 12 December 1999, and later published as *True Stories* (Sydney: ABC Books for the Australian Broadcasting Corporation, 1999). In 1998, land at Coranderrk was purchased by the Indigenous Land Corporation and returned to the Aboriginal people.

[41] C. M. H. Clark, *A History of Australia*, 6 vols (Melbourne: Melbourne University Press, 1978), IV, pp. 144–64.

[42] Patrick White, *Voss: A Novel* (London: Eyre and Spottiswoode, 1957), p. 45 and p. 94.

[43] John Rickard, 'Clark and Patrick White' in *Manning Clark: Essays on His Place in History*, ed. by Carl Bridge (Melbourne: Melbourne University Press, 1994), p. 48.

Such vocabulary resonates in medieval Cistercian culture, where the motif of a figurative desert is utilized to talk about a certain type of solitude, and where mastery of the natural environment is used to represent the permanence and subsequent *stabilitas* of a monastic foundation. In O'Farrell's description of the place of Tarrawarra as part of the longer history of white Australia, we might also see the interplay of these traditional historical narratives: on one hand, a historical trajectory which emphasizes progress and triumph over wilderness, and on the other, recourse to fairly traditional medieval models of describing monastic history. In both cases, it is the land itself that provides the means by which ideologies are expressed. The colonization history of the land — the very means by which the region was 'tamed' in the prehistory of the abbey's foundation — does not have a place in either paradigm. The region's indigenous inhabitants appear only as marginal, vague figures, who shared with the monastery some spiritual interest in the landscape, but whose subsequent disappearance from view goes unremarked.

Medievalism as Historical Choice

I have sketched a small part of the lives of the monks at Tarrawarra abbey in order to raise some broader ideas relating to how medieval past and postmodern present might be seen to meet in Australian culture. I have concentrated on the representational qualities of cultural forms, whether they be written, material or verbal, in order to begin an exploration of how such forms function within a broader historical language of culture. At Tarrawarra, the medieval origins of the Cistercian Order are acknowledged in both daily practice and in the imagination of the order's wider meaning within contemporary Australia. The language of the Cistercian enterprise, for example, continues to echo the foundational narratives of the twelfth and thirteenth centuries. At the same time, the abbey's history is given meaning by recourse to other Australian narratives, particularly those which build on the 'pioneer spirit' and those which stress the refashioning and taming of an alien, if not overtly hostile, landscape. In so far as the community at Tarrawarra negotiates its medieval origins via its presence in twenty-first century Australia, I would suggest that the abbey's place in Australia has provided important discursive opportunities to reaffirm the abiding premises of monastic life, and to emphasize, as did medieval Cistercians, just how important imagined and material landscapes and spaces remain in the articulation of community, identity and purpose.

For Tarrawarra abbey, however, an Australian identity is a white identity and a historical story that does not immediately address the black history of the land on which the community was eventually founded. The medieval past is the starting point in a historical trajectory that acknowledges white settlement and pastoralization but which ignores the dispossession on which white occupation was contingent. Medievalism, in this context, is a historical choice. Such a choice is not altogether surprising, given Tarrawarra abbey's institutional and spiritual debt to the worlds of the twelfth and thirteenth century. But I would suggest that the imagined medieval past and the white 'pioneer' past have created at Tarrawarra an Australian identity which is deliberately uncomplicated by issues of colonization and race. These are issues that we must confront when we explore what medievalism means in an Australian context. How does medievalism work to obscure difficult histories?

In more general terms, I stress the necessity for a cultural-historical approach to medievalism. How a culture describes and performs its identities and the ways in which such performance and representation may be read are of fundamental interest to cultural historians, as has long been recognized.[44] Exploring cultural practice is fundamental to delving into issues of historical appropriation, refashioning and imagination — issues that lie at the heart of the practices we call 'medievalism'. A community such as Tarrawarra, whose historical roots are deeply embedded in the landscape of the medieval past just as much as they are firmly planted in the Australian present, illuminates the profound and meaningful ways in which cultural production operates on historical, cultural and spiritual levels. The 'cultural universe' of contemporary monasticism thus affords us some insight into the negotiation, shaping and articulation of both modern and medieval worlds.

---

[44] *The New Cultural History: Essays*, ed. by Lynn Hunt (Berkeley: University of California Press, 1989).

A New Sort of Castle in the Air: Medievalist Communities in Contemporary Australia

ADINA HAMILTON

It is a question often asked. Why is the field of medieval studies in crisis in the academy, struggling to find ways of justifying its existence and demonstrating its relevance, when popular culture is fascinated with the Middle Ages, when the medieval is endlessly valorized (or sexily demonized) in books, movies, television programs, and computer games that are consumed by a mass audience, and fetishized in particular genres and media by cult audiences?

Answers are often sought in terms of power relations within the contemporary academy. But one part of the answer surely lies in the history of academic medievalism's engagement with those outside the academy. Kathleen Biddick has aptly summed up the process by which

> in order to separate and elevate themselves from popular studies of medieval culture, the new academic medievalists of the nineteenth century designated their practices, influenced by positivism, as scientific and eschewed what they regarded as less-positivist, 'non-scientific' practices, labelling them *medievalism* [...] Medievalism, a fabricated effect of this newly forming medieval studies, thus became visible as its despised 'other', its exteriority.[1]

It has become fashionable — even necessary — for medievalists like Biddick to cast a reflexive eye on the construction of their own discourse, and for critics to acknowledge some of the more accessible manifestations of medievalism flourishing in the fields of popular culture. Yet as Biddick also points out, the discipline of medieval studies is still in the thrall of the divide engineered by its founders. Academics can be mystified or annoyed by the preconceptions their students bring to the classroom; conversely, academic medievalism can seem beside the point to

---

[1] Kathleen Biddick, *The Shock of Medievalism* (Durham: Duke University Press, 1998), pp. 1–2.

many outside the academy. To draw on the metaphor used by Biddick and others, academic medievalism is like a castle. While those inside are certain of their privileged position in the landscape, differences in language and cultural understanding separate them from the 'popular' medievalists left outside the walls when the discipline was built. From the outside, the castle looks attractive, but the ways of its people are strange. And not necessarily better: these days, as I will discuss, some popular medievalists are not so certain that the image of the castle does in fact signify a power relationship at all. Likewise, an interest in the positivist study of medieval texts and artefacts is perceived as just one of many valid personal responses to the inspiration of the medieval. The peasants are not so much revolting as failing to notice that the people in the castle think they are in charge.

The purpose of this article, then, is to identify and deconstruct some of the tropes of just one of many contemporary manifestations of popular medievalism, one that is characterized by an interest in utopian community-building. The communities of interest to a medievalist enterprise of this type may be real or imagined, physical, virtual, or online. Their creation may be a literary undertaking, a practical project, or enacted through performances in a variety of venues and media. The particular utopian medievalist communities I have chosen to examine here are notable because their medievalism is entirely explicit and (self-)conscious, and the medieval past is deliberately invoked as inspiration and paradigm: it both justifies their existence and defines their nature. And yet, as I will show, their conceptualization of the medieval past and its relationship to the present differs from that of the scholarly community in fundamental ways, as do their understandings of the processes by which a true and meaningful understanding of the Middle Ages can legitimately be gained. In thus foregrounding and analyzing the lack of connection at a very basic level between academic medieval studies and this form of popular medievalism, some of the ways in which scholarly medievalism fails to engage the popular imagination — leaving it open within the academy to claims of irrelevance — will become apparent.

I will focus on three diverse but related examples of utopian medievalism from Australia in the last decade. Kerry Greenwood's children's science fiction novels set around a post-Holocaust Melbourne are a local example of an international subgenre, and include detailed imaginings of consciously medievalist communities that are presented as safe, civilized, utopian havens in a barbarous future world. The 'Principality of Lochac' is the local branch of the international Society for Creative Anachronism, whose members create medievalist virtual communities and temporary medievalist spaces, as well as pursuing a variety of medievally inspired craft activities and martial arts, as a leisure activity. Finally, the Crossroads Medieval Village Co-operative owns land outside Yass in New South Wales, and plans, in the coming years, to build there a village for its members to live in and for visitors to learn from. I will draw attention to shared thematic features of these three examples, explore the relationship they construct with the medieval past, and finally I will worry about their relationship with the Australian present. While I would characterize some aspects of this project as an act of translation, it would be entirely inappropriate for me to claim to speak for the people and texts I describe.[2] I should also stress that I characterize these examples of medievalism as utopian because of their aims and the meaning with which they invest the Middle Ages; I make no claims about the extent to which these groups (real or fictional) manage to achieve their utopian goals.

Melbourne Made Medieval

Australian science fiction and fantasy writing is currently experiencing a self-proclaimed golden age, and many of its practitioners are writing medievalist futures and fantasy worlds. (It is well beyond the scope of this article, but it is worth noting that there is also a renaissance of Gothic horror writing.) Isobelle Carmody, Kerry Greenwood, Sophie Masson, Victor Kelleher, Dave Luckett, Sara Douglass, and Sean McMullen are just some of the more prominent authors producing this sort of literature. Many of them write for children as well as adults.[3] Sometimes the settings have a distinctly Australian set of references, despite their medieval trappings; at other times the use of medieval motifs allows the creation and exploration of more generic (and perhaps therefore more internationally marketable) universes. The thriving Australian scene is a fractal corner of an enormous international (though US-dominated) market for the genre.

Kerry Greenwood's series of four science fiction novels, written for teenagers, is set in the not-too-distant future, ten years after malfunctioning military satellites have destroyed all the cities on earth.[4] Melbourne has been mostly melted to slag, with apparently only the north-western fringe of the central business district and some of the western suburbs still surviving. Government and other trappings of the state have disappeared, and people have formed new groupings — gangs, tribes and religious orders — to help them work together and survive. Each of the novels tells how traumatized teenagers find healing love, but each is also deeply concerned with the problems, in a fragmented and broken world, of rebuilding functional, healthy communities that will nurture good and happy people. Greenwood offers no single

---

[2] I have been involved with the Society for Creative Anachronism since 1986; I have never been a member of the Crossroads Co-operative, but received their newsletters for a period, and over the years have had many informal conversations with friends who are members; I know Kerry Greenwood very slightly but have not discussed medievalism or her books with her.

[3] An obvious name missing from this list is that of Catherine Jinks, a prolific writer for both children and adults. She writes both science fiction/fantasy and historical novels set in the Middle Ages, but has not yet combined the two.

[4] Kerry Greenwood, *The Broken Wheel* (Sydney: HarperCollins, 1996*)*; Kerry Greenwood, *Whaleroad* (Rydalmere: Hodder Headline, 1996); Kerry Greenwood, *Cave Rats* (Rydalmere: Hodder Headline, 1997); Kerry Greenwood, *Feral* (Rydalmere: Hodder Headline, 1998).

answer. The importance of valuing diversity and offering choice is one of her themes. But many of the successful groups and communities she creates have somewhat medievalist overtones, whether it be the Travellers of *The Broken Wheel* and *Whaleroad*, Father Redfern's Christian group in the ruins of the Supreme Court in *Cave Rats*, or the enclosed settlements along the Maribyrnong River in *Feral*. Most interestingly, two of the communities we see in most detail — the Barony of Thornguard and the Fortress of Whaleroad (organized differently, but both a part of the 'Kingdom of the West') — are shown as consciously and deliberately adopting the aesthetic and the ideals of medieval Europe.

Sarah, heroine of *The Broken Wheel,* makes her way down the Geelong Road and through a series of landscapes and encounters in the usual fashion of the post-Holocaust picaresque novel. Early on she is befriended by three benign travellers, but she does not reach a truly safe and civilized society until she is rescued from danger by the intervention of Baroness Anastasia of Thornguard. In Thornguard, safe behind its fairy-tale hedge of thorny plants, Sarah finds an idyllic and ideal place to live in a dangerous and unpleasant world. The love that she finds and the values that she learns there inspire her actions through the rest of the book and its sequel *Cave Rats*, as she confronts and then reforms the cruel new religion of the god Breaker. Thornguard is a self-consciously medievalist community, and the medievalism which makes it so successful and appealing in an uncivilized world had its roots before the disaster. The sage Eirene explains:

> For we were romantic people, unsatisfied with the real world, so we played a game, a recreation of the past — a long time ago, before the Three Days. It was a stratified society with a King and various ranks, such as Countess, Baroness. Most of us had put in money to build a medieval village here, as a tourist attraction and to amuse ourselves. It was stocked with food and with animals and it was a working farm [...] One by one or in nervous groups or pursued by bandits, we came here [...] We had to re-invent an agrarian society, you see, and we needed a social structure, so we kept our ranks and the incompetent rulers were sorted out within the first year or so.[5]

Thornguard people wear 'strange clothes' and armour, call each other 'Lord' and 'Lady' and adopt medieval-style names like 'Gunnar Ironhand' and 'Wulf Ringmaker'. They feast on stew in a hall and brew mead. And yet, although these obviously medieval affectations assure the reader that they are indeed medievalists, they do not limit the group's attempt to survive in the present. Thornguard is not anti-technology. Where the technology survives, they still use it to farm and to weave, and for anything else important to survival. Plastic bowls sit on their feasting tables beside wooden and ceramic ones; their houses are roofed with 'corrugated sun-block material'[6] as well as thatch. They have a whole room of computers, with which they manage to save the world from yet more blasting by the pre-programmed

---

[5] Greenwood, *Broken Wheel*, pp. 95–96.

[6] Greenwood, *Broken Wheel*, p. 95.

satellites. It is in fact their medievalist conception of a moral community — as Eirene explains, their whole way of life — which marks out them out as a safe and happy haven in a cruel world.

Thornguard is drawn as a utopia, impossibly perfect, the kindest and most successful community depicted in Greenwood's science fiction world. Its perfection offers little scope for drama, and little of the action takes place within its thorny walls. However, in *Whaleroad* we meet another settlement of the same medievalists, which is also portrayed in utopian terms, offering the fairest and most civilized way of life of all the communities depicted in that volume. But Whaleroad, situated in the 'castle' of the Queenscliff fort guarding the entrance to Port Phillip Bay, is a troubled (and therefore more dramatically interesting) utopia, because although it shares the medievalist ideal of community with Thornguard some of its ideals are pursued in an unbalanced way. Young knights are trained in a cold and rigid version of chivalry, and taught to keep themselves emotionally isolated from each other. Old friends have quarrelled for no good reason, and Memnon, whose knowledge is needed, has shut himself away as a hermit in his tower. The ultra-solemn approach to knightly virtue and hierarchical social structure within the Fortress has caused the Landsknecht — clever technicians who do not like to take anything too seriously — to leave Whaleroad and set up their own realm, and has made their alliance uncertain. Regaining the balance between emotion and reason, and reconciling groups and individuals divided by pointless old arguments is an important part of the drama of the novel (although the busy plot also manages to encompass an invasion by a gaming nerd with an army held by mind-control technology and the rescue of a girl telepathically linked with dolphins).

If the trappings of deliberate archaism serve to code Thornguard as medieval in *The Broken Wheel*, in *Whaleroad* these trappings actually symbolize the problems inherent in Whaleroad's version of a medievalist community. Inhabitants speak in a high-falutin' pseudo-medieval dialect, full of 'thees' and 'thous' and other archaisms, and they do not drop out of it even when speaking urgently to friendly outsiders. While Thornguard is effectively a matriarchy, Whaleroad is not: King Alexis Emerald leads more autocratically and more absolutely than the charismatic but consultative Baroness Anastasia. Whaleroad is marked as elitist and isolated from even its allies by its humourless insistence upon the mere trappings of medievalism.

Nonetheless, Greenwood shows Whaleroad as successful because it is fundamentally a compassionate and liberal community, where people have made a moral choice to work together for the good of each other. And, as in Thornguard, this is perceived by the characters as the real key to Whaleroad's medievalist nature. Maelgwyn, the King's Counsellor, is responsible for many of Whaleroad's flaws, but still lectures his young knights:

We have never forgotten that we survived because we held together. We are a community with one thought — to serve Whaleroad, to make it safer, more pleasant, more learned, more skilled, to feed and care for the lost ones and for our own sisters and brothers. You are knights. You have taken an oath of fealty which will hold you until you die or break your faith, and better you should break your heart or your bones than that you should be forsworn.[7]

There are several themes here to which I will return. Perhaps most important is the characterization of the true meaning and use of medievalism as being moral, about communal and individual good, rather than either scholarly or aesthetic achievement. The emphasis on diversity and fun is another key theme. Greenwood idealizes the serious game. But she also identifies paradoxes and dangers inherent in its logic. Because of the importance of participation, a baroness or king can lead autocratically only if they make the decisions everyone wants them to make; a person aspiring to a medievalized morality of honour and chivalry can use force only as a last resort, even in desperate times. More importantly, there are risks when games become too serious. *Whaleroad* in particular warns: be careful what games you play. If, like the villain, you play at being the Dark Lord, you will truly turn bad; conversely if, like the people of Whaleroad, you play too seriously at being good, you risk becoming a bunch of isolated bores with communication problems.

The source — or rather the lack of a source — for the medievalism in Greenwood's books is also important to remark upon. She allows her characters a generically 'medieval' aesthetic, which seems to take inspiration from many aspects and periods of the medieval past; the link with the medieval past is made explicit in the passage quoted above. However, the relationship of that past with the medievalism of the story's present has to be taken on faith. No medieval texts, artefacts or social forms are explicitly offered as historical legitimation. The only empirical reasoning which links the community to the medieval past relates to their practical experiences of 'sorting out' the ineffective leaders. While the medieval past is used to justify the community's existence, it becomes clear that, in fact, the medieval past is identified with whatever is considered necessary to sustain the medievalist present.

Re-creating Medieval Communities in Australia

The fictional communities of Greenwood's children's books are just that, but the Author's Note at the back of each book invites the reader to connect them with the Society for Creative Anachronism, offering a mailing address for the Melbourne branch.[8] The Society for Creative Anachronism (usually known as either 'the SCA'

---

[7] Greenwood, *Whaleroad*, p. x.

[8] Greenwood, *Broken Wheel*, p. 156; Greenwood, *Whaleroad*, p. 204. Kerry Greenwood was an early member of the SCA in Australia (as were fellow fantasy writers Dave Luckett

or 'the Society') was founded in Berkeley, California in 1966, growing out of a May Day theme party run by science fiction fans, which ended with the participants processing up through the streets in sixties Berkeley style, 'protesting the 20th century'.[9] It is now a worldwide organization, with approximately twenty-four thousand financial members, and several times that number estimated to regularly participate in activities.[10] There are branches throughout North America, Europe, Australia and New Zealand, and a scattered few elsewhere.

Just as medievalist science fiction and fantasy is currently a very popular phenomenon, so historical re-enactment, or 'living history' is becoming an increasingly dominant mode for explaining and learning about the past. While active participation remains very small-scale, living history gets mass exposure: heritage displays and television documentaries make increasing use of it to communicate with their markets. Particularly notable in this context is the popularity of the medieval period as a focus for such activity. The Australasian Register of Living History Organisations lists eighty-one groups interested in the Middle Ages across Australia (including eleven SCA groups, which is an underestimate). 'Medieval' is the single category with the most entries.[11] The phenomenon deserves more scholarly attention. However, for current purposes, it is worth noting that the SCA is not the usual sort of re-enactment group. In fact, it only rarely refers to its activities as 'living history' in either official or unofficial publications.[12] The term 're-enactment' is occasionally used, but it is more often carefully explained that re-

---

and Sean McMullen).

[9] The canonical account of the party was first published in a science fiction fanzine, but has been reprinted in every edition of the *Known World Handbook*. Diana Paxson, 'The Last Tournament', in *The Known World Handbook: Being a Compendium of Information, Traditions and Crafts Practiced in these Current Middle Ages in the Society for Creative Anachronism*, ed. by Alwyn Stewart, 3rd edn (Milpitas, CA: Society for Creative Anachronism, 1992), pp. 24–25. Diana Paxson is better known as a prolific writer of fantasy. Other fantasy writers were also early members, most notably Marion Zimmer Bradley who invented the name of the Society, Siegfried von Höflichkeit, 'A Brief Look at the Past', in *Known World Handbook*, p. 26.

[10] 'Life in the Current Middle Ages', heading 'Where did the SCA Come From?', http://www.sca.org.au/sca-intro.html, accessed 20 January 2002. This is the official introduction to the SCA, 'updated as necessary by order of the Board of Directors', and given prominence on both the Australian and US websites of the organization.

[11] http://www.members.ozemail.com.au/~adjutant/arlho/arl_sum.html, accessed 21 January 2002.

[12] One place where the phrase is used is in 'A Brief Introduction to the Society for Creative Anachronism', which forms part of the official governing documents of the Society, http://www.sca.org/docs/govdocs200201.pdf, p. 9, accessed 20 January 2002.

enactment is not what the SCA does.[13] The term most often used to describe the SCA's activities is 're-creation':

> The avowed purpose of the SCA is the study and recreation of the European Middle Ages, its crafts, sciences, arts, traditions, literature, etc.[14]

> 'Creative anachronism' takes the best qualities of the Middle Ages and selectively re-creates them in the modern world.[15]

> Members of the SCA strive to recapture the ambience of the Middle Ages and the Renaissance [...] more than research and practice, the SCA also attempts to embody those lost ideals that are found in the medieval romances: chivalry, courtesy, honor, and graciousness. This is re-creating the Middle Ages as they might have been.[16]

The liminal present-time in which the medieval is re-created is known as 'the Current Middle Ages', and engaging in the *active* process of re-creation is a more important indicator of 'membership' than paying the membership fee. This process is generally understood as a form of study, leading to legitimate knowledge about the medieval past:

> The thing that separates the SCA from a Medieval Studies class is the active participation in the learning process. To learn about period costume, you design and make the clothes.[17]

The Society is structured, both formally and informally, as a complicated set of nested and interwoven hierarchies, of both individuals and branches. The hierarchies of people are based on the 'rank' or 'precedence' that people acquire during their activities in the SCA. There is a plethora of titles that may be granted to participants under various circumstances, and which confer various levels of precedence. Such awards and titles are granted publicly, and usually as part of the ritual of a 'royal' or baronial 'court'. There are also offices (such as king/queen, baron/ess, seneschal, marshal) that financial members may hold, and which can also confer precedence

---

[13] 'The Society is a re-enactment and re-creation organisation, intended for participants rather than spectators', 'Forward Into the Past: An Introductory Guide to the S.C.A.', http://www.ansteorra.org/regnum/hospitaler/articles/fip.htm, , accessed 20 January 2002. But compare, 'you shouldn't adopt the name of a real historical person; the S.C.A. doesn't *re-enact* the events of those times, so historical figures don't belong at S.C.A. events'; http://www.grt-net.com/Heraldry/Names/An_SCA_Name___/an_sca_name___.html, accessed 20 January 2002.

[14] 'Life in the Current Middle Ages'.

[15] 'Forward Into the Past'.

[16] 'The Known World Around You: The SCA Today', *Known World Handbook*, p. 2.

[17] Rowan Perigrynne and Yseult de Lacy, *Barony of Rowany Beginners' Handbook* (Sydney: Barony of Rowany, 1995), p. 1.

while they are held, and sometimes result in an award or title afterwards. Participants take Society names, which are supposed to be both medieval in style and unique to the person; most importantly, no one can take the name of an actual historical figure, even a minor one. Some participants also develop more elaborate 'personas' attached to those fictional names.[18]

Just as individuals create new identities within the SCA, so branches re-inscribe and re-imagine the local geography. The hierarchy of branches — including Kingdoms, Principalities, Baronies, Shires and other 'medievally'-named units — is established according to both the number of members in a branch, and the nature of its relationship to nearby groups. The hierarchy of branches does not directly mirror the hierarchy of people; groups will usually contain individuals of various levels of SCA rank. Groups are usually encouraged to upgrade their status (from Shire to Barony, for example, or from Principality to Kingdom) once they can comfortably sustain the required minimum number of paid up members,[19] and this often means that a subgroup gains a greater portion of independence. Importantly, though, membership levels alone are not sufficient to initiate this process, because members must also indicate that there is a consensus in favour of the move and demonstrate that the group already possesses a separate identity.[20] Hence, while some groups are founded in geographical areas previously without an SCA branch, many are also generated from amongst established groups by a process like cell division. Either way, the 'Known World', as the international network of all SCA groups is called, expands. In addition to the official structures shared by all kingdoms, there are unofficial and less tangible structures that can weave a horizontal weft through the warp of the hierarchies. People with similar interests often keep in contact with each other regardless of where they live, increasingly through email lists. Sometimes such groupings give themselves names such as 'Households', 'Orders', 'Guilds', or 'Companies'; often they remain informal. Such interest groups can even relate to particular philosophical approaches to the SCA.[21]

---

[18] *The Completely Normal Person's Guide to the S.C.A. at Melbourne Uni. A Newcomer's Survival Manual* (Melbourne: n. pub., 1992), no pagination, advises: 'A persona is your SCA *alter ego*. Some people devise detailed family histories for their persona, while others just come up with a name.' While the extent to which a detailed persona is developed is a matter of choice, official Society publications provide two biographies for each author, a 'medieval' and a 'mundane' one, thus creating a normative pressure to create at least a minimal persona story.

[19] http://www.sca.org/docs/govdocs200201.pdf, accessed 20 January 2002, 'Corpora', pp. 6–8.

[20] 'Corpora', pp. 6–9

[21] See, for example, the website of the Company of St George, a 'tournament society' dedicated to promulgating a particular view of chivalry in the SCA; http://www.chronique.-com/george.htm, accessed 2 February 2002.

The Australian branch of the Society for Creative Anachronism was founded in the early 1980s. Originally the independent 'Society for the Current Middle Ages', members chose to ally themselves with the larger organization, and become the Crown Principality of Lochac, a part of the Kingdom of the West, which is based largely in northern California. Membership has grown sufficiently that the Australian branch will soon become a Kingdom.[22] There are branches in each capital city except Darwin, with subgroups in each, as well as in some regional centres. In Australia, the membership of the SCA is dominated by students and middle class professionals, with a heavy bias towards the computer industry and other scientific/technical professions.[23] Although the organization is incorporated in Australia for legal reasons, and is soon to become an independent kingdom (which means formal links with the Californian parent kingdom will be severed), the Australian group remains strongly connected to the wider society, since it accepts the 'Corpora' as the document defining the minimum shared rules of the game, and thus shares a basic structure, bureaucracy and 'flavour'.[24] Australian members of the SCA continue to perceive themselves en masse as part of the larger 'Known World', and may also develop personal relationships of various sorts with members from overseas. Australians participate in SCA-wide email lists and interest groups, host visitors from 'other kingdoms', and sometimes travel overseas to attend major events in other countries.

This is only the briefest and most superficial description of how the SCA works, and leaves out all the nuance and local variation that members usually take great pains to put in. Yet amidst this diversity, and despite the complexity of its rules, the SCA successfully functions as a community of communities; a machine for creating social capital. However, unlike the fictional groups of Greenwood's post-Holocaust fantasy, the communities the Society creates are imagined ones, constantly renegotiated, which people inhabit in their minds and in their spare time. The groups in Australia do not own land and have no permanent physical headquarters. They can achieve only temporary physical expression in such venues as a rented hall for a feast or a park for a tournament. They exist as voluntary networks of people who read and produce the same books, magazines and newsletters, who organize and attend the same meetings, workshops and training sessions, who belong to the same email lists and log on to the same web pages, who borrow each other's books and equipment and sleep on each other's lounge room floors when they travel. They also define themselves as people who share something further:

---

[22] http://www.sca.org.au/lochac/kingdom/index.htm, accessed 22 January 2002.

[23] Cary John Lenehan, 'Postmodern Medievalism: A Sociological Study of the Society for Creative Anachronism' (unpublished honours thesis, University of Tasmania, 1994), pp. 21–23.

[24] 'Corpora', p. 1.

A common interest — the aim of re-creating a society where personal integrity is important, honour and chivalry have real meaning, and the high ideals of the Middle Ages are not forgotten. You will sometimes hear this referred to as 'The Dream.' Not everyone has exactly the same idea of The Dream [...] but in our hearts this is what binds us all together.[25]

The defining features of this form of medievalism, then, are an emphasis on active participation, on community-building, and an essentially moral under-standing of what constitutes the medieval. It is undeniably 'other' in Biddick's terms, visibly outside the academic tradition of medieval studies, although the reverse is not necessarily true. After all, to *really* learn about medieval costume by making it, it can be helpful if someone else has already put some basic facts together about medieval clothes. Within this worldview, however, academic medievalism lacks a highly privileged status; it is seen as merely providing helpful technical information about objects and artefacts for those members who choose to make use of it in their re-creations. The products of the empirical tradition of research into the Middle Ages are perceived as just so much grist to the mill of a higher-level understanding that emphasizes a personal and active response to the inspiration of the medieval.

As for Greenwood's fictional medievalists, the existence of a medieval past authorizes contemporary medievalism, yet it is the practical experience gained in the present that is understood to truly bridge the two. In fact, when the (perceived) best of the medieval past is displaced into current Middle Ages, and participation in its activities is understood as a way to learn about the past, direct engagement with the original Middle Ages through the academically privileged medium of primary source texts becomes optional. While many members of the SCA in Australia are both highly educated and well read in academic medieval history and literature,[26] such a commitment is personal and voluntary. While reading or research in the academic sense can undoubtedly enrich the current Middle Ages, it is not essential to an individual's activities within the Society. Tellingly, in all the long and complex rules that define the operation of the Society, no medieval text or artefact is singled out as canonically authoritative. The canonical document — the key text that constructs the SCA as a textual community — is in fact the Corpora, the list of shared rules for all groups. Exactly what it is about the Middle Ages that makes them inspirational and worth re-creating — exactly what one's own version of The Dream is — is something that each individual must bring with them to the Society: members are equally as free to import it second-hand from a film or a fantasy novel as from a saga read in the original Old Norse.

---

[25] Perigrynne and de Lacy, *Barony of Rowany Beginners' Handbook*, p. 1. See also Lenehan, 'Postmodern Medievalism', pp. 39–40, where a similar point is made and discussed in terms of 'taste cultures'.

[26] Lenehan, 'Postmodern Medievalism', pp. 21–23.

A Castle Co-operative in Yass

The Crossroads Medieval Village Co-operative Ltd was registered as a co-operative in New South Wales in September 1992. Planning and organization had been going on for more than a year by that stage;[27] the first edition of the newsletter *Signpost* had been produced in December 1991. In mid-1994 183 hectares of land near Yass were purchased, and site improvement activities have taken place since then. The co-operative plans to build on the land, and although progress in this direction has been slow due to difficulties with Council approval and fundraising, it seems likely that the first building, a 'medieval barn', will be erected fairly soon.[28] The co-operative has always kept its eyes fixed on the future, however, and its website currently announces:

> We plan to build a medieval village on our property at Yass, New South Wales, Australia [...] The project has five main parts:
>
>> Five visitor cabins to accommodate 60 people, a kitchen/dining hall, and associated amenities. These will be used for medieval events and also available to community groups.
>>
>> A replica of the small French medieval castle, Chalençon, and its associated village.
>>
>> A residential subdivision with a medieval theme.
>>
>> A Centre for Heritage Crafts.
>>
>> A permaculture farm featuring old animal breeds and plant varieties.[29]

Permaculture is a system of environmentally sustainable agriculture, developed in the 1970s by Australian Bill Mollison, and now the centre of a global movement.[30] The aim of building such a farm may seem at odds with the plan to build a replica medieval castle and village, but is in fact central to the Crossroads plan. The group in fact defines its project as 'an initiative to build an ecologically sustainable community, with excellent facilities for medieval activities'.[31]

The very modern notions of equality, democracy, and ecological responsibility are core elements of the Crossroads vision of creating a medievally inspired community: 'our group was established as a co-operative because it guarantees all our members an equal say in the achievement of our common goal: a superb facility

---

[27] Ian McComb, 'Chair's Bit', *Signpost* (October, 1992), 3.

[28] 'Construction Progress', *Signpost* (March, 2000), 3.

[29] http://www.crossroads.org.au/crossroads/index.html, accessed 21 January 2002.

[30] http://www.permacult.com.au, accessed 2 February 2002

[31] http://www.crossroads.org.au/crossroads/index.html, accessed 21 January 2002.

for medievalists, and a model for environmentally sustainable development.'[32] In re-imagining the Middle Ages in this way, the co-operative has also re-inscribed many traditional medieval images and ideas with newer (and sometimes 'New Age') utopian understandings of community. This is perhaps most obvious in their use of the image of the castle. A photograph of the real Chalençon castle is the dominant image of the main page of their website. An early brochure distributed before Chalençon was settled upon as a model (as well as an earlier version of their website[33]) likewise focussed on role of the castle in the project, showing a drawing of an idealized medieval village beneath a castle on a hill, framed within a wreath of flowering wattle. The brochure explained 'the village vision' as including and centring around the castle:

> The Crossroads village nestles in a valley with green fields and some stripfarming around the village [...] From the common you can see a large stone castle with high curtain walls and many towers flying flags and pennants. Inside the castle is a great hall, a tavern, armouries, guild workshops and the list field. Around the castle is the medieval village [...] walking around, you will see a smithy, a bakery, and a village well [...][34]

Where one might expect the castle to appear in its traditional guise as a symbol of seigneurial authority (whether that is construed as good or bad), this is not in fact how it is imagined here. In the Crossroads vision, the castle is envisaged as part of the common resources for the village, and contains the tavern and the guild workshops. In the more down-to-earth presentation of the current web page, it is again bracketed with the village as an important part of the building plans, but distinguished from the 'residential subdivision' where members will in fact live. The aesthetically appealing image of the castle is clearly central to the co-operative's vision of what is properly medieval — but this idea is subordinated to the more powerful connection of the 'medieval' with the idea of a flourishing and harmonious community. Thus the castle becomes a resource that a medieval community should hold in common and share with visitors, rather than the community being ruled over or exploited by the inhabitants of the castle.

A deep interest in the medieval European past certainly abides at the heart of the Crossroads project. The decision to build a castle which is a replica of an original medieval building — and the central significance that this castle occupies in the co-operative's publicity and planning — is a sure indication of this. To build an accurate replica of the Chalençon castle, Crossroads will need to engage with scholarly discourses, to make use of 'scientific' (to use Biddick's phrase) ways of knowing about the medieval past. They will need to find and synthesize concrete data about the Chalençon castle and the region; and indeed the co-operative has

---

[32] http://www.crossroads.org.au/crossroads/coop.html, accessed 21 January 2002.

[33] http://www.crossroads.org.au/vision.jpg, accessed 5 February 1999.

[34] 'Introducing the Crossroads Project', undated brochure.

already commissioned a local French historian as a researcher. To this extent, it seems that the Crossroads project is the exception to the rule the two previous examples have illustrated; in order to enact and reify its own medievalist vision, it does need to enter into a relationship with the medieval which privileges both the processes and the products of the academy's form of medievalism.

And yet, the Crossroads website offers the replica castle and village as just one of the five 'main parts' of the project. An analysis of the other four shows that by their nature they set limits on the extent to which a 'scientific' understanding of the Middle Ages can dominate the project. Visitor cabins available to community groups; a residential development where only a medieval 'theme' is required: these privilege the everyday requirements of modern lifestyles, rather than the positivist project of acquiring detailed knowledge about a specific and particular time and place. A 'heritage' (as opposed to medieval) craft centre and a permaculture farm, if they were to come to fruition, would by definition actively promote post-medieval crafts, agricultural techniques and ways of thinking and working; yet they would do this in a context which encouraged these post-medieval forms of production to be understood through a medievalist filter, as part of a 'medieval' whole. Once again the medieval is understood to be important because it provides a desirable aesthetic and a shared source of inspiration for what is fundamentally a community-building project, engaging with present-day needs, and born out of a desire to find ways to re-integrate the fragmentation by which modern society is perceived to be beset. The traditions of the academy appear then to be co-opted to support this goal, rather than recognized as worthy ends in themselves.

Idealizing the Medieval and Medievalizing the Australian Experience

If, then, some contemporary popular medievalism mediates its understanding of the medieval past through the (re-)creation or use of isolated physical or literary objects, rather than a coherently historicized view of the Middle Ages, this does not mean these understandings are themselves incoherent, isolated or fragmented. As I have shown, for many present-day people who find medievalism appealing, the coherence and relevance of the period is conceived not in the language of academic history or literary criticism, but rather of popular moral philosophy and psychology.

A shared vision of an inspirational Middle Ages unites individuals and factions who might otherwise have little in common, and allows them to work together in building communities. However, the vision or the dream is often left deliberately ill-defined, because closer definition would vitiate precisely this aspect of its usefulness. While aesthetic issues are important, the Middle Ages are perceived as important and worthy of re-creation not only because they look good, but because they seem to offer models for personal relationships and social organization which are better and more fulfilling than modern ones. Yet these models are often populated by a substantial amount of entirely modern content, represented by

Greenwood's computers and plastic, Crossroads' devotion to environmental sustainability, or the SCA's reliance on email and sewing machines. This blending of medieval and modern ideas, practices and objects to achieve a medievalist goal often calls for negotiations about the requirements and limits of 'authenticity', but as a basic practice it is not problematized.[35] The process of participation, and the exercise of creativity, receives more attention.

Diversity, inclusiveness and a playful and creative form of participation are important principles in each of the examples I have discussed. In the SCA organizers of feasts or tournaments cannot specify a particular year or region to which costumes and accessories must belong, but must accept any comer dressed in 'an attempt at pre-17th century clothing'.[36] While Crossroads is basing its replica castle and village on a French example, the cabins and other buildings that will be constructed first are derived from English examples,[37] and when the residential subdivision takes place there will no doubt be an even wider range of times and places represented.[38] SCA literature places a great emphasis on the practice of 'courtesy' to those who are doing things differently, and one of Crossroads' early goals was 'forging links between different parts of the broader medieval movement'.[39] Both organizations value participation more highly than financial membership (the Crossroads Co-operative requires members to put in time as well as money to be considered active and to exercise voting rights).[40] Participation and inclusiveness are also encouraged by the cultivation of a light touch, even when matters are actually taken very seriously. Participating in the SCA in Australia is often referred to as 'playing', while Crossroads members run pub nights and other friendly get-togethers, and have

---

[35] See the discussion on authenticity and fun in Alura the Twinn, 'How to Get What You Want out of the SCA', *Known World Handbook*, pp. 34–36. *Signpost* (October, 1992), published the results of a questionnaire put out in Issue 2, which showed that 19% of respondents thought that 'authenticity' was 'extremely important', 53% thought it 'very important' and 28% thought it 'somewhat important'. In response, Crossroads came up with a system of different 'levels' of authenticity to be expected in different places and contexts. I cannot find a current document outlining these levels, but they have been explained in previous versions of their website.

[36] 'Corpora', p. 4.

[37] 'The Crossroads Cabins', insert in *Signpost* (July 2001), no pagination.

[38] The website notes: 'Within the residential area, clusters of houses may choose special themes, such as a re-creation of a particular medieval housing style, and then additional design criteria may apply'; http://www.crossroads.org.au/crossroads/residential.html, accessed 21 January 2002.

[39] 'Courteous and honourable behaviour is at the core of the Society. It is difficult to be too polite' warns 'Forward into the Past'. See also 'Gossip', in Perigrynne and de Lacy, *Barony of Rowany Beginners' Handbook*, p. 16; http://www.crossroads.org.au, accessed 4 February 1999; *Signpost* (October 1992), p. 4.

[40] http://www.crossroads.org.au/crossroads/coop.html, accessed 21 January 2002.

kept their publications determinedly cheerful in tone for ten years, despite some frustrating periods of financial difficulty and bureaucratically-imposed delay.[41] Even Greenwood's fictional medievalists — in a post-Holocaust world where survival is at stake — find that it is disadvantageous to take their medievalism, or their world, too seriously.

To sum up, then, in keeping with the diversity that these groups encourage in other ways, as *organizations* they neither offer nor impose a monolithic conception of the Middle Ages. The medieval past itself is their text, and it is a palimpsest that can continually be revisited and re-inscribed to inspire and authorize their creations. Rather than calling such an approach — which is also to be found beyond the examples dealt with here — medievalist, it might be more appropriate to describe it as medieval*izing*. Armed with an idealized conception of the medieval, the present can be re-made as ideal by re-making it as medieval, and in turn, idealized aspects of the present can be reinterpreted as more truly medieval in spirit than any mere historical facts.

So it becomes necessary to ask, why are twenty-first-century *Australians* doing this? Why are they re-creating their world through the mirror of Europe hundreds of years ago? Before trying to offer some answers to this question, it is worth noting that this does not seem to be something that is important either to ask or to answer within this strand of medievalism. The assumptions that give rise to the query are in fact some of the assumptions that separate academic medievalism from many contemporary forms of medievalism.

The examples examined here all present themselves as importantly but unproblematically Australian, anchored to the rest of the world by a keen sense of place. Greenwood's characters move through a landscape full of recognizable names and landmarks. The Principality of Lochac shows a map of Australia (indicating the location of its branches) on the front page of its website, right next to its 'medieval' coat of arms, which features the stars of the Southern Cross only slightly abstracted.[42] Crossroads values its links with the Yass community, and devotes a generous section of its website to the native wildlife to be found on its land.[43] And even while they share a desire to re-imagine and re-inscribe Australian spaces, this process does not reinterpret those spaces as European, or completely overwrite their Australianness. Rather, they find opportunities to imagine specifically Australian

---

[41] Play should be fun, but serious. The science fiction examples have already been discussed. The *Known World Handbook*, p. 245, explains that the SCA is 'a special kind of fun that is found in very few places in our modern culture. It encourages us to play at who we really are [...]. The SCA lets us play at being our best selves, the selves we could be in a perfect, fantasy world [...].'

[42] http://www.sca.org.au, accessed 21 January 2002. On the other side of the coat of arms is a picture of a castle. Although the drawing looks rather forbidding, it is intended to symbolize a welcoming gateway to the 'contact information' for Australian SCA groups.

[43] http://www.crossroads.org.au/crossroads/creatures.html, accessed 21 January 2002.

forms of medievalism, and to build local landscape, language and culture into their utopian dreamings.

However, although this sort of Australianness is presented as important, issues of Australian identity and nationality are not. Neither Greenwood's science fiction nor the public literature of the Principality of Lochac and the Crossroads Co-operative display any interest in nationalist discourses, either to support or contest them. Nor, in general, do they show a great deal of engagement with Australian history (although, in a solitary, brief exception, Greenwood suggests that their medievalized morality prevents her characters from engaging in acts of aggression and dispossession which can be equated with the white colonization of Australia).[44] On the contrary, these texts demonstrate an awareness of their place in a series of wider contexts that are likewise inclusive, such as the genre of science fiction, the permaculture movement, or the international presence of the SCA and the wider world of living history. They celebrate the local whilst referencing the global.

Perhaps this is not so surprising. If the medieval past is not understood in terms of its place in a newly problematized grand narrative of European progress and domination, but the Australian past is, there is no reason at all to connect the two. The ahistorical character of a medievalism where all the bad things in history (and thus the bad things in the present) have been purged from the commemorative process of re-creation liberates such medievalists from the consequent burdens of postcolonial history. The freedom to inform the category of 'medieval' with almost any historical or literary content that appeals to the individual also offers a safe space to negotiate one's own peace with issues of ethnicity and heritage, whether by constructing a persona as a ninth-century Welshman or by building a house from Renaissance Italy. Or by any number of other means which achieve the same end.

This insistence on a de-historicized (or perhaps it would be more accurate to say, an only incidentally historicized), de-nationalized conception of the medieval is the fundamental way in which this sort of popular medievalism fails to connect with academic medievalism. The academic discipline of medieval studies was born in an era when the empirical study of medieval history and languages was understood to be a way of possessing and defending a national past, and thus of asserting a relevance to the present. While a good deal of contemporary scholarship is devoted to deconstructing and rejecting the racist, sexist and imperialist agendas with which previous generations of academics were complicit, and the language has changed greatly, academic medievalist discourse still defines its relevance in what are essentially nineteenth-century terms. Those terms are entirely other to those of popular utopian medievalisms, where the project of engaging with the medieval is understood to be about the creative construction of an inclusive and integrated way of living in the present, rather than the possession and exploitation of the past.

I started this essay by drawing on the image of academic medievalism as an ivory tower, an enclosed castle keep, occupied by an elite defined by their possession of

---

[44] *Broken Wheel*, p. 105.

knowledge and their means of acquiring it, but also an instrument in the maintenance of those power relations. I would like to finish by reiterating that, at least for some contemporary medievalists, that is not what a castle is, and it is not what a castle does. In contemporary popular imaginings, castles can be shared resources that sustain communities and inform the inner life of individuals. To the extent that academic medievalism can do such a job, it will seem relevant and useful to those 'unscientific' medievalists who teem outside its walls.

'The Only Limitation Is Your Imagination': Quantifying the Medieval and Other Fantasies in *Dungeons and Dragons*

MATTHEW CHRULEW

> Every society always manifests somewhere the formal rules which its practices obey. [...]
> First of all, in the specific *games* of each society.[1]

Fantasy role-playing games (FRPGs) like *Dungeons and Dragons* (*D&D*) are fascinating late twentieth-century cultural products that re-create and perform medieval and other cultural and historical materials in simulated and quantified fantastic worlds.[2] Preceding the video of the recent *D&D* movie is an advertisement for the role-playing game itself that bears the following slogan: 'The only limitation is your imagination'. As an exercise in cultural studies, this essay will focus on the distinctive mode in which FRPGs recreate the Middle Ages and other times and cultures, interrogating the particular historical form of imagination that occasions these objects of popular subculture. Starting with this motto, I will examine the ways in which FRPGs actually delimit and constrain the supposedly unbounded imaginative resources of their players.

Examining *Dungeons and Dragons* yields a powerful understanding of the systematic, tabular and iconographic forms in which medieval and other cultural fantasies are simulated in these games, in interactive tension with their performative nature as practices aspiring to active play. I will argue that FRPGs appropriate a

---

[1] Michel de Certeau, *The Practice of Everyday Life*, trans. by Steven Rendall (Berkeley: University of California Press, 1984), pp. 21–22.

[2] Thanks to Dave Cake, Andrew Lynch, and Stephanie Trigg for their help with this essay.

multitude of images to populate constructed fantastic worlds into which players 'escape', and that they select, translate and codify those images into data according to the ideological imperatives of a capitalism that is postmodern, consumerist, and disciplinary.

Limited Imaginations

FRPGs are group games in which players enact character roles in a fictional world, under the guidance of a gamemaster.[3] They are a type of interactive storytelling, or psychodrama, with the events determined not only (or perhaps not even) by an external plot but also by the interactions between the players. In what are commonly called 'tabletop role-playing games', players create characters defined by quantified statistics and shared fantastic images and tropes, who take shape in their imaginations and verbal interplay. They must negotiate with each other, and the fictional world, within the context of an extensive quantified rule system applied by the gamemaster, which determines the outcomes of these negotiations.[4] FRPGs have no simple correspondence, however, to the normal competitive mode found in most games. Despite this strongly rule-driven aspect — or perhaps because of it — they are in many other ways quite flexible.

Gaming is very much a subcultural phenomenon, strongly linked to science fiction fandom and to gothic subcultures. Members share distinctive interests, particularly common popular culture influences. Participation may require specialized knowledge, not only of the game rules, but also in areas such as military history, science fiction, fantasy, mythology, history, science, mysticism, and sociology. However, some participation is possible with even the most general exposure to the tropes and patterns of 'fantasy' in Western popular culture, and to bureaucratic forms of definition and organization. Typical adventures involve the exploration of dungeons, forests, or other sites, where the characters face challenges both from monsters and the natural and built environment. Typical tasks include solving puzzles, travelling, interacting with non-player characters, and fighting. The

---

[3] The gamemaster — called the Dungeon Master in *D&D* — has the job of controlling the game. Before the game they organize the adventure; many go so far as to create the whole campaign setting themselves. During the scenario, they narrate what the characters see, and mediate their interactions with each other and the game-world environment through adjudication of the rules.

[4] For a more detailed exposition, see Daniel Mackay, *The Fantasy Role-Playing Game: A New Performing Art* (Jefferson, NC: McFarland, 2001), pp. 4–5. He defines the FRPG as 'an *episodic* and *participatory* story-creation *system* that includes a set of quantified *rules* that assist a group of *players* and a *gamemaster* in determining how their fictional *characters'* spontaneous interactions are resolved.' (Italics in original.)

tropes of fantasy — dungeons, dragons, magic, treasure, quests, traps, and maps —
are highly conspicuous. If players are lucky and play well, their characters return
home with treasure and experience. If not, they won't make it out alive.

Their multi-sided nature makes FRPGs complex and rewarding texts to scrutinize.
In addition to sociological examination of the social contexts of role-playing,[5] they
can be approached through rulebooks, dungeon modules, and various other
associated textual products; but the performative variation of actual gameplay serves
to complicate such approaches. FRPGs stand in an uneasy relation to normal fictive
modes, differing from stock textual narratives in many respects: their closest cousins
include computer-driven hypertexts, spontaneous performance, and wargames.
FRPGs are highly intertextual; they exist largely in the imaginations of the players;
they are collectively negotiated, requiring the contributions of a group of people; and
they consist of spontaneous and largely oral storytelling. Like the art of
conversation, these are 'verbal productions in which the interlacing of speaking
positions weaves an oral fabric without individual owners'.[6] This is certainly a site
where the 'death of the author' obtains: FRPGs break down conventional categories
of genre and textuality, increasing the roles of readers and fans, who creatively
participate in either established fantasy settings or worlds of their own devising.[7]

These aspects of interstitiality, performance, and — as we shall see — pastiche,
tempt us to describe FRPGs as subversively 'postmodern' texts. As the ad said, 'The
only limitation is your imagination'. But imagination, of course, is limited — and
shaped — in many important ways by powerful cultural forces which determine the
nature of gaming itself. These influences provide both the tropes and narratives used,
and the manner in which they are combined, archived and manipulated. In fact, these
forces are very much part of postmodernism seen as the counterpart of late
capitalism: consumeristic, commodifying, disciplinary and governmental.

Simulating the Middle Ages (and More)

The medievalism in which the Australian authors and players of FRPGs participate
is not so much a heritage of British colonialism, driven by a nostalgia focussed on an
idealized chivalric past: rather, it is part of Australia's larger participation in a global
semiosphere driven by the American culture industry, where nostalgia tends on the
whole to be more eclectic. Here medievalism re-creates fantasy as substitute history,

---

[5] The exemplary text of such study is Gary Alan Fine, *Shared Fantasy: Role-Playing Games as Social Worlds* (Chicago: University of Chicago Press, 1983).

[6] Certeau, *The Practice of Everyday Life*, p. xxii.

[7] Players and Dungeon Masters are encouraged to modify published rules and modules for their own games.

a surrogate site gratifying the unscrupulous desire for the past. The various settings and tropes of FRPGs are contrasted with the present as *other* — as the site of fantasy — but despite their content, judgement of their value is generally suspended; rather, they are *performed*.

The form and content of FRPGs varies widely. Game types range from freeform Live Action Role Playing, to miniaturized wargaming, to computer games; however, I am particularly concerned here with the tabletop models described above. Settings extend from fantasy and science fiction to war, Western, superhero, and more, and the inner coherence of these genres is also variable. Many FRPGs attempt to simulate historical or fictional settings with a high degree of accuracy and internal consistency. However, a general eclecticism is evident in the proliferation of many such individually accurate games, each based on a different setting. Meanwhile, other FRPGs (like *D&D* and *Shadowrun*) include a much wider range of historical and cultural material *within* the one setting. In order to focus the discussion, I will comment on these pastiche models; but some of these remarks might easily be extended to the general field of FRPGs.

Dungeons and Dragons was the original FRPG, developed from simulation war games, and originally published commercially by Dave Arneson and E. Gary Gygax in 1974. Despite (and perhaps also feeding off) some negative public reactions, it became highly popular, and is once again a focus of interest with the recent publication of the third edition of its rules. *D&D* is more general in outlook than many other FRPGs, and tends more towards adventure gaming than sociological simulation. Highly particular game-worlds are of course used — the *Forgotten Realms*, *Dragonlance*, and other campaign settings have been published in conjunction with various novels and other products — but the *D&D* rule system is intended to suit a wide variety of possible fantastic worlds. However, these generally flow from a generic setting: a broad medieval fantasy framework, parasitic not only on fantasy literature, particularly Tolkien,[8] but also modern conceptions of the Middle Ages, and an abundance of New Age, occult and Eastern material.

D&D is extremely broad in its scope: as an exemplary rule-system designed to be compatible with any number of different settings, it provides the matrix in which these diverse worlds meet. As Mackay puts it:

> *Dungeons & Dragons* fantasy is characterized by a certain ahistorical, piecemeal conflation of courtly romance literature, supernatural and gothic literature, folklore,

---

[8] See Matthew Chrulew, 'Sub-Created Earths, Middle- or Otherwise: Tolkien as Archetypal Dungeon Master', *Masquerade Swancon 2001: Academic Proceedings*, ed. by Cathy Cupitt (Perth: Western Australian Science Fiction Foundation, 2002), pp. 27–37, for a discussion of Tolkien's relationship to FRPGs.

mythology, contemporary politics, social mores, morals, and ethics, and as Eurasian history, all within the popular imagination of Americans.[9]

The new third edition of the rules represents the culmination of this constant growth to include even more elements, some from non-Western cultures.

One way to frame this characteristic pastiche, distilled from the mechanical aspects particular to FRPGs, is via the *Dungeons and Dragons* movie.[10] Although science fiction and sword and sorcery films have been common Hollywood outputs since *Star Wars*, around the time of the inception of FRPGs, a movie version of *D&D* has only recently been released. The film has been tellingly compared in popular and critical reviews to the imaginary entertainment-environment of *Star Wars*.[11] There are in fact some very specific similarities: the visual characteristics of the mythical creatures; the young but wise princess ruling the kingdom (who must oppose the corrupt council, and who knows deep in her soul that all people should live freely and equally); the special effects of the fantastic cities; even aspects of the music. More broadly, though, the quest narrative, the characters' party or fellowship formation, the ontological certainty of good and evil, and the Romantic universe exemplify the familiar nostalgic genre that we can recognize as dominating contemporary fantasy.

However, the iconic surface of role-playing *D&D* today overflows from the generic fantasy of the *D&D* film. While Tolkien combined influences from Norse mythology, Old English, and other roots into an aesthetically consistent world, and movies like *Star Wars* likewise combined a number of elements into its own particular brand of romantic science fiction, one rather finds in pastiche FRPGs like *D&D* and *Shadowrun* a loose conglomeration of cultures, geographies, professions, and images culled from a variety of inconsistent sources. Umberto Eco suggests that this element is itself a very medieval one:

> An art not systematic but additive and compositive, ours and that of the Middle Ages: Today as then the sophisticated elitist experiment coexists with the great enterprise of popularization [...] with interchanges and borrowings, reciprocal and continuous; and the evident Byzantinism, the mad taste for collecting, lists, assemblage, amassing of disparate things is due to the need to dismantle and reconsider the flotsam of a previous world, harmonious perhaps, but by now obsolete.[12]

---

[9] Mackay, *The Fantasy Role-Playing Game*, p. 22.

[10] *Dungeons and Dragons*, dir. by Courtney Solomon (Sweetpea Entertainment/Silver Pictures, 2000).

[11] See Mackay, *The Fantasy Role-Playing Game*, pp. 26–33, for his introduction of the term 'imaginary entertainment-environment', and a discussion of other ideas related to world-creation.

[12] Umberto Eco, 'The Return of the Middle Ages,' *Travels in Hyperreality: Essays*, trans. by William Weaver (San Diego: Harcourt, Brace, Jovanovich, 1986), pp. 59–85 (p. 83).

For those who lived in medieval times this 'previous world' may have been the culture of classical Greece, but for contemporary Westerners it is commonly the medieval history of Europe, and, increasingly, other non-Western cultures also encoded as 'previous'. Although still descending from the nostalgic tradition of the medieval imaginary, continuing the fascination with the customs, values and practices of the Middle Ages, FRPGs are also driven by an imperative for encompassing imaginative play, and extract 'cultural resources' from variegated periods, places, and cultures, which are then slotted into a broadly 'medieval' template. Starting with a general medieval structure, diverse mythologies, legends, creatures and other elements are added to form a heterogeneous setting.[13] For this postmodern pastiche, the past is an imaginary museum, a source of possible styles to be raided at will.

The dominant filter for these images is the American popular culture that dominates the West. As Mackay shows, game players reassemble an internalized score of popular culture memes imprinted from a shared mass media, film and literary culture.[14] In the contemporary semiosphere, multiple ways of portraying the medieval coexist, and none are ignored in the recreative processes of FRPGs, whose performed experiments in medievalism are unashamedly broad. If we ask with Umberto Eco 'what kind of Middle Ages are we talking about?'[15] when we consider *D&D*, one answer would seem to be: *all of them, and more*.

The main character-types (or 'classes') available in *D&D* illustrate this eclectic mix of the tropes of medieval representation. In keeping with the positive image of the Middle Ages as the 'Age of Chivalry', one can choose to play a Paladin, a forceful yet honourable crusader for good. Alternatively, one might wish, in keeping with the negative image of the medieval as the 'Dark Ages' and 'Gothic', to play a Barbarian, illiterate, brutal, and prone to rage. FRPG worlds can be both realms of high adventure and *at the same time* crude and dangerous domains. Other character options include the Fighter, Bard, Wizard and Rogue. Our ideas of the Middle Ages have fluctuated, ever since the period ended, between 'dark' and 'golden' images, along with every conceivable composite between; and it sometimes seems as if pastiche FRPGs attempt to include all of these combinations.

---

[13] Interestingly, although *Shadowrun* is set in the twenty-first century, and juxtaposes a wide variety of 'authentic' native cultures to the West's megacorporate capitalism, the general setting is somewhat fantastic and neomedieval. Magic abounds since the 'Awakening', fantastic races merge with the human population, resources are scarce, and life is on the whole more perilous and insecure.

[14] Mackay, *The Fantasy Role-Playing Game*, pp. 73–82. However, beyond the restoration of popular culture 'fictive blocks' through performance, Mackay gives limited consideration to the cultural sources and content of medieval and other images as they are constructed in this field.

[15] Eco, 'The Return of the Middle Ages', p. 72.

However, the FRPG assortment of images does not cease with the limits of conceivable Middle Ages. The third edition of *D&D* includes amongst its choices of available character-types the Druid, a geomancer with an essential link with nature, and the Monk — not a pacifist transcriber of texts, but a contemplative warrior using only her bare hands or exotic weapons resembling those of the Orient. These Monks tap into an energy called *ki*. A similar phenomenon occurs in games like *Magic: The Gathering*, with the concept of 'mana' taken from Polynesian and Melanesian cultures (through the intermediary of primitivist anthropology) to refer to magical power. Often mythological or symbolic notions are given literal interpretations, such as when totemic animals or mythical beasts are taken to assume physical forms. Many 'Other' cultures — Eastern, Native American, Aztec and so on — are subject to this treatment, with images selected, removed and slotted into a generic (originally European medieval) fantasy world.

It seems perhaps surprising then that *D&D* has thus far failed to include material derived from traditional Australian Aboriginal culture. However, the images of totemism and shamanism which pervade popular conceptions of African and Australian 'primitive' cultures are commonly encountered, a sign that in a sense, a detailed engagement is not needed. The idealized conceptions and structures that all but predetermine the way the culture will be portrayed have already been systematized.

However, one *Shadowrun* supplement does take Australia as its main focus. *Target: Awakened Lands* is a sourcebook designed to provide background material on an Australian setting for *Shadowrun* games.[16] It describes a neo-medieval twenty-first century Australia that, like the rest of the world, has been altered by the advent of various technologies, along with the rise of almost unrestricted multinational corporations, and the 'Awakening', whereby magic has become a force in the world. The game generally plays off the juxtaposition of 'authentic' native or traditional cultures with the technological and capitalist West; in the Australian context the tribal and magical Aborigines of the 'Outback' are set against the multicultural population inhabiting the urban sprawls.

The book utilizes Australian stereotypes and slang as guides narrate local information to prospective 'down-under' shadowrunners. Although it is recognized that there are multiple and various Aboriginal cultures,[17] a somewhat typical literal presentation of a mostly homogeneous culture is still given. Powerful shamanistic magic is accepted as real, as are many aspects of mythological tradition.

This is typical in the general context of the *Shadowrun* game. A pastiche FRPG like *D&D*, it also incorporates many non-Western cultures, particularly Native

---

[16] Rob Boyle and others, *Target: Awakened Lands: A Shadowrun Sourcebook* (Milwaukee: FanPro LLC, 2001).

[17] Boyle and others, *Target*, p. 46.

American. The various traditions are subject to comparative inquisition: the types of magic are interrelatable, as various paths (of the Shaman, the Adept, the Voodoo priest, the Quabbalist, etc.) with similar patterns, which all associate with similar types of 'metaplanes' and spirits. Consider 'things in the Outback called "song lines" or "dreaming tracks" [... some] say they're similar in most respects to what are called "manalines" elsewhere, or "dragon lines" in the Far East.'[18] Although providing description and data on particular (magical) Australian locations — including Uluru, the Great Barrier Reef, the Kakadu Rainforest, and a Tasmania that has 'truly gone wild'[19] — the next section of the same book deals with various other 'Awakened Sites' from around the world, including Anasazi Ruins, the Bermuda Triangle, the Nazca plateau and Teotihuacan.[20]

Through this eclecticism, the Middle Ages are also constructed according to the same colonial procedures as all of the other 'Others' to the postmodern West — whether primitive, oriental or occult — and consumed as part of this pastiche imaginary entertainment-environment. As with the notion of chivalry, the essentialisms of shamanism or monasticism, for example, are only self-referentially 'played' as part of a fantasy. One important effect of this proliferation of images is to efface the difference between various cultural sources: both 'Other' cultures, and Western (medieval) history when constructed as 'Other', become decontextualized resources for imaginative play. These games simplify and idealize what are of course contested and complex periods and cultures. They provide an alluring point of difference: the fantastic instead of the mundane; the authentic instead of the alienated; the exciting and adventurous instead of the monotonous. To fulfill the desire for a more authentic and meaningful world, this plethora of landscapes, identities, and adventures are made available to the postcolonial market in commodity form as historically and culturally displaced experience. The irony is that this usage in fact empties the tropes of meaning, creating a vacuum which in turn feeds the desire even more. The end product is a simulacrum of free-floating signifiers, stripped of meaning, all inhabiting the same pre-defined fantastic space.

The best model by which to understand the 'creation' of these pastiche worlds seems then to be that of the 'simulacrum' as theorized by Jean Baudrillard. Today '[s]imulation is no longer that of a territory, a referential being or a substance. It is the generation by models of a real without origin or reality: a hyperreal.'[21] In this process what Eco describes as 'the need to dismantle and reconsider the flotsam of a

---

[18] Boyle and others, *Target*, p. 55.

[19] Boyle and others, *Target*, p. 118.

[20] In fact, the colonialist practice of cartography is a central technique by which FRPGs subdue and synthesize their multiple geographies.

[21] Jean Baudrillard, 'Simulacra and Simulations', *Selected Writings*, ed. by Mark Poster (Stanford: Stanford University Press, 1988), pp. 166–84 (p. 166).

previous world'[22] is taken to its extreme; cultural images and structures are subjected to fragmentation, patterning and then re-assemblage, not as imitative representations of a past reality, but rather as a recreated model by which the past can be understood, made real: a hyperreal simulation.

Quantifying the Medieval and Other Fantasies

One of the most surprisingly distinctive features of *fantasy* role-playing games is the degree of quantification involved. The different cultural images of the simulacrum, originally distinct and contradictory, do not merely co-inhabit the same imaginative space ('fantasy') enjoying accidental, approximate equality. These images are remade through simulation in the role-playing system, but only through a very particular set of foundational definitions and structures that govern these worlds, the images they can contain, and players' interactions with those worlds. This wealth of material is recorded and accessed in a manner that fetishizes control, statistics, and data.

The shared, interactionist nature of gameplay requires that very weak, very strong, or plot-based characters are generally non-player characters, that is, characters controlled by the Dungeon Master.[23] The Gandalf-type figure remains conspicuous in FRPGs as the organizer of quests; but unfortunately, when characters are being decided, you generally cannot stick your hand up first and say 'I'll be Gandalf thanks', unless others also play a character of this strength. This also goes for the likes of poor Bilbo; gamers generally would prefer to play a thief with some skills. These skills, importantly, must be qualities which can give a comparative, quantifiable advantage in relation to other character-types, in place of forgone magical and combative prowess; thus one is ranked according to levels of proficiency in abilities such as hiding, moving silently, picking locks, disarming traps, searching and so on.[24] Other, non-quantifiable aspects are not mentioned in the rules; they may be described, but they are not regulated, and thus give no disadvantage or advantage in terms of game mechanics.

Thus democratization figures heavily in the transformation of medieval fantasy worlds for the purposes of role-playing, particularly to facilitate fairness and variety. In addition to character class, the different races are balanced, so there is no domination — each have their own distinctive advantages and limitations. Despite

---

[22] Eco, 'The Return of the Middle Ages', p. 83.

[23] These types are still required despite the narrative control given to Player Characters.

[24] Importantly, this equality *serves* difference — character types each have distinctive niches they fill in the gaming activity. In restricted situations such as combat, some character types are manifestly superior; but other situations make up for this.

the extreme variety of images available, intense effort is put into ensuring all characters are created equal. Maintaining balance is the most important rule for Dungeon Masters to remember.[25] However, this multicultural democratization is heavily regulated.

The game rules, or 'mechanics', entwine detailed descriptions of game aspects, full of strongly defined jargon and procedures for situation resolution, with statistical charts by which many aspects of the fantasy worlds are quantified. Character attributes[26] and skills are given integer values in a manner reflecting the practice of IQ testing. The medieval and postmodern 'mad taste for collecting, lists, assemblage, amassing of disparate things',[27] bordering on an obsession with accumulation and categorization, is controlled by the provision of extensive rules for determining outcomes and possibilities, fixing 'medieval' verisimilitude, and ensuring mathematical equality and fairness. Although encouraged to make their own 'house-rule' modifications, Dungeon Masters are also strongly warned against breaking the important gaming balance. Dungeon Masters interested in rule adjustments, such as altering character races, are warned to 'handle this radical change to the campaign with care'.[28] The class (that is, occupation) boundaries are similarly balanced to cooperate or conflict 'well' in society or adventuring parties, and any changes to these highly defined categories are made by strictly monitoring the quantification of attributes. Fairness, and the possibility of fantasy and freedom, flow forth only from this firm regulatory control.

Magic is broadly accessible in *D&D*, beyond the domain of a cloister of wizards in order to allow access for lower-level characters. But magic is not only democratized to place wizards and warriors on more equal standing; it is highly rule-bound to facilitate its usage within all possible games. Magic spells are defined in terms of components, casting time, range, duration and so on, to the extent that nothing distinguishes them from mundane weapons and effects in terms of comprehensibility and the application of their effects at the most basic level of the game. In one sense, magic is no longer magical.

In fact, the relative character abilities of fighters, magic-users, and wielders of *ki* are all quantified, defined in terms of particular integers, to place them all on similar — and comparable — levels. The various magical paths of *Shadowrun*, although providing a choice of cultural images, are comparable through similarly defined mechanics: a voodoo priest can duel an Aboriginal shaman, and the results would be

---

[25] Monte Cook and others, *Dungeons and Dragons: Dungeon Master's Guide*, 3rd edn (Renton: Wizards of the Coast, 2000), pp. 10–11.

[26] These include the numerical definition of not only 'strength' and 'dexterity', but aspects closer to character personality such as 'wisdom' and 'charisma'.

[27] Eco, 'The Return of the Middle Ages', p. 83.

[28] Cook, *Dungeon Master's Guide*, p. 22.

determined as an interaction largely of numerical attributes and dice rolls. The particularly Australian totems are often merely iconographically different from their Native American or other counterparts: the Dingo is the 'Australian version of Jackal',[29] while the Wombat is the 'Australian version of Badger'.[30] Page references are given to the corresponding sections of another rulebook. The problems of inter-cultural communication — the difficulties of broaching (let alone understanding) unfamiliar language-games — are solved through the application of numerical methods, with logical and mathematical simulations given ontological primacy. Rules are vital for systematizing the contradictory material that makes up the cultural and iconographic element of FRPGs.

This quantifying aspect does not only apply to the *D&D* or *Shadowrun* style pastiche of medieval and/or non-Western images. Even in the numerous FRPGs where the gaming world is closely based on a particular source — whether it be 'actual' twelfth-century Britain or Tolkien's Middle-Earth — the world is still commonly defined in these very strict terms. Nor does the historical precision of many FRPGs avoid this desire to define and assign numbers; rather, the FRPG impulse to quantify and control reflects and intensifies the contemporary emphasis on historical accuracy. This is the ideology of gaming: the historical 'ethos' of the very structure of the games is that of a bureaucratic and disciplinary society that orders knowledge and administers social control through an obsession with statistical definition and archiving. The performance of FRPGs is entangled with the articulation of the historical forms of knowledge of contemporary culture into which the disciplines of history, sociology and medievalism are entwined.

These games do not translate and quantify a formerly un-defined 'reality'; rather they reflect and perform the manner in which 'reality' is seen — i.e. organized and simulated — by the culture that produced them. These forms of description and definition are typical of the society in which these games are created and played, and its methods of defining and controlling its own populace. In FRPGs, these strategies constitute a version of Foucault's 'governmentality', whereby the production of knowledge about their fictional constituencies is coextensive with the operation of power.[31] Mackay describes the creation of 'doubles' through archiving details of both people and characters,[32] and the gamemaster's position of panoptic

---

[29] Boyle and others, *Target*, p. 105.

[30] Boyle and others, *Target*, p. 106.

[31] See Michel Foucault, 'Governmentality', *Power: Essential Works of Foucault 1954-1984*, ed. by James D. Faubion, trans. by Robert Hurley and others, vol. 3 (Harmondsworth: Penguin, 2002), pp. 201–22.

[32] He compares character attributes and other aspects of what he calls the 'drama sphere' to 'credit ratings, income tax returns, IQ tests, student exams, job evaluations, consumer habits, and so forth'. Mackay, *The Fantasy Role-Playing Game*, p. 68.

surveillance,[33] considering the possibility that the FRPG 'form replicates the structures of power operating within society'[34] as described by Foucault in *Discipline and Punish*. Most prominent is the painstaking discrimination of game-world characteristics: like the human sciences, FRPGs descend from the procedure of the examination 'that places individuals in a field of surveillance [and] also situates them in a network of writing; it engages them in a whole mass of documents that capture and fix them.'[35] But FRPGs reflect more than just this disciplinary bureaucratization; they also exemplify the biopolitical aspect of Foucauldian governmentality whereby the concept of population is treated as an object for definition. The *Dungeon Master's Guide* and *Monster Manual* are full of tables documenting the frequency of different races and monsters and their social composition, as well as their combat properties.

This quantification extends in the simulated possible worlds of FRPGs beyond the numerical definition of individuals and populations. The extensive *freedom* of FRPGs simultaneously (and ironically) necessitates comprehensive *rules*, extending to every possibility they may be required to adjudicate: the direction a missed arrow flies, the degree of drunkenness a character feels,[36] and so on. The endless possibilities of fantasy takes quantification — as the dominant organization model available for understanding the 'world' — to its extreme, requiring its applicability to every situation and action.[37] The game rules even incorporate their own 'physics' based on tables and dice.

Of course, performance, interpretation and narrative are also important elements of FRPGs; the tension between these facets and quantification is pivotal to role-playing. The *Dungeon Master's Guide* distinguishes two extremes between which most gameplay falls: the 'kick in the door' and 'deep-immersion storytelling' styles of play. In the former, action-oriented style, 'character motivation need be no more developed than a desire to kill monsters and acquire treasure. Rules and game

---

[33] Mackay, *The Fantasy Role-Playing Game*, pp. 95–96.

[34] Mackay, *The Fantasy Role-Playing Game*, p. 93.

[35] Michel Foucault, *Discipline and Punish: The Birth of the Prison*, trans. by Alan Sheridan (Harmondsworth: Penguin, 1991 [1977]), p. 189. Indeed, as Foucault himself writes, 'if from the early Middle Ages to the present day the "adventure" is an account of individuality, [...] it is also inscribed in the formation of a disciplinary society' (p. 193).

[36] The assigned strength of drinks is compared with the character's numerical 'constitution' value.

[37] See Mackay, *The Fantasy Role-Playing Game*, pp. 103–04, for an interesting consideration of how those elements of life *not* quantified — sex, emotions etc. — penetrate the nondiegetic situation in a carnivalesque overflow.

balance are very important in this style of play',[38] whereas the latter style places less importance on game mechanics and more on story and performance.

There are, of course, varieties of FRPGs (or their relatives such as Live Action Role-Playing) that avoid the imperative to quantify their world-setting. Experienced gamers commonly report that eventually the focus turns away from competition and statistical character improvement, until the games become more about role-playing and the development of character motivation and persona. Mackay argues that in an 'ongoing role-playing game narrative',[39] where players have a greater chance to interact and reach mutual understanding, the quantified, competitive and manipulative elements decline in importance;[40] thus he proposes the FRPG as *A New Performing Art*, engaging its aesthetic dimensions against the grain of much contemporary criticism.[41] Certainly, the worlds and characters imagined by the players are not entirely reducible to their mechanized form. Quantified attributes can be interpreted to mean a variety of things in terms of personality;[42] Mackay describes how the 'dissected units of the game are assembled into a character concept',[43] and Role Playing Game rulebooks are emphatic that character survival depends more on role-play than numerical advantage, as they are that their rules are neither exhaustive nor adamantine.

---

[38] Cook, *Dungeon Master's Guide*, p. 8.

[39] Mackay, *The Fantasy Role-Playing Game*, p. 100.

[40] In Mackay's terms, the 'script sphere, theater sphere, and performance sphere begin to assume a more important structural role in the role-playing game performance' (p. 100) over the mechanized elements of the 'drama sphere'.

[41] He even claims that '[t]hese imaginary events are then rarefied into an aesthetic object, the creation of which subverts the structures of power [...] the performance's participation in disciplinary power structures and the exclusionary aspect of the quantified character recordsheet' (Mackay, *The Fantasy Role-Playing Game*, p. 108). It is partly to counterweight his emphasis on aesthetics that I accentuate quantification.

[42] In fact, role-play and theme have been made part of game structure in order to motivate players towards more 'sophisticated' engagement. For example, Dungeon Masters give 'story awards' consisting of experience points for dramatic skill in role-play. Some role-playing games avoid quantified structural elements as much as possible, such as *Everway*, whose 'brand of fantasy is the generic, piecemeal approach with American Indian and African shamanistic tribal culture added to *D&D's* European emphasis', and which has an 'abstract and vague' rules system. In seeking to focus on theme and the 'aesthetic elements of story creation and character development', *Everway*'s creators have quantified thematic elements within the formal rules (Mackay, *The Fantasy Role-Playing Game*, pp. 46–47). Mackay, however, rejects this on artistic grounds, arguing that this control over narrative and theme can actually debilitate it.

[43] Mackay, *The Fantasy Role-Playing Game*, p. 67.

But quantification is not an accidental aspect of FRPGs, which must be shed if they are to reach their true performative potential; it is a defining characteristic which, although perhaps a remainder from wargames,[44] is one which is still enormously influential today with little sign of disappearing. More sophisticated gaming is not, at present, representative; moreover, Mackay, who is eager to legitimate FRPGs despite their involvement in quantification, argues that it is only within a quantified system that performative freedom is achieved.[45] It is still the quantified mechanics that determine the outcomes of conflicting game-world activity. Many aspects of game content are in fact determined by the game mechanics, and only retrospectively rationalized in terms of some game-world explanation. For example, the nature of magic spells, and how characters memorize and cast them, is in *D&D* a result of the necessity of spellcasting being a temporally viable option in combat.[46]

In fact, FRPGs often do not simply reflect disciplinary quantification, but actually fetishize its methods. Commonly, the players' enjoyment of FRPGs lies in the strategic manipulation of rules; games can become such that the fantastic icons are merely an overlay of the strategy, while gaming is largely a competition (or demonstration) of skill in interpretation and control of rules and information. An example of this gaming style is the 'rort', a tournament of combat encounters with characters specifically created — within limits to ensure fairness — to maximize the advantages that could possibly be interpreted from the rules. Mechanization is always at least a defining factor with which narrative and performance must contend, marking gaming as at best a highly ambiguous activity.

Entrepreneurial Adventurers

The striking prominence of both aspects of fantasy and control in FRPGs may seem puzzlingly anachronistic at first, but both sides of this apparent contradiction in fact stem from the same source. The regulatory control of disparate, simulated images in FRPGs is best illuminated as encoding the consumer capitalism of the late twentieth century.

---

[44] A paraphrasing of what Mackay thinks is the case with both combat (pp. 102–03) and the dice-based system (p. 7).

[45] For Mackay, it is the quantification of the world (and not story — see n. 37 above) in *D&D* that allows the freedom to create art (Mackay, *The Fantasy Role-Playing Game*, pp. 43–48). This sits uneasily, however, with his rejection elsewhere of the efficacy of quantification.

[46] In Mackay's terms (although more than he recognizes), the nature of the different FRPG 'spheres' interacts and interferes with the others to a large degree; most notably, the quantification of the 'drama sphere' determines many elements of the other aspects of gaming.

The intense fervour of late capitalism sustains both the governmental techniques of societal definition and control, and the cultural cannibalism of multiple images in an encompassing simulacrum. In Eco's words, the Middle Ages and other cultures are 'messed up in order to meet the vital requirements'[47] of our period: the consuming subject of Western capitalism takes on these fantastic mantles for entertainment, while controlling them according to its own methods of definition. The postmodern proliferation of images is itself a product of a hyperconsumptive capitalism. Little attempt is made to understand the cultures raided for these tropes in their own terms. Rather, they are chosen, accumulated and then defined according to a system of rules that accentuates definition and strategy.[48] Although quite willing to take on many different new identities and lives, these games are highly structured at the core by the modes of definition of contemporary society, while also motivated by the incessant desire of consumer capitalism.

In the medieval social system as imagined in FRPGs, no one has to be a peasant at all, due to the abundance of travelling adventurers. These enterprising questers are self-consciously above average, possessing not only money, but also most importantly the skills and capabilities to contend in these competitive worlds. Role-playing scenarios are structured according to a system of challenge and reward: in turn for successfully overcoming obstacles, characters receive items, experience points, treasure and fame. Looking beyond the quest narratives within each scenario, a greater narrative spans and joins these together into 'campaigns'. What we find in FRPGs is not a Tolkienesque *bildungsroman* — a story of the moral education and development of the characters towards a time of testing — but a different model of character development that is largely determined by the capitalistic ethos. The formative period comprises not moral but skillful improvement, with the entrepreneurial advancement of the adventurers through experience, levels, skills, statistics, money, and equipment. Facing greater challenges as they themselves become greater, and receiving rewards (treasure, magical items, etc.) for their efforts and abilities, they are constantly improving statistics on the character sheet. This narrative of improvement can be a large part of what drives the desire to gameplay.[49]

---

[47] Eco, 'The Return of the Middle Ages', p. 68.

[48] Susan Stewart can help us understand the form of fetishism involved in these collections of cultural icons: she follows Baudrillard's argument 'that the desire and *jouissance* characterizing fetishism result from the systematic quality of objects rather than from the objects themselves [...]. In the collection such systematicity results in the quantification of desire. Desire is ordered, arranged, and manipulated'. *On Longing: Narratives of the Miniature, the Gigantic, the Souvenir, the Collection* (Baltimore: Johns Hopkins University Press, 1984), p. 163.

[49] Single-player fantasy computer games commonly intensify this narrative, submerging much of the game mechanics, simplifying the presentations of plot and quest devices, and focusing on combat with monsters and character improvement ('level-ups'). The monsters

One aspect of the implicit ideology that Fine recognizes as written into FRPG worlds is the myth of infinite availability: 'The structure of dungeons and fantasy worlds reflects the American image of a potentially unlimited supply of treasure.'[50] These fascinating, meticulously expounded worlds are to a large degree constructed and defined in terms of challenges to be overcome by the characters, and what they can gain in return. Many of the rules and statistical tables function to ensure everyone gets what they deserve,[51] and no more, no less; sometimes, it seems that FRPGs are fantasizing a perfect capitalist system. One can see these games as models of ideal competition: everyone starts different but equal, and if they try hard and overcome the challenges, they will be successful.

The versions of medieval bestiaries that appear in FRPGs are reconstructed according to the same imperatives. The third core rulebook of *D&D* is an extensive list of monsters that can be encountered within gaming sessions.[52] This pastiche of monstrosity is sourced from the fantastic denizens that filled medieval bestiaries, as well as fantasy literature, many mythologies, records of real animals and dinosaurs, and new chimeras created particularly for the game. The *Shadowrun* Australian sourcebook provides information on bunyips, drop bears, and many other native Australian fauna altered by the magical Awakening (including dingoes, kangaroos, redback spiders, and cloned thylacines).[53] But whereas the medieval bestiaries were obsessed with providing a Christian moral message derived from the animals' characteristic behaviour, those in FRPGs describe the animals in terms of the challenge they pose to the adventurers. Simultaneously, they present a fantastic, alluring image, and delimit the creature in terms of the characters' (mostly combative) encounters. Many are defined according to aspects of governmental 'population' definition: in terms of climate/terrain, frequency of appearance, social structure and so on. But they are further circumscribed according to the attributes that facilitate hostile confrontations, such as their 'hit points', damage, speed and skills.

The activities of the players (as opposed to the characters they play) are very much concerned with the control of information. The skills required for success in FRPGs include interpreting cultural images and tropes, making decisions according to rules, and manipulating and interpreting information — definitively middle class

---

here are displayed on screen according to fantastic iconography, but exist in computer code and game-world effects as digitally defined entities for strategic encounters.

[50] Fine, *Shared Fantasy*, p. 76.

[51] Success is often determined by effort and ingenuity, and less commonly by luck. See Fine, *Shared Fantasy,* pp. 90–106, on the efficacy of the dice.

[52] Monte Cook and others, *Dungeons and Dragons: Monster Manual*, 3rd edn (Renton: Wizards of the Coast, 2000).

[53] Boyle, *Target*, pp. 66–73.

and entrepreneurial activities. This 'heroic' adventure is actually highly involved in skills important for success in contemporary capitalistic culture: the very world from which the gameplayers are (supposedly) trying to escape. The desire to escape from a mundane, alienated economic existence, in search of fantasy, becomes controlled by consumer capitalism in its cannibalistic search for images of authenticity. As an attempt to escape from contemporary technological society, this retreat into a fantastic world is compromised by its own drives to control and quantify that world, drives that reveal a deeper underlying allegiance to capitalist modes of governance.

The Danger of Performance

Mackay believes that the creation of a traditional narrative structure distilled from the spontaneous performance is the predominant cultural and social value of FRPGs.[54] However, let me propose for the moment that the interstitial, spontaneous and performative elements themselves, unappropriated by retelling structured by memory and conventional narrative, are more particular and central to the experience and value of gaming. We might then better follow de Certeau in understanding anecdotal '*accounts* of particular games' as '*repertories of schemas of action* between partners [...] these mementos teach the tactics [of resistance] possible within a given (social) system'.[55]

From early in their history, FRPGs have been constructed as 'dangerous' in a manner that has long been associated with the Gothic: 'Such terrors, emerging from the gloom of a castle or lurking in the dark features of the villain [...] critics feared, encouraging readers' decline into depravity and corruption.'[56] Although this dubious yet oft-heard accusation, largely from the religious and cultural right, is no doubt fueled by the occult elements included in many FRPGs, the force behind the accusation that they are 'dangerous' seems also to be a response to their creative and performative aspects.[57] In contrast to the relatively passive entertainment of media such as film, FRPGs' particular 'engrossment [in alternate worlds] that transcends mere reading or viewing'[58] involves active participation in the performance of cultural scripts in an act of self-conscious play. Built into role-playing is an unavoidable awareness of the scripted nature of the contained performances.

---

[54] Mackay, *The Fantasy Role-Playing Game*, pp. 121–31.

[55] Certeau, *The Practice of Everyday Life*, pp. 22–23.

[56] Fred Botting, *Gothic* (London: Routledge, 1996), pp. 6–7. See also Kurt Lancaster, 'Do Role-Playing Games Promote Crime, Satanism and Suicide among Players as Critics Claim?' *Journal of Popular Culture*, 28 (1994), 67–79.

[57] Mackay, *The Fantasy Role-Playing Game*, p. 68.

[58] Fine, *Shared Fantasy*, p. 124.

The subversive possibilities of FRPGs are certainly best located in this consciousness: the awareness of the arbitrariness and mutability of these modes of defining people and the world; the recognition of the manner in which we construct classifications of things, and perform parts according to culturally defined scripts. FRPGs unavoidably betray their own vagaries; beyond masking 'the *absence* of a basic reality [... they] dissimulate that there is nothing'.[59] For FRPGs do not merely reflect these power-filled aspects of contemporary society — they play with them. As little is sacred, and all can be performed, and thus mocked and subverted, FRPGs avoid the danger of reifying the forms of knowledge they use. They thus open up room for the collective negotiation of different ways of imagining our past and ourselves, challenging and interrogating the methods of construction and the habits of viewing involved in our power-filled social structures, and resisting the naturalisation and restriction of the cultural 'world'. The *possibility* of creating different ways of being, the imaginative exploration and critique of ourselves and/through others, lies in the playful and fantastic. According to one attentive, if slightly optimistic gamer:

> What do people do in life, other than play roles? [...] Apart from the fact that RPGs can be just plain fun, they can help us survive in our shifting cultural environment by restoring our childish ability to vary the number of roles we can play in 'real' life, and by allowing us to explore the nature of that 'reality' through engaging in fantasy.[60]

FRPGs are (as Blonsky paraphrases Mackay) 'a (perhaps futile) way of mastering that other gaming, the game playing we all do in everyday life'.[61]

This subversive dream perhaps seems at best naïve in the context of the reading of *D&D* I have presented above. It is, however, precisely FRPGs' resistance to the necessity of their objects that provokes their simultaneous fetishization. Gaming's self-consciousness of simulation is itself reflective of contemporary postmodern culture and theory, whose subversive possibilities present their own obstacles to vision and change. The legacy of the simulacrum is the awareness of arbitrariness, which betrays the difficulty of imagining or justifying a different or better model; thus FRPGs accept and repeat cannibalizing tropes and disciplinary systems. In this FRPGs are truly postmodern texts: unalterably aware of their own circumstantiality, they are debilitated by this all-encompassing simulation. Unable to escape the endless circulation of images and numbers, and locked into their repetition by an insatiable desire, FRPGs become frustratingly trapped in the endless simulation that is the predicament of postmodernism.

---

[59] Baudrillard, 'Simulacra and Simulations', p. 170.

[60] Fine, *Shared Fantasy*, p. 54, quoting Stephen L. Lortz, 'My Life and RPGs', *Different Worlds*, 1 (1979), 26–27 (p. 27).

[61] Mackay, p. 162.

The 'UnAustralian' Goth: Notes Towards a Dislocated National Subject

KEN GELDER

T he massacre of students at Columbine High School in Denver, Colorado, in April 1999 was amongst other things the catalyst for a positive retrieval of modern Goth identity.[1] Young Goths were subsequently distinguished from the more nihilistic, pro-violence 'Trench Coat Mafia', even though both groups may have shared some musical and other tastes as well as a 'structural' position at secondary school, marginal to a dominant pedagogical culture directed towards good citizenship, sports prowess and nation building. In Melbourne, the *Age* newspaper's editorial for 23 April 1999 also attributed the massacre to the influence of 'global culture' and its counter-effect of producing newer and smaller 'tribalisms'.[2] The editorial noted that globalization — the eradication of once taken-for-granted cultural and social boundaries in particular — brought the Columbine massacre 'closer to home', that is, closer to Australia. There was, indeed, serious concern about just such a high school massacre happening here, leading to the investigation of a student at a high school in Sydney following the Columbine events. A few days after the *Age* editorial, journalist Sharon Gray published a short piece in the same newspaper as part of the subsequent recovery of a Goth identity maligned as simultaneously too global and too tribal. Her punning title, 'Vamping It Up's Goth to Be Fun', signals its intention to detach a Goth subculture from the high anxieties which had built themselves around the Columbine school events, giving it a very different kind of identity. She looks in particular at her Goth son's infatuation with the American fantasy role-playing game *Camarilla*, and makes the following key points:

---

[1] A different version of this essay was written for a collection entitled *Goth: Undead Subculture*, to be published in 2005 by Duke University Press. It is used here with permission.

[2] 'Editorial: A Horror Not So Far Away', *The Age*, 23 April 1999.

— that the game 'has more rules than you can think of' (that is, it is not anarchic or out of control; it is disciplinary)[3]

— that the game is played, as she says, 'from the waist up' (that is, it is non-sexual and non-violent)

— that the game is 'problem-solving' (that is, it has a positive pedagogical function; it is therapeutic)

— and most importantly, that the game is creative, relying on the participants' invention of characters and their ability to tell a story to a small group of co-players.

This latter feature takes the game out of the context of global culture, returning it to the localized realm of the storyteller as famously outlined by Walter Benjamin, where the role-playing game transmits narratives directly to listeners, with everything that is said prescribed by shared and accepted regulatory codes of behaviour; where everything is conventional.[4] Together, these points all seem to suggest a very particular mode of Goth cultural practice — as therapeutic, localizing, creative, non-violent — which then enables it to be distinguished from the 'Trench Coat Mafia's' more destructive and self-alienating fantasy/role-playing activities. The Melbourne *Camarilla* domain, called Flavus Periculum, is, Gray notes, the second-largest in the world, with its own website and magazine, and now, a clearly-defined 'chapter' (http://www.users.bigpond.com/harlquin.flavusp/). 'Chapters', Gray goes on, 'tend to stay together and become close friends, and blood runs thick'. When she goes to Perth with her Goth son, he emails ahead and chapter members 'picked him up within an hour of our arrival, took him to games and clubs all over town, and dropped him back the night before our departure. Better than Rotary', she concludes.[5]

The Melbourne chapter of *Camarilla* is one of many expressions of a contemporary Goth identity and is located in Australia in the post-Columbine framework of a mother's spirited defence of her son's subcultural interests. It works here to bridge the generational divide in a way that may be untypical of relations between parent cultures and other youth subcultures.[6] More particularly, the return to storytelling, to generic rules or conventions and regulated behaviour (rather than

---

[3] For a similar argument, see Matthew Chrulew's essay in this collection.

[4] See Walter Benjamin, 'The Storyteller', *Illuminations*, trans. by Harry Zohn (London: Fontana, 1936).

[5] Sharon Gray, 'Vamping It Up's Goth to Be Fun', *The Age* (Melbourne), 26 April 1999. For another article distinguishing Goths from the 'Trench Coat Mafia' and violence, see Rachel Gibson, 'Cultists Repudiate the Creed of the Killers', *The Age*, 25 April 1999. 'Goths are generally more into melancholy than murder', Gibson suggests.

[6] See the classic Birmingham School account of subcultures on this topic of generational differences between youth subcultures and the 'parent' culture: *Resistance Through Rituals*, ed. by Stuart Hall and Tony Jefferson (1975; repr. London: Routledge, 1990).

violence, anarchy and destruction) is broadly symptomatic of what seems to be a creative, highly literate and *literary* subculture. I speak here of Goth in terms of its mediated or textualized forms of self-expression; this essay is not an ethnographic project along the lines of, for example, Paul Hodkinson's recent study of actual Goth subcultures in the UK (which talks primarily about Goth styles and Goth self-identification as 'insiders' with consistently-held tastes, interests and practices).[7] My interest is instead in Goth literariness, Goth textual production. In fact, Goth subcultures are both creative (they produce a great deal of literature) and routinely citational, returning over and over to a set of generically-prescribed or canonical literary quotations, especially from Oscar Wilde, Tennyson and other Victorians, as well as various Romantic poets. Goth literary self-expression can seem anachronistic as a consequence: out of time, as well as out of place. This feature can seem all the more striking in a country like Australia, where the relation between national culture and a subculture such as this can be tangential at best. This predicament was played out some time ago in the Australian soap opera *Home and Away* through its own resident Goth, Edward Dunglass, a character utterly out of place on the otherwise normative Australian beaches of Summer Bay. Australian Goths — involved in role-playing games like *Camarilla* or, like Dunglass, reading French existential literature — might well be thought to have disengaged from the nation altogether, attracted to a set of *other* places (imaginary as well as real) in what could be seen as an act of mute resistance: neither passive nor active (and certainly never violent), and perhaps not even critical, but simply as an occupation of some other place or 'structure of feeling' (in Raymond Williams's phrase) elsewhere that offers pleasures that Australia's national culture cannot satisfy.

On its own, however, this view also runs the risk of relaxing into the prevailing Goth subcultural stereotype of alienation — a stereotype exploited in much Goth mediated- and self-expression as viewers of *Home and Away* would probably know, and used as the primary trope in accounting for the troubled condition of the 'Trench Coat Mafia'. Even so, Richard Davenport-Hines, a major commentator on Goth and Gothic identity, invokes this stereotype in a way that is useful in the Australian context when he suggests that Goth (he takes it as a transnational cultural practice) stands for 'no homeliness, no reconciliation'.[8] Australia, of course, has an official cultural policy of reconciliation with its indigenous people, and it has been recently obsessed with the issue of homeliness, intensified in 2001 through the centenary of Federation (revisiting the unification of its constituent states and the foundational moment of the nation) as well as in a range of cultural/political/spiritual tracts

---

[7] See Paul Hodkinson, *Goth: Identity, Style and Subculture* (Oxford: Berg, 2002). Hodkinson emphasizes what he calls the 'cultural substance' of Goth subcultures: that they live their subcultural lives creatively and emotionally, relying on the particularity of their interests and style to distinguish themselves from a 'mainstream' they actively disdain.

[8] Richard Davenport-Hines, *Gothic: Four Hundred Years of Excess, Horror, Evil and Ruin* (London: Fourth Estate, 2000), p. 10.

currently in circulation that address and often yearn for contemporary Australian forms of belonging.[9] Following Davenport-Hines, we could imagine Australian Goths to be indifferent to these features of a national culture, in particular, national self-identity as 'Australian'. However, I want to argue in this chapter that although Goths may well be indifferent to or even downright dismissive of the dominant preoccupations of national culture in Australia, they may nevertheless engage these preoccupations in a dialectical way. Working against the stereotype of alienation, there are indeed forms of Goth belonging in Australia — the need to be *here* — that sit alongside forms of Goth longing to be *elsewhere*.[10]

Daniel Nettheim's *Angst* (2000) is the first Australian feature film to have a Goth as one of its protagonists. The film centres around Dean, who lives with some friends in Kings Cross in inner-city Sydney. Dean works in a video store and is passionate about lowbrow horror films, modelling himself on Quentin Tarantino perhaps, as he spends his idle time at the store writing schlock horror film scripts. One day, a Goth girl walks in — a character called May, played by Abi Tucker — and immediately captures his attention. Dean has an ex-girlfriend who lives in prosperous, suburban Sydney and who is now engaged to a clean-cut young man with entrepreneurial ambition. Kings Cross, by contrast, is cast as a desolate place, with homeless, unemployed men wandering the streets: something that horrifies Dean, giving him a sense of his own possible future. He confides in May as they become romantically linked, and they decide to go to his former girlfriend's suburban home — she still lives with her parents — to exorcize his demons. The trip by taxi to the suburbs begins an act of desecration directed at the prosperous suburban home and all that it stands for: an Australianness that is both conformist and infantilized in this case, with the former girlfriend's bedroom filled with pink fluffy pigs — one of which, some time ago, Dean had accidentally ejaculated over, thus ending their otherwise non-sexual relationship. May and Dean break into the house, and go up to the bedroom. The pink toys are arranged and then discarded as the couple themselves have sex together, completing the desecration. Two features are worth noting in this sequence: first, that Dean's fear of homelessness is cured paradoxically by the desecration of what is in effect a sacred space in a suburban home; and second, that it is the Goth girl, May, who supplies this cure. May retains her Goth image as someone without respect for *homeliness* (suburban homeliness, at least). In the process, however, she cures Dean's fear of *homelessness*. During the sex that follows after she undoes her brassiere, her identity is rendered almost maternal as the camera focuses on her breasts from underneath and then on her

---

[9] See, for example, Peter Read, *Belonging* (Cambridge: Cambridge University Press, 2000); also John Moloney, *The Native Born* (Melbourne: Melbourne University Press, 2000); and David Tacey, *Re-Enchantment* (Sydney: HarperCollins, 2000).

[10] I take this juxtaposition of belonging and longing, rather loosely, from Susan Stewart, *On Longing: Narratives of the Miniature, the Gigantic, the Souvenir, the Collection* (Baltimore: Johns Hopkins University Press, 1984).

reassuring gaze down at Dean as she sits on top of him. The Goth girl thus has both a desecrating and a therapeutic function: no homeliness, certainly, but no homelessness either. Hers is the body through which Dean's future is settled. In so far as he is cast as a national subject (since he wants to 'fit in', that is, to belong), the Goth girl functions as a nation builder as much as she figures an indifference to the nation through her Goth-ness.

This dialectic of engagement and disengagement — being both of the nation and indifferent to or dismissive of it — offers a way of productively conceiving of relations between a subculture and a national culture, with Goths as my example. In Australia, there is now a national Goth magazine, *Goth Nation* (published out of Melbourne, the first issue in 2002), and there are two national Goth websites. The first (although it closed in July 2003) is http://www.gothic.net.au, titled 'gothic-netau', a state-by-state, city-by-city network of Goth activity and Goth email addresses, each with their Goth nickname ('Abyss', 'Dark Maiden', 'Solitaire', 'Miasma', and so on) and sound bite profiles of self-identification. Like *Goth Nation*, this site produced a national identity and a Goth identity simultaneously, distinguishing them from each other even as it necessarily folded them together. The second national website is http://www.aethersanctum.net, intitially titled 'The Aether Sanctum: dark culture with a quizzical antipodean twist' (and now, simply, 'dark culture'), a much denser, beautifully designed e-zine with reviews and articles as well as Goth news, articles about club life and so on. The subtitle evokes both its national identity and its Goth difference. Again, there are city-by-city listings of relevant events; Australian cities might even be claimed as 'Goth' in accounts that map Goth geographies by identifying Goth clubs to go to, shops to visit, and a range of other Goth-identified sites. In Melbourne, for example, there are the Goth nightclubs Heresy and Revelations (both in Flinders Lane), Abyss (in Bourke Street), and Belfry (Smith Street in Collingwood). There are boutique Goth clothing shops such as Gown of Thorns on Brunswick Street in Fitzroy and Victorian Gothic on Sydney Road, Brunswick. Each of these venues has its own website. There is at least one specialist Goth record shop, too: Heartland, in North Melbourne. These venues collectively produce a set of Goth nodal points across the city — the inner city, not the suburbs which are always in receipt of Goth contempt — announcing a particular kind of inhabitation of inner urban territory. Other Australian cities can be equally transformed: an entry on 'The Aether Sanctum' website from 18 April 2001 announces 'Sydney Gothic is now open!', linking to a 'Sydney Gothic' website which both territorializes and commodifies (with news about Goth fetish shops and Gothic features on the Mercedes Australian Fashion Week Festival, for example). The *Goth Nation* magazine similarly talks of 'east coast Gothic', drawing three eastern Australian cities together — Melbourne, Sydney and Brisbane — through their Goth music and nightclubs.[11]

---

[11] Martin le Marchant, 'East Coast Gothic', *Goth Nation*, 2 (Feb-Mar–Apr 2003), no pagination.

On the other hand, commodified Goth identities imprinted upon cities can also be rejected: to deterritorialize, perhaps, that is, to reassert (often defiantly) Goth identity as marginal. In November 2000, there were many media reports about Michael Rymer's filming of Anne Rice's novel *Queen of the Damned* in Melbourne, one of them — from the *Herald Sun* of 15 November — announcing that 'Melbourne is officially the goth capital of Australia'. The article is posted on 'The Aether Sanctum' website and given short shrift with these remarks: 'Melbourne tabloid rag *The Herald Sun* recently printed some piece which is based on a chat one of their people had with one of the guys working on that I'm-so-fucking-sick-of-hearing-about-it *Queen of the Damned* movie. I find the attitude to be pretty shonky show-biz fare. Makes me wonder if goths are too recognisable. I think we are really'. The 'recognisability' of Goths is both crucial to their subcultural aesthetic (their style) and constantly disavowed. On the one hand, many Goth websites and magazines — and not just those from Australia — work hard to make Goth identity more recognizable than ever by providing often quite elaborate genealogies of Goth cultural activity, for example, or working carefully through definitions of Goth. On the other hand, these websites and magazines also relish the various kinds of eccentricities or idiosyncrasies that characterize this subculture. The homepage of Miasma, http://www.gothic.net.au/~miasma says, 'And so we come to the place where one usually finds a description of the being that has made this page. Well why should I be any different?' Alongside this rather resigned acceptance of sameness, the name Miasma is given its own peculiar Goth identity, as a word invoking an 'unwholesome or unpleasant atmosphere', and is thus rendered utterly eccentric. Her identity is then thickened through a set of literary citations, references to a range of fantasy literature that is claimed as Goth (from Terry Pratchett novels to Anne McCaffrey and Isobelle Carmody: the website quotes passages which use the word 'miasma' from each of these novelists works).

The Goth snubbing of the filming of *Queen of the Damned* and its cinematic occupation of Melbourne stems also from distinctions between the subcultural e-zine (with its restricted, discriminating Goth audience) and the tabloid newspaper (with its far less restricted and — by implication — less discriminating, mainstream Australian readership). These are taste differences, of course, which align the Goth website with higher cultural concerns, reflected in particular through its commitment to literary cultural production. Goth, as I have noted, is a literate and literary subculture: it can be canonical (drawing from Tennyson, Wilde, etc.) and marginal (turning to fantasy literature outside of the canon). Both gothicnetau and 'The Aether Sanctum' contain much Goth fiction and poetry and clearly encourage literary self-expression amongst its regular users. For 'The Aether Sanctum', poetry is especially central to Australian Goth self-identification, and a considerable amount of virtual space is devoted to it. This is a space that also knows about the mainstream Australian literary canon. Issue 6 of the e-zine, featured a section in its literary pages titled 'Goth Bush Poetry': lovingly crafted Goth rewritings of Australian bush poetry classics. Here is a sample from 'The Goth from Snowy Riva', a version of Banjo

Paterson's famous poem 'The Man from Snowy River', so central to mainstream national self-expression. It is crafted (or 'translated', as the website suggests) by Barbara Welton:

> There was movement at the nightclub, for the word had passed around
> That a Homie's younger sister had gone astray,
> And had joined the wild goth gang — she'd been known to hang around,
> So all the Homies gathered for the fray.
> All the old and jaded gothics from the nightclubs far and near
> Had mustered at the Hell Club on that night,
> For the gothics love hard chiding where there's Homies on which to sneer,
> And the gossip snuffs the battle with delight.
>
> There was Azriel, who dressed up as the Tarot's Page of Cup,
> The young man with his hair as black as jet;
> But few could sneer beside him when his blood-alcohol was up —
> No one had ever shown him up as yet.
> And Romancy of the Overblown came down to lend a hand,
> No better one-up-man had they yet seen;
> No other intellect could throw him while he was sober 'nough to stand,
> And he looked damn fine in those shiny jeans.
>
> And he was there, a gothling — a small and weedy beast,
> He was something like an Eldritch, undersized,
> With a touch of Peter Murphy — three pints thoroughbred at least —
> And as such by goth women muchly prized.
> He was hard and tough and wiry — just the sort that won't say die —
> There was courage in his quick impatient tread;
> And he bore the badge of gameness in his black-rimmed, mascared eye,
> And the spiked and lofty plumage of his head.[12]

There are parodic tributes to other Australian bush anthems, turning them into spaces through which to write mock Goth epics. As I see it, this process involves both a canny engagement with a national literary canon — the latter now clichéd and overwrought, as well as redundant (especially in relation to Goth inner-city self-identification) — and, through the Goth 'translation' or, we might say, desecration of these poems, a celebration of subcultural marginality. These are not poems that arise out of indifference, in other words; they are not *dis*engaged with national culture. Indeed, Goths rewrite these bush poems precisely to give their own place (their geographical place) in that national culture some clarity. In another example, the

---

[12] 'The Aether Sanctum', http://www.aethersanctum.net/about/archives/6/bushpoetry.html, accessed 6 May 2003.

pseudonymous poet 'ephemerae' reworks the famous Australian bush song 'Nine Miles from Gundagai', each verse ending with the refrain, 'And the goths sat on the Town Hall steps / 'Neath cloudy Sydney skies'.

These Goth makeovers of Australian bush poetry — relocating them to an identifiably Goth inner city of nightclubs and Goth-inhabited public spaces — certainly present a (still unfolding) relationship to the national literary canon. But, as noted already, Australian Goth writing is inevitably also transnational. An Australian Goth literary genealogy would, of course, begin with the iconic Goth singer/composer Nick Cave, whose first novel, *And the Ass Saw the Angel* (1989), is a Faulkner-esque work set in the American Deep South, labouring under the heavy influence of *Revelations* in its unfolding of a story of aberrance and persecution. With his bands The Birthday Party and The Bad Seeds, Cave himself helped to identify Melbourne as the 'goth capital of Australia' and many Goth websites elsewhere locate Cave and his music as foundational to Goth subcultural identity. Cave's many commentaries often bear out the disjuncture between recognizability as a Goth ('I'd hate to go down in history as the number one Goth, the man who spawned a thousand goth bands with stacked hairstyles, no personality, pale sick people') and a Goth-underwritten sense of the eccentric or idiosyncratic or marginal ('I seem so totally at odds with the modern world [...] some oddity of novelty that has ceased to be important').[13] An earlier collection of writing, *King Ink* (1988) — a bicentennial publication that never once mentions the nation, nor has anything to do with it — includes five very short dramatic variations on the Oscar Wilde play, *Salomé*. Its literary citations turn away from contemporary Australia (as Cave himself did not long afterwards), drawing attention instead to the book's otherworldliness: its inhabitation of somewhere else (Old Testament narrative mediated through Wilde's decadent aesthetic, the American Deep South, and so on), its longing to be elsewhere.

There are now signs of a newer 'second generation' of Goth novelists in Australia. My focus here is strictly on novels with identifiably Goth characters written by identifiably Goth authors: there is, indeed, so often a strong 'fit' between the two, a direct projection of authorial Goth sensibilities onto the protagonists. This is one feature that places a novel like Milissa Deist's *Bloodlust* (1999) — an Australian vampire novel based, much like the film *Angst*, in inner-city Sydney — outside the Goth subgenre.[14] This is certainly a self-consciously citational piece of work, naming its vampire heroine Carmilla after the Irish writer J. Sheridan Le Fanu's 1872 vampire story and offering a range of transnational references to other vampire and related writing (the last line invoking a novel by American writer Poppy

---

[13] See interviews with Nick Cave in *Sounds*, July 1986, and *New Musical Express*, August 1988.

[14] I am grateful to McKenzie Wark for drawing my attention to this novel, published by Vintage.

Z. Brite) as well as to Romantic poets such as William Blake. But although it is generically related, this novel is not Goth in the way I have outlined it above. For one thing, its unhinged female heroine is too destructive: when she unclasps her brassiere it signals death, not, as for May in *Angst*, therapy and redemption. Indeed, she is a perpetually homeless character who relishes her alienation, becoming, eventually, a suicide. It makes this novel closer in kind to the darker world of the 'Trench Coat Mafia' from whom, as I've noted, Goths had subsequently been carefully distinguished. The second generation of Goth novels are thus quieter, more inclined to yearn than to destroy, producing the peculiar combination of alienation and the longing-to-belong already described: not (self-)destructive, but trans-formative.

Cameron Rogers's *The Music of Razors* (2001) is a horror fantasy also heavily under the influence of *Revelations*, with its fallen Angels and its characters who yearn to be transformed, to be something else in some other place. An opening section is titled, precisely, 'The Art of Longing'. Here, a Goth girl, Hope, 'pink haired and pierced', is cast as an old soul grown tired of the world: a soul about to become otherworldly. The novel turns away from the Australian ideal of the family suburban home, staging its rejection — in typical Goth fashion — of 'the bland eternal scenarios that existed just beyond the happy lie of high school's end, the horrible, mediocre things that *happened to everyone else*'.[15] In place of suburban mediocrity, the novel offers an otherworldly fantasy that finds its earthly resonance in an inner-city alleyway: a Goth place that is both marginal and appropriately full of significance, as Hope sees when she passes by it:

> She had looked into it [...] and fancied she could see huddled ghosts curled in the refuse, memories of memories looking back at her out of the corners of old eyes.

> Thick grime layered the brickwork. The stuff was like a dried, crumbly paste of talcum and mucus, with the occasional cancerous fleck of faded red here and there, the markings of some forgotten vandal. The stuff on the walls had made her think of growth rings in trees, or layers of earth [...] To Hope, that little alleyway was a cathedral to what happened when life tossed you into what lies outside.[16]

Here is a Goth place that is welcoming in its alienation; homely in its invocation of homelessness: a place that is both empty and inhabited, bringing together utter estrangement with what the Australian historian Tom Griffiths has called 'deep belonging'. Nostalgia here — expressed through a central character whose own life at home has become traumatic and unsustainable (but who, like May in the film *Angst*, goes on to perform an essentially therapeutic role) — provides the impetus for

---

[15] Cameron Rogers, *The Music of Razors* (Ringwood: Penguin, 2001), pp. 260–61.

[16] Rogers, *The Music of Razors*, p. 91. Thanks to Lucy Sussex for drawing my attention to this novel.

a Goth future where place itself is perpetually cast as otherworldly: where every place (even the suburban home) is always already a gateway to some other place.

Kim Wilkins is another Goth horror novelist who has published six novels to-date, as well as a series of novels for teenagers. She also has a website (http://www.welcome.to/KimWilkins) which once opened with a quotation from Alfred Lord Tennyson's 'Ulysses': 'Yet all experience is an arch wherethrough/ Gleams that untravelled world whose margin fades / Forever and forever when I move'. The Goth yearning for otherworldliness (a gateway into 'that untravelled world') stands in contrast to the various diary entries in Wilkins's website, beginning in 1997 and working through to the present day, which self-consciously map a very *worldly* career in popular fiction built around new publications, awards won (especially the Aurealis Award for horror fiction, which Wilkins has won several times over), deals made with publishers, book launches, reviews received, and so on. A novelistic identity is developed online that seamlessly integrates commercial imperatives (promoting her work, outlining her career) with an authorial Goth voice that seems at last somehow unmediated, intimate and confessional, absorbed in the craft of literature for its own sake, presenting it as its *own* otherworld, both therapeutic and deranging:

> I love writing more than I can adequately express. It is the balm for my soul — I love to lose myself in a story, and I get so attached to the characters that it's not unusual for me to go to pieces emotionally while finishing a book. Everything I write is written with the utmost care and attention; I can honestly say that my heart is in my work.

Kim Wilkins comes from Queensland, already reconstructed here as a place intrinsically suited to the budding Goth author ('I grew up near the seaside in a creepy old Queenslander. Underneath it I had a cubby-hole where I used to go to write'). Brisbane, where she now lives, is itself represented as Goth city, with its vibrant Goth club and music scenes and Goth magazines and boutiques. But it is also sometimes cast as parochial, and so often too hot for a Goth 'to think'. For her book launches, Wilkins would sometimes come down to Slow Glass Books in Melbourne — a science fiction, fantasy and horror book shop near the centre of the city which had also hosted the launch (attended by Goths) of Cameron Rogers's *The Music of Razors*: another nodal point in urban Australian Goth cultural geography (but now, sadly, closed down). Her novels are published in Britain and Europe, too, translated into German in one case; Wilkins comments on 'an overseas junket' that takes her to London and Berlin, 'the coolest place in the universe', and so maps out an Australian/transnational network of Goth-inflected cities comparable to Nick Cave's post-*King Ink* infatuation with Berlin — although Wilkins does not share his more developed literary and musical fascination with the American Deep South. Indeed, her own literary connections are often northern: Yorkshire in England, or London, or in one novel the Norwegian coast. This is far too specific and restricted in its range to be considered under the diffuse heading of 'global culture'. Indeed, it works at creating a highly localized, resonating cultural geography, networked into a set of places that — in relation to an available Goth sensibility (as well as in relation to so much settler Australian experience, still attached to British and Western European locations) — are already highly familiar, enabling those first trips to London and Berlin to be cast nostalgically. The Goth attachment to places that 'being Goth' has already rendered familiar works against the grain of the usual romanticizing of Goth found in so much cultural criticism these days. Csaba Toth's article on Industrial Goth music, for example, links its practitioners to Judith Halberstam's claim that Goth 'marks a peculiarly modern preoccupation with boundaries and their collapse', thus enabling 'multiple interpretations and a plurality of locations of cultural resistance'.[17] But this particular fantasy about Goth art (seen routinely by commentators as *avant garde*, cutting edge) is simply not realized in the case of Australian Goth horror fiction which, like popular fiction broadly speaking, certainly does *not* enable 'multiple interpretations'. It relies instead on a shared, recognizable and (recalling 'The Aether Sanctum' website) perhaps 'too recognisable' set of conventions. Nor is there a 'plurality of locations of cultural resistance' here; as I have noted, the cultural geography of Goth is restricted and familiar, a means of conserving identity rather than seeing it collapse. It produces not the unhomeliness of Davenport-Hines but a renewal of homeliness-away-from-home, the kind of homeliness that can be traced in a fairly clear way through Wilkins's second novel, *Grimoire* (1999).

This novel is certainly citational in a conventionally Goth sense: its characters read Poe, Byron, Coleridge, Keats, Goethe, and the English decadent poet Ernest Dowson. One of its two epigraphs comes from Tennyson, and the demons one of its characters conjures up have their names taken from Edmund Spenser. This is a strikingly literary novel, in fact, concerning a graduate student, Holly, who comes down to cold, wintry Melbourne from northern Queensland to begin her studies — research into British Victorian poetry — at a place called Humberstone College. We can note the structural homology between this character and Wilkins herself, a graduate student at the University of Queensland researching British Romantic poetry: the novel is 'close' to the author in this sense ('I can honestly say that my heart is in my work'), charting the lives of literary studies graduate students who live somewhere between the 'young adult' demographic Wilkins has also explored in her fiction and the more 'mature' end of the literary marketplace (the point, perhaps, at which Goth horror fiction becomes Gothic Literature). The novel's comment that Holly was awarded a scholarship 'to start her Masters in Victorian literature at one of the most elite institutions in the southern hemisphere'[18] might suggest that

---

[17] Cited in Csaba Toth, '"Like Cancer in the System": Industrial Gothic, Nine Inch Nails, and Videotape', in *Gothic: Transmutations of Horror in Late Twentieth Century Art*, ed. by Christoph Grunenberg (Boston: Institute of Contemporary Art/MIT Press, 1997), p. 89.

[18] Kim Wilkins, *Grimoire* (Sydney: Arrow Books, 1999), p. 7. All further references are to this edition.

Humberstone College is a fictional cipher for the heavily self-promoting University of Melbourne. But Wilkins instead gives the college its own idiosyncratic Goth genealogy, as an Australian outpost of a fictional university in York, England, built in Melbourne in 1857 by a scandalous Victorian named Howard Humberstone in the Gothic architectural style, of the kind that Brian Andrews, in a book on Gothic architecture in Australia, has cast as 'increasingly irrelevant [to] our national consciousness'.[19] The old college has two key features for the novel: a library, where the characters do their research; and a set of subterranean tunnels where the current owner of the college and some of the academics there try to call up demons in order to gain eternal life. It becomes central to the 'old' Melbourne created in the novel that Holly increasingly makes into her home: a place that, in spite or perhaps because of the discomfort it brings with it (cold, rain, wind, run-down accommodation), nevertheless calls forth 'infinite promise' (p. 22).

Holly is joined by two other students: Prudence, an outgoing Goth girl whose wealthy parents are living in Hong Kong and who has a huge collection of occult books in her own library at home; and Justin, an orphaned boy who comes to live with the Humberstones themselves and who is studying the works of Dante Gabriel Rossetti. Holly, too, is distanced from her family, leaving a failed marriage in Queensland and gaining the disapproval of her mother and father for doing so. This east coast Goth novel would seem, then, to be emphasizing (in Davenport-Hines's terms) the 'unhomeliness' of its symptomatic characters: Justin's comment, 'I don't know how to behave in a family' (p. 225), becomes representative of the graduate students' condition and returns to the more typical subcultural rendering of parent culture/youth subculture divisions. Holly's predicament is more traumatic, pulled back to the Queensland town of Daybrook by her domineering parents, especially her mother, as if Daybrook is her rightful place, her home: the real place, a place of responsibility and duty, in relation to which the old imported Gothic architecture of Humberstone College is just a nostalgic and (from the mother's point of view) irresponsible Goth fantasy. But the novel reverses this structure, turning Daybrook and Queensland — and Holly's mother — into the unreal part of the Goth equation, as Holly realizes when she wakes up there one morning:

> Holly was completely disoriented when she woke. The smells and sounds were familiar but didn't seem right somehow. It took her a moment or two before she remembered she was back at her mother's place [...] Time seemed to be slipping away from her too swiftly, as though Daybrook were fairyland and for every hour she spent here, a week or two was going by in the real world. The world where she really belonged. (pp. 174–75)

The return to Melbourne — and the ghostly young lover she has become infatuated with there — is thus 'intoxicating' to Holly, increasingly securing it as her

---

[19] See Brian Andrews, *Australian Gothic: The Gothic Revival in Australian Architecture from the 1840s to the 1950s* (Carlton South: Miegunyah Press, 2001), p. 142.

rightful place: homeliness away from home. Her two graduate student friends help this security in the midst of demonic events, bonding together — gossiping, telling secrets, comforting each other, sometimes talking quite aimlessly — as they race to prevent the piecing together of a book of demonology, the 'grimoire' of the novel's title, pitching themselves against the diabolical Humberstone and the rather clumsy, bumbling academics in his charmed circle.

This kind of homeliness without a home sees a structure of belonging invoked not in 'Australia' as such, but in a uniquely Goth and highly nostalgic cultural and literary geography that moves from an oppressively hot and conservative Queensland down to a wintry but nevertheless exhilarating Melbourne, and then into a Victorian netherworld connected romantically — quite literally, through Holly's ghostly lover — to the dark streets and quaint, strange houses of London. Such a homeliness without a home is also given expression through the character Prudence, a promiscuous girl who is having an affair with one of the college's academics, Dr Aswell. In a sequence that serendipitously recalls Dean and May in the film *Angst* as they go by taxi out to the suburbs to desecrate an old girlfriend's bedroom, Prudence — feeling jilted by her teacher — goes to Aswell's house to confront her own particular demons. The house is a 'picture of suburban happiness' (p. 255), with Aswell and his wife Mandy away. Prudence breaks in and goes up to the bedroom, just as Dean and May had done — and finds Mandy's dresses in the wardrobe, all coloured beige: 'Did people who wore beige *want* to fade into the background?' (p. 285), she wonders, meditating on the topic of subcultural recognizability. Aswell suddenly returns home and Prudence is caught; she leaves quietly, determined next time to break into his office instead. The novel spends some time getting Aswell out of her system; it does this in order to bind the three graduate students ever closer together (sexually, amongst other ways). Finally, with the demonic Humberstone defeated and the 'grimoire' and the demons laid to rest, the three characters express a set of fantasies that see themselves 'chained' together as a 'family' that replaces conventional family structures (as a family without parents, for example). It does so, however, not by invoking 'homelessness' or playing witness to the collapse of 'boundaries', but by rewriting a set of generic conventions appropriate to being Goth in Australia over the top of those local conventions that have been rejected: conventions linked to suburban-ness, worldliness, mainstream national culture, parochialism, bad fashion sense and the suffocating pressures of the parent culture.

The effect is to make Australian Goth identity — in its textualized, mediated form, at least — both less Australian and more homely-in-Australia: more other-worldly and yet *here*. Through the self-conscious establishment of an all 'too recognisable' set of cultural and literary markers (literary citations, inner city cultural geographies, highly particularized transnational associations), this alternative but conventional subculture thus achieves self-definition, coherence and a certain amount of comfort in the knowledge that living in Australia and being Goth can indeed be reconciled.

Rituals of Nationhood: Medievalism, Neo-Traditionalism and Republicanism

PAUL JAMES AND STEPHANIE TRIGG

In 1901, Australia as a nation-state was born modern but with an abiding sense of political tradition.[1] This was expressed both ritualistically and institutionally, with ties bound strongly to a far-away monarchical empire and to a parliament whose own traditions stretched back to medieval England. The opening proclamation of the first sitting of the Australian Federal Parliament was delivered with the full force of ancient formalities and medieval titles:

> Australia, To Wit. By His Excellency the Right Honourable the EARL of HOPE-TOUN, a member of His Majesty's Most Honorable Privy Council; Knight of the Most Ancient and Most Noble Order of the Thistle; Knight Grand Cross of the Most Distinguished Order of Saint Michael and Saint George; Grand Knight Cross of the Royal Victorian Order; Governor-General and Commander-in-Chief of the Commonwealth of Australia [...] appoint Thursday, the ninth day of May proximo, as the day for the said Parliament to assemble [...] GOD SAVE THE KING![2]

And so begins the history of a contradictory nation-state. The inaugurating phrase 'Australia, To Wit' and the formalities that follow suggest that Australia's political scribes wrote with uncertain distance from any assumption about the naturalness of an already-existent nation. Their new nation-state had not only to be politically confirmed, but also to be given the legitimacy of deep tradition. Unlike its European progenitor, Australia as a settler colony did not claim a local cultural-political past that went back in the mists of time, and so the symbols and rituals of extant European tradition were gathered tightly around the political process.

---

[1] Our thanks to Helen Hickey, Melissa Raine and Douglas McQueen-Thomson for research assistance.

[2] The Parliament of the Commonwealth of Australia, Votes and Proceedings, vol. 1, 1901, p. 1.

The legitimacy of the modern nation-state was expressed in many different forms. In keeping with the way in which the female figure was increasingly being used to stand in for the people of the abstract nation, in countries around the globe, the invitation to the official occasion to celebrate the opening of the Australian parliament depicts two mythological women. Timeless Britannia stands with her shield, and the young maiden of Australia wears the white robes of a Greek goddess. They embrace an unfurled scroll with the shield of the lion and the unicorn, all markers of a traditional lineage. The scroll bears the words: 'His Majesty's Ministers of State for Australia have the honor to invite [...] to an evening reception'. With these words the Minsters of State, or 'Cabinet of Kings' as they were also known, affirmed their own power to include selected members of the population in the celebration of a political nation. At the same time, the invitation effectively signed the state into existence as a traditional-modern, old-young polity.

Some cultural tensions would remain continuous until the turn of the next century. At the beginning of the twenty-first century, 'Australia' continues to project itself as a young nation built upon an ancient southern continent. However, other contradictions changed in telling ways. Across the turn of the nineteenth into the twentieth century, Australia was a new polity, one conscious of the novelty of its political experiment with federalism, and yet steeped in the sense that its heritage lay elsewhere — in the halls of Westminster and in what Rudyard Kipling called the 'Hall of Our Thousand Years'. It is indicative that the year 1901 was actively celebrated in Australia as simultaneously the year of federation and the millennial anniversary of the death of Alfred, King of the West Saxons.[3] By comparison, across the cusp of the twenty-first century, we find a transformed, though related, tension. In the present century, the Australian parliament continues to draw upon and debate the historical conventions and political lineages of its British motherland just as it did at the end of the nineteenth century. However, when we move from the original formation of the nation-state of Australia to the recent republican debates over the continuing relevance of the monarchical system and its medieval origins, we find paradoxically a more self-consciously insecure nation. Even its most ardent neo-traditionalists are sensitive to the accusation that Australia's sovereignty is qualified. This chapter explores the various expressions of this subjectivity by considering the history of debates over national ritual practice in Australia.

Currently, Australia is a nation caught between four conflicting 'moments' of ontological disquiet. The first is a conservative fear of change, most often translated as a defensive neo-traditionalism, but one very clearly belonging to the modern world as its taken-for-granted mooring in past traditions slowly rots. The second is a classical modern anxiety that aims (once, and for all) to clarify the institutions that underpin national identity and make it all consistently modern: one head of state for

---

[3] Gavin Souter, *Lion and Kangaroo: Australia, 1901–1919* (Sydney: Fontana, 1978), pp. 52–53.

one nation. The third is a late-modern instrumentalism leading, at least in its crudest form, to assertions of political independence from the old country as part of a national branding of 'Australia' as it competes in a globalizing capitalist market. The fourth is a postmodern embarrassment, a concern that by maintaining traditional English political trappings Australia tarnishes the possibilities of an increasingly mobile, pluralistic and fluid sovereignty. Political debate over the past five years has been dominated by a cleavage between two dominant forces. On one side are the neo-traditionalists or monarchists in a strange alliance with the instrumentalists. In this, some figures such as Prime Minister John Howard sustain a contradictory position of being both neo-traditional and instrumentally modern at the same time by arguing for foundational ties to monarchy in the cultural realm and competitive deregulation in the economic. On the other side we find an equally uneasy and often-times disintegrating alliance between the classical modernists (the core of the republicans), some instrumental modernists and the political postmodernists. This latter group of republicans includes postmodern critics such as Don Watson,[4] a speech-writer who gained prominence for a period in the mid-1990s under the Prime Ministership of Paul Keating. By the turn of the century these critics had lost political centre-stage and had mostly returned to being satirists, academics and writers.

The debate, then, has many layers. For the monarchists the issue appears to be simple: if the system is not broken, then why fix it? By contrast, for all three variations of the republican push, Australia may have been born modern in social terms at the end of the nineteenth century, and then reinforced as modern in institutional terms over the course of the twentieth century, but in one important respect it remains hampered by medieval anachronism. For contemporary republicans the symbolic function of the Queen of England as putative head of state does not make sense. As we will illustrate, the republicans are happy to live with most of the conventional rituals and institutional forms of the past — that is, so long as those rituals are thoroughly abstracted from their medieval origins and post-medieval transformations, and so long as Australia severs ties to the person 'over there' who reminds them of the tensions over national sovereignty. In short, their anguish is concentrated around the continuing symbolic power of monarchy with an absent embodied incumbent. This is because, in Mary Douglas's terms, the Crown in Australia has never become an 'empty symbol', a ritualized ritual.[5] In other words, if the modern had emptied out the traditional completely then deference to the Crown

---

[4] In 1993, the prime-ministerial adviser gives a speech advocating that Australia become the first postmodern republic. First reported in *The Age* (Melbourne) 26 March 1993, and later reproduced in full as 'Birth of a Post-Modern Nation', *The Australian* (Sydney), 24 July 1993. It was also published in the *The Times Literary Supplement*, 20 August 1993, with the title 'How to Become a Young Country at Last'.

[5] Mary Douglas, *Natural Symbols* (Harmondsworth: Penguin, 1973), Chapter 1.

would be either an anachronistic irrelevance or a procedural ritual rather than something so passionately contested.

This argument is founded on the methodological premise that just as it is possible to talk about ontologically different kinds of ways of being in the world — tribalism, traditionalism, modernism and postmodernism — it is possible to talk about different kinds of medievalism, different ways of taking hold of the subjectivities and practices that we now associate with the Middle Ages. The first kind of medievalism relevant here, *traditional medievalism*, became available even before people started to talk about a thing or epoch called 'the medieval'. By traditional medievalism we mean any kind of reference to a medieval practice, discourse or icon that takes for granted its self-evident truth. This sensibility assumes that the meaning of this (medieval) object is palpably present to us, both then and now, through an unbroken lineage of embodied or ritualistic connection. While there are hints of this in the Australian debates at the turn of each of the two centuries, in both cases such a subjectivity is rare.

Neo-traditionalists, in comparison to traditionalists, tend to be already modern in form even if they romanticize the content of a 'medieval past'. They defend themselves against critical modernists (or satirical postmodernists) using the terms of their modernist assailants: appeals to historiography, empiricism, rationality and rules of evidence. Put in more theoretical terms, they allow their own putatively traditionalist arguments to be reconstituted in terms of modernist approaches to time and epistemology. This might most pointedly be called 'modern neo-traditionalism', incidentally the grounding basis for most contemporary monarchism. It is thus one pathway taken by a second kind of medievalism, *modern medievalism*. The third form, *postmodern medievalism*, tends to occur either as ironical reference or as romanticizing pastiche. While postmodern romanticism is prevalent in the fringe cultures of gothic groups and societies of medieval re-enactment, in the political realm we tend to find only the ironical self-deprecating kind of postmodern medievalism where pseudo-medieval references are used for rhetorical effect against those who still believe in actual tradition.

There are counter-examples to this generalization about the limits of cross-over between postmodern aesthetics and the modern political symbolic in the Australian context, but they are rare. One such counter-example is the notice by the Blue Mountains community at Glenbrook, New South Wales, celebrating the 2001 centenary of Australia's federation with both 'Ye Olde Federation style Celebrations' on a 'village green' alongside medieval re-enactments.[6] A more typical example is the forty-two-metre long Federation tapestry for the new Parliament House in Canberra, the most expensive piece of public art ever commissioned in Australia. In an act of *modern* medievalism, the tapestry's production co-ordinator, Sue Walker, spoke on national television of its resonance with the Bayeux

---

[6] http://www.bluemts.com.au/centenary/press.htm, accessed 28 June 2002.

embroidery, but it became clear that she was more enthralled with the possibilities of tourists making pilgrimages to visit the work than she was with its romantic ties of meaning to an ever-present past.[7]

A more prevalent form of boundary crossing is found amongst the ritual objects used in parliamentary practice, as they are considered alternately as traditional or modern signs of authority and power. Traditional-modern ritual objects such as the parliamentary Mace, or Black Rod, have an ambiguous medieval reference. That is, to the extent that they act as signs of traditional continuity rather than actually being produced in the past, they are beset by ambiguity. The medieval military mace, for example, was originally an instrument of violent combat and had been gradually abstracted, first as the sign of the medieval sergeant's power to make arrest, and then as a ceremonial object in parliamentary process with its head-crushing spikes replaced by jewels and national or state insignia. This process is obvious when pointed out, but in ritual practice is usually forgotten. The metaphor had been buried for centuries in the British parliamentary tradition as an abstracted icon long before it arrived in Australia during the age of the 'invention of traditions'. When maces began to be used in the colonial parliaments they were taken to be a natural part of the trappings of legitimized power. These objects were flexibly accumulated, conferred with tradition, and moved around, in the practice of the exertion of modern power. For example, in Victoria, one of the first states in the continent of Australia, the parliament drew upon Westminster tradition from its inception in 1856.[8] Its original mace was lost (as we will see below) and its second, a humbler, wooden model, was handed over to the Federal parliament for its first meeting in 1901. When it was returned in 1951 it went into a display rack above the entrance door of the parliamentary library. How could such a gift be returned? Quite simply, the federal House of Representatives was given another one by the House of Commons after a directive from King George VI that Australia be presented with an object suitable to mark the jubilee of Federation.

The rest of this chapter is intended as an initial foray into documenting and unravelling the intricate complexities and genealogy of contemporary *political* medievalism in Australia, an area in which virtually nothing has been written.[9] In order to do so, the next section takes us back to the nineteenth century and the original formation of the Australian nation-state. It argues that, while the context of

---

[7] 7.30 Report, Australian Broadcasting Commission, 8 May 2001.

[8] Its current website talks at length about this tradition, noting that 'The conduct and behaviour of Victoria's Presiding Officers therefore closely resembles that of the Speaker in the House of Commons whose position has evolved over hundreds of years. England's first Speaker assumed office in 1377'; http://www.parliament.vic.gov.au/pres.html, accessed 18 April 2002.

[9] Essays with enticing titles such as 'Medievalism and Australian Culture', John T. Gilchrist in *Twentieth Century*, 14 (1960), 295–302, come up in library searches, but they all turn out to be overgeneralized meditations with little or no analytical content.

this self-instituting state was a growing self-consciousness about the meaning of tradition, the oft-cited 'invention of tradition' thesis does not do justice to the contradictory depth of attachment *and* flexibility about the medieval iconography inherited from Australia's imperial motherland. If association with monarchy was simply an invented tradition or a superficial transplant to the colonies would we find such passionate defence or revulsion a hundred years later? This contemporary passion-play between the monarchists and the republicans becomes the subject of the later parts of the essay. Along the way, we weave a second argument about the nature of political ritual practice as it occurs across the intersection of traditional and modern formations. These formations are not understood in epochal or temporal terms but rather as overlapping ways of being and thinking. As the intersection between them is traversed by objects — mysterious traditional-modern objects such as maces and rods, harking back to the medieval but without the legitimizing authenticity of an object that was actually fabricated in the medieval period — they become carriers of all the uncertainties, ambivalences and insecurities of ambiguously conferred political authority.

Ritual Practice and the Modern Invention of Tradition

In the literature on nationalism the dominant modernist theoretical approaches tend to espouse the 'cultural invention' thesis. Ernest Gellner writes: 'It seems to me to be obvious that modern nationalism has nothing to do with the reassertion of atavistic loyalties (other than invoking or inventing them for its convenience)'.[10] This argument, for us, flattens out the way in which traditionalism was important to the formation of the modern nation, even if it was not the dominant constitutive condition of that formation. Eric Hobsbawm and Terence Ranger are responsible for the most sophisticated rendition of that one-dimensional argument. It is put forward in their edited collection, *The Invention of Tradition*, and it is worth spending a little time on the strengths and weaknesses of their approach. Hobsbawm's argument begins with the premise that the nation is a pseudo-community.[11] Secondly, he argues that the nation and the nation-state 'rest on exercises in social engineering which are often deliberative and always innovative, if only because historical novelty implies innovation'.[12] And thirdly, as Hobsbawm and his colleagues document at length, the period of the late-nineteenth century to early-twentieth

---

[10] Ernest Gellner, *Culture, Identity and Politics* (Cambridge: Cambridge University Press, 1987), p. 113.

[11] Eric Hobsbawm, 'Introduction: Inventing Traditions', in *The Invention of Tradition*, ed. by Eric Hobsbawm and Terence Ranger (Cambridge: Cambridge University Press, 1983), p. 10.

[12] Hobsbawm, 'Introduction', p. 13.

century (associated with the uneven consolidation of the nation-state) was a period of intensive mass-production of 'tradition'.

The first point does not warrant any response, except to say that Hobsbawm does not understand that an abstract community of strangers can still be a real community. Like any community, nations are lived as subjective-objective projections in actual histories and in relation to actual places. The second point about social engineering is partly true but overstated. It is the third point, however, that we have to take very seriously. The empirical evidence is overwhelming. The nineteenth century is the period of intensification of national and public consciousness about the past. Across the world, states began to issue manuals of direct instruction, often directed first towards primary schools, training their people how to be good citizens and to follow in the footsteps of the nation's founding heroes. In the USA, from the 1890s, children began the tradition of daily saluting the flag. This is also the period that saw the mass production of public ceremonies across Europe. In France, Bastille Day was instituted in 1880 not in 1789 as one might have expected — just as the anthem, La Marseillaise, became so in 1879 not 1789. Public monuments were erected in their thousands in England and its settler colonies, including Australia. In Scotland, two prominent early examples are the Walter Scott monument in Edinburgh, built in 1830, and the William Wallace monument in Stirling, from 1869. In Germany, after Bismarck's death in 1898, four hundred and seventy municipalities decided to erect monuments to him. In France, Jeanne d'Arc was elevated to sainthood in 1870 and numerous monuments were subsequently raised to testify to the glories of this medieval warrior. What does it all add up to? It suggests that at a time of modernizing upheaval the new nation-states were establishing and re-establishing their conscious lineages with old and new traditions. In short, we suggest, rather than popular nationalism being an expression of an invention of tradition (or resting on the social engineering of official nationalism), the 'mass production' of public testimony to past continuities that peaked in the nineteenth century is the outcome of massive social transformation. It is much beyond this essay even to begin theorizing the rise of this new sense of historicity, but we can consider what it meant for the new parliaments in the settler states such as Australia that had no continuous spatial link to a medieval past.

Across the settler states of the British Empire, from Australia to South Africa, the rules, rituals and traditions of the Westminster system were actively embraced in the nineteenth century as symbols of 'continuous' political authority. These traditions were not so much invented as taken to be self-evidently necessary for the legitimacy of a new polity. In Alberta, Canada, the first legislature rushed to find a suitable mace. It is worth quoting the current Canadian website at length to pick up the postmodern incredulity that accompanies the description of that history:

> Here in Alberta the first Legislature was caught off guard just before its first sitting: there was no Mace. Because nobody so much as suggested that a sitting could be held without it, Alexander Rutherford's Liberal government ordered the rush construction

of one from Watson Brothers jewelry in Calgary. Watson Brothers hired Rufus E. Butterworth, a Canadian Pacific Railway employee from Calgary, to do the job. He came up with Alberta's first Mace in only a few weeks' time, and it was made entirely of scrap. Its shaft was plumbing pipe mounted on a toilet tank float, some ornamental decorations around the orb were made from old shaving mug handles, and bits of an old bedstead and other scraps of wood formed the rest. A piece of red velvet and a coat of gold paint provided the finishing touches […].[13]

This spectacular piece of bricolage was firmly installed by the neo-traditionalists at the symbolic heart of the modern democratic system. The pipe was used for half a century until 1956 when it was replaced by a presentation from the provincial employees' union on the occasion of Alberta's Golden Jubilee. In a fantastically flexible mix of medievalism and localism, two coats of arms adorned the ball of the new Mace, those of Canada and of the British monarch, as well as a hand-carved beaver and a ring of precious stones with initials that spell 'Alberta', starting with amethyst.

Not every parliament has a Black Rod, but interestingly, a number of Black Rods in Commonwealth parliaments are relatively recent. The Victorian Parliament's Gentleman Usher started using a Black Rod only in 1951, while Alberta inaugurated this office only as recently as 1991. In Britain, too, the rituals of parliamentary practice are subject to change. In 1998, the BBC filed a special report on some changes to the rituals for the State Opening of Parliament, changes that had the effect of streamlining and shortening the ceremony. Some, though not all officials were no longer required to walk backwards away from the monarch, and Black Rod was no longer to wait for the Queen to be seated before he summoned the members of the House of Commons. According to the BBC report, 'In the past the MPs have kept the Queen waiting for some time as they deliberately dawdled on the trip between the two houses, reluctant as they are to acknowledge that the Lords is, traditionally at least, the senior chamber'.[14] The recent war of words between Black Rod and the Prime Minister's Office in Britain, over whether Tony Blair had asked to play a greater role, or not, in the Queen Mother's lying-in-state in Westminster Hall, is testimony to the ease with which these ritual offices can become embroiled in contemporary party politics. In South Africa, the new regime after the dismantling of apartheid planned to get rid of the Sergeant-at-Arms and Usher of the Black Rod as symbols of British monarchy.

In all these cases, even in South Africa, the emphasis on tradition remains. The central question to be negotiated is how best the modern nation can carry tradition forward while adjusting its relation to and against the medieval past of a common imperial heritage. In the present, even without considering the possibility of reform

---

[13] http:// www.assembly.ab.ca/pub/gdbook/Part3/page7.htm, accessed 18 April 2002.

[14] http://www.news.bbc.co.uk/hi/english/special_report/1998/11/98/queen_speech-/newsid_216000/216684.stm, accessed 18 April 2002.

or constitutional or political change, the symbolic language of Australian parliamentary nationalism is already complex, and must tread a careful line in negotiating the
rival claims and appeal of tradition and modernity. These claims are especially
evident on parliamentary websites that seek to codify the rituals of current practice
and outline their antecedents. The Australian federal website and most state
parliamentary websites feature a 'historical note' or an 'education page', or equivalent, which often traces 'ceremony and traditional practices derived from those of
the United Kingdom Parliament'.[15] These 'traditional practices' are now typically
presented in relatively bland and neutral language, even though they may actually
derive from contentious incidents. Most notable is the convention that neither the
queen nor the governor-general may enter the House of Representative chamber
during proceedings. This practice dates from 1642, when Charles I entered the
chamber of the House of Commons with an armed guard, seeking to arrest five of its
members. The attempt failed, and the members escaped, and 'since then no
Sovereign has entered the House of Commons Chamber during proceedings and this
tradition has continued in the Commonwealth Parliament'.[16]

These traditions of parliamentary ritual practice are visible at several levels: in the
forms of process and protocol; and in the material signs of office and ritual, such as
the various coats of arms, the ceremonial dress and other appurtenances of office and
ceremonial behaviour. In these relationships we can read several levels and stages in
the struggle between tradition and modernity that characterize public ritual practice.
As soon as the 'modern era' begins to mark its difference from the medieval, a range
of possibilities arise: claiming an unbroken line with those traditions; dispensing
with tradition altogether and rejecting the stranglehold of the past in the
characteristic mode of modernity and reform; analysing that tradition critically; and
lastly, reflecting self-consciously on the meaning of that tradition.

Two central objects or symbols of this practice, the Mace and the Black Rod,
stand as tangible links to the mother parliament, as it is frequently called, without
embarrassment, in the early twentieth century. This tangible link is underlined by the
traditional court costume worn by their bearers. In their design, too, they are typical
agglomerations of traditional design and distinctive Australian features; they
incorporate native woods (for example, the fiddleback blackwood, instead of ebony
for Victoria's Rod) and feature Australian fauna and flora in their designs.

Like the icons, the rituals and designations of office, however highly codified,
have been open to change and to overlays of meaning. We know that the office of
Black Rod has its origins in Edward III's foundation of the Order of the Garter in
1348. According to the home page of the South Australian Parliament, 'Black Rod is
an ancient office with great traditions associated primarily with the Sovereign and
subsequently the Imperial Parliament [...]. From ancient times the staff has been the

---

[15] http://www.aph.gov.au/house/info/infosheets/fs09.htm, accessed 17 April 2002.

[16] http://www.aph.gov.au/house/info/infosheets/fs09.htm, accessed 17 April 2002.

symbol of authority'.[17] The Legislative Assembly in Alberta, Canada, however, appeals to the medieval origins of Black Rod to mark its own legitimacy as a separate sovereign state: the Black Rod's first duties, they suggest, were to exclude uninvited guests from the Garter festivities at Windsor Castle in 1348, and thus by extension it has come to signify the independence of the assembly from the crown.[18] In Australia, as elsewhere, Black Rod's modern duties are rather more bureaucratically oriented. In addition to arranging ceremonies and security for the parliament, Black Rod's office is also responsible for the management of office accommodation and equipment, publishing and printing, for example, while the office also houses the human resources and financial management sections of the parliament.

As ritual components, the objects used in bureaucratic management seem to stand as silent testimony to tradition. However, that tradition is not worn lightly: parliamentary webpages and information booklets abound, explaining the origin of the sergeant's Mace and the office of the Black Rod. The NSW booklet painstakingly naturalizes the official's dress:

> It is not surprising that the current dress of Black Rod is Old Style Court Dress, as he was originally an active member of the Royal Court. The form of dress in New South Wales is the same as that worn by the Gentleman Usher of the Black Rod in the House of Lords consisting of a black cloth, tailed coat, stand collar, gauntlet cuffs with three notched or false holes and buttons and three-pointed pocket flaps complete with a button beneath each point. A black silk wig-bag is attached to the coat at the back of the neck. A black waistcoat with similarly treated three-pointed flaps to those on the coat is also worn. Black knee breeches, with marcasite buckles, black silk stockings and ecclesiastical shoes with silver buckles and black kid gloves are worn at all times in the house of Lords, but in New South Wales, for some inexplicable reason, these items of apparel are replaced by ordinary black shoes and long black trousers except for ceremonial occasions.[19]

We quote this passage at length to draw attention to its curious mixture of response to tradition. At first, this response seems entirely uncritical: court costume — with all its arcane details of the wig-bag and the careful placement of buttons — is explained simply in terms of the British parliament, rather than by explaining why old style court dress should continue to govern parliamentary convention, in England or in Australia. But when it comes to stockings, black gloves and marcasite buckles, an ingenuous tone expresses surprise that these items are worn only for 'ceremonial' use. This careful articulation of the relation between traditionalism (the 'natural'

---

[17]   http://www.parliament.sa.gov.au/legcouncil/2_1_2_officers.shtm, accessed 18 April 2002.

[18]   http://www.assembly.ab.ca/pub/gdbook/Part3/page7.htm, accessed 18 April 2002.

[19]   *The Usher of the Black Rod* (Parliament of New South Wales, 1974), pp. 11–13.

inheritance of court dress) and modernism (the 'natural' resistance to certain aspects of court dress) is typical of parliamentary practice and protocol.

These tensions are evident in the performance of ritual, too. When the lower house is summoned to the upper house for a joint sitting at the commencement of parliament, Black Rod takes the message from queen, or governor, or governor-general to the lower house, where the doors are slammed in his or her face, to signify that the lower house maintains its prerogative of 'freedom of speech and uninterrupted debate'.[20] Only after knocking three times with the tip of the rod is Black Rod admitted. This ritual of refusal and then admission is a perfect example of ritual practice: the symbolic re-enactment of a significant historical moment, whose significance now lies in its superstitious repetition, rather than the risk of any real transgression.

A curious document in the Victorian parliamentary library seems to be a typed draft of some notes about the office and history of Black Rod. Recalling that the office was instituted in 1951, only three years before the queen's visit to Australia, it includes notes about the history of the office, and, as it were, stage directions for the joint sitting of parliament. It contains the extraordinary sentence: 'On receipt of the command from Her Majesty I will proceed to the Legislative Assembly where the door is slammed in my face.' It is a sentence that can belong only to the world of ritual, where refusal or transgression is formalized as a necessary component of symbolic practice, where *not* to slam the door in the face of the official would be to transgress. The convention of dragging a reluctant new Speaker to his or her chair plays a similar role. Acts of transgression, or resistance, are harnessed through ritualized repetition until they come, themselves, to represent tradition, in all its contradictions.

The material objects of ritual sometimes struggle to hold together these contradictory meanings. The Victorian Black Rod, and the Federal and Victorian Mace have all enjoyed some rather salacious and contentious histories which have the effect of emphasizing a rather less stable relationship with tradition. In these contexts, debate and disagreement about the symbolic meanings attached to these instruments of office are foregrounded.

The state of Victoria instituted the Office of Black Rod only in 1951, when the parliament celebrated the centenary of its first Legislative Council. The first rod was an elaborate design, but was made only of gold-covered plaster, apart from the rod itself. The maker, John Gogerly, of the Department of Public Works, meant to make a wooden cap to replace the plaster one for the famous ceremony where the usher beats on the door, but time ran short and it was not available. To beat on the door with the plaster tip would have shattered it, 'So Mr Tierney strode to the door and, as had his predecessors since 1856, he instead kicked the door three times with the heel

---

[20] *The Usher of the Black Rod*, p. 14.

of his shoe, thereby preserving the plaster Rod.'[21] So up until this point, the ceremony had taken place without the office of Black Rod; but instituting its own local variant, its own century-old tradition, of kicking on the door. Hearing reports of this, the Victorian Chamber of Manufactures wrote to the premier and offered to make a 'proper' Black Rod, the one in use today.

Victoria's Mace has an even more scandalous history, concerned with its theft from parliament in 1891. This remains an unsolved crime, and a reward was recently offered for its recovery. Various theories have been propounded: it was stolen to be sold; it was taken as a prank by drunken parliamentarians who could not return it, and so passed it on to some underworld figures who dumped it in the Maribyrnong river; or it was smuggled aboard an American ship to be returned to London, but perished in the Great Fire of San Francisco.[22] The story seized the popular imagination, especially the part of the story that imagines the Mace in Annie Wilson's brothel, Boccaccio House, in Lonsdale St, where it was used, according to the *Ballarat Courier*, in 'low travesties of parliamentary procedure', which seem to have involved the parodic repetition of the historic phrase: 'remove that bauble'.[23] This itself dates back to Cromwell, who referred to the parliamentary mace in these terms, as he dissolved the Long Parliament in 1653: 'Remove that fool's bauble!' Historical explanations abound, saying he was referring only to the monarch's orb with surmounted cross at the end of the mace, which he ordered to be replaced with an acorn. (This is a prime early example of modernity defining a sharp difference from received tradition, by replacing one symbol with another.) The phrase has passed into parliamentary tradition, and 'bauble' has become a conventional term of familiar ritual abuse for the mace.

When Victoria's Mace was stolen, Andrew Symmonds wrote in the *Argus:*

> More than once some predatory Captain Blood has made attempts upon the Crown Jewels, but never until yesterday has an instance been known in which any sacrilegious hand dared to disturb the inviolate sanctity of the emblem of constitutional liberty — the Mace.

He used the conventional description, too, calling it the 'golden bauble'. There were disputed accounts of its value, which the police inspector downplayed, describing it as a 'mere bauble'. And it was, indeed, not golden, but silver, with gold coating, and valued at just three hundred pounds, a revelation that provoked further embarrassment. The *Argus* wrote, 'How can Parliament inspire the lawless with respect and awe when its emblem of power and strength is a sham?'[24]

---

[21] 'Victoria's First Black Rod'.

[22] Robert Wilson, 'As It Was', *The Canberra Times*, 26 October 1991, quoting Harry Gordon*, An Eyewitness History of Australia* (Ringwood: Penguin, 1988).

[23] *The Ballarat Courier*, 6 January 1893.

[24] Quoted in Robert Travers, *Rogues' March: A Chronicle of Colonial Crime in Australia* (Melbourne: Hutchinson of Australia, 1973), p. 204.

Theoretically, of course, the symbolic value of a mace clearly outweighs its material value, but the theft threw up a remarkable variety of responses. Melbourne was, and remains fascinated by the story about the Mace's sojourn in Boccaccio House (it was already well known as the location of one of the first telephones in Melbourne), though official discourse discouraged public speculation about the nature of the 'low travesties'. The owner of the *Ballarat Courier*, for example, was summoned before the bar of the house and received a public admonition from the speaker. But the Sydney *Bulletin* was prepared to elaborate, saying that various drunken politicians used to lay the Mace on the table with the whisky-and-soda, and shout in chorus, 'Take away that bauble!'[25]

Far from being universally revered, then, these ritual objects often seem to participate in accidents, in parodies, or transgressions of their own history, or rather, to feature as boundary-crossing objects as if their public visibility invites an instability between their secularized sacred and carnivalesque modes. The prime example here is the Order of the Garter, whose disputed narrative of origins famously involves the king retrieving a lady's dropped garter and transforming it into a symbol of great honour. This story continues to tantalize through its imbrication of medieval sexuality and chivalry in a system of national honour. The sexualized aspects of transgression persist, moreover. In the case of the two recent incidents involving inebriated Australian politicians (in the Federal and in the New South Wales parliaments), both men displayed their drunkenness in assaults on female members of parliament.

The unrecovered 1890s Victorian Mace was replaced by a modest wooden carved one, which, as noted earlier, was given to the new Federal parliament in 1901. Even here, however, its use was not without controversy. In 1911, Speaker McDonald ordered the Mace removed, and ruled any discussion of its removal out of order. The Mace was restored in 1913 by Speaker Johnson, who similarly refused to discuss its restoration, though he was put under considerable pressure to do so by Mr Mathews and Mr Higgs, who asked 'whether it is under your instructions, sir, that *this bauble* was placed [on the Table] [...].' At one point in the heated debate, Mathews commented, 'The Mace is such a miserable devil, too.' Mr Anstey commented that the Government had 'restored once more all the signs and symbols of fourteenth century government. Once more the Mace is paraded before us.'[26] Here the 'medieval' is a target for abuse, under the sign of irrelevance. After being ruled out of order by the Speaker, since his predecessor had ruled that any reference to the absence of the Mace from the table would not be allowed, Mr Anstey commented, 'I watch with very anxious care the manner in which this little piece of wood is placed in its little bed and taken out again.'[27] Trivializing the symbolic import of material

---

[25] *The Bulletin*, 23 January, quoted in Travers, p. 207.

[26] *Hansard*, 2 September 1913, p. 772.

[27] *Hansard*, 2 September 1913, p. 772.

objects is the simplest way to mock ritual practice; however, as we have been suggesting, for as long as its ambiguities persist, such parody in turn contributes to the continuing saliency of the tradition.

Despite, or rather because of this ambivalent care, the next year the Mace disappeared for a week until it was discovered under one of the Opposition benches — this was followed later by a confession from Webster and Higgs. The Mace was used until McDonald was re-elected speaker again in 1914, when the Mace was once more removed until Johnson returned to the office in 1917. These discussions take place in the context of similar discussions about the necessity for the formal wigs and gowns in public rituals of various kinds. Such costumes are easy to ridicule as outmoded habiliments, just as ritual objects become 'baubles', or half demystified as 'little pieces of wood', but they are less easy to displace. Similarly, successive speakers, in refusing to engage in discussion about the removal or restoration of maces, did little to diminish the standing of the icon.[28]

The Mace was again the subject of controversy when Speaker Makin ordered its removal from the table the day after his election, in November 1929. In response to a question the next day, he made an extraordinary speech, saying he had searched the standing orders and he had not found

> any good reason for its appearance on the Table. The Mace is a relic of barbarism. It is a symbol of power, which comes to us from a time when turbulence was met with brute force; it is associated with methods and manners that should have no place in our public or private life. Its ceremonial employment in Parliament has no significance as evidencing our loyalty to the Crown, or as testifying or expressing in any way our association with the King and Empire. The Mace is merely, as I have said, a symbol of power — in this case a symbol of the power of the Speaker in this House. But, although it symbolises, its use in no way increases the authority of the Chair, and I consider that I am quite capable of asserting that authority without it.

In contrast to the earlier reticence, or the easy dismissal of traditional forms, the Speaker provides an excellent example of critical modernism, as he interrogates the history and meaning of the symbol, reminding us of its origins as a military weapon and as the instrument of violence and summary justice in the medieval period. He also goes one step further in reflexivity, though, acknowledging that the Mace symbolizes his own power as speaker in the house, while also diminishing the necessity of that symbol: 'I consider that I am quite capable of asserting that authority without it.'

His speech raised considerable ire in the heart of Empire, when one correspondent wrote to *The Times* in dismay, remarking that the speaker's words 'have shocked

---

[28] Even when decades later a mace is seized as an expression of rage, or frustration, rather than as any challenge to the symbolic order — as when Michael Heseltine grabbed the Mace in the House of Commons at Westminster, in 1976 — it becomes another story in the annals of the object.

those who regard the continuity of procedure in the great Dominion assemblies as one of the firmest and most lasting links of Empire'.[29] However, the appeal to continuity was quickly set aside to fulminate against the upstart colony, as the letter writer went on, 'Relic of barbarism indeed! Is it not a relic of ignorance for a mushroom capital to speak with such scant reverence of the ancient Mace?'

Continuity and tradition are always being remade and re-invented, with a variable mix of appeals to heritage and relevance. The colonial parliaments foreground this issue beautifully, as seen in the varied procedures set in place for the queen's visit to Australia and New Zealand in 1954. The Federal parliament took the view that the Mace symbolized the queen, and so the Mace did not accompany the speaker into the senate when the queen opened parliament that year, but was left outside, covered in a green cloth. The New Zealand parliament had taken a different view, however, by carrying the Mace into the upper house into the queen's presence. The Victorian Parliament followed Wellington's procedure, however, with the clerk of the Legislative Assembly commenting that by order of 1856, the Victorian Mace represents not royal authority but the authority of the speaker, and so it must accompany him when he is acting in his official capacity.[30]

The symbolic and ritual practices in Australian parliaments have rich and disputed histories, here, as in other Commonwealth countries. Remarkably, though, whenever the question of parliamentary or constitutional reform is raised, debate about this traditional inheritance invariably flattens this history into the polarized opposition between medieval and modern. In order to take this discussion further we turn now to an episode in Australia's recent political history when the bland and neutral language of state was left aside in the full and passionate debate about whether Australia should maintain even symbolic ties to this past.

Modern Republicanism Meets Modern Medievalism

In October 1999, Eddie McGuire, the well-known sporting commentator, quiz- and football-show host, and president of the Collingwood Football Club, launched the 'Yes' case in the national referendum on whether Australia should become a republic, and tapped into a powerful opposition between the medieval and the modern. According to the report in *The Australian*, he said 'that the alternative to an Australian president was to move into the new millennium with a "medieval system where King Charles III will be Australia's next head of state"'.[31] McGuire's phrase

---

[29] A. R. Browning, *The Mace, House of Representatives* (Canberra: Australian Government Publishing Service, 1970), p. 7.

[30] John Dunn, 'A Problem in Procedure,' *The Sun* (Melbourne), 15 February 1954.

[31] *The Australian*, 18 October 1999. The referendum motion was defeated, though most commentators agree that Australians were rejecting a particular model of republicanism on offer, involving parliamentary nomination, as opposed to popular election of the president.

describing the 'medieval system' is historically correct. As we have been describing, the Australian 'Westminster system' does indeed have its foundations in symbolic practices and institutions dating back to the thirteenth and fourteenth centuries. However, his authority also drew upon a more popular understanding of the 'medieval', as archaic and tradition-bound, shading into its more pejorative popular associations, as irrelevant, even barbaric. In McGuire's formulation, the key sense of medieval is as the opposite, or the Other, we may say, to what is modern, new, relevant, and appropriate to the new millennium. Implicit in his set of alternatives is the mutual exclusivity of the concepts 'medieval' and 'Australia'. The unfamiliar prolepsis of 'King Charles III' was designed to shock Australians into a sense of just how inappropriate a title this might be for their next head of state.

In the debates about the possibility of constitutional change, the traditional aspects of the monarchy are frequently invoked, though granted different political weight and rhetorical valencies by different groups. Unsurprisingly, those in favour of republican reform tend, like McGuire, to draw out a contrast between the medieval and the modern, while those in favour of retaining the constitutional monarchy repeatedly mount the argument from beneficent tradition and continuity. The regular award of royal honours, and recent milestones for the royal family — the Queen's Golden Jubilee in 2002, for example — provide an important focus for polarized debates and views on the relevance of the monarchy to contemporary Australia. In this section, we want to consider some of the discursive strategies by which Australians use the monarchy and its medieval associations to construct arguments and debates about national identity. More than that, we want to extend our argument that at certain times and for particular individuals within the monarchist grouping the strategies are not simply rhetorical ploys. Rather they are part of a deeply embedded tradition that has at one level continued into the present despite being increasingly anachronistic in rationalist modernist political and legal terms.

The Constitutional Convention, held in Canberra, in February 1998, involved just over one hundred and fifty delegates. Discussion was governed by parliamentary-style processes that were less familiar (and so more intimidating) to some delegates than to others. Its detailed daily reports in Hansard constitute an extraordinary printed record of relatively formal and considered discourse about Australian tradition, society and governance from a range of perspectives, clustered around precisely the questions that drive this essay collection: the relation between tradition and modernity in Australian society and culture. Most discussion focussed on modern questions of the relative merits of various republican models, about the means of electing a president, and the relative powers to be invested in that office. However, when delegates spoke to the question of whether Australia should become a republic at all, they were more likely to appeal to cultural considerations — to tradition or, conversely, to a modernity that is directly opposed to tradition. The monarchy and the present royal family were frequently aligned with a medieval inheritance; what varied was the positive or negative rhetorical valency attached to this inheritance.

As we might expect, defenders of the constitutional monarchy (and also some republican advocates) praised Australia's connection with the literature, law, social and political practices of Britain. Prime Minister John Howard acknowledged that 'Australia's emotional ties to the Crown have diminished', yet remarked that this nation 'will forever be in debt to Britain for her gifts of law, language, literature and political institutions' (2 February 1998, p. 2). Less formally, Geoff Hourn, from Australians for a Constitutional Monarchy, remarked that 'the Crown is [...] interwoven into the fabric of our society. The Crown is no more alien to Australians than cricket, soccer, rugby or Shakespeare' (4 February 1998, p. 281). Lloyd Waddy, QC, from Australians for Constitutional Monarchy, appealed to 'our founders' who 'freely chose at the time of Federation [...] the accumulated wisdom of one thousand years of evolution of the British monarchy, the second oldest institution in Europe after the papacy' (2 February 1998, p. 12). Waddy uses the naturalizing metaphor of evolution, while at the same time emphasizing the 'free choice' made by Australians at Federation. Among others, Rob Borbidge, Premier of Queensland, drew a connection to Magna Carta (2 February 1998, p. 49), while David Mitchell, from the Australian Monarchist League, drew a longer bow, back to 888 and the declaration by King Alfred of 'the Ten Commandments read in the light of the New Testament and Old Testament to be the Constitution of England, and so it has remained ever since' (2 February 1998, p. 76). Alasdair Webster, from the Christian Democratic Party (Fred Nile Group), began with King Ethelbert of Kent in the sixth century, who 'limited his own powers — an expression of Christ-like compassion for those he governed', commenting that Australia's parliamentary conventions 'connect us with the world's richest vein of freedom' (11 February 1998, p. 771). Brigadier Alf Garland, from the Australian Monarchist League, drew a more personal connection to historical continuity, and shaded his sentiments with what appeared to be traditional expressions of medievalism. Without any of the embarrassment that a modernist would usually feel in using such a rhetorical ploy, he began a long speech on his own family's connections to the Capetian dynasty in tenth-century France, and had progressed as far as Henry III of England, before he was interrupted (5 February 1998, p. 353).

Most of these instances are recognizable examples of a culture of medievalism — the invocation of medieval history or tradition for the purposes of revival, or the defence of traditional forms. However, as we have been concerned to document, medievalism takes various forms. On the negative side of the debate were many examples of what we may call a kind of 'anti-medievalism', where the medieval is not invoked as any kind of positive model, any kind of imaginative space for fiction, for play, for fantasy, for spiritualism, but rather as representing the antithesis of the modern. This negative reading of medievalism assumes that Australia must be, or must become modern, by rejecting its negatively valued medieval traditions. Mike Elliott (Leader of the Australian Democrats in South Australia) drew a specific contrast between the medievalism of children's literature and the needs of contemporary Australia:

As a young child, I read stories of kings and queens, princesses and princes — the latter of which appeared to be interchangeable with frogs. As far as Australia is concerned, I do think the place for kings and queens really is within storybooks and history books, certainly no longer within the Australian Constitution (6 February 1998, p. 448).

Senator Faulkner presented the case more formally, arguing that the monarchy represents an archaic institution, by definition irrelevant to contemporary Australia:

I believe that many characteristics of the British monarchy stand in stark contrast to essential Australian value. Indeed, hereditary succession itself is antithetical to Australian values such as equality of opportunity and religious beliefs. The monarch occupies the throne of England by birthright, regardless of merit. The monarch must be of the Anglican faith, and mandatory preference is given to male descendants over female. Surely such archaic restrictions on who can become the Australian head of state would be complete anathema to modern Australian thinking and the egalitarian practices we advocate.

In the argument from anachronism and archaism, Australia is implicitly defined as a 'young' and 'modern' nation. Other delegates were less formal in their rhetoric, but could still be quite concerned with the rhetorical forms that accompany the monarchy with the spread of empire. Paul Tully (Queenslanders for a Republic) attempted to turn that rhetoric against itself. Reminding the convention that the Australian constitution is an act of the British parliament, he cited the preamble to that constitution: 'enacted by the Queen's most Excellent Majesty, by and with the advice and consent of the Lords Spiritual and Temporal, and Commons'. Tully's comments express common modern frustration: 'What a load of monarchical claptrap' (3 February 1998, p. 100).

This polarizing rhetoric, and the dualism in the representation of tradition (usually, though not always represented as specifically medieval tradition) is not surprising in the context of a debate over issues of such crucial importance as national self-definition, and indeed, the language in which such self-definition would be framed, in the event of a revised constitution. Nor should it surprise us to realize that the rhetorical twists and turns could become quite sophisticated and problematic. In particular, the argument against hereditary principles did not always run smoothly, or along expected courses. Peter Costello, the Federal Treasurer, spoke passionately: 'The temper of the times is democratic; we are uncomfortable with an office that appoints people by heredity. In our society in our time we prefer appointment by merit' (3 February 1998, p. 128). But Professor Geoffrey Blainey, controversial conservative historian, turned the debate against the republicans:

There are valid arguments against the hereditary principle embodied in the monarchy and I am mindful of them. The arguments sometimes have to be taken with a grain of salt. Mr Keating, in attacking our constitutional monarchy, our *de facto* republic, said that the hereditary principle was outrageous, but he was slightly indignant when it was pointed out to him that his own chosen version of the native title legislation relied more comprehensively on the hereditary principle than any law hitherto passed by an Australian parliament. If it is right to uphold the hereditary principle in this important law, we should be a little more discreet in denouncing other hereditary institutions which are essentially symbolic (4 February 1998, p. 221).

Here we get duplicity from both sides. The conservative monarchist here is playing a rhetorical game with what we earlier identified as tensions and contradictions inherent in the intersection of different ways of being. In talking of '*the hereditary principle*' he is no different from the modernists in collapsing two quite different ontological formations — tribalism and traditionalism — into each other. On the other hand, he is right that the Keating government had fudged the issue of native title, framing the whole process with modern property law, but talking of symbolic difference. Without explicitly recognizing different formations of sovereignty and subjectivity — in this case, tribalism, traditionalism and modernism — the whole issue descends into a mess of claim and counterclaim. To compound the complexity of the problem, several indigenous Australians spoke in favour of retaining a monarchy; if not by appealing to hereditary inheritance, at least by appealing against unnecessary change. George Mye, representing Torres Strait Islanders, spoke in this way, followed several days later by Neville Bonner, Australia's first Aboriginal senator, who urged the convention to put aside its fascination with the new, and to focus on social issues affecting indigenous peoples.

> How dare you? I repeat: how dare you? You told my people that your system was best. We have come to accept that. We have come to believe that. The dispossessed, despised adapted to your system. Now you say that you were wrong and that we were wrong to believe you. Suddenly you are saying that what brought the country together, made it independent, ensured its defence, saw it through peace and war, and saw it through depression and prosperity, must all go (4 February 1998, p. 221).

It was Olympic athlete Nova Peris-Kneebone who made the clearest attempt to distinguish between different forms of lineage and responsibility. She spoke of the need for a clearer Australian identity in international contexts, while appealing to a much older heritage, her 'traditional responsibilities for country around Cannon Hill in the Kakadu National Park': 'My responsibilities are more than 60,000 years old. That is a lot of tradition to maintain. It is a tradition that is much older than anything the monarchists support' (4 February 1998, p. 221).

The Cultural Power of Dead Symbolism?

It is telling that during the Australian Constitutional Convention, relatively little attention was paid to the question of parliamentary ceremonials. A number of speakers commented on the pleasures of speaking in the old Parliament House building and attention was paid to the question of changing the national flag.

However, no attention was paid to the many medieval rituals and appellations discussed earlier that still permeate parliament: the Sergeant-at-Arms, Guardian of the Mace, the Usher of the Black Rod, and even the Office of the Speaker.[32] In his opening address to the Constitutional Convention, John Howard commended the monarchy precisely for its 'separation of the ceremonial and executive functions' (4 February 1998, p. 221). In response, the republican speakers focussed upon the effect of these ceremonial functions on 'our' image. Malcolm Turnbull of the Australian Republican Movement spoke of attending the Australian bicentennial celebrations of 1988:

> It was said to be the celebration of a nation, yet the star turn — the principal speech — was given not by an Australian but by Prince Charles. Throughout that year, as every great public ceremony came around, we imported another member of the British royal family to preside. Rather than celebrating our nationhood, we denied it. When the world looked to Australia, we showed them what they knew was the monarchy of another country. What was so deficient about us, we asked, that we could not celebrate our nationhood, our achievements, without an endless stream of British royals? Was there no Australian who could safely handle a pair of scissors? (4 February 1998, p. 221).

Turnbull's rhetoric argues contradictorily for the symbolic significance of these ceremonials, while at the same time diminishing the royal 'work' of cutting the ribbon. The more traditional ceremonial aspects could themselves be spoken of in reverential or dismissive terms. Paul Tully could speak of 'monarchical claptrap', while Alasdair Webster from the Christian Democratic Party found every alternative to be

> shallow when compared with appointment at a coronation service, where our head of state accepts a Bible as 'the most valuable thing that this world affords' [...] And, before any heir to the throne can get their hands on the sceptre, which is the symbol of kingly power, they must first accept the orb — a golden sphere mounted by a cross — with the following words: 'Take this to remind you that the whole world is subject to the power and empire of Christ our redeemer'. (4 February 1998, p. 221)

By contrast, Matt Foley, remarked:

> We need an Australian republic which replaces the old dogma of the divine right of kings and queens with the democratic authority which springs from the people. 'Dieu et mon droit' — God and my right — may be a slogan appropriate for the lion and the unicorn which adorn the Speaker's chair in this chamber. But that slogan is a quaint irrelevance for the people of suburban Brisbane whom I represent (4 February 1998, p. 221).

---

[32] The *House of Representatives Infosheet*, no. 3, April 2002, p. 3, describes the office of the speaker as 'a very ancient one, dating back eight hundred years to 13th century England'.

This is a powerful rhetorical argument to run: nothing seems simpler than to isolate an arcane medieval element in another language and draw a contrast with life in the Australian suburbs. When an Australian woman gives up her citizenship to become the Crown Princess of Denmark, for example, it is simplest to conceptualize this as a 'fairy-tale' romance, as media reports did consistently in 2004, focusing on the almost magical transformation of Mary Donaldson from Hobart into a member of European royalty (even while they also stressed the strict grooming and training of the bride). It is much harder to 'invent' an appropriate symbol for a nation, as the debate about a new constitutional preamble revealed. John Howard's facile attempt to write the virtues of 'mateship' into the constitution foundered for this reason, among others. Here we confront the very real difficulties of *producing* a meaningful and lived symbolic language. In the argument of the present chapter the institutions of the Australian polity were not invented *ex nihilo*. They were drawn out of the British parliamentary tradition and translated into a new context and time. It is quite possible, as evidenced by the energy shown in the debates around what Australians should call their head of state, that the monarchy is an irrelevance to modern/postmodern Australia. Certainly the debate about the republic is a distraction from far more important social issues including the rights of indigenous peoples. However, whichever be the case, the continuing controversy suggests that even almost-dead symbols carry enormous cultural weight, enough to provoke intense and ongoing debate. Australia does not look anything like a medieval society; yet the terms in which we frame our cultural and national identity are still powerfully driven by the complex legacy of medievalism.

Select Bibliography

Ackland, Michael, ed., *Henry Kendall: Poetry, Prose and Selected Correspondence* (St Lucia: University of Queensland Press, 1993).

Andrews, Brian, *Australian Gothic: The Gothic Revival in Australian Architecture from the 1840s to the 1950s* (Melbourne: Miegunyah Press and Melbourne University Press, 2001).

Baldick, Chris, ed., *The Oxford Book of Gothic Tales* (Oxford: Oxford University Press, 1992).

Barry, Elaine, *Fabricating the Self: The Fictions of Jessica Anderson* (St Lucia: University of Queensland Press, 1996).

Baudrillard, Jean, *Selected Writings*, ed. by Mark Poster (Stanford: Stanford University Press, 1988).

Biddick, Kathleen, *The Shock of Medievalism* (Durham: Duke University Press, 1998).

Bloch, R. Howard, and Stephen G. Nichols, ed., *Medievalism and the Modernist Temper* (Baltimore: Johns Hopkins University Press, 1996).

Botting, Fred, *Gothic* (London: Routledge, 1996).

Brooks, Chris, *The Gothic Revival* (London: Phaidon, 1999).

D'Arcens, Louise, 'Europe in the Antipodes: Australian Medieval Studies', *Studies in Medievalism*, 10 (1998), 13–40.

D'Arcens, Louise, 'From Holy War to Border Skirmish: The Colonial Chivalry of Sydney's First Professors', *Journal of Medieval and Early Modern Studies*, 30 (2000), 519–45.

Dahood, Roger, ed., *The Future of the Middle Ages and the Renaissance* (Turnhout: Brepols, 1998).

Davenport-Hines, Richard, *Gothic: Four Hundred Years of Excess, Horror, Evil and Ruin* (London: Fourth Estate, 2000).

Davidson, Jim, 'Tasmanian Gothic', *Meanjin*, 48 (1989), 307–24.

De Certeau, Michel, *The Practice of Everyday Life*, trans. by Steven Rendall (Berkeley: University of California Press, 1984).

Eco, Umberto, *Travels in Hyperreality. Essays*, trans. by William Weaver (San Diego: Harcourt, Brace, Jovanovich, 1986).

Fine, Gary Alan, *Shared Fantasy: Role-Playing Games as Social Worlds* (Chicago: University of Chicago Press, 1983).

Foucault, Michel, *Discipline and Punish: The Birth of the Prison*, trans. by Alan Sheridan (1977; Harmondsworth: Penguin, 1991).

Foucault, Michel, *Power: Essential Works of Foucault 1954–1984*, ed. by James D. Faubion, trans. by Robert Hurley and others, vol. 3 (London: Penguin, 2002).

Frow, John, *Time and Commodity Culture: Essays in Cultural Theory and Postmodernity* (Oxford: Clarendon Press, 1997).

Gamer, Michael, *Romanticism and the Gothic: Genre, Reception, and Canon Formation* (Cambridge: Cambridge University Press, 2000).

Gilchrist, John, 'Medievalism and Australian Culture', *Twentieth Century*, 14 (1960), 293–301.

Girouard, Mark, *The Return to Camelot: Chivalry and the English Gentleman* (New Haven: Yale University Press, 1981).

Grunenberg, Christoph, ed., *Gothic: Transmutations of Horror in Late Twentieth Century Art* (Boston: Institute of Contemporary Art/MIT Press, 1997).

Hodkinson, Paul, *Goth: Identity, Style and Subculture* (Oxford: Berg, 2002).

Holsinger, Bruce, 'Medieval Studies, Postcolonial Studies and the Genealogies of Critique', *Speculum*, 77 (2002), 1195–1227.

Hunt, Lynn, ed., *The New Cultural History: Essays* (Berkeley: University of California Press, 1989).

Ingham, Patricia, and Michelle R. Warren, eds, *Postcolonial Moves, Medieval to Modern* (New York: Palgrave, 2003).

Kerr, Joan, and James Broadbent, *Gothick Taste in the Colony of New South Wales* (Sydney: David Ells Press, in association with the Elizabeth Bay House Trust, 1980).

Klein, Kerwin Lee, 'On the Emergence of *Memory* in Historical Discourse', *Representations*, 69 (2000), 127–50.

Kucich, John, and Dianne F. Sadoff, eds, *Victorian Afterlife: Postmodern Culture Rewrites the Nineteenth Century* (Minneapolis: University of Minnesota Press, 2000).

Lowenthal, David, *The Past is a Foreign Country* (Cambridge: Cambridge University Press, 1985).

Lukács, Georg, *The Historical Novel* (Lincoln: University of Nebraska Press, 1983).

McDougall, Russell, ed., *Henry Kendall, the Muse of Australia* (Armidale: Centre for Australian Language and Literature Studies, 1992).

Mackay, Daniel, *The Fantasy Role-Playing Game: A New Performing Art* (Jefferson, North Carolina: McFarland, 2001).

McKenzie, Bertha, *Stained Glass and Stone: The Gothic Buildings of the University of Sydney* (Sydney: University of Sydney, 1989).

Mancoff, Debra N., *King Arthur's Modern Return* (New York: Garland, 1998).

Mancoff, Debra N., *The Arthurian Revival in Victorian Art* (New York: Garland, 1990).

Matthews, David, *The Making of Middle English, 1765–1910* (Minneapolis: University of Minnesota Press, 1999).

Menz, Christopher, *Morris & Company: Pre-Raphaelites and the Arts and Crafts Movement in South Australia* (Adelaide: Art Gallery Board of South Australia, 1994).

Patterson, Lee, *Negotiating the Past: The Historical Understanding of Medieval Literature* (Madison: University of Wisconsin Press, 1967).

Reed, T. T. ed., *The Poetical Works of Henry Kendall* (Adelaide: Libraries Board of South Australia, 1966).

Rosenthal, Bernard, and Paul E. Szarmach, eds, *Medievalism in American Culture* (Binghamton: Medieval and Renaissance Texts and Studies, 1989).

Smith, Andrew, and William Hughes, eds, *Empire and the Gothic: The Politics of Genre* (New York: Palgrave Macmillan, 2003).

Stewart, Susan, *On Longing: Narratives of the Miniature, the Gigantic, the Souvenir, the Collection* (Baltimore: Johns Hopkins University Press, 1984).

Strohm, Paul, *Theory and the Premodern Text* (Minneapolis: University of Minnesota Press, 2000).

Turney, Clifford, Ursula Bygott, and Peter Chippendale, *Australia's First: A History of the University of Sydney, Vol. I, 1850–1939* (Sydney: Hale and Iremonger, 1991).

Utz, Richard, and T. A. Shippey, eds, *Medievalism in the Modern World: Essays in Honour of Leslie J. Workman* (Turnhout: Brepols, 1998).

Webb, Francis, *Collected Poems* (Sydney: Angus and Robertson, 1969).

Weisl, Angela, *The Persistence of Medievalism: Narrative Adventures in Contemporary Culture* (New York: Palgrave Macmillan, 2003).

Wright, Patrick, *On Living in an Old Country* (London: Verso, 1985)

Zacher, Christian K. *Curiosity and Pilgrimage* (Baltimore: Johns Hopkins University Press, 1976).

Contributors

Geraldine Barnes teaches in the Department of English at the University of Sydney. Her most recent book is *Viking America: The First Millennium* (Boydell & Brewer).

Megan Cassidy-Welch teaches medieval history at the University of Melbourne. She is the author of *Monastic Spaces and their Meanings: Thirteenth-Century English Cistercian Monasteries* (Brepols). She is currently writing a cultural history of medieval imprisonment, 1100–1500.

Matthew Chrulew is writing a PhD in the Centre for Studies in Religion and Theology at Monash University. His Master's dissertation, completed at the University of Western Australia, was a Foucauldian study of zoological gardens.

Louise D'Arcens is a lecturer in medieval, medievalist, and contemporary literature in the English Literatures Program at the University of Wollongong. She has published a number of articles on academic and creative medievalism in Australia, and is co-editor of *Maistresse of My Wit: Medieval Women, Modern Scholars* (Brepols).

Victoria Emery has a doctorate in history from the University of Melbourne, on 'Reading and After: Literary Community, Identity and Practice in Melbourne, c. 1886–1910'. She is the Human Research Ethics officer at Deakin University.

Ken Gelder teaches popular fiction and global literature in the Department of English at the University of Melbourne. His books include studies of Australian fiction and cultural politics, subcultures, and vampire film and fiction. His most recent book is *Popular Fiction: The Logics and Practices of a Literary Field* (Routledge).

Adina Hamilton has an MA in medieval history from the University of Melbourne. She is a member of the Society for Creative Anachronism.

Paul James is Director of the Globalism Institute at RMIT University (Melbourne), an editor of *Arena Journal*, and author or editor of seven books including *Nation Formation: Towards a Theory of Abstract Community* (Sage).

Valerie Krips teaches cultural and critical theory, and children's literature in the English Department at the University of Pittsburgh. Her most recent publications include *The Presence of the Past: Memory, Heritage and Childhood in Postwar Britain* (Garland).

Andrew Lynch teaches in the discipline of English, Communication, and Cultural Studies at The University of Western Australia. His publications include *Malory's Book of Arms* (Brewer). This is his fourth article on Francis Webb's poetry.

David Matthews teaches medieval literature and Australian literature in the discipline of English, School of Language and Media, University of Newcastle. He is the author of *The Making of Middle English 1765–1910* (University of Minnesota Press).

Jenna Mead teaches medieval and medievalist literature, and film studies at the University of Tasmania. She is the editor of *Bodyjamming: Sexual Harassment, Feminism and Public Life* (Vintage). Two recent articles read race, colour and nation in Chaucer's *Treatise on the Astrolabe*.

Adrian Mitchell teaches in the Department of English at the University of Sydney. His current research is into the literature of cultural contact in the early modern period.

Peter Otto teaches in the Department of English at the University of Melbourne. His recent publications include *Blake's Critique of Transcendence* (Oxford University Press), and *Gothic Fiction*, a large microfilm collection of Gothic novels and chapbooks published between 1764 and 1830 (Adam Matthews Publishers).

Sarah Randles is completing a PhD on medieval narrative textiles at the Australian National University. She is also the Vice-Principal of Sancta Sophia College at the University of Sydney.

Margaret Rogerson teaches medieval and modern literature in the Department of English at the University of Sydney. Her current research project investigates medievalism in action in the modern revivals of the York Mystery Plays in the city of their origin: 'The York Mystery Plays 1951–2002: A History'.

Stephanie Trigg teaches in the Department of English at the University of Melbourne. She has published works on Australian literature and medieval English literature. Her most recent book is *Congenial Souls: Reading Chaucer from Medieval to Postmodern* (Minnesota University Press).

Index

In this index, notes are designated with an 'n'. The numbers of notes are included where there are multiple notes on a page. Page numbers of figures are in **bold**.